SOMETHING ABOUT THE AUTHOR®

Something about
the Author *was named
an "Outstanding
Reference Source,"*
*the highest honor given
by the American
Library Association
Reference and Adult
Services Division.*

ISSN 0276-816X

SOMETHING ABOUT THE AUTHOR®

**Facts and Pictures about authors
and Illustrators of books for Young People**

volume 186

GALE
CENGAGE Learning™

Detroit • New York • San Francisco • New Haven, Conn • Waterville, Maine • London

GALE
CENGAGE Learning

Something about the Author, Volume 186

Project Editor: Lisa Kumar

Editorial: Dana Ferguson, Amy Elisabeth Fuller, Michelle Kazensky, Jennifer Mossman, Joseph Palmisano, Mary Ruby, Amanda D. Sams, Marie Toft

Permissions: Margaret Abendroth, Mollika Basu, Aja Perales

Imaging and Multimedia: Leitha Etheridge-Sims, Lezlie Light

Composition and Electronic Capture: Amy Darga

Manufacturing: Drew Kalasky

Product Manager: Janet Witalec

For product information and technology assistance, contact us at
Gale Customer Support, 1-800-877-4253.
For permission to use material from this text or product,
submit all requests online at **www.cengage.com/permissions.**
Further permissions questions can be emailed to
permissionrequest@cengage.com

While every effort has been made to ensure the reliability of the information presented in this publication, Gale, a part of Cengage Learning, does not guarantee the accuracy of the data contained herein. Gale accepts no payment for listing; and inclusion in the publication of any organization, agency, institution, publication, service, or individual does not imply endorsement of the editors or publisher. Errors brought to the attention of the publisher and verified to the satisfaction of the publisher will be corrected in future editions.

EDITORIAL DATA PRIVACY POLICY: Does this publication contain information about you as an individual? If so, for more information about our editorial data privacy policies, please see our Privacy Statement at www.gale.cengage.com.

Gale
27500 Drake Rd.
Farmington Hills, MI, 48331-3535

LIBRARY OF CONGRESS CATALOG CARD NUMBER 62-52046

ISBN-13: 978-0-7876-9935-2
ISBN-10: 0-7876-9935-7

ISSN 0276-816X

This title is also available as an e-book.
ISBN-13: 978-1-4144-3838-2
ISBN-10: 1-4144-3838-9
Contact your Gale sales representative for ordering information.

Printed in the United States of America
1 2 3 4 5 6 7 12 11 10 09 08

Contents

Authors in Forthcoming Volumes

Below are some of the authors and illustrators that will be featured in upcoming volumes of SATA. These include new entries on the swiftly rising stars of the field, as well as completely revised and updated entries (indicated with *) on some of the most notable and best-loved creators of books for children.

Stephen Alter ▌ Born and raised in India, Alter is an American author and educator whose writing has been inspired by the country of his birth. His critically acclaimed works include the autobiography *All the Way to Heaven: An American Boyhood in the Himalayas* and the young-adult fantasy novel *The Phantom Isles.* Alter's novels for adults reflect on the aftermath of the British Raj by illuminating the lives of India's ethnically mixed descendants, while his nonfiction work, *Elephas Maximus,* examines the role of the Indian elephant in the region's myth, history, and culture.

*Ying Chang Compestine ▌ Compestine, born in the People's Republic of China, is the author of several cookbooks featuring Asian cuisine, and her love of cooking is a key ingredient in her children's books *The Runaway Rice Cake* and *The Real Story of Stone Soup. Revolution Is Not a Dinner Party,* Compestine's critically acclaimed novel, is based on her experiences growing up during China's Cultural Revolution. Now living in the United States, she shares her cultural insights in lighthearted fare geared for the very young, among them the alphabet book *D Is for Dragon Dance* and the picture books *The Story of Kites* and *The Story of Noodles,* which follow the amusing adventures of two young brothers.

*Deborah Ellis ▌ Ellis's political activism and social concerns fuel her writings for young adults. In *Looking for X* an eleven-year-old girl struggles to deal with the challenges of growing up in a single-parent family, until a friendship with a mysterious homeless woman changes her perspective. In *The Breadwinner,* another novel geared for young teens, the Canadian writer takes readers to Iran and provides a child's-eye view of life under the Taliban regime. Ellis's story is related by eleven-year-old Parvana, a girl who is separated from her family due to regional violence. A sequel, *Parvana's Journey,* continues the girl's adventures in a repressive, wartorn society as she bravely sets out to locate her missing relatives.

Peter Hannan ▌ Hannan was the class cartoonist in middle school, and he successfully parlays his talent for creating bizarre creatures in his adult life as an illustrator. He is the creative talent behind Nickelodeon's popular *CatDog* television series, even composing and performing the theme song. Hannan's cartoon drawings have also been collected in *The Adventures of a Huge Mouth,* and his "Super Goofballs" book series for elementary-grade readers introduces a roster of offbeat super heroes that includes Amazing Techno Dude and Bodacious Backwards Woman.

Jeff Kinney ▌ Kinney started his career as a cartoonist in college, but he later had to content himself with publishing his original comic strip, "Diary of a Wimpy Kid," online at Funbrain.com. After six years of self-publishing, however, Kinney's online work was captured in print as the graphic novel *The Diary of a Wimpy Kid: Greg Heffley's Journal.* Inspired by events in Kinney's own family, *The Diary of a Wimpy Kid* chronicles the hilarious misadventures of a clueless and self-absorbed middle-grader in the seventh grade.

*Neal Layton ▌ Although much of Layton's quirky art has been published in conjunction with texts by such writers as Frieda Wishinsky, Jenny Oldfield, Nicola Davies, and Sally Grindley, the British illustrator has also created original picture books such as the award-winning *Oscar and Arabella.* Another self-illustrated work, *Smile If You're Human,* finds an alien family living on Earth undercover while they secretly study the habits of humans. Featuring his unique cartoon style and sly humor, Layton's artwork continues to turn up in numerous picture books, among them *Poop: A Natural History of the Unmentionable,* by Davies, *Howler,* by Michael Rose, and the "Totally Tom" reader series by Oldfield.

Jean-Claude Mourlevat ▌ Mourlevat is a French novelist, translator, and short-story writer. He addresses a younger readership with his critically acclaimed young-adult novel *The Pull of the Ocean,* Mourlevat's first work to be published in English translation. *The Pull of the Ocean* is a contemporary take on Charles Perrault's classic fairy tale "Tom Thumb." In the French author's hands, the well-known story is reconfigured, and readers follow a mute ten-year-old boy and his six older brothers as they escape from a violent parent and take a picaresque journey to the French coast in search of a new home.

Gretchen Olson ▌ A native of rural Oregon, Olson writes young-adult novels that center on contemporary social issues. In *Joyride,* an upper-class teen drives his car through a local farmer's bean field and ultimately pays for the damages by joining the farmer's migrant labor force. Praised for its realism, Olson's novel is based on its author's experience working with migrant workers on her family's blueberry farm. In another novel featuring contemporary themes, *Call Me Hope,* the novelist centers on a young girl who is struggling to deal with her mother's verbal abuse.

*Lemony Snicket ▌ Snicket—the pen name of writer Daniel Handler—is the author of the wildly popular "A Series of Unfortunate Events" books. The thirteen-volume series, which follows the grim misadventures of the orphaned Baudelaire children, includes the compellingly titled *The Bad Beginning, The Reptile Room, The Wide Window,* and *The Grim Grotto.* Critics and fans alike have praised Snicket's droll tales, noting that the appeal of his stories lies in his unique mix of irony, humor, and melodrama.

James Warhola ▌ Warhola, an illustrator and author, credits the encouragement of his famous uncle, artist and filmmaker Andy Warhol, with inspiring his own creative career. Beginning by creating book-cover art for hundreds of science-fiction and fantasy novels, Warhola shifted his focus to children's-book illustration in the late 1980s. Memories of his beloved uncle inspired Warhola's first self-illustrated book, *Uncle Andy's: A Faabbbulous Visit with Andy Warhol.*

Introduction

Something about the Author (*SATA*) is an ongoing reference series that examines the lives and works of authors and illustrators of books for children. *SATA* includes not only well-known writers and artists but also less prominent individuals whose works are just coming to be recognized. This series is often the only readily available information source on emerging authors and illustrators. You'll find *SATA* informative and entertaining, whether you are a student, a librarian, an English teacher, a parent, or simply an adult who enjoys children's literature.

What's Inside *SATA*

SATA provides detailed information about authors and illustrators who span the full time range of children's literature, from early figures like John Newbery and L. Frank Baum to contemporary figures like Judy Blume and Richard Peck. Authors in the series represent primarily English-speaking countries, particularly the United States, Canada, and the United Kingdom. Also included, however, are authors from around the world whose works are available in English translation. The writings represented in *SATA* include those created intentionally for children and young adults as well as those written for a general audience and known to interest younger readers. These writings cover the entire spectrum of children's literature, including picture books, humor, folk and fairy tales, animal stories, mystery and adventure, science fiction and fantasy, historical fiction, poetry and nonsense verse, drama, biography, and nonfiction. Obituaries are also included in *SATA* and are intended not only as death notices but also as concise overviews of people's lives and work. Additionally, each edition features newly revised and updated entries for a selection of *SATA* listees who remain of interest to today's readers and who have been active enough to require extensive revisions of their earlier biographies.

Autobiography Feature

Beginning with Volume 103, many volumes of *SATA* feature one or more specially commissioned autobiographical essays. These unique essays, averaging about ten thousand words in length and illustrated with an abundance of personal photos, present an entertaining and informative first-person perspective on the lives and careers of prominent authors and illustrators profiled in *SATA*.

Two Convenient Indexes

In response to suggestions from librarians, *SATA* indexes no longer appear in every volume but are included in alternate (odd-numbered) volumes of the series, beginning with Volume 57.

SATA continues to include two indexes that cumulate with each alternate volume: the Illustrations Index, arranged by the name of the illustrator, gives the number of the volume and page where the illustrator's work appears in the current volume as well as all preceding volumes in the series; the Author Index gives the number of the volume in which a person's biographical sketch, autobiographical essay, or obituary appears in the current volume as well as all preceding volumes in the series.

These indexes also include references to authors and illustrators who appear in *Gale's Yesterday's Authors of Books for Children, Children's Literature Review,* and *Something about the Author Autobiography Series.*

Easy-to-Use Entry Format

Whether you're already familiar with the *SATA* series or just getting acquainted, you will want to be aware of the kind of information that an entry provides. In every *SATA* entry the editors attempt to give as complete a picture of the person's life and work as possible. A typical entry in *SATA* includes the following clearly labeled information sections:

PERSONAL: date and place of birth and death, parents' names and occupations, name of spouse, date of marriage, names of children, educational institutions attended, degrees received, religious and political affiliations, hobbies and other interests.

ADDRESSES: complete home, office, electronic mail, and agent addresses, whenever available.

CAREER: name of employer, position, and dates for each career post; art exhibitions; military service; memberships and offices held in professional and civic organizations.

MEMBER: professional, civic, and other association memberships and any official posts held.

AWARDS, HONORS: literary and professional awards received.

WRITINGS: title-by-title chronological bibliography of books written and/or illustrated, listed by genre when known; lists of other notable publications, such as plays, screenplays, and periodical contributions.

ADAPTATIONS: a list of films, television programs, plays, CD-ROMs, recordings, and other media presentations that have been adapted from the author's work.

WORK IN PROGRESS: description of projects in progress.

SIDELIGHTS: a biographical portrait of the author or illustrator's development, either directly from the biographee—and often written specifically for the *SATA* entry—or gathered from diaries, letters, interviews, or other published sources.

BIOGRAPHICAL AND CRITICAL SOURCES: cites sources quoted in "Sidelights" along with references for further reading.

EXTENSIVE ILLUSTRATIONS: photographs, movie stills, book illustrations, and other interesting visual materials supplement the text.

How a *SATA* Entry Is Compiled

SATA editors examine a wide variety of published sources to gather information for an entry. Biographical and bibliographic

sources are consulted, as are book reviews, feature articles, published interviews, and material sometimes obtained from the biographee's family, publishers, agent, or other associates. Whenever possible, the author or illustrator is sent a copy of the entry to check for accuracy and completeness.

Entries that have not been verified by the biographees or their representatives are marked with an asterisk (*).

Contact the Editor

We encourage our readers to examine the entire *SATA* series. Please write and tell us if we can make *SATA* even more helpful to you. Give your comments and suggestions to the editor:

Editor
Something about the Author
Gale, Cengage Learning
27500 Drake Rd.
Farmington Hills MI 48331-3535

Toll-free: 800-877-GALE
Fax: 248-699-8070

Something about the Author Product Advisory Board

The editors of *Something about the Author* are dedicated to maintaining a high standard of excellence by publishing comprehensive, accurate, and highly readable entries on a wide array of writers for children and young adults. In addition to the quality of the content, the editors take pride in the graphic design of the series, which is intended to be orderly yet inviting, allowing readers to utilize the pages of *SATA* easily and with efficiency. Despite the longevity of the *SATA* print series, and the success of its format, we are mindful that the vitality of a literary reference product is dependent on its ability to serve its users over time. As literature, and attitudes about literature, constantly evolve, so do the reference needs of students, teachers, scholars, journalists, researchers, and book club members. To be certain that we continue to keep pace with the expectations of our customers, the editors of *SATA* listen carefully to their comments regarding the value, utility, and quality of the series. Librarians, who have firsthand knowledge of the needs of library users, are a valuable resource for us. The *Something about the Author* Product Advisory Board, made up of school, public, and academic librarians, is a forum to promote focused feedback about *SATA* on a regular basis. The nine-member advisory board includes the following individuals, whom the editors wish to thank for sharing their expertise:

Eva M. Davis
Youth Department Manager,
Ann Arbor District Library,
Ann Arbor, Michigan

Joan B. Eisenberg
Lower School Librarian,
Milton Academy,
Milton, Massachusetts

Francisca Goldsmith
Teen Services Librarian,
Berkeley Public Library,
Berkeley, California

Susan Dove Lempke
Children's Services Supervisor,
Niles Public Library District,
Niles, Illinois

Robyn Lupa
Head of Children's Services,
Jefferson County Public Library,
Lakewood, Colorado

Victor L. Schill
Assistant Branch Librarian/Children's Librarian,
Harris County Public Library/Fairbanks Branch,
Houston, Texas

Caryn Sipos
Community Librarian,
Three Creeks Community Library,
Vancouver, Washington

Steven Weiner
Director,
Maynard Public Library,
Maynard, Massachusetts

something ABOUT the AUThOR

ALKOUATLI, Claire

Personal

Born in Canada; married; husband's name Saadi. *Education:* Attended college. *Religion:* Muslim.

Addresses

Home and office—Canada.

Career

Author and editor.

Member

ASMA Society.

Writings

Islam, Marshall Cavendish (Tarrytown, NY), 2007.

Biographical and Critical Sources

PERIODICALS

Booklist, February 15, 2007, Hazel Rochman, review of *Islam,* p. 71.

School Library Journal, March, 2007, Ann W. Moore, review of *Islam,* p. 223.

ONLINE

ASMA Society Web site, http://www.asmasociety.org/ (January 3, 2007), Claire Alkouatli, "Notes from the Ka'ba."*

*　　*　　*

ALSENAS, Linas 1979-

Personal

Born August 10, 1979, in Bedford, OH. *Education:* Harvard University, B.A. (history of art and architecture), 2001.

Addresses

Home and office—Stockholm, Sweden. *E-mail*—linas@alsenas.com.

Career

Author and illustrator. Worked previously as a children's book editor for Harry N. Abrams, New York, NY.

Awards, Honors

Oppenheim Toy Portfolio Award, 2008, for *Peanut.*

In his text and pictures for **Mrs. Claus Takes a Vacation,** *Linas Alsenas presents readers with a fresh take on a well-known, loving relationship.* (Scholastic Press, 2006. Text and illustrations copyright © 2006 by Linas Alsenas. Reprinted by permission of Scholastic Inc.)

Writings

Mrs. Claus Takes a Vacation, Scholastic (New York, NY), 2006.

Peanut, Scholastic (New York, NY), 2007.

Gay America: Struggle for Equality, Amulet Books, (New York, NY), 2008.

Contributor to periodicals, including *Architectural Digest.*

Sidelights

Linas Alsenas has always been interested in children's books. Although he studied art history in college and considered a career in architecture, his job as an editorial assistant for a New York City publisher convinced Alsenas that he would rather have a career that involved books. He worked as a children's book editor for several years before taking the step to become an author. His self-illustrated picture-book debut, *Mrs. Claus Takes a Vacation,* was published in 2006.

Mrs. Claus Takes a Vacation takes a unique approach to the tradition of Christmas by centering its tale on Mrs. Claus. Although her husband, Santa Claus, has ample opportunity to travel, Mrs. Claus has a desire to see the world that has yet to be fulfilled. Every year, when Christmas duties take Santa away from the North Pole on his round-the-world gift-delivery route, Mrs. Claus is left at home to bake gingerbread cookies. After one holiday, however, she finally gets her pportunity for travel, hopping on a sleigh bound for such exotic locations as Japan, India, and Scandinavia. While Mrs. Claus is off exploring the world, Mr. Claus also has a chance to see what he has been missing: he stays busy at the North Pole baking his own cookies! Mara Alpert, in her review of *Mrs. Claus Takes a Vacation* for *School Library Journal,* commented that the author/illustrator's "acrylic illustrations are the perfect accompaniment to the tender tale," while a *Publishers Weekly* critic cited Alsenas for portraying his tale "in a series of humorous, well-chosen scenes."

Peanut, Alsenas's second picture book, tells the story of Mildred, a lonely elderly woman who finds a stray puppy in the park and names it Peanut. Peanut is not like other dogs, however: He does not roll over and never fetches. In addition, his nose is much, much bigger than that of a poodle, a terrier, or a pug. It turns out that Peanut is an elephant, and when a man from the circus retrieves him, Mildred is left by herself again . . . until a very strange kitten comes by . . . , a very tall kitten with two humps on its back.

In addition to picture books, Linas is the author of the nonfiction history book *Gay America: Struggle for Equality.* Geared for teens and heavily illustrated with photographs, the book serves as an introduction to the history of gay men and women in America since the late nineteenth century.

Biographical and Critical Sources

PERIODICALS

Horn Book, November-December, 2006, Kitty Flynn, review of *Mrs. Claus Takes a Vacation,* p. 687.
Kirkus Reviews, November 1, 2006, review of *Mrs. Claus Takes a Vacation,* p. 1126; July 1, 2007, review of *Peanut,* p. 659.
Publishers Weekly, September 25, 2006, review of *Mrs. Claus Takes a Vacation,* p. 69.
School Library Journal, October, 2006, Mara Alpert, review of *Mrs. Claus Takes a Vacation,* p. 94; December 1, 2007, Linda M. Kenton, review of *Peanut.*

ONLINE

Children's Bookwatch Web site, http://www.midwestbookreview.com/ (December 1, 2006), review of *Mrs. Claus Takes a Vacation.*
Linas Alsenas Home Page, http://www.linasalsenas.com (December 11, 2007).

*   *   *

ANDERSON, Laurie Halse 1961-

Personal

Surname rhymes with "waltz"; born October 23, 1961, in Potsdam, NY; daughter of Frank A., Jr. (a Methodist minister) and Joyce (in management) Halse; married Gregory H. Anderson (a chief executive officer), June 19, 1983 (divorced); married Scot Larrabee, 2005; children: (first marriage) Stephanie, Meredith; (stepchildren) Jessica, Christian. *Education:* Onandaga County Community College, A.A., 1981; Georgetown University, B.S.L.L., 1984. *Politics:* "Independent." *Religion:* Quaker (Society of Friends). *Hobbies and other interests:* Reading, running, skiing, hiking, basketball, history, travel, genealogy.

Addresses

E-mail—laurie@voicenet.com.

Career

Author.

Member

Society of Children's Book Writers and Illustrators.

Awards, Honors

Pick of the Lists designation, American Booksellers Association, 1996, for *Ndito Runs;* National Book Award finalist, and Michael L. Printz Award Honor Book designation, both 1999, both for *Speak;* Best Book for Young Adults selection, American Library Association, 2003, for *Catalyst.*

Writings

Ndito Runs, illustrated by Anita Van der Merwe, Henry Holt (New York, NY), 1996.
Turkey Pox, illustrated by Dorothy Donohue, Albert Whitman & Co. (Morton Grove, IL), 1996.
No Time for Mother's Day, illustrated by Dorothy Donohue, Albert Whitman & Co. (Morton Grove, IL), 1999.
Speak, Farrar, Straus & Giroux (New York, NY), 1999.
Fever 1793, Simon & Schuster (New York, NY), 2000.
Saudi Arabia, Carolrhoda Books (Minneapolis, MN), 2001.
The Big Cheese of Third Street, illustrated by David Gordon, Simon & Schuster (New York, NY), 2002.
Catalyst, Viking (New York, NY), 2002.
Thank You, Sarah: The Woman Who Saved Thanksgiving, illustrated by Matt Faulkner, Simon & Schuster (New York, NY), 2002.
Prom, Viking (New York, NY), 2005.
Twisted, Viking (New York, NY), 2007.
Independent Dames: The Women and Girls of the American Revolution, illustrated by Matt Faulkner, Simon & Schuster (New York, NY), 2008.
The Hair of Zoe Fleefenbacher, illustrated by Ard Hoyt, Simon & Schuster (New York, NY), 2009.

"WILD AT HEART" SERIES

Fight for Life, American Girl (Middleton, WI), 2000.
Homeless: Sunita, American Girl (Middleton, WI), 2000.
Trickster, American Girl (Middleton, WI), 2000.
Say Good-Bye, American Girl (Middleton, WI), 2001.
Storm Rescue, American Girl (Middleton, WI), 2001.
Teacher's Pet, American Girl (Middleton, WI), 2001.
Trapped, American Girl (Middleton, WI), 2001.
Fear of Falling, American Girl (Middleton, WI), 2001.
Time to Fly, American Girl (Middleton, WI), 2002.
Race to the Finish, American Girl (Middleton, WI), 2002.
Masks, American Girl (Middleton, WI), 2002.
End of the Race, American Girl (Middleton, WI), 2002.
Manatee Blues, G. Stevens (Milwaukee, WI), 2003.
Say Good-bye, G. Stevens (Milwaukee, WI), 2003.

Adaptations

Speak was adapted as a television film in 2004 by Speak Film Inc.

Sidelights

Laurie Halse Anderson writes for children and young adults, her work ranging from lighthearted folktales such as *Ndito Runs* to earnest morality tales for the "American Girl" series to taut dramas for older teens, such as *Speak* and the historical thriller *Fever 1793*. Noting the variety of genres in which Anderson works, Cynthia Leitich Smith wrote on *Cynsations* online that the author is "always taking chances—writing books that are very different from one another—and still hitting it out of the literary ballpark." *Speak,* a first-person narrative written in the voice of a young rape victim, was a Michael L. Printz Award Honor Book the first year the prize was awarded. In her acceptance speech for this honor, as reprinted in *Booklist,* Anderson spoke of her admiration for her adolescent audience: "I love teenagers because they are honest. I love teenagers because they are raw and passionate. They think in black and white and are willing to go to extremes to defend their beliefs. . . . I love teenagers because they challenge me, and because they frustrate me. They give me hope. They give me nightmares. They are our children, and they deserve the best books we can write."

Anderson knew she wanted to be an author from a young age. As she once told *SATA,* after her second-grade teacher introduced her to writing poetry, she "spent hours and hours and hours reading every book in my school library. The books took me everywhere—ripping through time barriers, across cultures, experiencing all the magic an elementary school library can hold." She also traveled across cultures in her first published picture book, *Ndito Runs,* which was published in 1996. The book follows a young Kenyan girl as she makes her lighthearted and cheerful journey from her home to her school. Ndito leaves her village and enters the countryside, imagining herself to be any number of animals and birds indigenous to the African savanna. As Hazel Rochman commented in a *Booklist* review of *Ndito Runs,* Anderson's "simple, poetic words . . . express Ndito's exhilaration and her connection with nature and with people." A reviewer for *Publishers Weekly* wrote that "both narrative and art paint an appealing portrait of an unusually vivacious heroine," and in *School Library Journal* Tom S. Hurlburt asserted that few multicultural titles share a similar "melding of illustration and text."

A more-humorous picture book, *Turkey Pox* introduces readers to young Charity who wakes up with chicken pox on Thanksgiving Day, just as her family is preparing to drive to Nana's house to celebrate the holiday. In the car on the way there, the girl's chicken pox are discovered, and the family returns home amidst a swirling snowstorm. Disappointed at the thought of spending her first Thanksgiving without the presence of her beloved

Cover of Laurie Halse Anderson's novel **Fever 1793**, *which focuses on a deadly outbreak of yellow fever that errupted in the United States during the late eighteenth century.* (Simon & Schuster, 2000. Illustration © 2000 by Lori Earley. Reproduced by permission.)

Nana, Charity is overjoyed when the woman arrives with a perfectly roasted turkey, helped by four snow-plow drivers who are also invited to dinner. Nana has "dressed up" the turkey skin with numerous cherries, imitating Charity's affliction and creating the "turkey pox" of the title. Charity returns in *No Time for Mother's Day,* and here she is puzzled by what to give her tremendously busy mother for Mother's Day. Ultimately, it dawns on the girl that the best gift of all would be to turn off all the clocks and machines in the house since these timekeepers seem to be the cause of her mom's stress. "Featuring a satisfying story and appealing illustrations, [*Turkey Pox*] . . . is just right for reading aloud to classes," Carolyn Phelan noted in *Booklist.* Janice Del Negro wrote in the *Bulletin of the Center for Children's Books* that the combination of illustrations and text in the book creates "just the right note of jolly delirium."

The Big Cheese of Third Street is a charming story told from the perspective of Benny Antonelli, a very small kid in a neighborhood filled with tremendously large men, women, and older kids. Benny's ability to climb is often the only thing that saves him from good-humored torture by older children, until the day of the neighborhood block party. Benny's triumph in climbing a greased pole to capture the cheese at the very top makes him a tiny hero that any kid can relate to. "Anderson's urban tall tale is a hoot, from her cheeky take on the woes of runt-hood to her plain use of exaggeration and sassy street talk," observed a contributor to *Publishers Weekly.*

The picture book *Thank You, Sarah: The Woman Who Saved Thanksgiving* describes Sarah Hale's efforts to turn Thanksgiving Day into a national holiday through her appeals to President Abraham Lincoln. A *Kirkus Reviews* contributor wrote of the book that "Anderson offers readers both an indomitable role model and a memorable, often hilarious glimpse into the historical development of this country's common culture." Louise L. Sherman, writing in *School Library Journal,* described *Thank You, Sarah* as "fresh, funny, and inspirational."

Focusing on older readers, Anderson's first young-adult novel, *Speak,* was nominated for two prestigious literary awards. The narrator of *Speak* is a high-school freshman who is rendered almost mute as a result of being singled out by her classmates. Melinda has beeen ostracized since phoning 911 during a teen drinking party the previous summer. Although she can hardly bring herself to speak to her peers or teachers, Melinda's written narrative is bursting with language that is angry, sardonic, frightened, sad, and sometimes even funny, according to reviewers. "An uncannily funny book even as it plumbs the darkness, *Speak* will hold readers from first word to last," predicted a *Horn Book* contributor. Other reviewers focused on Anderson's realistic depiction of adolescent life. According to a *Publishers Weekly* critic, the author "uses keen observations and vivid imagery to pull readers into the head of an isolated teenager." A popular novel, *Speak* was also adapted as a television movie.

Also geared for teens, *Fever 1793* is an historical novel set during a yellow-fever epidemic that swept through Philadelphia, which was then the capital of the United States. Like *Speak, Fever 1793* features a first-person narrative, this time that of a fourteen-year-old girl who runs a coffeehouse with her widowed mother and grandfather. Matilda reports, with growing horror, on her life as her community is struck by yellow fever, resulting in the death of thousands in a matter of a few months. "Anderson has carefully researched this historical event and infuses her story with rich details of time and place," remarked Frances Bradburn in *Booklist.* Kathleen Isaacs, reviewing *Fever 1793* for *School Library Journal,* concluded that "readers will be drawn in by the characters and will emerge with a sharp and graphic picture of another world."

Catalyst follows the consequences of eighteen-year-old Kate's decision to only apply to the college attended by her late mother. When she is rejected by the school, she must confront issues regarding her identity as an independent young woman. Also dealing with feelings of loss, Kate gains an insight into the life of her intimidating fellow student, Teri. A series of revelations show the difficult life Teri has survived, and when tragedy strikes, Kate decides to put her life on hold and help her friend. Noting that Kate had intended to study chemistry, Paula Rohrlick wrote in *Kliatt* that "the chemistry metaphor is cleverly employed throughout, and readers will quickly become caught up in Kate's and Teri's dramas and struggles." A *Kirkus Reviews* critic described *Catalyst* as "intelligently written with multi-dimensional characters that replay in one's mind." Noting that the book is set in the same high school as *Speak,* Lauren Adams wrote in *Horn Book* that "readers will return for Anderson's keen understanding and eminently readable style."

Lighter in tone, *Prom* describes an ordinary teen named Ashley as the girl becomes drawn into her best friend's plan to save their school's senior prom. Because one of their teachers embezzled the funds intended to fund prom, Ashley and Natalia need to come up with a way

Cover of Anderson's teen novel **Prom,** *which focuses on one of high school's most memorable rituals.* (Photograph © 2005 by Marc Tauss. Reproduced by permission of Speak, an imprint of Penguin Group, USA.)

to finance the entire operation. "Teens will love Ashley's clear view of high-school hypocrisies, dating, and the fierce bonds of friendship," wrote Gillian Engberg in *Booklist*. A *Kirkus Reviews* contributor noted that "modern teen life just outside Philadelphia is vividly drawn" in Anderson's text, while Laurie Adams wrote in *Horn Book* that "Ashley and her friends could be any American teens, less defined by their background than by their dreams." In *Publishers Weekly* a reviewer predicted that readers "will be enraptured and amused by Ashley's attitude-altering, life-changing commitment to a cause," and Karyn N. Silverman concluded in *School Library Journal* that *Prom* "will delight readers who want their realism tempered with fun."

In *Twisted* nerdy Tyler goes from social outcast to local legend when he is caught spraying graffiti on school property. Although he initially likes the attention he receives as a result, Tyler soon begins to wish that he could go back to being invisible, especially after queen bee Bethany accuses him of posting nude photos of her on the Internet. "Anderson skillfully explores identity and power struggles that all young people will recognize," wrote Engberg. Erin Schirota, reviewing *Twisted* for *School Library Journal*, observed that, "with gripping scenes and a rousing ending, Anderson authentically portrays Tyler's emotional instability" as he contemplates increasingly desperate ways to change his situation. A *Publishers Weekly* critic concluded of the book that Anderson's "dark comedy gives a chillingly accurate portrayal of the high-school social scene."

In addition to picture books and novels for teens, Anderson has also written the "Wild at Heart" novel series for older elementary-aged readers. Part of the "American Girl" library, the novels feature a preteen named Maggie and her adventures surrounding a veterinary clinic run by Maggie's grandmother and staffed by teenage volunteers. In the first installment, *Fight for Life: Maggie*, Maggie begins to suspect that a puppy mill may be operating in the neighborhood when a litter of ten sick puppies is brought to the clinic. "Pet lovers will identify with the young characters as well as with their strong need to solve a real problem," remarked Janie Schomberg in *School Library Journal*. The series continues with *Homeless: Sunita*, which centers on a young girl's desire for a cat of her own, despite her parents' objections and a recent outbreak of rabies among wild cats in the area. Another book in the series, *Say Good-Bye*, adds a new character, Zoe, whose volunteer work at the Wild at Heart Clinic helps her learn how to housebreak her new puppy and teaches her about therapy-pets.

Anderson once told *SATA*, "Despite evidence to the contrary, I believe the world has an abundance of goodness. Not all children get to see this, sadly. I would like to think my books serve up some goodness—with hot fudge, whipped cream, and a cherry on top. Becoming a children's author has been an incredible privilege.

The thought that some kid is reading a book of mine in the library makes me feel like I can fly. I have the coolest job in the world."

Biographical and Critical Sources

PERIODICALS

American Libraries, April, 2006, "Jambotastic," p. 16.

Booklinks, January, 2007, Chris Liska Carger, review of *Speak,* p. 38.

Booklist, March 15, 1996, Hazel Rochman, review of *Ndito Runs,* p. 1268; September 1, 1996, Carolyn Phelan, review of *Turkey Pox,* p. 35; February 15, 1999, Ilene Cooper, review of *No Time for Mother's Day,* p. 1073; November 15, 1999, Stephanie Zvirin, review of *Speak,* p. 18; May 1, 2000, Lauren Peterson, review of *Fight for Life,* p. 1665; October 1, 2000, Frances Bradburn, review of *Fever 1793,* p. 332; November 15, 2000, Stephanie Zvirin, review of *Speak,* p. 632; January 1, 2001, Stephanie Zvirin, "The Printz Award Revisited," p. 932; March 15, 2001, Jean Hatfield, review of *Speak,* p. 1412; April 1, 2001, Stephanie Zvirin, review of *Fever 1793,* pp. 1486, 1494; December 1, 2001, Ilene Cooper, review of *The Big Cheese of Third Street,* p. 644; September 15, 2002, Ilene Cooper, review of *Catalyst,* p. 222; December 15, 2002, Ilene Cooper, review of *Thank You, Sarah: The Woman Who Saved Thanksgiving,* p. 764; January 1, 2005, Gillian Engberg, review of *Prom,* p. 852; January 1, 2007, Gillian Engberg, review of *Twisted,* p. 78; September 15, 2007, Heather Booth, review of *Twisted,* p. 82.

Bulletin of the Center for Children's Books, November, 1996, Janice Del Negro, review of *Turkey Pox,* pp. 89-90; December, 2002, review of *Catalyst,* p. 141; February, 2003, review of *Thank You, Sarah,* p. 225; February, 2005, Deborah Stevenson, review of *Prom,* p. 242; April, 2007, Karen Coats, review of *Twisted,* p. 323.

Horn Book, September, 1999, review of *Speak,* p. 605; September, 2000, Anita L. Burkam, review of *Fever 1793,* p. 562; November-December, 2002, Lauren Adams, review of *Catalyst,* p. 746; March-April, 2005, Lauren Adams, review of *Prom,* p. 196; March-April, 2007, Lauren Adams, review of *Twisted,* p. 191; November-December, 2007, Philip Charles Crawford, review of *Twisted,* p. 704.

Journal of Adolescent and Adult Literacy, March, 2000, Sally Smith, review of *Speak,* p. 585; September, 2005, James Blasingame, review of *Prom,* p. 71.

Kirkus Reviews, September 1, 2002, review of *Catalyst,* p. 1300; October 1, 2002, review of *Thank You, Sarah,* p. 1462; January 15, 2005, review of *Prom,* p. 115; February 15, 2007, review of *Twisted.*

Kliatt, September, 2002, Paula Rohrlick, review of *Catalyst,* p. 6; May, 2003, Sunnie Grant, review of *Catalyst,* p. 43; March, 2005, Paula Rohrlick, review of *Prom,* p. 6; January, 2006, Sally Tibbetts, review of *Prom,* p. 49; March, 2007, Myrna Marler, review of *Twisted,* p. 6.

New York Times Book Review, November 19, 2000, Constance Decker Thompson, review of *Fever 1793*, p. 45; June 3, 2007, John Green, review of *Twisted*, p. 35.

Publishers Weekly, March 18, 1996, review of *Ndito Runs*, pp. 68-69. September 13, 1999, review of *Speak*, p. 85; December 20, 1999, Jennifer M. Brown, "In Dreams Begin Possibilities," p. 24; July 31, 2000, review of *Fever 1793*, p. 96; July 16, 2001, John F. Baker, "Laurie Halse Anderson," p. 70; November 19, 2001, review of *The Big Cheese of Third Street*, p. 67; July 22, 2002, review of *Catalyst*, p. 180; January 24, 2005, review of *Prom*, p. 245; January 15, 2007, review of *Twisted*, p. 52.

Register-Guard (Eugene, OR), November 12, 2007, "Book Picks," p. C18.

School Librarian, winter, 2005, Angela Lepper, review of *Prom*, p. 209.

School Library Journal, May, 1996, Tom S. Hurlburt, review of *Ndito Runs*, p. 84; October, 1996, p. 84; April, 1999, Roxanne Burg, review of *No Time for Mother's Day*, p. 85; October, 1999, Dina Sherman, review of *Speak*, p. 144; January, 2000, Claudia Moore, review of *Speak*, p. 76; March, 2000, "Author Turns Loss into Gain," p. 109; July, 2000, Janie Schomberg, review of *Fight for Life: Maggie*, p. 100; August, 2000, Kathleen Isaacs, review of *Fever 1793*, p. 177; December, 2000, Ronni Krasnow, review of *Homeless: Sunita*, p. 138; January, 2001, Carol Johnson Shedd, review of *Saudi Arabia*, p. 112; March, 2001, Tina Hudak, review of *Fever 1793*, p. 84; July, 2001, Jennifer Ralston, review of *Say Good-Bye*, p. 102; February, 2002, Genevieve Gallagher, review of *The Big Cheese of Third Street*, p. 96; October, 2002, Lynn Bryant, review of *Catalyst*, p. 154; December, 2002, Louise L. Sherman, review of *Thank You, Sarah*, p. 116; February, 2003, Jane P. Fenn, review of *Catalyst*, p. 77; February, 2005, Karyn N. Silverman, review of *Prom*, p. 132; January, 2006, Claudia Moore, review of *Prom*, p. 83; May, 2007, Erin Schirota, review of *Twisted*, p. 128.

Voice of Youth Advocates, April, 2005, Anita Beaman, review of *Prom*, p. 35; April, 2007, Heather Pittman, review of *Twisted*, p. 42; August, 2007, Teri S. Lesesne, review of *Twisted*, p. 223.

ONLINE

Cynsations, http://cynthialeitichsmith.blogspot.com/ (January 31, 2005), Cynthia Leitich Smith, review of *Prom*.

Laurie Halse Anderson Blog site, http://halseanderson.livejournal.com/ (December 18, 2007).

Laurie Halse Anderson Home Page, http://www.writerlady.com (December 18, 2007).

TeenReads Web site, http://www.teenreads.com/ (December 18, 2007), interview with Anderson.*

*   *   *

ANDREASEN, Dan

Personal

Married; children: three.

Addresses

Home—Orlando, FL. *Agent*—Shannon Associates, 630 9th Ave., New York, NY 10036.

Career

Artist and illustrator. Also worked as a sculptor for American Greetings Corporation.

Writings

SELF-ILLUSTRATED

(Adaptor) *Rose Red and the Bear Prince*, HarperCollins (New York, NY), 2000.

With a Little Help from Daddy, Margaret K. McElderry Books (New York, NY), 2003.

A Special Day for Mommy, Margaret K. McElderry Books (New York, NY), 2004.

The Giant of Seville: A "Tall" Tale Based on a True Story, Abrams Books for Young Readers (New York, NY), 2007.

The Baker's Dozen: A Counting Book, Henry Holt (New York, NY), 2007.

ILLUSTRATOR

Dianne Case, *Love, David*, Lodestar Books (New York, NY), 1991.

Alison Cragin Herzig, *The Boonsville Bombers*, Viking (New York, NY), 1991.

Valerie Tripp, *Meet Felicity: An American Girl*, Pleasant Company Publications (Middleton, WI), 1991.

Valerie Tripp, *Felicity Learns a Lesson: A School Story*, Pleasant Company Publications (Middleton, WI), 1991.

Valerie Tripp, *Felicity's Surprise: A Christmas Story*, Pleasant Company Publications (Middleton, WI), 1991.

Barthe DeClements, *The Bite of the Gold Bug: A Story of the Alaskan Gold Rush*, Viking (New York, NY), 1992.

Valerie Tripp, *Changes for Felicity: A Winter Story*, Pleasant Company Publications (Middleton, WI), 1992.

Valerie Tripp, *Felicity Saves the Day: A Summer Story*, Pleasant Company Publications (Middleton, WI), 1992.

Valerie Tripp, *Happy Birthday, Felicity!: A Springtime Story*, Pleasant Company Publications (Middleton, WI), 1992.

Virginia T. Gross, *The President Is Dead: A Story of the Kennedy Assassination*, Viking (New York, NY), 1993.

Alison Cragin Herzig, *The Boonsville Bombers*, Puffin (New York, NY), 1993.

Susan Shreve, *Joshua T. Bates Takes Charge*, Knopf (New York, NY), 1993.

Steven Kroll, *By the Dawn's Early Light: The Story of the Star-spangled Banner*, Scholastic (New York, NY), 1994.

Elaine Moore, *Grandma's Garden*, Lothrop, Lee & Shepard (New York, NY), 1994.

Kathleen Leverich, *Brigid Bewitched*, Random House (New York, NY), 1994.

Kathleen Leverich, *Brigid Beware!*, Random House (New York, NY), 1995.

Kathleen Leverich, *Brigid the Bad*, Random House (New York, NY), 1995.

Elaine Moore, *Grandma's Smile*, Lothrop, Lee & Shepard (New York, NY), 1995.

Steven Kroll, *Pony Express!*, Scholastic (New York, NY), 1996.

Tres Seymour, *Black Sky River*, Orchard Books (New York, NY), 1996.

Maria D. Wilkes, *Little House in Brookfield*, HarperCollins (New York, NY), 1996.

Joseph Bruchac, *Eagle Song*, Dial Books (New York, NY), 1997.

Roger Lea MacBride, *New Dawn on Rocky Ridge*, HarperCollins (New York, NY), 1997.

Jean Van Leeuwen, *Touch the Sky Summer*, Dial Books (New York, NY), 1997.

Maria D. Wilkes, *Little Town at the Crossroads*, HarperCollins (New York, NY), 1997.

Susan S. Adler, *Meet Samantha: An American Girl*, Pleasant Company Publications (Middleton, WI), 1998.

Susan S. Adler, *Samantha Learns a Lesson: A School Story*, Pleasant Company Publications (Middleton, WI), 1998.

William Anderson, *Pioneer Girl: The Story of Laura Ingalls Wilder*, HarperCollins (New York, NY), 1998.

Mary Chapin Carpenter, *Halley Came to Jackson* (with audiocassette), HarperCollins (New York, NY), 1998.

Roger Lea MacBride, *On the Banks of the Bayou*, HarperCollins (New York, NY), 1998.

Maxine Rose Schur, *Samantha's Surprise: A Christmas Story*, Pleasant Company Publications (Middleton, WI), 1998.

Tres Seymour, *We Played Marbles*, Orchard Books (New York, NY), 1998.

Valerie Tripp, *Changes for Samantha: A Winter Story*, Pleasant Company Publications (Middleton, WI), 1998.

Valerie Tripp, *Happy Birthday, Samantha!: A Springtime Story*, Pleasant Company Publications (Middleton, WI), 1998.

Valerie Tripp, *Samantha Saves the Day: A Summer Story*, Pleasant Company Publications (Middleton, WI), 1998.

Maria D. Wilkes, *Little Clearing in the Woods*, HarperCollins (New York, NY), 1998.

Roger Lea MacBride, *Bachelor Girl*, HarperCollins (New York, NY), 1999.

Valerie Tripp, *Felicity's New Sister*, Pleasant Company Publications (Middleton, WI), 1999.

Valerie Tripp, *Samantha's Winter Party*, Pleasant Company Publications (Middleton, WI), 1999.

Rosemary Wells, *Streets of Gold*, Dial Books (New York, NY), 1999.

Melissa Wiley, *Little House by Boston Bay*, HarperCollins (New York, NY), 1999.

Valerie Tripp, *Samantha Saves the Wedding*, Pleasant Company Publications (Middleton, WI), 2000.

Maria D. Wilkes, *On Top of Concord Hill*, HarperTrophy (New York, NY), 2000.

Julie Clay, *The Stars That Shine*, Simon & Schuster (New York, NY), 2000.

Naomi Judd, *Naomi Judd's Guardian Angels* (with compact disc), HarperCollins (New York, NY), 2000.

Valerie Tripp, *Felicity's Dancing Shoes*, Pleasant Company Publications (Middleton, WI), 2000.

Susan S. Adler, Maxine Rose Schur, and Valerie Tripp, *Samantha's Story Collection*, Pleasant Company Publications (Middleton, WI), 2001.

Verla Kay, *Tattered Sails*, Putnam (New York, NY), 2001.

Ann McGovern, *If You Lived in the Days of the Knights*, Scholastic (New York, NY), 2001.

Valerie Tripp, *Felicity Takes a Dare*, Pleasant Company Publications (Middleton, WI), 2001.

Valerie Tripp, *Felicity's Story Collection*, Pleasant Company Publications (Middleton, WI), 2001.

Valerie Tripp, *Samantha and the Missing Pearls*, Pleasant Company Publications (Middleton, WI), 2001.

Melissa Wiley, *On Tide Mill Lane*, HarperCollins (New York, NY), 2001.

Celia Wilkins, *Across the Rolling River*, HarperCollins (New York, NY), 2001.

Marion Dane Bauer, *Love Song for a Baby*, Simon & Schuster (New York, NY), 2002.

Margaret Wise Brown, *Sailor Boy Jig*, Margaret K. McElderry Books (New York, NY), 2002.

(With Ann Boyajian) Tamara England, Michelle Jones, and Peg Ross, *Samantha's Friendship Fun*, Pleasant Company Publications (Middleton, WI), 2002.

S.A. Kramer, *Night Flight: Charles Lindbergh's Incredible Adventure*, Grosset & Dunlap (New York, NY), 2002.

Valerie Tripp, *Felicity Discovers a Secret*, Pleasant Company Publications (Middleton, WI), 2002.

Valerie Tripp, *Samantha's Blue Bicycle*, Pleasant Company Publications (Middleton, WI), 2002.

Rosemary and Tom Wells, *The House in the Mail*, Viking (New York, NY), 2002.

Melissa Wiley, *The Road from Roxbury*, HarperCollins (New York, NY), 2002.

Douglas Wood, *A Quiet Place*, Simon & Schuster (New York, NY), 2002.

William Anderson, *River Boy: The Story of Mark Twain*, HarperCollins (New York, NY), 2003.

Bruce Balan, *The Balloon Man*, Simon & Schuster (New York, NY), 2003.

(With Troy Howell) Sarah Masters Buckey, *Samantha's Special Talent*, Pleasant Company Publications (Middleton, WI), 2003.

Shana Corey, *Joan of Arc*, Random House (New York, NY), 2003.

Celia Wilkins, *Little City by the Lake*, HarperCollins (New York, NY), 2003.

Sharlee Glenn, *Keeping up with Roo*, Putnam (New York, NY), 2004.

B.G. Hennessy, *The Attic Christmas*, Putnam (New York, NY), 2004.

Alison Jeffries, *Sam and the Bag*, Harcourt (Orlando, FL), 2004.

Melissa Wiley, *Across the Puddingstone Dam,* HarperCollins (New York, NY), 2004.

Alyssa Satin Capucilli, *Little Spotted Cat,* Dial Books (New York, NY), 2005.

Bunny Crumpacker, *Alexander's Pretending Day,* Dutton (New York, NY), 2005.

Rhonda Gowler Greene, *Firebears: The Rescue Team,* Henry Holt (New York, NY), 2005.

Sandra Day O'Connor, *Chico,* Dutton (New York, NY), 2005.

Celia Wilkins, *A Little House of Their Own,* HarperCollins (New York, NY), 2005.

Lisa Church, reteller, *20,000 Leagues under the Sea* (based on the novel by Jules Verne), Sterling Publishing (New York, NY), 2006.

Kristin Earhart, *Starlight,* Scholastic (New York, NY), 2006.

Oliver Ho, reteller, *The Adventures of Huckleberry Finn* (based on the novel by Mark Twain), Sterling Publishing (New York, NY), 2006.

Kathleen Olmstead, reteller, *Oliver Twist* (based on the novel by Charles Dickins), Sterling Publishing (New York, NY), 2006.

Kathleen Olmstead, reteller, *White Fang* (based on the novel by Jack London), Sterling Publishing (New York, NY), 2006.

Valerie Tripp, *Felicity's Short Story Collection,* Pleasant Company Publications (Middleton, WI), 2006.

(With Troy Howell) Valerie Tripp and Sarah Masters Buckey, *Samantha's Short-Story Collection,* Pleasant Company Publications (Middleton, WI), 2006.

Tania Zamorsky, reteller, *The Story of King Arthur and His Knights,* Sterling Publishing (New York, NY), 2006.

Bill Cochran, *The Forever Dog,* HarperCollins (New York, NY), 2007.

Joy N. Hulme, *Stable in Bethlehem: A Christmas Counting Book,* Sterling Publishing (New York, NY), 2007.

Stephen Krensky, *Too Many Leprechauns; or, How That Pot o' Gold Got to the End of the Rainbow,* Simon & Schuster (New York, NY), 2007.

(With others) Teri Witkowski and Jennifer Hirsch, *Minute Mysteries Two: More Stories to Solve,* Pleasant Company Publications (Middleton, WI), 2007.

Karen Kingsbury, *Let's Go on a Mommy Date,* Zonderkidz (Grand Rapids, MI), 2008.

Michelle Meadows, *Pilot Pups,* Simon & Schuster (New York, NY), 2008.

Eileen Spinelli, *Hug a Bug,* HarperCollins (New York, NY), 2008.

Sidelights

Dan Andreasen is the illustrator of several highly regarded picture books, including Steven Kroll's *By the Dawn's Early Light: The Story of the Star-spangled Banner* and Douglas Wood's *A Quiet Place.* A former sculptor for American Greetings Corporation, Andreasen has also provided the artwork for Valerie Tripp's *Felicity Takes a Dare* and numerous other titles in Pleasant Company's popular "American Girls" book series. In

Dan Andreasen's detailed paintings bring to life Douglas Wood's imaginative picture book **A Quiet Place.** (Aladdin Paperbacks, 2002. Illustrations copyright © 2002 Dan Andreasen. All rights reserved. Reprinted with the permission of Simon & Schuster Books for Young Readers, an imprint of Simon & Schuster Children's Publishing Division.)

addition, he has produce self-illustrated volumes such as *The Giant of Seville,* a picture book that a *Publishers Weekly* contributor praised as "a folksy, big-hearted tale."

Andreasen, whose detailed oil paintings have been used by such companies as Fanny Farmer and Marshall Fields, has enjoyed successful picture-book collaborations with Rosemary Wells, Tres Seymour, and other talented authors. In one of his illustration projects, *Grandma's Garden* by Elaine Moore, a young girl makes a spring visit to her grandmother's country home, where the two prepare the land for planting. "Andreasen's realistic, earth-tone paintings ably portray the wealth of feelings shared by the pair," observed *Booklist* critic Kay Weisman. The illustrator also teamed with Kroll on *Pony Express!,* which chronicles the history of the nineteenth-century mail service. Andreasen's paintings, "rendered with near photographic quality, clearly convey the human cost of this effort," Weisman stated, and a *Publishers Weekly* reviewer noted that his illustrations showcase the riders' "unflagging spirit and determination as they battled to get the mail through on time."

A Kentucky farm is the setting of Seymour's *We Played Marbles,* which recounts a U.S. Civil War battle. According to *Booklist* critic Helen Rosenberg, Andreasen's oil paintings "beautifully capture the drama of the past as well as the serenity of the present." In *The House in the Mail,* written by Rosemary and Tom Wells, a family constructs a house using a kit offered in the 1928 Sears, Roebuck catalogue. "Andreasen's art adheres to the scrapbook premise, sacrificing a more dynamic rhythm and palette to offer neatly compiled images in muted colors," observed a reviewer in *Publishers Weekly.* A young boy learns to enjoy the pleasures of solitude in *A Quiet Place.* "The pretty, framed, full-page pictures have an old-fashioned *Saturday Evening Post* feel to them," remarked Hazel Rochman in a *Booklist* review of the book, and a *Kirkus Reviews* contributor stated that Andreasen's "lifelike illustrations provide just the right accompaniment on this imaginative journey."

Andreasen has also earned praise for his self-illustrated titles. In *With a Little Help from Daddy,* a "simple celebration of a loving relationship," noted *School Library Journal* critic Gay Lynn Van Vleck, a tiny blue elephant spends a joyful day with its father. The illustrations "make it clear that this is a real team," a *Publishers Weekly* reviewer stated, and Doug Ward, writing in the *New York Times Book Review,* noted that Andreasen "fashions a tight weave between his reassuring pictures and his gentle words." A piglet's messy but humorous attempts to surprise its mother are the focus of *A Special Day for Mommy.* A critic in *Kirkus Reviews* called Andreasen's "'50s-period illustrations and colors so right they are like comfort food," and a *Publishers Weekly* contributor stated that "the sturdy, rounded shapes and warm colors of Andreasen's oil paintings exude domestic comfort even as they suggest play."

In *The Baker's Dozen: A Counting Book,* a work told in verse, Andreasen introduces a jolly baker whose delicious pastries draw thirteen customers to his door. According to Rochman, young readers "will find the messy baking play as much fun as the food." Based on a true story, *The Giant of Seville* concerns Captain Martin Van Buren Bates, a retired circus performer standing nearly eight feet tall who decides to settle down in Seville, Ohio. When Bates and his equally large wife have problems adjusting to small-town life, the residents pitch in to make the couple feel welcome. "Andreasen extends the tale's old-fashioned feel in detailed, color-washed ink drawings of townspeople in nineteenth-century dress," observed Gillian Engberg in *Booklist,* and a contributor in *Kirkus Reviews* described the work as "a clever blend of tall-tale telling, historical anecdote and giant-sized appeal that truly measures up."

Biographical and Critical Sources

PERIODICALS

Booklist, June 1, 1994, Kay Weisman, review of *Grandma's Garden,* p. 1842; April 15, 1995, Lauren Peterson, review of *Brigid Bewitched,* p. 1509; December 15, 1995, Stephanie Zvirin, review of *Brigid the Bad,* p. 705; March 1, 1996, Kay Weisman, review of *Pony Express!,* p. 1177; February 15, 1998, Helen Rosenberg, review of *We Played Marbles,* p. 1020; October 15, 1998, Carolyn Phelan, review of *Halley Came to Jackson,* p. 426; May 1, 1999, Hazel Rochman, review of *Streets of Gold,* p. 1593; January 1, 2001, Stephanie Zvirin, review of *The Stars That Shine,* p. 956; February 15, 2002, Hazel Rochman, review of *A Quiet Place,* p. 1023; September 1, 2002, Kathy Broderick, review of *Love Song for a Baby,* p. 134; January 1, 2004, Ilene Cooper, review of *Keeping up with Roo,* p. 876; April 1, 2004, Julie Cummins, review of *A Special Day for Mommy,* p. 1367; February 1, 2007, Gillian Engberg, review of *The Giant of Seville: A "Tall" Tale Based on a True Story,* p. 45; July 1, 2007, Hazel Rochman, review of *The Baker's Dozen: A Counting Book,* p. 63.

Kirkus Reviews, March 15, 2002, review of *A Quiet Place,* p. 429; May 1, 2003, review of *With a Little Help from Daddy,* p. 673; March 1, 2004, review of *A Special Day for Mommy,* p. 217; March 15, 2005, Alyssa Satin Capucilli, review of *Little Spotted Cat,* p. 348; December 1, 2006, review of *Too Many Leprechauns; or, How That Pot o' Gold Got to the End of the Rainbow,* p. 1222; January 15, 2007, review of *The Giant of Seville,* p. 69; March 1, 2007, review of *The Forever Dog,* p. 218.

New York Times Book Review, June 1, 2003, Doug Ward, review of *With a Little Help from Daddy,* p. 24; December 19, 2004, Constance Decker Thompson, review of *The Attic Christmas,* p. 27; May 15, 2005, Jessica Bruder, review of *Little Spotted Cat,* p. 20.

Publishers Weekly, February 5, 1996, review of *Pony Express!,* p. 90; December 8, 1997, review of *Pioneer Girl,* p. 72; January 14, 2002, review of *The House in the Mail,* p. 60; April 14, 2003, review of *With a Little Help from Daddy,* p. 68; March 29, 2004, review of *A Special Day for Mommy,* p. 61; August 8, 2005, review of *Firebears: The Rescue Team,* p. 232; March 12, 2007, review of *The Giant of Seville,* p. 56.

School Library Journal, July, 2002, Jody McCoy, review of *A Quiet Place,* p. 102; May, 2003, Gay Lynn Van Vleck, review of *With a Little Help from Daddy,* p. 108; July, 2004, Jane Marino, review of *A Special Day for Mommy,* p. 66; April, 2005, Lisa Gangemi Kropp, review of *Alexander's Pretending Day,* p. 96; June, 2005, Blair Christolon, review of *Little Spotted Cat,* p. 106; July, 2005, Wendy Woodfill, review of *Firebears,* p. 74; March, 2006, Marlene Johnson, review of *Very Funny, Elizabeth!,* p. 203; August, 2006, Cheri Dobbs, review of *The Story of King Arthur and His Knights,* p. 132; February, 2007, Kirsten Cutler, review of *Too Many Leprechauns,* p. 90; April, 2007, Robin L. Gibson, review of *The Giant of Seville,* p. 119.

ONLINE

Shannon Associates Web site, http://www.shannonassociates.com/artists/ (December 20, 2007), "Dan Andreasen."*

ATTEBERRY, Kevan J.

Personal

Male.

Addresses

Home and office—P.O. Box 40188, Bellevue, WA 98015. *E-mail*—kevan@oddisgood.com.

Career

Illustrator.

Member

Picture Book Artists Association (Web master, 2004).

Awards, Honors

Best Juvenile Book designation, Oklahoma Writers Federation, 2006, for *Lunchbox and the Aliens.*

Illustrator

Tish Rabe, *Lots of Letters,* Innovative Kids (Norwalk, CT), 2006.

Bryan W. Fields, *Lunchbox and the Aliens,* Henry Holt (New York, NY), 2006.

Lola M. Schaefer, *Frankie Stein,* Marshall Cavendish (New York, NY), 2007.

Bryan W. Fields, *Froonga Planet,* Henry Holt (New York, NY), 2008.

Sidelights

As a children's book illustrator, Kevan J. Atteberry is known for creating stylistic art using both computer programs and more-traditional means. In his illustra-

tions for *Frankie Stein* by Lola M. Schaefer, Atteberry brings to life the story of a married Frankenstein-like couple whose child is cute and cuddly. The perplexed couple attempts to make their adorable little boy scarier by dying his hair purple and plastering fake warts on his face. According to *Booklist* contributor Ilene Cooper, Atteberry's "glossy graphic-style artwork," generated by computer, enhances Schaefer's story and "takes every opportunity to find the sly aside" featured in the author's text. Donna Atmur, reviewing the book in *School Library Journal,* remarked on Atteberry's bold use of color in *Frankie Stein,* concluding that the illustrator's use of purple and green highlights "the cartoony creepiness of the Stein house."

Biographical and Critical Sources

PERIODICALS

Booklist, September 15, 2007, Ilene Cooper, review of *Frankie Stein,* p. 72.

Publishers Weekly, September 24, 2007, review of *Frankie Stein,* p. 72.

School Library Journal, October, 2006, Cynde Suite, review of *Lunchbox and the Aliens,* p. 110; September, 2007, review of *Frankie Stein,* p. 175.

ONLINE

Children's Bookwatch Web site, http://www.midwestbookreview.com/ (November 1, 2006), review of *Lunchbox and the Aliens.*

Kevan J. Atteberry Home Page, http://oddisgood.com/ (December 11, 2007).

B

BAE, Hyun-Joo

Personal
Born in South Korea. *Education:* Ewha Women's University (Seoul, South Korea), graduate; attended Hankook Illustration School. *Hobbies and other interests:* Studying traditional Korean culture and folktales.

Addresses
Home—South Korea.

Career
Author and illustrator.

Writings

(Self-illustrated) *New Clothes for New Year's Day,* Kane/Miller Book Publishers (La Jolla, CA), 2007.

Biographical and Critical Sources

PERIODICALS

Booklist, February 1, 2007, Jennifer Mattson, review of *New Clothes for New Year's Day,* p. 48.
Children's Bookwatch, February, 2007, review of *New Clothes for New Year's Day.*
Washington Post Book World, December 10, 2006, Jabari Asim, review of *New Clothes for New Year's Day,* p. 8.

ONLINE

Kane Miller Web site, http://www.kanemiller.com/ (January 3, 2007), "Hyun-joo Bae."*

BARAKAT, Ibtisam 1963-

Personal
Born October 2, 1963, in Beit Hanina, E. Jerusalem, Palestine; immigrated to United States June 9, 1986. *Education:* Birzeit University, degree (English literature); University of Missouri—Columbia, M.A. (journalism), M.A. (human development and family studies). *Hobbies and other interests:* Reading, especially works by Nobel Prize winners in literature; photography; languages; music.

Addresses
Home and office—Columbia, MO. *E-mail*—i_barakat@yahoo.com.

Career
Memoirist, poet, songwriter, speaker, journalist, Mideast scholar, educator, photographer, and translator. Human rights activist; U.S. delegate to third United Nations World Conference for the Elimination of Racial Discrimination. Stephens College, instructor of language ethics; founder and leader of Write Your Life seminars.

Awards, Honors
American Library Association Notable Book designation, National Council of Social Studies/Children's Book Council Notable Trade Book in the Field of Social Studies designation, and Middle East Outreach Council Best Literature Award, all 2007, all for *Tasting the Sky.*

Writings

Tasting the Sky: A Palestinian Childhood, Farrar, Straus & Giroux (New York, NY), 2007.

Poetry included in anthologies such as *The Flag of Childhood*, edited by Naomi Shihab-Nye, Aladdin (New York, NY), 2002, and online. Essays included in *What a Song Can Do*, edited by Jennifer Armstrong, Knopf (New York, NY), 2004, and in periodicals and online sites.

Sidelights

Ibtisam Barakat has long lived under the shadow of war. At age three, she fled with her family from their home in the Palestinian city of Ramallah to Jordan to escape the terror of the Six-Day War. After the war ended, the Barakat family returned to Ramallah and lived under the Israeli occupation. "Ever since the Six-Day War I have had a huge amount of fear that separated me from my mind and my memory, from all sorts of things in me," the author later explained to interviewer Robert Hirschfield for the *Washington Report on Middle East Affairs*. "Fear is another level of occupation. . . . It holds your life energy hostage. My life's goal is to create bridges across the fear to new possibilities." In 1986, Barakat moved to New York City to work as an intern at the *Nation* magazine. She then studied journalism and human develpment at the University of Missouri—Columbia and began writing what would become her memoir for young adults, *Tasting the Sky: A Palestinian Childhood*. She taught language ethics at Stephens College, and founded Write Your Life seminars "because the society needs everyone's voice and everyone's story," as she told *SATA*. Barakat eventually became a U.S. delegate to the third United Nations World Conference for the Elimination of Racial Discrimination.

Barakat's memoir begins in 1981 when, at age seventeen, she was returning home to Ramallah by bus after visiting her post-office box in a neighboring town. Stopped at a check point run by Israeli soldiers, Barakat was told by a soldier that her city was destroyed. She, along with everyone else on the bus, was transferred to a detention center. The experience brought back all her memories of fear during the Six-Day War. "What makes the memoir so compelling is the immediacy of the child's viewpoint," wrote Hazel Rochman in a review of *Tasting the Sky* for *Booklist*. A critic for *Publishers Weekly* noted that Barakat's "understated tone lacks self-pity and thus allows readers to witness her fear and hope." Nomi Morris, writing in *Biography*, called the memoir "a lyrical journey through dislocation and occupation," and Kathleen Isaacs commented in *School Library Journal* that Barakat's description of her homeland and culture "brings to life a Palestinian world" readers "will come to know and appreciate."

Although introducing young readers to Palestinian life and culture was not Barakat's first goal, it is a goal in keeping with her efforts to help in healing the hurts of racial injustices and prejudice. "In the face of destructive thoughts and the stereotypes that accompany political strife, human kindness really goes very far," she told Rick Margolis in a *School Library Journal* interview. Discussing why she geared her memoir for teen readers, she told Hirschfield: "Part of me has remained a child because of that war. So, part of me is in complete empathy with all children, and the parts of people that are children."

"My biggest struggle and achievement in writing *Tasting the Sky* was in sorting through the relationship betweenthe young voice and the adult voice," Barakat explained to *SATA*. "In order to allow the voice of the young person to speak freely and to tell this story, I had to fight continually to make sure the adult mindset did not interfere, but rather did the hard work of getting out of the way. It was like pushing the walls of the society to create a larger playground for a child, and making sure all the playing is on the young person's terms.

"I think that to remember what it was like to be a young person is to remember the core and the root of ourselves. As a child I was very concerned with the joy of simply being alive and the understanding of every thing in my environment. As I remain true to that intent, I maintain a sense of continuity. I can look into my inner mirror and recognize who I am no matter where I happen to be."

Biographical and Critical Sources

PERIODICALS

Biography, summer, 2007, Nomi Morris, review of *Tasting the Sky: A Palestinian Childhood,* p. 413.

Booklist, March 15, 2007, Hazel Rochman, review of *Tasting the Sky,* p. 48.

Publishers Weekly, April 2, 2007, review of *Tasting the Sky,* p. 59.

School Library Journal, May, 2007, Rick Margolis, "Give Peace a Chance," p. 32, and Kathleen Isaacs, review of *Tasting the Sky,* p. 148.

Voice of Youth Advocates, June, 2007, Suzi Steffen, review of *Tasting the Sky,* p. 170.

Washington Report on Middle East Affairs, July, 2007, Robert Hirschfield, "Author Ibtisam Barakat Unites English Language, Palestinian Memory," p. 62.

ONLINE

Ibtisam Barakat Home Page, http://www.ibtisambarakat. com (November 28, 2007).

National Book Critics Circle Board of Directors Blog, http://www.bookcriticscircle.blogspot.com/ (May 14, 2007), interview with Barakat.

Wisconsin International Outreach Consortium Web site, http://www.wioc.wisc.edu/ (November 28, 2007), "Ibtisam Barakat."

BARASCH, Lynne 1939-

Personal

Born March 23, 1939, in New York, NY; daughter of Robert Julius and Elaine Marx; married Kenneth Robert Barasch (an ophthalmologist), June 20, 1958; children: Wendy, Jill (deceased), Nina (deceased), Cassie, Dinah. *Education:* Attended Rhode Island School of Design, 1957-58; Parsons School of Design, B.A., 1976. *Politics:* Democrat. *Religion:* Jewish. *Hobbies and other interests:* Theater, ballet, art.

Addresses

Home—New York, NY. *Agent*—Jean V. Naggar Literary Agency, Inc., 216 E. 75th St., New York, NY 10021. *E-mail*—llbarasch@aol.com.

Career

Children's author and illustrator.

Member

Authors Guild, Authors League.

Awards, Honors

Outstanding Science Trade Book for Children designation, National Science Teachers Association/Children's Book Council (CBC), 1993, for *A Winter Walk;* Oppenheim Toy Portfolio Gold Award, for *The Reluctant Flower Girl;* Notable Children's Book selection, *Smithsonian* magazine, 2000, Notable Children's Book selection, American Library Association, 2001, and Pick of the Lists selection, American Booksellers Association, Best Children's Books of the Year selection, Bank Street College of Education, and Oppenheim Toy Portfolio Gold Award, all for *Radio Rescue;* Paterson Prize for Books for Young People, and Notable Social Studies Trade Book, National Council for the Social Studies/CBC, both 2005, both for *Knockin' on Wood;* Parents' Choice Award, 2005, for *Ask Albert Einstein.*

Writings

SELF-ILLUSTRATED PICTURE BOOKS

Rodney's Inside Story, Orchard Books (New York, NY), 1992.
A Winter Walk, Ticknor & Fields (New York, NY), 1993.
Old Friends, Farrar, Straus & Giroux (New York, NY), 1998.
Radio Rescue, Frances Foster Books (New York, NY), 2000.
The Reluctant Flower Girl, HarperCollins (New York, NY), 2001.
Knockin' on Wood: Starring Peg Leg Bates, Lee & Low Books (New York, NY), 2004.

Lynne Barasch (Reproduced by permission.)

A Country Schoolhouse, Farrar, Straus & Giroux (New York, NY), 2004.
Ask Albert Einstein, Farrar, Straus & Giroux (New York, NY), 2005.
Hiromi's Hands, Lee & Low Books (New York, NY), 2006.

ILLUSTRATOR

Jane Cutler, *Commonsense and Fowls,* Farrar, Straus & Giroux (New York, NY), 2005.
Mona Kerby, *Owney, the Mail Pouch Pooch,* Farrar, Straus & Giroux (New York, NY), 2008.

Sidelights

Lynne Barasch is the author of several critically acclaimed works for young readers, including *Knockin' on Wood: Starring Peg Leg Bates* and *Hiromi's Hands.* Barasch once told *SATA* that she found "picture books . . . a very gratifying means of expression." As she also remarked to *Cynsations* online interviewer Cynthia Leitich Smith, "As an illustrator, I am always writing with pictures in my head. I don't use paragraphs when a few words will do!"

Barasch developed an interest in the arts early in life, as she told Smith. "All my life I have painted \and done drawings," she recalled. "I went to art classes as a child and to the Art Students League on Saturdays when I was in high school." After high school, Barasch attended the Rhode Island School of Design and later graduated from the Parsons School of Design. It was not until her daughter, Cassie, was ten years old, however, that she began writing and illustrating in earnest. She published her debut work, *Rodney's Inside Story,* in 1992.

Barasch followed that effort with *A Winter's Walk,* a quiet tale about a day in winter when Sophie and her mother go for a stroll. Describing the outdoors in a simple text, Barasch accompanied the story with watercolor illustrations, eliciting praise from a *Kirkus Reviews* contributor for putting together a "quiet book with special appeal for the observant child."

In another work, *Old Friends,* Barasch explores the unusual topic, for picture books, of reincarnation. Henrietta is an older woman who has outlived her acquaintances, and very much misses her childhood friend, Anna. One day, she meets a little dog that seems to communicate with her, reminding her of Anna. Henrietta realizes a connection with the dog and they remain friends until the woman dies. Reviewing this work for *School Library Journal,* Jody McCoy lauded Barasch's "soft focus" illustrations and "thoughtful text."

In 2001 Barasch wrote and illustrated *The Reluctant Flower Girl,* a book about young April and the wedding of her older sister, Annabel. Fearing she is losing her best friend, April attempts to thwart the upcoming nuptials, telling her sister's fiancé that Annabel both snores and wets the bed. However, discovering that her brother-in-law has a fine sense of humor and play, April realizes that she is not losing a sister, but instead gaining a brother. Writing in *Publishers Weekly,* a critic remarked that "Barasch gets to the heart of a girl's jumble of feelings regarding her sister's wedding with both humor and honesty." "In simple, perfectly paced text and appealing pen-and-watercolor drawings," found *Booklist* reviewer Gillian Engberg, the author and illustrator "nicely captures a young girl's sense of loss, leavening it with plenty of humor and lighthearted detail."

In *Knockin' on Wood,* Barasch chronicles the life of Clayton "Peg Leg" Bates, a remarkable one-legged tap dancer. Bates, a sharecropper's son who lost his left leg in a machine accident at the age of twelve, learned to walk and dance with the aid of a wooden leg. After performing for years on the vaudeville circuit, he rose to fame, appearing on television's *Ed Sullivan Show* and before the king and queen of England. On the Lee & Low Books Web site, Barasch stated: "If I had to single out one thing that this story says to me it would be: The pursuit of an art has the power to carry you through life no matter what obstacles may present themselves. There is no finer endeavor." *Knockin' on Wood,* which garnered the Paterson Prize for Books for Young People, was described as "a very neat story, told briefly but effectively," by a contributor to *Kirkus Reviews,* and Marianne Saccardi remarked in *School Library Journal* that

"Barasch's watercolor-and-ink cartoon paintings capture the poverty of the dancer's early life, the adulation of his falls, and his joyous love of dancing."

A grandfather recounts a piece of his childhood in *A Country Schoolhouse,* "an undeniably engaging look back," according to *Booklist* critic GraceAnne A. DeCandido. While reminiscing with his grandson, the senior citizen describes the three-room country schoolhouse he attended during the 1940s, fondly recalling the wood-burning stove that kept students warm, his love of spelling and geography bees, and even the lack of indoor plumbing. A critic in *Kirkus Reviews* described Barasch's self-illustrated tale as "a child-friendly history lesson made relevant with details," and *School Library Journal* contributor Catherine Threadgill remarked that the book's "watercolor-and-ink illustrations create a solid sense of time and place."

Based on a 1952 *New York Times* article, *Ask Albert Einstein* focuses on the efforts of seven-year-old April to help her older sister, Annabel, a high-schooler who is struggling with math. After she fails in her own efforts to solve one particularly vexing problem, April pens a letter to the celebrated physicist, requesting his assistance. "There's a lot to like here: sprightly pen-and-ink art, a clever presentation of Einstein's famous sayings, easily understood biographical material," Ilene Cooper commented in *Booklist.* Holly Sneeringer, reviewing the work for *School Library Journal,* wrote that Barasch's "nostalgic cartoon illustrations and numerous quotes from the international figure add charm to this enchanting tale."

In *Hiromi's Hands,* an "upbeat, contemporary immigration story," according to *Booklist* critic Hazel Rochman, Barasch offers a biography of Hiromi Suzuki, one of

Barasch focuses on the importance of cultural traditions in her self-illustrated picture book **Hiromi's Hands.** *(Lee and Low Books, Inc., 2007.*

New York City's first female sushi chefs. "I first met Hiromi as an adorable, shy, five-year-old kindergartener in my daughter Dinah's class," the author remarked on the Lee & Low Books Web site, adding, "Their teacher predicted that they would be lifelong friends, and her prediction came true!" The work follows not only the life of Hiromi but also that of her father, Akira Suzuki, a restaurateur who taught his daughter the culinary arts. "The muted ink-and-watercolor illustrations are spare but expressive," observed *Horn Book* contributor Jennifer M. Brabander. A critic in *Kirkus Reviews* described *Hiromi's Hands* as "a fascinating family story."

Biographical and Critical Sources

PERIODICALS

Booklist, May 1, 2001, Gillian Engberg, review of *The Reluctant Flower Girl*, p. 1688; June 1, 2004, Ilene Cooper, review of *Knockin' on Wood: Starring Peg Leg Bates*, p. 1760; September 1, 2004, GraceAnne A. DeCandido, review of *A Country Schoolhouse*, p. 129; September 1, 2005, Ilene Cooper, review of *Ask Albert Einstein*, p. 126; March 15, 2007, Hazel Rochman, review of *Hiromi's Hands*, p. 50.
Children's Book Review Service, November, 1993, review of *A Winter's Walk*, p. 25.
Five Owls, February, 1995, review of *A Winter's Walk*, p. 55.
Horn Book, May-June, 2007, Jennifer M. Brabander, review of *Hiromi's Hands*, p. 299.
Kirkus Reviews, July 15, 1993, review of *A Winter's Walk*, p. 930; January 15, 1998, review of *Old Friends*, p. 109.
Miami Herald, August 20, 2004, Sue Corbett, "Author Barasch Passes Things on from Past to Future."
Publishers Weekly, April 30, 2001, review of *The Reluctant Flower Girl*, p. 76; May 1, 2004, review of *Knockin' on Wood*, p. 438; July 15, 2004, review of *A Country Schoolhouse*, p. 681; March 1, 2005, review of *Common Sense and Fowls*, p. 285; October 1, 2005, review of *Ask Albert Einstein*, p. 1076; February 15, 2007, review of *Hiromi's Hands*.
School Library Journal, September, 1993, Starr LaTronica, review of *A Winter's Walk*, p. 204; April, 1998, Jody McCoy, review of *Old Friends*, p. 91; June, 2004, Marianne Saccardi, review of *Knockin' on Wood*, p. 122; August, 2004, Catherine Threadgill, review of *A Country Schoolhouse*, p. 82; March, 2005, Deanna Romriell, review of *Common Sense and Fowls*, p. 170; January, 2006, Holly T. Sneeringer, review of *Ask Albert Einstein*, p. 116; May, 2007, Wendy Lukehart, review of *Hiromi's Hands*, p. 113.

ONLINE

Cynsations Web site, http://cynthialeitichsmith.blogspot.com/ (March 28, 2007), Cynthia Leitich Smith, interview with Barasch.
Lee & Low Books Web site, http://www.leeandlow.com/ (December 20, 2007), "Booktalk with Lynne Barasch."
Lynne Barasch Home Page, http://www.lynnebarasch.com (December 20, 2007).

* * *

BAYOC, Cbabi
(Clifford Miskell)

Personal

Born in Fort Dix, NJ; son of Sandra Louise Miskell; married; wife's name Reine (an artist); children: Jurni Moon, Ajani Day. *Education:* Belleville Area College (now Southwest Illinois College), A.A. (liberal arts); Grambling State University, B.A. (drawing and painting).

Addresses

Home and office—St. Louis, MO. *Office*—Bayoc Studio, 4177 Cleveland Ave., St. Louis, MO 63110. *E-mail*—bayoc@bayocstudio.com.

Career

Illustrator. Worked previously as a caricaturist at Six Flags (amusement park), 1997.

Member

New Power House (honorary member).

Illustrator

Ruth Forman, *Young Cornrows Callin out the Moon: Poem*, Children's Book Press (San Francisco, CA), 2007.

Sidelights

As artist Cbabi Bayoc noted on his home page, his mission in life is to create "art which reflects [my] . . . love of music and family." Bayoc's full name, which he created, is also a representation of himself as an artist: it is an acronym in which Cbabi stands for "Creative Black Artist Battling Ignorance" and Bayoc stands for "Blessed African Youth of Creativity."

Bayoc began his artistic career working as a caricaturist at Six Flags amusement park, and he has bone on to find success creating caricatures for musicians' album covers. In addition to creating his unique caricatures, Bayoc has also created illustrated works for large corporations, such as Coca-Cola, Anheuser-Busch, and SIDS Resource. In an interview for the University of Missouri—St. Louis Web site, Bayoc advised aspiring artists to "create as much as you can with 100 percent effort, and then find a great college with a great art department with a great staff with great connections to the outer art world."

Bayoc's first illustration project, the children's book *Young Cornrows Callin out the Moon: Poem* follows Ruth Forman's rhyming text as she reminisces about summers as a child in South Philly. The rhyming text recalls hot summer days spent playing games and eating ice cream, having her hair braided in cornrows, and watching the moon in the night sky. Bayoc's illustrations capture these memories, employing "thick lines and bright colors in exaggerated folklore style" according to Hazel Rochman in *Booklist.* Mary Hazelton, writing in *School Library Journal,* commented that Bayoc's images for *Young Cornrows Callin out the Moon* "swirl with energy, movement, and color," and Clarence V. Reynolds wrote in *Black Issues Book Review* that the energetic illustrations "don't miss a beat" in keeping the rhythm of Forman's poetry.

Biographical and Critical Sources

PERIODICALS

Black Issues Book Review, March-April, 2007, Clarence V. Reynolds, review of *Young Cornrows Callin out the Moon: Poem,* p. 23.
Booklinks, March, 2007, Angela Leeper, review of *Young Cornrows Callin out the Moon,* p. 32.
Booklist, February 1, 2007, Hazel Rochman, review of *Young Cornrows Callin out the Moon,* p. 60.
Bulletin of the Center for Children's Books, June, 2007, Deborah Stevenson, review of *Young Cornrows Callin out the Moon,* p. 414.
School Library Journal, March, 2007, Mary Hazelton, review of *Young Cornrows Callin out the Moon,* p. 195.

ONLINE

Cbabi Bayoc Home Page, http://www.bayocstudio.com (December 15, 2007).
New Power Clique Web site, http://www.newpowerclique.com/ (December 15, 2007), "Cbabi Bayoc—Painter and Illustrator."
St. Louis Artists' Guild Web site, http://www.stlouisartists guild.org/ (December 15, 2007), "Cbabi Bayoc: Emerging Local Artists, on the National Scene."
University of Missouri—St. Louis Web site, http://www.um sl.edu/ (December 15, 2007), interview with Bayoc.*

*   *   *

BEATY, Andrea

Personal
Born in IL.

Addresses
Home—Chicago, IL. *E-mail*—andreabeaty@gmail.com.

Andrea Beaty (Courtesy of Andrea Beaty.)

Career
Children's book author.

Member
Society of Children's Book Writers and Illustrators.

Awards, Honors
Barbara Karlin Honor grant for picture-book writing, 2006, Society of Children's Book Writers and Illustrators, for *When Giants Come to Play;* Parents' Choice Silver Honor, and *Time* magazine Top Ten Children's Book, both 2007, both for *Iggy Peck, Architect.*

Writings

When Giants Come to Play, illustrated by Kevin Hawkes, Abrams (New York, NY), 2006.
Iggy Peck, Architect, illustrated by David Roberts, Abrams (New York, NY), 2007.
Cicada Summer (middle-grade novel), Amulet Books (New York, NY), 2008.
Dr. Ted, illustrated by Pascal Lemaître, Margaret K. McElderry Books (New York, NY), 2008.
Firefighter Ted, illustrated by Pascal Lemaître, Margaret K. McElderry Books (New York, NY), 2009.
Hush, Baby Ghostling, illustrated by Pascal Lemaître, Margaret K. McElderry Books (New York, NY), 2009.
Master Ted, True Artiste, illustrated by Pascal Lemaître, Margaret K. McElderry Books (New York, NY), 2010.

Sidelights

Born and raised in the Midwest, Andrea Beaty instills each of her picture books with a sense of fun and whimsy. In addition to the simple, rhyming texts she has created to entertain young children in books such as *When Giants Come to Play, Iggy Peck, Architect,* and *Dr. Ted,* Beaty also addresses older readers in *Cicada Summer,* a novel for middle graders in which a preteen deals with the guilt she feels over her brother's death.

Beaty's first picture book, *When Giants Come to Play,* focuses on a day of fun as Anna finds traditional games such as hide and seek and jump rope taking on a new twist when two giants are her playmates. Playing a game of catch, for example, is particularly exciting for Anna when she serves as the ball and is tossed from giant to giant. Praising *When Giants Come to Play* in *School Library Journal,* Sally R. Dow dubbed Beaty's book "a delightful romp, full of imagination, told in lyrical prose." In *Booklist,* Randall Enos made particular note of the illustrations by Kevin Hawkes, which Enos described as softly toned and portraying the giants with a "slight resemblance to [American film comedians] Laurel and Hardy." The author uses an "economical and straightforward text," noted a *Kirkus Reviews* contributor, concluded of the book that "Beaty's language and Hawkes's pictures make it enormously appealing."

In her second award-winning picture book, *Iggy Peck, Architect,* Beaty and illustrator David Roberts team up to focus on a little boy whose only joy is building things. Iggy does not need wooden blocks, or Legos or any other toy in order to indulge in his favorite pastime; he can build using anything at hand. A problem comes in second grade, however, when his teacher Miss Greer puts the kibosh on construction. During a school fieldtrip that takes Miss Greer's class to a park where a faulty footbridge strands the group on a small island, Iggy's talent proves invaluable: he creates a suspension bridge with roots, string, and assorted scrounged objects and helps the group return safely home. "Youthful irreverence and creativity find a champion in this tale," noted a *Publishers Weekly* contributor, concluding of *Iggy Peck, Architect* that "the structured rhymes and controlled illustrations fit the architectural theme" of Beaty's tale. Margaret R. Tassia wrote in *School Library Journal* that Roberts' cartoon drawings "capture the emotion and action of [Beaty's] . . . imaginative story."

In an interview with Cynthia Leitich Smith for *Cynsations* online, Beaty noted of her childhood: "Our mother was a voracious reader and filled our house with books so when I wasn't on an adventure or blowing soda out my nose from laughing too hard, I was reading. I had about a hundred things I was going to be when I grew up: spy, detective, arctic explorer, interpreter for the U.N., pirate, English veterinarian, head of the CIA, pool shark. . . .

In When Giant's Come to Play *Beaty's playful story is injected with visual humor by illustrator Kevin Hawkes.* (Abrams Books for Young Readers. Illustration © 2006 by Kevin Hawkes. Reproduced by permission.)

"I think the great thing about being a writer is that I can still be all of those things if I just keep writing! I guess I've already been a giant, an architect, and a bear doctor! What's next?"

Biographical and Critical Sources

PERIODICALS

Booklist, September 15, 2006, Randall Enos, review of *When Giants Come to Play,* p. 65.
Bulletin of the Center for Children's Books, November, 2006, Deborah Stevenson, review of *When Giants Come to Play,* p. 113.
Kirkus Reviews, August 1, 2006, review of *When Giants Come to Play,* p. 781; September 15, 2007, review of *Iggy Peck, Architect.*
Publishers Weekly, October 23, 2006, review of *When Giants Come to Play,* p. 49; November 26, 2007, review of *Iggy Peck, Architect,* p. 52.
School Library Journal, October, 2006, Sally R. Dow, review of *When Giants Come to Play,* p. 102; November, 2007, Margaret R. Tassia, review of *Iggy Peck, Architect,* p. 86.

ONLINE

Andrea Beaty Blog site, http://andreabeaty.blogspot.com/ (January 10, 2007).

Andrea Beaty Home Page, http://www.andreabeaty.com (January 10, 2007).

Cynsations Web site, http://cynthialeitichsmith.blogspot. com/ (March 1, 2003), Cynthia Leitich Smith, interview with Beaty.

Society of Children's Book Writers and Illustrators, Illinois Web site, http://www.scbwi-illinois.org/ (January 20, 2008), "Andrea Beaty."

*   *   *

BELTON, Sandra 1939-
(Sandra Yvonne Belton)

Personal

Born March 1, 1939, in Bluefield, WV; daughter of Alphonso David (a physician) and Alice Elizabeth Belton; married James Sidney Hammond (a music teacher and choral director); children: Allen Douglass. *Education:* Howard University, B.A. (English, sociology, and German), 1960; attended Boston Conservatory of Music, 1962; George Washington University, M.A. (elementary education), 1967.

Addresses

Home—Chicago, IL. *Office*—Scott Foresman, 1900 E. Lake Ave., Glenview, IL 60025. *Agent*—Edite Kroll, 20 Cross St., Saco, ME 04072.

Career

Children's book author and editor. District of Columbia Public Schools, Washington, DC, teacher at West Elementary School, 1964-69; Scott, Foresman, Glenview, IL, associate editor, 1969-72, executive editor, 1978—; Lyons & Carnahan, Chicago, IL, editor, 1972-74; Encyclopaedia Britannica Educational Corp., Chicago, senior editor; City Colleges of Chicago, reading teacher, 1976-78.

Member

Delta Sigma Theta.

Awards, Honors

Young People's Literature Award, Friends of American Writers, and finalist, Children's Books of Distinction Award, both 1994, both for *From Miss Ida's Porch;* Notable Children's Trade Books in the Field of Social Studies, National Council of Social Studies (NCSS)/ Children's Book Council (CBC), 1995, for *May'naise Sandwiches and Sunshine Tea;* Best Children's Books of the Year selection, Bank Street College of Education, 2000, and Notable Children's Trade Books in the Field of Social Studies, NCSS/CBC, 2001, both for *McKendree.*

Writings

PICTURE BOOKS

From Miss Ida's Porch, illustrated by Floyd Cooper, Four Winds Press (New York, NY), 1993.

May'naise Sandwiches and Sunshine Tea, illustrated by Gail Gordon Carter, Four Winds Press (New York, NY), 1994.

Pictures for Miss Josie, illustrated by Benny Andrews, Greenwillow Books (New York, NY), 2003.

Beauty, Her Basket, illustrated by Cozbi A. Cabrera, Greenwillow Books (New York, NY), 2004.

The Tallest Tree: The Paul Robeson Story, Greenwillow Books (New York, NY), 2008.

"ERNESTINE AND AMANDA" SERIES

Ernestine and Amanda, Simon & Schuster (New York, NY), 1996.

Summer Camp Ready or Not!, Simon & Schuster (New York, NY), 1997.

Members of the C.L.U.B., Simon & Schuster (New York, NY), 1997.

Mysteries on Monroe Street, Simon & Schuster (New York, NY), 1998.

YOUNG-ADULT NOVELS

McKendree, Greenwillow Books (New York, NY), 2000.

Store-bought Baby, Greenwillow Books (New York, NY), 2006.

OTHER

Sparks (nonfiction; for adults), University Research Corp. Press, 1973.

Sidelights

Sandra Belton has published a number of well-received picture books for children in addition to novels for young adults that include the award-winning *McKendree.* She is perhaps best known for her "Ernestine and Amanda" series about two African-American girls growing up in the 1950s. In an interview with Janice Del Negro for the *Bulletin of the Center for Children's Books* online, Belton noted that the series is enriched by her own experiences as a youngster growing up in small-town West Virginia. "Ernestine and Amanda are the keepers of my childhood memories and dreams," the author remarked. "Their voices echo the ones I heard while chasing lightning bugs and playing at twilight with the kids down the street. The homes they live in and the schools and churches they attend paint a picture of the neighborhoods that nurtured all of us. The events of their lives and the heroes they celebrate are the ones of our heritage."

Belton found success with her debut book for children, *From Miss Ida's Porch,* published in 1993. Miss Ida's porch becomes the gathering place for the neighborhood. Adults come to relax and enjoy a place of storytelling and reminiscing, while children come to hear true stories about African Americans such as musicians Marian Anderson and Duke Ellington and their contributions to history. Elizabeth Hanson, writing in *School Library Journal,* called the book "outstanding in its depth of emotion and evocative depiction of poignant historical moments." In *Horn Book,* Lois F. Anderson praised the "rich, descriptive language," going on to assert that Belton "successfully blends together fact and fiction and, in the process, creates a distinctive mood and memorable, believable characters." Belton's second book for children, *May'naise Sandwiches and Sunshine Tea,* again features an older generation passing along stories to young people. In this book, Big Mama tells her grandchild about an experience she had as a child that influenced her to become the first member of her family to attend college.

In 1996, Belton issued the first of her "Ernestine and Amanda" books. In *Ernestine and Amanda,* the two girls meet at Miss Elder's house, where they are both taking piano lessons. Both take an instant dislike for each other, not realizing that each is struggling with personal problems. In Ernestine's case it is her weight that bothers her, and in Amanda's case it is her parents' marriage that she is worried about. The narrative alternates between the two girls, with each getting an alternating chapter. Belton uses the story to explore both the personal issues the girls are struggling with and the social reality of being African American in the 1950s. Susan Dove Lempke praised Belton's quality of prose, lauding her in a *Booklist* review for "beautifully capturing the voices of her characters."

At the beginning of the second book in the series, *Summer Camp, Ready or Not!,* Amanda is struggling with her parent's divorce, while Ernestine has recently learned that her father has lost his job. As with the first book in the "Ernestine and Amanda" series, the narrative alternates between the girls. Shipped off to camp for the summer, Amanda ends up in a nearly all-white camp, while Ernestine attends an all-black camp. Once again, Belton uses their experiences to highlight social issues of the day, including racial prejudice. Lempke wrote in another *Booklist* review that, although the two girls hardly meet in the book, "Belton captures everyday life for middle-class black children during the 1950s with poignancy and freshness." A *Kirkus Reviews* critic further noted that while Belton deals directly with significant and difficult social issues of the day, her "novel translates well to classroom use" because it presents the issues in such a thoughtful manner.

In series installment *Members of the C.L.U.B.,* Belton focuses on Amanda's attempts to launch an exclusive club she is sure Ernestine will not qualify for. Ernestine, on the other hand, is sad because she does not have a best friend in class. As the book progresses, Ernestine makes friends with the beautiful Wilhelmina, while Amanda discovers that not many people are very enthusiastic about her exclusive club. Writing in the *Bulletin of the Center for Children's Books,* Del Negro noted that in this book of "alternating points of view," Belton "strikes just the right balance between humor and pathos."

In *Mysteries on Monroe Street* the girls are excited about the launch of a new dance studio in their town. As Amanda enjoys the dancing lessons, Ernestine is still conscious about her weight and instead opts to play the piano during the lessons. Although the narrative alternates between the girls, in this book the two have established a somewhat precarious, though continuously stormy relationship. Once again, Belton was praised by critics for her realistic portrayal of life in the 1950s, Del Negro remarking on the writer's ability to keep "her characters and her series firmly in hand as she leads them out of the 1950s and toward a promising if potentially stormy future."

In *Pictures for Miss Josie,* Belton creates a picturebook biography of celebrated African-American educator Josephine Carroll Smith, who helped desegregate schools in Washington, DC, and served as that city's director of elementary education. In the work, a young boy visits Smith's home, where she once welcomed the youngster's father when he was a student. As the years pass, the relationship between Smith and the boy deepens, and she encourages him to pursue his interest in art. *Pictures for Miss Josie* earned praise for Belton's spare, inviting text and illustrator Benny Andrews's elegant artwork. According to *School Library Journal* reviewer Heather E. Miller, Andrews's "large, brightly colored folk paintings, done in oil and collage, are in harmony with the quiet, lyrical narrative," and a critic in *Publishers Weekly* similarly noted that "the illustrations . . . solidly depict action only implied in the narrative, thus complementing Belton's economy of language while propelling the story." A *Kirkus Reviews* contributor described *Pictures for Miss Josie* as a "gracious, gentle-hearted story" and "a fine tribute."

Featuring artwork by Cozbi A. Cabrera, *Beauty, Her Basket* introduces readers to a young girl spending a summer with her Nana, a member of the Gullah community living on the Sea Islands off the coast of Georgia. During her time there, the narrator learns about the African heritage of her ancestors, as well as the history of the sea grass baskets her grandmother weaves. "Belton once again uses a narrative tale to illuminate priceless nuggets of African American history," Terry Glover remarked in *Booklist.* The author "has a lovely way with a phrase," observed a critic in *Publishers Weekly,* who called the tale "a quiet treasure."

Turning to older readers, in *McKendree,* Belton tells a coming-of-age story about Tilara Haynes, a teen struggling to find her identity. Through the course of the book, Tilara learns to appreciate the diversity and richness of her own African-American roots. Spending the summer working with her Aunt Cloelle in McKendree, a retirement home for black seniors, she learns to take pride in her own heritage. The author's "love for the characters and for the time and place of her period setting is infectious," remarked *Booklist* contributor Michael Cart. A reviewer for *Publishers Weekly* called Belton's portrayal of her protagonist's growth "persuasive and thought-provoking," while Lisa Denton, writing in *School Library Journal,* remarked on the quality of Belton's writing and imagery, also lauding her "finely crafted characterizations."

A high school sophomore must deal with grief and loneliness following the death of her adopted older brother in *Store-bought Baby,* Belton's 2006 novel for young adults. After a car accident takes the life of her beloved sibling, Leah copes with her sorrow by seeking Luce's birth parents. In the process, she comes to a greater understanding of Luce's special relationship with his adoptive mother and father. "Leah's voice is consistent throughout," commented *Horn Book* reviewer Deborah Taylor, "and her misery and confusion are palpable." *Store-bought Baby* "is an affecting novel dealing with a difficult loss and emphasizing the redemptive power of family," commented Janis Flint-Ferguson in *Kliatt,* and Hazel Rochman stated in *Booklist* that "Belton's powerful novel opens up the meaning of 'real' family."

Biographical and Critical Sources

PERIODICALS

Booklist, January, 1997, Susan Dove Lempke, review of *Ernestine and Amanda,* p. 855; August, 1997, Susan Dove Lempke, review of *Summer Camp, Ready or Not!,* p. 1898; November 15, 1997, Susan Dove Lempke, review of *Members of the C.L.U.B.,* p. 557; July, 1998, Susan Dove Lempke, review of *Mysteries on Monroe Street,* p. 1881; August, 2000, Michael Cart, review of *McKendree,* p. 2133; May 1, 2003, Hazel Rochman, review of *Pictures for Miss Josie,* p. 1604; March 1, 2004, Terry Glover, review of *Beauty, Her Basket,* p. 1192; May 1, 2006, Hazel Rochman, review of *Store-bought Baby,* p. 79.

Black Issues Book Review, July-August, 2003, Suzanne Rust, review of *Pictures for Miss Josie,* p. 64; March-April, 2004, Erica Dollan, review of *Beauty, Her Basket,* p. 67.

Bulletin of the Center for Children's Books, September, 1997, Janice M. Del Negro, review of *Summer Camp, Ready or Not!,* p. 6; February, 1998, Janice M. Del Negro, review of *Members of the C.L.U.B.,* p. 194; September, 1998, Janice M. Del Negro, review of *Mysteries on Monroe Street,* p. 7.

Horn Book, November, 1993, Lois F. Anderson, review of *From Miss Ida's Porch,* p. 743; May-June, 2003, Maria Salvadore, review of *Pictures for Miss Josie,* p. 325; May-June, 2006, Deborah Taylor, review of *Store-bought Baby,* p. 310.

Kirkus Reviews, May 15, 1997, review of *Summer Camp, Ready or Not!,* p. 797; April 1, 2003, review of *Pictures for Miss Josie,* p. 531; December 15, 2003, review of *Beauty, Her Basket,* p. 1446.

Kliatt, May, 2006, Janis Flint-Ferguson, review of *Store-bought Baby,* p. 4.

Publishers Weekly, July 26, 1993, review of *From Miss Ida's Front Porch,* p. 73; October 1, 1996, review of *Ernestine and Amanda,* p. 84; June 5, 2000, review of *McKendree,* p. 95; March 17, 2003, review of *Pictures for Miss Josie,* p. 76; January 12, 2004, review of *Beauty, Her Basket,* p. 54.

School Library Journal, November, 1993, Elizabeth Hanson, review of *From Miss Ida's Porch,* p. 76; August, 1997, Starr LaTronica, review of *Summer Camp, Ready or Not!,* p. 154; November, 1997, Tammy J. Marley, review of *Members of the C.L.U.B.,* p. 114; July, 2000, Lisa Denton, review of *McKendree,* p. 100; May, 2003, Heather E. Miller, review of *Pictures for Miss Josie,* p. 108; June, 2006, Carol A. Edwards, review of *Store-bought Baby,* p. 146.

Tribune Books (Chicago, IL) June 8, 2003, review of *Pictures for Miss Josie,* p. 5.

ONLINE

Bulletin of the Center for Children's Books Web site, http://bccb.lis.uiuc.edu/ (October 2, 1998), Janice Del Negro, "Rising Star: Sandra Belton."

Sandra Belton Home Page, http://www.sandrabelton.com (December 20, 2007).*

*   *   *

BELTON, Sandra Yvonne
See BELTON, Sandra

*   *   *

BRASSARD, France 1963-

Personal

Born 1963, in Quebec, Canada; children: Luke. *Education:* Studied interior design and graphic art.

Addresses

Home—Saint-Armand, Quebec, Canada. *E-mail*—fbrassard@aei.ca.

Career

Illustrator and portrait artist.

Member

Canadian Society of Miniature Painters and Gravers.

Illustrator

Carolyn Jackson, *If I Had a Dog,* Tundra Books (Toronto, Ontario, Canada), 2006.

Deborah Hodge, *Lily and the Mixed-up Letters,* Tundra (Toronto, Ontario, Canada), 2007.

Sidelights

A miniaturist who specializes in creating detailed watercolor images, Canadian artist France Brassard has been fascinated with the magical power of children's picture books since childhood. Although she studied interior design and graphic art during college, Brassard has since rekindled her early interest in illustration, particularly the miniature images in treasured books from her own library. Brassard, a resident of Quebec, has also been inspired by her own young son, Luke. Her book-length illustration projects include Deborah Hodge's *Lily and the Mixed-up Letters* and Carolyn Jackson's *If I Had a Dog.* Praised for her ability to depict young children, Brassard also creates custom small-scale watercolor portraits for individual clients.

Praising Brassard's detailed paintings for *Lily and the Mixed-up Letters, School Library Journal* contributor Linda L. Walkins wrote that the artist's "detailed watercolors infuse the story with genuine emotion that is somewhat lacking in the narrative." Brassard's art "tenderly show[s] Lily's every emotion as she struggles with learning to read," a *Kirkus Reviews* critic stated in reviewing the same book, the critic adding that Brassard's art surpasses Hodge's "rather shallow treatment of reading difficulties." Calling her illustrations for *If I Had a Dog* the "strengths" of the picture book, *Resource Links* contributor Linda Berezowski added that Brassard "does a commendable job of infusing interest by varying the perspective, adding visual details and using an attractive palette. The factual tone of the book is reflected in the illustrations, which closely chronicle the storyline."

Biographical and Critical Sources

PERIODICALS

Canadian Book Review Annual, 2006, Janet Collins, review of *If I Had a Dog,* p. 450.
Kirkus Reviews, February 15, 2007, review of *Lily and the Mixed-up Letters.*
Resource Links, April, 2006, Linda Berezowski, review of *If I Had a Dog,* p. 5.
School Library Journal, April, 2007, Linda L. Walkins, review of *Lily and the Mixed-up Letters,* p. 108.

ONLINE

Arts Quebec Web site, http://www.artsquebec.net/ (January 1, 2008), "France Brassard."*

* * *

BREEN, Steve 1970-

Personal

Born 1970, in Los Angeles, CA; married; wife's name Cathy; children: two sons. *Education:* University of California at Riverside, B.S. (political science), 1992. *Hobbies and other interests:* Playing guitar, reading, running, old movies.

Addresses

Home and office—San Diego, CA. *E-mail*—steve. breen@uniontrib.com.

Career

Author and editorial cartoonist. Asbury Park Press, Neptune, NJ, editorial cartoonist, 1994-2001; San Diego Union-Tribune, San Diego, CA, editorial cartoonist, 2001—.

Awards, Honors

Charles M. Schulz Award for Best College Cartoonist, Scripps Howard Foundation, 1991; John Locher Award for Outstanding College Editorial Cartoonist, Association of American Editorial Cartoonists, 1991; Pulitzer Prize for editorial cartooning, 1998; Wilbur Award, Religion Communicator's Council, 1999, for *Grand Avenue.*

France Brassard joins author Deborah Hodge in focusing on the problems of dyslexia in the picture book **Lily and the Mixed-up Letters.**
(Tundra Books. Illustration © 2007 by France Brassard. Reproduced by permission.)

Writings

Your Grandma Rocks, Mine Rolls: A Grand Avenue Collection, Dial Books for Young Readers (New York, NY), 2001.

Stick, Dial Books for Young Readers (New York, NY), 2007.

Violet the Pilot, Dial Books for Young Readers (New York, NY), 2008.

Sidelights

Steve Breen's career as an editorial cartoonist had an auspicious start. While attending the University of California, Riverside, Breen got a job creating editorial cartoons for the university newspaper. Readers responded positively, and soon the student cartoonist began receiving recognition from outside the university campus, including from the Scripps Howard News Service, which awarded Breen the Charles M. Schulz Award for top college cartoonist. In 1998, while working for the Asbury Park Press, Breen received a Pulitzer prize for editorial cartooning. Breen, who now creates cartoons for the *San Diego Union-Tribune,* has also ventured into the world of children's literature. In 2007 his self-illustrated children's book debut, *Stick,* was published, introducing younger readers to his detailed cartoon art.

With a minimal amount of words, *Stick* follows the adventures of an independent-minded frog. A curious amphibian, Stick wants to experience everything on his own and he does so, even when his mother disapproves. It seems that Mother Frog may have known best when Stick is carried aloft after attempting to eat a dragonfly. Returning to earth, he moves from one form of transportation to another—from a horse's nose to a balloon floating by—while making his way back home. Breen's story is conveyed in a "frenetic pace and [with] loads of humor," according to *School Library Journal* reviewer Ieva Bates, the critic adding that the cartoonist's "art perfectly conveys the frog's childlike exuberance" in a "lighthearted mood." A *Publishers Weekly* reviewer also commented on Breen's lively illustrations, noting that his "detailed artwork . . . supplies the heft to this tale with few words."

Cartoonist Steve Breen pairs text and art to introduce readers to an unusual little hero in his quirky picture book Stick. (Dial Books for Young Readers. Illustration © 2007 by Steve Breen. Reproduced by permission.)

Biographical and Critical Sources

PERIODICALS

Booklinks, September-October, 2007, Denise B. Geier, review of *Stick,* p. 60.

Booklist, March 15, 2007, Gillian Engberg, review of *Stick,* p. 50.

Kirkus Reviews, February 1, 2007, review of *Stick,* p. 120.

Mediaweek, April 10, 2000, Joanna Wlper, "Life after the Pulitzer," p. 60.

Publishers Weekly, March 12, 2007, review of *Stick,* p. 57.

School Library Journal, May, 2007, Ieva Bates, review of *Stick,* p. 86.

ONLINE

Comics.Com, http://www.comics.com/ (December 15, 2007), profile of Breen.

Penguin Group Web site, http://us.penguingroup.com/ (December 15, 2007), "Steve Breen."

San Diego-Union Tribune Online, http://www.signonsan diego.com/ (December 15, 2007), "Steve Breen."*

C

CAIN, Sheridan 1952-

Personal

Born 1952, in England.

Addresses

Home—Canvey Island, Essex, England.

Career

Children's book author.

Writings

Look out for the Big Bad Fish!, illustrated by Tanya Linch, Little Tiger Press (Waukesha, WI), 1998.

Why So Sad, Brown Rabbit?, illustrated by Jo Kelly, Dutton Children's Books (New York, NY), 1998.

Little Turtle and the Song of the Sea, illustrated by Norma Burgin, Crocodile Books (New York, NY), 2000.

The Crunching, Munching Caterpillar, illustrated by Jack Tickle, Tiger Tales (London, England), 2000, Tiger Tales (Wilton, CT), 2003.

Run Little Fawn, Run!, illustrated by Gavin Rowe, Little Tiger (London, England), 2001.

The Teeny Weeny Tadpole, illustrated by Jack Tickle, Tiger Tales (Wilton, CT), 2005.

By the Light of the Moon, illustrated by Gaby Hansen, Tiger Tales (Wilton, CT), 2007.

Adaptations

The Crunching Munching Caterpillar and *The Teeny Weeny Tadpole* were adapted as audiobooks and board books by Little Tiger Press.

Sidelights

An English writer, Sheridan Cain is the author of simple texts that have been transformed into entertaining picture books through the work of illustrators such as Jo Kelly, and Norma Burgin, and Jane Chapman working under the whimsical pseudonym Jack Tickle. Cain specializes in simple stories featuring young animal characters that deal with toddler-like situations. In her first book, *Look out for the Big Bad Fish!*, for example, Tadpole is worried because he is the only one of his animal friends who cannot jump. *Why So Sad, Brown Rabbit?* focuses on a young rabbit whose wish for a family seems to be answered when a trio of ducklings adopt him as their mother, and *Little Turtle and the*

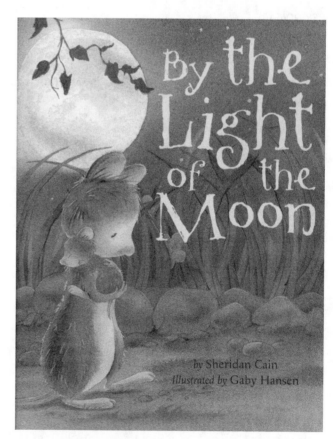

Cover of Sheridan Cain's picture book **By the Light of the Moon,** *featuring artwork by Gaby Hansen.* (Tiger Tales, 2006. Illustration © 2006 by Gaby Hansen. Reproduced by permission.)

Song of the Sea follows newly hatched Turtle as it takes its crucial first steps toward the sea and safety. A mother mouse worries that her young son is not sleeping in the right spot in *By the Light of the Moon,* while in *The Crunching Munching Caterpillar* a hungry caterpillar does what it does best—eat!—but grows increasingly lonely as each of its friends spread their wings and fly away.

Reviewing *The Crunching Munching Caterpillar* for *School Library Journal,* Piper L. Nyman wrote that "Cain's simple language and Tickle's engaging illustrations make it acceptable for [group] sharing," and Julie Corsaro predicted in *Booklist* that readers of *Look out for the Big Bad Fish!* will enjoy "the action and humor of the simple, repetitive, cumulative text." Cain's *Why So Sad, Brown Rabbit?* was praised by a *Publishers Weekly* contributor who cited the book's "economical but warm text," which "keeps the story moving" and pairs well with Jo Kelly's energetic illustrations. Noting the story's appeal for toddlers, *Booklist* critic Lauren Petersen dubbed *Why So Sad, Brown Rabbit?* "heartwarming" and featuring an engaging "what happens next" premise.

Biographical and Critical Sources

PERIODICALS

Booklist, January 1, 1998, Lauren Peterson, review of *Why So Sad, Brown Rabbit?,* p. 822; July, 1998, Julie Corsaro, review of *Look out for the Big Bad Fish!,* p. 1884.

Kirkus Reviews, February 15, 2007, review of *By the Light of the Moon.*

Publishers Weekly, January 19, 1998, review of *Why So Sad, Brown Rabbit?,* p. 377; December 18, 2000, review of *Why So Sad, Brown Rabbit?,* p. 80.

School Library Journal, July, 1998, Sally R. Dow, review of *Look out for the Big Bad Fish,* p. 71; December, 2000, Betty S. Evans, review of *Little Turtle and the Song of the Sea,* p. 104; September, 2003, Piper L. Nyman, review of *The Crunching Munching Caterpillar,* p. 175; May, 2007, Debbie Stewart Hoskins, review of *By the Light of the Moon,* p. 86.*

*　　*　　*

CAMP, Madeleine L'Engle
See L'ENGLE, Madeleine

*　　*　　*

CASANOVA, Mary 1957-

Personal

Born February 2, 1957, in Duluth, MN; daughter of Eugene (a business manager) and Joyce (a homemaker) Gazelka; married Charles Casanova (an insurance

Mary Casanova (Reproduced by permission of Mary Casanova.)

agent), July 1, 1978; children: Katie, Eric. *Education:* University of Minnesota, B.A., 1981. *Religion:* "Judeo-Christian/Lutheran." *Hobbies and other interests:* Reading, writing, cross-country and downhill skiing, camping, canoeing, hiking, running, horseback riding, playing the piano.

Addresses

Home and office—P.O. Box 141, Ranier, MN 56668. *Agent*—Andrea Cascardi, Transatlantic Literary Agency, Inc., P.O. Box 349, Rockville Centre, NY 11571.

Career

Author and speaker. Presenter at conferences and speaker; visiting author to elementary and middle schools.

Member

Society of Children's Book Writers and Illustrators, Children's Literature Network, Loft Literary Center, International Reading Association.

Awards, Honors

Emily Johnson Award, Children's Literature Conference, 1990, for "Father's Boots"; Minnesota State Arts Board career development grant, 1992; Arrowhead Regional Arts Council career opportunity grants, 1992-94; Arrowhead Regional Arts Council/McKnight Foundation fellowship in literature, 1995; Flicker Tale Children's Book Award, North Dakota Library Association, 1997, and Iowa Readers' Choice Book Award, and Indian Paintbrush Book Award, both 1998, all for *Moose Tracks;* Quick Picks for Reluctant YA Readers citation, American Library Association (ALA), Oklahoma Children's Crown Award list, and Sequoyah Book Award listee, all for *Riot;* Wyoming Indian Paintbrush Book Award listee, 1999-2000, Indiana Best-Read Alouds listee, 1999-2000, Iowa Children's Choice Award listee, 2000-2001, Lamplighter Award listee, 2000-2001, and Missouri Mark Twain Book Award listee, all for *Wolf Shadows;* Top 100 Books for 2000 citation, New York Public Library, Notable Children's Book citation, ALA, Minnesota Book Award, 2001, Gold Award, Parent's Choice, Pick of the List, American Bookseller's Association, Aesop Accolade, American Folktale Society, and Blue Ribbon List, *Bulletin of the Center for Children's Books,* all for *The Hunter;* Minnesota Book Award, 2001, for *Curse of a Winter Moon;* Iowa Children's Choice Award, 2002-03, for *Stealing Thunder;* National Parenting Publications Award Honor designation, 2002, for *Jess.*

Writings

FOR CHILDREN

The Golden Retriever (nonfiction), Crestwood House/Macmillan (New York, NY), 1990.

Moose Tracks (middle-grade novel), Hyperion (New York, NY), 1995.

Riot (middle-grade novel), Hyperion (New York, NY), 1996.

Wolf Shadows (middle-grade novel; sequel to *Moose Tracks*), Hyperion (New York, NY), 1997.

Stealing Thunder (middle-grade novel), Hyperion (New York, NY), 1999.

Curse of a Winter Moon (middle-grade novel), Hyperion (New York, NY), 2000.

(Reteller) *The Hunter: A Chinese Folktale* (picture book), illustrated by Ed Young, Atheneum (New York, NY), 2000.

When Eagles Fall (middle-grade novel), Hyperion (New York, NY), 2002.

Cécile: Gates of Gold ("American Girl" series), illustrated by Jean-Paul Tibbles, Pleasant Company (Middleton, WI), 2002.

One-Dog Canoe (picture book), illustrated by Ard Hoyt, Farrar, Straus & Giroux (New York, NY), 2003.

Jess ("American Girl" series), illustrated by Jean-Paul Tibbles, Pleasant Company (Middleton, WI), 2005.

Some Dog! (picture book), illustrated by Ard Hoyt, Farrar, Straus & Giroux (New York, NY), 2007.

Mary Casanova and You (memoir), Libraries Unlimited (Westport, CT), 2007.

The Klipfish Code, Houghton Mifflin (Boston, MA), 2007.

Utterly Otterly Day (picture book) illustrated by Ard Hoyt, Simon & Schuster (New York, NY), 2008.

"DOG WATCH" SERIES

Trouble in Pembrook, illustrated by Omar Rayyan, Aladdin (New York, NY), 2006.

Dog-napped, illustrated by Omar Rayyan, Aladdin (New York, NY), 2006.

Danger at Snow Hill, illustrated by Omar Rayyan, Aladdin (New York, NY), 2006.

To Catch a Burglar, illustrated by Omar Rayyan, Aladdin (New York, NY), 2007.

Extreme Stunt Dogs, illustrated by Omar Rayyan, Aladdin (New York, NY), 2007.

The Turtle-hatching Mystery, illustrated by Omar Rayyan, Aladdin (New York, NY), 2008.

Sidelights

In her award-winning books for middle-grade readers, Mary Casanova blends a love for the outdoors with insightful coming-of-age stories that pull no punches. Her linking novels *Moose Tracks* and *Wolf Shadows* focus on wildlife preservation, while *Stealing Thunder* tells an heroic story about animal cruelty and saving a horse. With historical novels such as *Curse of a Winter Moon* and *The Klipfish Code,* Casanova takes readers back to seventeenth-century France and World-War II Norway, respectively, and her modern family drama *When Eagles Fall* is set in the northern Minnesota wilderness near the author's home. In addition to her work for preteen readers, Casanova attracts younger readers in her "Dog Watch" books, which are set in her home state and feature a group of bright, observant canines. Her picture books include *The Hunter: A Chinese Folktale, One-Dog Canoe,* and *Some Dog!*

"When I set out to write for children, I had two main goals," Casanova once told *SATA:* "To write books that kids couldn't put down and to write books that matter. Coming from a family of ten children—seven boys and three girls—I was always active: riding horses, playing tag off the pontoon boat in the summer and ice-hockey with our own 'team' in the winter. I was also a reluctant reader. I loved being outside, and if a book was going to hold my attention it had to be a fast-paced story."

Moose Tracks, Casanova's first novel, is geared for readers like the author was in middle school. In the story, twelve-year-old Seth tries to save a wounded moose calf from poachers. Out hunting with his stepfather's shotgun but without the man's permission, Seth shoots a rabbit and takes its foot as a good-luck charm. However, the boy is tormented by his action, partly because his stepfather is the local game warden, and partly because he feels guilty. When he later observes poachers killing a cow moose, the boy is warned by them not to tell his stepfather. As a way to set things right, Seth is determined to save the injured moose calf the men have orphaned. Joined by his friend Matt, Seth soon finds himself trapped in an abandoned mine by the poachers. Now he is forced to draw on his outdoors skills to save the calf and bring the poachers to justice.

Cover of Casanova's chapter book Moose Tracks, *featuring artwork by* **Kam Mak.** (Hyperion Books for Children, 1995. Text copyright © 1995 by Mary Casanova. Jacket illustration © 1995 by Kam Mak. Reprinted by permission of Hyperion Books for Children. All rights reserved.)

A contributor to *Kirkus Reviews* wrote of *Moose Tracks* that "the attention-grabbing action and emotional struggles of the hero will hook reluctant readers." In *School Library Journal* Todd Morning wrote that "Casanova's precise and evocative descriptions" add depth to the story's building suspense. Reviewing the book in *Publishers Weekly,* a critic noted that Casanova's novel "earnestly conveys the ugliness of killing animals for financial gain."

Wolf Shadows takes place a week after *Moose Tracks* ends. Seth's life is still complicated by the impending birth of a first child to his mother and stepfather. Added to this, Matt has decided to fight the efforts of a wolf protection program because it appears wolves have been killing his family's livestock. Further complications come from the orphaned moose calf; Seth knows he should release the animal soon, but he is fearful of doing so as the first day of deer hunting season approaches. That day, Seth's mother goes into labor with the new baby, and Seth joins Matt for the opening of the season. When Matt illegally shoots a wolf, the act causes a rift in the boys' friendship that may not be able to heal. In

Booklist Chris Sherman once again had praise for Casanova, noting that in *Wolf Shadows* she "offers a well reasoned argument for wolf protection in this tense, fast-paced story."

As Casanova admitted, "I love to throw my character in the midst of issues . . . I can't quite get my arms around. *Riot* is that kind of story. After living through a two-year labor dispute that erupted into violence in my small northern town in 1989, I knew I'd have to write about it and somehow make sense of it. The result is the fictionalized account of a riot through twelve-year-old Bryan Grant's eyes;" In Casanova's story, Bryan's dad is a worker at a local paper mill, and when work dries up, he joins the protests. Bryan's mom, a union member and teacher, objects to protesting, hoping instead to find a peaceable, constructive outcome to the battle between employer and employee. In *Riot,* Casanova "create[s] . . . an exciting, realistic novel," according to *School Library Journal* contributor Cheryl Cufari. Although Elizabeth Bush complained in her *Bulletin of the Center for Children's Books* review that the author's "good guy/bad guy treatment of the labor action grossly oversimplifies" the social and economic issues surrounding the protest, Lauren Peterson concluded in *Booklist* that *Riot* features a "fast-paced story [that] poses challenging questions that have no easy answers."

In *Stealing Thunder* a preteen desperately wants to save an Appaloosa horse from danger. Inspired by Casanova's own love of horses, the novel introduces Libby, who has always longed for her own horse. Libby's neighbor, Jolene Porter, has let the girl care for her own horse, Thunder. Although the animal was initially skittish around her new caretaker, girl and horse have become close. However, when Jolene leaves her husband, Libby finds herself cut off from Thunder as a result. Although her family cannot afford to buy the horse from Mr. Porter, when Libby discovers that Thunder is being mistreated, she resolves to save the horse. Libby and her friend Griff, whom she has enlisted into the cause, soon find themselves over their heads in trouble in this "fast-paced adventure," filled with "precise and evocative" descriptions, as Janet Gillen described the novel in *School Library Journal.* Gillen further commented that Libby and Griff are "personable characters" who enhance Casanova's "compelling story of intrigue and heroism."

In *When Eagles Fall* thirteen-year-old Alex Castille-Reid has gotten into trouble in San Jose. Now she is sent to the wilderness of northern Minnesota, joining her father, an eagle researcher, while he conducts field work. In an attempt at rebellion, Alex steals off to remove a lure from an eagle's nest and ends up stranded in bad weather with an injured eaglet. "Casanova has written an eco-adventure story that also provides valuable information about eagle research," wrote *School Library Journal* contributor Doris Losey. Describing *When Eagles Fall* as "a good choice for reluctant readers," *Booklist* critic Jean Franklin dubbed the novel "an obviously well-researched survival novel with lots of local color and a teenage heroine who turns out to have plenty of grit."

With *Curse of a Winter Moon,* Casanova departs from her usual outdoors scenario and transports readers to sixteenth-century France. Because of family hardship, young Marius must postpone his apprenticeship in order to take care of his six-year-old brother, Jean-Pierre. The younger boy's birth on Christmas Eve, which took their mother's life, has given rise to rumors that that Jean-Pierre is a werewolf. Local villagers' misguided belief is fueled by Catholic superstition and the Church's zeal in exposing heretics. Soon Marius finds his world turned upside down when his father is condemned as a heretic and Jean-Pierre is also taken into custody. Barbara Scotto, writing in *School Library Journal,* called *Curse of a Winter Moon* a "solid look at a period not often written about in novels for this age group," while *Booklist* critic Ilene Cooper noted that Marius "comes across as a real boy in extraordinary circumstances."

Moving to another historical epoch, World War II-era Scandinavia, *The Klipfish Code* focuses on ten-year-old Marit Gundersen, who is sent to her grandfather's home on Godoy Island with her younger brother Lars after the Germans bomb Norway. Missing her parents, who are working for the Resistance, Marit endures another separation when her beloved aunt Ingeborg, a teacher who lives with them, is deported by the Nazis months later. When her grandfather refuses to stand up to the German troops, the girl grows frustrated, and when she discovers a wounded resistance member she willingly takes up his mission. In *Kirkus Reviews,* a critic called *The Klipfish Code* "worthwhile book about a rarely documented facet of" World War II, and commended Casanova for captures the essence of island life during wartime "uncommonly well." Dubbing the book "suspenseful," Anne O'Malley added in *Booklist* that the novel successfully opens a window for young readers onto "the grim reality of war and its effects on ordinary citizens."

Casanova again turns to history in her first contribution to the "American Girls" series. *Cécile: Gates of Gold* follows the life of twelve-year-old Cécile Revel, a servant at the court of King Louis XIV who, in 1711, finds following royal protocol a challenging task. Writing in *School Library Journal,* reviewer Kristen Oravec wrote that in *Cécile* the story's "action builds steadily and will sustain readers interest," and *Booklist* critic Shelle Rosenfeld praised Casanova's heroine as "a likeable character." A second contribution to the series, *Jess,* returns to the present day and contemporary concerns regarding the environment in its story about a fourth-grade girl who joins her archeologist parents on a dig at Mayan ruins in Belize. Calling the novel's plot "well thought out," Krista Tokarz concluded in *School Li-*

brary Journal that in *Jess* the author "seamlessly integrate[s]" information about Mayan history and archeology into her story.

Casanova retells a Chinese folktale in *The Hunter,* in which Hai Li Bu learns to understand the language of animals and becomes a more effective hunter. However, in a time of scarce game, he must sacrifice himself in order to save the lives of his villagers. "The tale of his sacrifice is well told in measured, poetic prose, unified by repeating word patterns," wrote *School Library Journal* critic Margaret A. Chang, the reviewer concluding that *The Hunter* is a "handsome addition to any folktale collection." David Russell, writing in *Five Owls,* commented that the "union of a moving and simply told tale and subtly evocative illustrations make this an especially beautiful picture book—one that deserves to be treasured."

Other picture books by Casanova include *One-Dog Canoe, Some Dog!,* and *Utterly Otterly Day,* all of which feature illustrations by Ard Hoyt. In *One-Dog Canoe* a little girl and her dog take a trip in her canoe, and when other animals gradually climb aboard, the canoe gradu-

Casanova's "Dog Watch" series includes Trouble in Pembrook, *a novel featuring cover art by Omar Rayyan.* (Aladdin Paperbacks, 2006. Illustrations copyright © 2006 by Omar Rayyan. Reprinted with the permission of Aladdin Paperbacks, an imprint of Simon & Schuster Children's Publishing Division.)

The canine crew of Casanova's "Dog Watch" series returns in **Danger at Snow Hill,** *a book featuring artwork by Omar Rayyan.* (Aladdin Paperbacks 2006. Illustrations copyright © 2006 by Omar Rayyan. Reprinted with the permission of Aladdin Paperbacks, an imprint of Simon & Schuster Children's Publishing Division.)

ally becomes unstable and all the passengers end up in the water. *Some Dog!* finds George the Basset hound frustrated when a bouncy stray turns up, is adopted by George's human family, and turns the sedate, older dog's quiet life upside down. *Utterly Otterly Day* focuses on a young otter that learns, during a day's worth of adventures, that family is important even when one is all grown up. *One-Dog Canoe* is enriched by Casanova's "lively rhyming text and . . . wry sense of humor," according to *School Library Journal* contributor Jane Marino, the critic adding that Hoyt's "watercolor illustrations give the animals lots of personality." Readers of *Some Dog!* "will . . . embrace this story of each individual's importance and place in a family," wrote *School Library Journal* contributor Genevieve Gallagher, and in *Kirkus Reviews* a critic praised the picture book as "well-written" and with a "wonderfully dramatic climax."

"If it's true that writers should 'write to express, not to impress,' then nowhere is this more important than in writing for children," Casanova noted on her home page. "They are the toughest critics, demanding first and foremost a good story. It's the writer's responsibility to write honestly, from the heart, and to give something of lasting value to the reader. Every writer offers a unique gift; if expressed clearly enough, true enough, it is a gift of story that a young reader will remember for a long time."

Biographical and Critical Sources

BOOKS

Casanova, Mary, *Mary Casanova and You* (memoir), Libraries Unlimited (Westport, CT), 2007.

PERIODICALS

Booklist, July, 1995, Chris Sherman, review of *Moose Tracks,* p. 1878; November 1, 1996, Lauren Peterson, review of *Riot,* p. 497; October 1, 1997, Chris Sherman, review of *Wolf Shadows,* p. 328; October 15, 2000, Ilene Cooper, review of *Curse of a Winter Moon,* p. 437; June 1, 2002, Jean Franklin, review of *When Eagles Fall,* p. 1704; October 15, 2002, Shelle Rosenfeld, review of *Cécile: Gates of Gold,* p. 404; February 15, 2003, Diane Foote, review of *One-Dog Canoe,* p. 1072; May 1, 2007, Julie Cummins, review of *Some Dog!,* p. 96; October 15, 2007, Anne O'Malley, review of *The Klipfish Code,* p. 48.

Bulletin of the Center for Children's Books, January, 1997, Elizabeth Bush, review of *Riot,* p. 165.

Five Owls, March-April, 2001, David Russell, review of *The Hunter,* p. 90.

Horn Book, March-April, 2007, Robin Smith, review of *Some Dog!,* p. 178.

Kirkus Reviews, May 15, 1995, review of *Moose Tracks,* p. 708; December 15, 2002, review of *One-Dog Canoe,* p. 1846; February 15, 2007, review of *Some Dog!;* August 1, 2007, review of *The Klipfish Code.*

Publishers Weekly, June 19, 1995, review of *Moose Tracks,* p. 60; August 21, 2000, review of *Curse of a Winter Moon,* p. 74; December 9, 2002, review of *One-Dog Canoe,* p. 81.

Saint Paul Pioneer Press, January 3, 2006, Maja Backstrom, "Real-life Experience Shapes New 'American Girl' Tale."

School Library Journal, June, 1995, Todd Morning, review of *Moose Tracks,* p. 108; October, 1996, Cheryl Cufari, review of *Riot,* p. 120; October, 1997, Claudia Morrow, review of *Wolf Shadows,* p. 131; October, 1999, Janet Gillen, review of *Stealing Thunder,* p. 148; August, 2000, Margaret A. Chang, review of *The Hunter,* p. 168; October, 2000, Barbara Scotto, review of *Curse of a Winter Moon,* p. 156; July, 2002, Doris Losey, review of *When Eagles Fall,* p. 114; September, 2002, Kristen Oravec, review of *Cécile,* p. 220; March, 2003, Jane Marino, review of *One-Dog Canoe,* p. 178; September, 2006, Krista Tokarz, review of *Jess,* p. 161; March, 2007, Genevieve Gallagher, review of *Some Dog!,* p. 96.

ONLINE

Mary Casanova Home Page, http://www.marycasanova.
    com (January 15, 2008).
Meet Authors and Illustrators Web site, http://www.
    childrenslit.com/ (April 9, 2002), "Mary Casanova."*

* * *

CASTROVILLA, Selene 1966-

Personal

Born 1966; married (divorced); children: two sons. *Education:* New York University, B.A. (English); New School University, M.F.A.

Addresses

Home—Long Island, NY.

Career

Writer.

Awards, Honors

New School Chapbook Award, for *Evolution.*

Writings

By the Sword: A Young Man Meets War, illustrated by Bill Farnsworth, Boyds Mills Press (Honesdale, PA), 2007.

Also author of *Evolution* (chapbook).

Sidelights

Selene Castrovilla lives close to the Revolutionary War site of the Battle of Long Island, which was fought in August of 1776, and it is this piece of history that inspired her children's book *By the Sword: A Young Man Meets War.* A fictional account that is based on the life and journal of Benjamin Tallmadge, Castrovilla's picture book for older readers draws on primary source documents and a great deal of research, and includes a time line and bibliography.

Inspired by his belief in the principals that inspired the American colonies' fight for independence, twenty-two-year-old Tallmadge was a minister's son and Yale College graduate. Teaching at a school in Connecticut, Tallmadge took his horse, Highlander, and traveled to New York, where he was appointed a lieutenant in the army of General George Washington. After training, he ultimately found himself confronting a large force of Hessian mercenaries on the battlefield. The Battle of Long Island, which was fought in Brooklyn Heights, ended with the British capture of New York City and

the colonial army's retreat across the river under the cover of fog. For Tallmadge, the battle did not end here, however. Realizing that Highlander was still in Long Island, the lieutenant returned to Brooklyn in an attempt to rescue his faithful mount. In an endnote, Castrovilla explains that Tallmadge went on to become one of General Washington's most respected spies and officers.

In his *Booklist* review of *By the Sword,* Ian Chipman wrote that Castrolvilla successfully portrays "the tension and dread an unweathered soldier would feel in the face of battle without resorting to the grisly details" that might distress younger readers. Farnsworth's "impressionistic" oil paintings for the book were cited by Ann Welton, who noted in her *School Library Journal* review of *By the Sword* that Castrovilla spins a "plausible historical narrative that also adds a human face" to one of the many battles that forged a new nation. Referencing the author's copious research in her review for *Childhood Education,* Connie Green commented on the "authenticity" in *By the Sword,* adding that Farnsworth's somber paintings "reflect . . . the fear and stark reality" expressed in Castrovilla's story."

Discussing the timeliness of *By the Sword* relative to life in the United States over two centuries after the nation's founding, Castrovilla commented on her home page: "I write about people, and the emotions which

In **By the Sword** *artist Bill Farnsworth joins with author Selene Castrovilla to bring to life an episode from Revolutionary-era U.S. history.* (Calkins Creek, an imprint of Boyds Mills Press, Inc., 2007. Illustrations copyright © 2007 by Bill Farnsworth. Reproduced by permission.)

drive them to their actions. It could be 1776, it could be four o'clock this morning—we're all the same. History repeats itself because people repeat themselves."

Biographical and Critical Sources

PERIODICALS

Booklist, February 15, 2007, Ian Chipman, review of *By the Sword: A Young Man Meets War,* p. 74.
Childhood Education, fall, 2007, Connie Green, review of *By the Sword,* p. 48.
Kirkus Reviews, March 15, 2007, review of *By the Sword.*
School Library Journal, March, 2007, Ann Welton, review of *By the Sword,* p. 225.

ONLINE

Selene Castrovilla Home Page, http://www.selenecastro villa.com (January 10, 2008).*

*   *   *

CHAMBLISS, Maxie

Personal

Female. *Hobbies and other interests:* Sailing.

Addresses

Home and office—Somerville, MA. *Agent*—Jane Feder Literary Agency, 305 E. 24th St., New York, NY 10010.

Career

Illustrator.

Illustrator

D. Leb Tannenbaum, *Baby Talk,* Avon (New York, NY), 1981.
Steven Kroll, *Bathrooms,* Avon (New York, NY), 1982.
Mike Thaler, *It's Me, Hippo!,* Harper & Row (New York, NY), 1983.
Stephanie Calmenson, *Ten Furry Monsters,* Parents Magazine Press (New York, NY), 1984.
Beverly Keller, *When Mother Got the Flu,* Coward-McCann (New York, NY), 1984.
Zibby Oneal, *Maude and Walter,* Lippincott (Philadelphia, PA), 1985.
Marjorie Weinman Sharmat, *Who's Afraid of Ernestine?,* Coward-McCann (New York, NY), 1986.
Mike Thaler, *Hippo Lemonade,* Harper & Row (New York, NY), 1986.
Stephanie Calmenson, *The Giggle Book: Favorite Riddles,* Parents Magazine Press (New York, NY), 1987.
Stephanie Calmenson, *Fido,* Scholastic (New York, NY), 1987.

Nancy Evans Cooney, *Donald Says Thumbs Down,* Putnam (New York, NY), 1987.
Ann McGovern, *Eggs on Your Nose,* Macmillan (New York, NY), 1987.
Stephanie Calmenson, *Where's Rufus?,* Parents Magazine Press (New York, NY), 1988.
Harry A. Sutherland, *Dad's Car Wash,* Atheneum (New York, NY), 1988.
Pat Lowrey Collins, *Taking Care of Tucker,* Putnam (New York, NY), 1989.
Paul Fehlner, *Dog and Cat,* Grolier (Danbury, CT), 1989.
Diane Namm, *Monsters!,* Grolier (Danbury, CT), 1989.
Elizabeth Lee O'Donnell, *I Can't Get My Turtle to Move,* Morrow (New York, NY), 1989.
Nancy Evans Cooney, *Go Away Monsters, Lickety Split!,* Putnam (New York, NY), 1990.
Marcia Leonard, *Hannah the Hamster Hunter,* Silver Press (Englewood Cliffs, NJ), 1990.
Mike Thaler, *Mole's New Cap,* Early Education (Orlando, FL), 1990.
Jillian Wynot, *The Mother's Day Sandwich,* Orchard (New York, NY), 1990.
Barbara Ann Porte, *Fat Fanny, Beanpole Bertha, and the Boys,* Orchard (New York, NY), 1991.
Mike Thaler, *Come and Play, Hippo,* HarperCollins (New York, NY), 1991.
Jamie Gilson, *You Cheat!,* Bradbury Press (New York, NY), 1992.
Kathryn Hook Berlan, *Andrew's Amazing Monsters,* Simon & Schuster (New York, NY), 1993.
Katharine Kenah, *Eggs over Easy,* Dutton (New York, NY), 1993.
Barbara Ann Porte, *When Grandma Almost Fell off the Mountain, and Other Stories,* Orchard (New York, NY), 1993.
Carol Snyder, *One up, One Down,* Atheneum (New York, NY), 1994.
Harry A. Sutherland, *Dad's Car Wash,* Aladdin (New York, NY), 1994.
Ginger Wadsworth, *Tomorrow Is Daddy's Birthday,* Caroline House (Honesdale, PA), 1994.
Marianne Borgardt, *What Do You Do with a Potty,* Western (New York, NY), 1994.
Virginia Haviland, *Favorite Fairy Tales Told in England,* Beech Tree (New York, NY), 1994.
Christine Loomis, *We're Going on a Trip,* Morrow (New York, NY), 1994.
Barbara Ann Porte, *When Aunt Lucy Rode a Mule, and Other Stories,* Orchard (New York, NY), 1994.
Joanna Cole, *How I Was Adopted: Samantha's Story,* Morrow (New York, NY), 1995.
Ellen Jackson, *Monsters in My Mailbox,* Troll (Mahwah, NJ), 1995.
Angela Shelf Medearis, *Here Comes the Snow,* Scholastic (New York, NY), 1996.
Mary Smith, *My Teacher Is the Tooth Fairy,* Troll (Mahwah, NJ), 1996.
Kathryn Siegler, designer, *I'm Going to the Doctor: A Pop-up Book,* Ladybird (New York, NY), 1997.
Willabel L. Tong, designer, *I'm Going to the Dentist: A Pop-up Book,* Ladybird (New York, NY), 1997.

Joanna Cole, *I'm a Big Brother,* Morrow (New York, NY), 1997.

Joanna Cole, *I'm a Big Sister,* Morrow (New York, NY), 1997.

Paul Z. Mann, *Meet My Monster,* Reader's Digest (Pleasantville, NY), 1999.

Joanna Cole, *My Big Boy Potty,* HarperCollins (New York, NY), 2000.

Joanna Cole, *My Big Girl Potty,* HarperCollins (New York, NY), 2000.

Joanna Cole, *When Mommy and Daddy Go to Work,* HarperCollins (New York, NY), 2001.

Joanna Cole, *When You Were Inside Mommy,* HarperCollins (New York, NY), 2001.

Pat Brisson, *Hobbledy-Clop,* Boyds Mills (Honesdale, PA), 2003.

Joanna Cole, *Sharing Is Fun,* HarperCollins (New York, NY), 2004.

Joanna Cole, *My Friend the Doctor,* HarperCollins (New York, NY), 2005.

Eve Bunting, *Baby Can,* Boyds Mills (Honesdale, PA), 2007.

Sidelights

Illustrator Maxie Chambliss has provided artwork for a number of picture books. Known for what a *Publishers Weekly* contributor described as "wholesome, cheery watercolors" in a review of Chambliss's contribution to Christine Loomis's *We're Going on a Trip,* the artist has contributed illustrations to tales about monsters, stories of everyday life, and fairy tales. Among her many collaborations are those with writer Joanna Cole, which have resulted in books that help young children understand where they came from, how to prepare for a new sibling, or why potty training is important.

Chambliss uses predominantly watercolor and line illustrations for her work, although she occasionally also in-

Maxie Chambliss contributes her engaging artwork to several picture books, among them Tomorrow Is Daddy's Birthday *by Ginger Wadsworth.*

***Chambliss's comfortingly rotund figures are a perfect match for Eve Bunting's humorous story in* Baby Can.** (Boyds Mills Press, 2007. Illustrations copyright © 2007 by Maxie Chambliss. Reproduced by permission.)

corporates muted, soft-edged pastels. She introduces creatures ranging from happy human families to monsters, and she gears her art to be kid-friendly rather than frightening. In her illustrations for *Andrew's Amazing Monsters,* for example, Chambliss "creatively transforms" the "homespun monsters" in Kathryn Hook Berlan's story "into festive, full-size party-goers," according to a *Publishers Weekly* contributor. Chambliss also helps keep doctors looking friendly, even when a young character has to get a shot; "Clean line drawings . . . help create the upbeat tone," wrote Carolyn Phelan in her *Booklist* review of Chambliss's work for Cole's *My*

Friend the Doctor. In her illustrations for Barbara Anne Porte's *When Aunt Lucy Rode a Mule, and Other Stories,* the artist's "sprightly watercolors depict a rambunctious family of strong women," wrote a *Publishers Weekly* critic. Mary Harris Veeder, reviewing the same title in *Booklist,* deemed Chambliss's images "winning," particularly in "depicting the exuberant faces and bodies" of the main characters, from children to grandparents.

Chambliss's work is often noted for its humor. In her art for Jillian Wynot's *The Mother's Day Sandwich,* she contributes "pencil and pastel illustrations" that depict the two main characters "in winning, good-humored fashion," according to a *Publishers Weekly* contributor, while in *When Grandma Almost Fell off the Mountain, and Other Stories* her "pencil and watercolor illustrations boost the comedy" of Porte's story, according to another *Publishers Weekly* critic. Writing about the same title, Hanna B. Zeiger wrote in *Horn Book* that Chambliss's illustrations "add a touch of humor to this delightful reminiscence."

In her work with Cole and others, Chambliss incorporates images of loving families as a way of reassuring young children. In *One up, One Down*, Carol Snyder's story about a big sister helping her parents in caring for twins, her "illustrations express the affection of the family," according to *Booklist* contributor Hazel Rochman. "Chambliss' sweet illustrations add warmth" to Cole's *How I Was Adopted: Samantha's Story*, concluded *Booklist* contributor Stephanie Zvirin. A *Publishers Weekly* critic wrote of the same book that the "exuberant watercolors . . . sustain a friendly and positive mood throughout." *I'm a Big Sister* and *I'm a Big Brother*, both with a text by Cole, both feature images that "glow with playfulness and warmth," according to *Booklist* critic Carolyn Phelan. Writing in the same periodical, Kathy Broderick noted that "Chambliss's watercolor illustrations" for Cole's *My Big Girl Potty* "show smiles all around." In another Cole-Chambliss collaboration, *When Mommy and Daddy Go to Work*, "the [artist's] delicately toned illustrations complement this soothing story," in the opinion of *School Library Journal* contributor Marilyn Ackerman. "The gentle colors and benevolent portrayals of characters help create a reassuring tone," wrote Phelan of the same title. For Eve Bunting's book about sibling rivalry, *Baby Can*, "Chambliss's charming watercolors showcase Baby James's development," wrote a *Kirkus Reviews* contributor.

Biographical and Critical Sources

PERIODICALS

Booklist, September 1, 1994, Mary Harris Veeder, review of *When Aunt Lucy Rode a Mule, and Other Stories,* p. 54; June 1, 1995, Hazel Rochman, review of *One up, One Down,* p. 1789; August, 1995, Stephanie Zvirin, review of *How I Was Adopted: Samantha's Story,* p. 1955; August, 1996, Ilene Cooper, review of *Here Comes the Snow,* p. 1910; March 1, 1997, Carolyn Phelan, review of *I'm a Big Sister* and *I'm a Big Brother,* p. 1170; December 15, 1997, Ilene Cooper, review of *I'm Going to the Doctor: A Pop-up Book,* p. 700; February 1, 2001, Kathy Broderick, review of *My Big Girl Potty,* p. 1055; August, 2001, Carolyn Phelan, review of *When Mommy and Daddy Go to Work* and *When You Were Inside Mommy,* p. 2124; January, 2005, Carolyn Phelan, review of *My Friend the Doctor,* p. 1929; February 15, 2007, Julie Cummins, review of *Baby Can,* p. 82.

Horn Book, May-June, 1993, Hanna B. Zeiger, review of *When Grandma Almost Fell off the Mountain, and Other Stories,* p. 330.

Kirkus Reviews, March 15, 2003, review of *Hobbledy-Clop,* p. 459; December 15, 2006, review of *Baby Can,* p. 1265.

Publishers Weekly, March 16, 1990, review of *The Mother's Day Sandwich,* p. 68; March 22, 1991, review of *Fat Fanny, Beanpole Bertha, and the Boys,* p. 80; March 8, 1993, review of *when Grandma Almost Fell off the Mountain, and Other Stories,* p. 77; March 29, 1993, review of *Andrew's Amazing Monsters,* p. 54; February 14, 1994, review of *We're Going on a Trip,* p. 88; August 1, 1994, review of *When Aunt Lucy Rode a Mule, and Other Stories,* p. 79; October 2, 1995, review of *How I Was Adopted,* p. 74; October 2, 2000, review of *Me, Me, Me,* p. 83.

School Library Journal, November, 2000, Jane Marino, review of *My Big Boy Potty,* p. 112; November, 2001, Marilyn Ackerman, review of *When Mommy and Daddy Go to Work,* p. 113; December, 2001, Kathleen Kelly MacMillan, review of *When You Were Inside Mommy,* p. 97; February, 2003, Marlene Gawron, review of *Hobbledy-Clop,* p. 102; August, 2004, Rachel G. Payne, review of *Sharing Is Fun,* p. 85; September, 2005, Laurel L. Iakovakis, review of *My Friend the Doctor,* p. 167; May, 2007, Martha Topol, review of *Baby Can,* p. 86.

ONLINE

Boyds Mills Press Web site, http://www.boydsmillspress.com/ (December 19, 2007), "Maxie Chambliss."

HarperCollins Web site, http://www.harpercollinschildrens.com/ (December 19, 2007), profile of Chambliss.

Jane Feder Literary Agency Web site, http://www.janefeder.com/ (December 19, 2007), "Maxie Chambliss."*

*   *   *

CHELUSHKIN, Kirill 1968-

Personal

Born 1968, in Abramtsevo, USSR (now Russia). *Education:* Institute of Architecture (Moscow, Russia), graduated, 1994.

Addresses

Home—Moscow, Russia.

Career

Illustrator and artist. *Exhibitions:* Artwork exhibited in Belgium, Czech Republic, France, Russia, and United States. Work included in permanent collections of museums, including Bozano Art Museum, Bologna, Italy; State Art Gallery, Kalingrad, Russia; Itabashi Art Museum, Tokyo, Japan; and Museum Ludvig, Köln, Germany.

Awards, Honors

Classics of Russian Literature in Contemporary Editions for Children award first prize, 2000; Russian Classical Literature Illustrations award nomination, Taipei International Book Exhibition; numerous other art awards.

Writings

Anna Carew-Miller, *Hans Christian Andersen: Denmark's Famous Author,* Mason Crest (Philadelphia, PA), 2003.

John Cech, *The Elves and the Shoemaker,* Sterling Publishers (New York, NY), 2007.

Illustrator of books published in Russia.

Sidelights

Breaking with the traditions that unify much illustration work for children's books, Russian artist Kirill Chelushkin creates unique images that draw readers in to the fantastic. Trained as an architect, he plays with perspective in imaginative ways, and inhabits his Escher-like settings with imaginatively disproportionate characters. In addition to his unique images, Chelushkin also breaks with another artistic standard: rather than use pencil and paper, he draws with various shades of graphite on plastic sheets, keeping his palette limited primarily to shades of grey. In addition to his picture-book work, Chelushkin is a well-known fine artist whose architectural-inspired drawings have been exhibited internationally.

One book featuring Chelushkin's art that has reached English-language readers is John Cech's retelling the traditional story "The Elves and the Shoemaker." Praised by *School Library Journal* contributor Kirsten Cutler as "strikingly illustrated and well-written," *The Elves and the Shoemaker* finds an impoverished and overworked shoemaker leaving his humble shop each night, then returning the following morning only to find that new shoes have been crafted from the scraps of leather on his work bench. Ultimately, when it is determined that these new shoes are being crafted by elves, the shoemaker and his grateful wife must figure out how to thank their nocturnal helpers. Chelushkin characteristically "plays with perspective and shadows" in his illustrations for Cech's tale, prompting Cutler to worry that the book's "slightly eerie look" might not be appropriate for younger children. In *Booklist,* Carolyn Phelan described the illustrator's "monochromatic" drawings as "dark, dense, and a bit puzzling," but dubbed *The Elves and the Shoemaker* "artistically accomplished" and "imaginative."

Biographical and Critical Sources

PERIODICALS

Booklist, March 15, 2007, Carolyn Phelan, review of *The Elves and the Shoemaker,* p. 50.

Bulletin of the Center for Children's Books, July-August, 2007, Hope Morrison, review of *The Elves and the Shoemaker,* p. 454.

School Library Journal, April, 2007, Kirsten Cutler, review of *The Elves and the Shoemaker,* p. 120.

ONLINE

Krokin Gallery Web site, http://www.krokingallery.com/ (August 1, 2003), Selma Stern, "Kirill Chelushkin."*

*　　*　　*

CLEARY, Brian P. 1959-

Personal

Born October 1, 1959, in Lakewood, OH; son of Michael J. (an international businessman) and Suzanne Cleary; children: Grace, Ellen, Emma. *Ethnicity:* "Irish-American." *Education:* John Carroll University, B.A., 1982. *Religion:* Roman Catholic.

Addresses

Home and office—16505 Southland Ave, Cleveland, OH 44111. *E-mail*—baberuth60@aol.com.

Career

Humor writer and freelance copywriter. American Greetings, senior editor.

Awards, Honors

Children's Choice selection, International Reading Association/Children's Book Council, 1996, for *Give Me Bach My Schubert* and *Rainbow Poetry;* Pick of the List citations, American Booksellers Association, 1999, 2000; Benjamin Franklin Award for Best Juvenile/Young Adult Nonfiction, 2002, for *To Root, to Toot, to Parachute: What Is a Verb?;* Honor Book designation, Society of School Librarians International, 2002.

Writings

Jamaica Sandwich?, illustrated by Rick Dupre, Lerner (Minneapolis, MN), 1996.

It Looks a Lot like Reindeer, illustrated by Rick Dupre, Lerner (Minneapolis, MN), 1996.

Give Me Bach My Schubert, illustrated by Rick Dupre, Lerner (Minneapolis, MN), 1996.

You Never Sausage Love, illustrated by Rick Dupre, Lerner (Minneapolis, MN), 1996.

A Mink, a Fink, a Skating Rink: What Is a Noun?, illustrated by Jenya Prosmitsky, Carolrhoda Books (Minneapolis, MN), 1999.

Hairy, Scary, Ordinary: What Is an Adjective?, illustrated by Jenya Prosmitsky, Carolrhoda Books (Minneapolis, MN), 2000.

Brian P. Cleary (Self-portrait reproduced by permission.)

To Root, to Toot, to Parachute: What Is a Verb?, illustrated by Jenya Prosmitsky, Carolrhoda Books (Minneapolis, MN), 2001.

Under, Over, by the Clover: What Is a Preposition?, illustrated by Brian Gable, Carolrhoda Books (Minneapolis, MN), 2002.

Nearly, Dearly, Insincerely: What Is an Adverb?, illustrated by Brian Gable, Carolrhoda Books (Minneapolis, MN), 2003.

I and You and Don't Forget Who: What Is a Pronoun?, illustrated by Brian Gable, Carolrhoda Books (Minneapolis, MN), 2004.

Rainbow Soup: Adventures in Poetry, illustrated by Neal Layton, Carolrhoda Books (Minneapolis, MN), 2004.

Pinch and Throw, Grasp and Know: What Is a Synonym?, illustrated by Brian Gable, Carolrhoda Books (Minneapolis, MN), 2005.

The Mission of Addition, illustrated by Brian Gable, Millbrook Press (Minneapolis, MN), 2005.

How Much Can a Bare Bear Bear?: What Are Homonyms and Homophones?, illustrated by Brian Gable, Millbrook Press (Minneapolis, MN), 2005.

Stop and Go, Yes and No: What Is an Antonym?, illustrated by Brian Gable, Millbrook Press (Minneapolis, MN), 2006.

A Lime, a Mime, a Pool of Slime: More about Nouns, illustrated by Brian Gable, Millbrook Press (Minneapolis, MN), 2006.

Rhyme and Punishment: Adventures in Wordplay, illustrated by J.P. Sandy, Millbrook Press (Minneapolis, MN), 2006.

Eight Wild Nights: A Family Hanukkah Tale, illustrated by David Udovic, Kar-Ben (Minneapolis, MN), 2006.

The Action of Subtraction, illustrated by Brian Gable, Millbrook Press (Minneapolis, MN), 2006.

Peanut Butter and Jellyfishes: A Very Silly Alphabet Book, illustrated by Brian Gable, Millbrook Press (Minneapolis, MN), 2007.

Quirky, Jerky, Extra-Perky: More about Adjectives, illustrated by Brian Gable, Millbrook Press (Minneapolis, MN), 2007.

Slide and Slurp, Scratch and Burp: More about Verbs, illustrated by Brian Gable, Millbrook Press (Minneapolis, MN), 2007.

How Long or How Wide?: A Measuring Guide, illustrated by Brian Gable, Millbrook Press (Minneapolis, MN), 2007.

The Laugh Stand: Adventures in Humor, illustrated by J.P. Sandy, Millbrook Press (Minneapolis, MN), 2008.

On the Scale: A Weighty Tale, illustrated by Brian Gable, Lerner (Minneapolis, MN), 2008.

Contributor of humor articles, essays, features, and cartoons to magazines.

Sidelights

Humorist Brian P. Cleary has filled his children's books with good clean fun. His picture books *Jamaica Sandwich?, It Looks a Lot like Reindeer, Give Me Bach My Schubert,* and *You Never Sausage Love* rely heavily on pun-filled wordplay and are geared to entertain. His more-recent books have another purpose: to explain in an entertaining way several fundamental parts of speech: nouns, verbs, adjectives, adverbs, homophones, synonyms, antonyms, and prepositions. As Cleary once told *SATA,* "I believe humor increases vocabulary, ignites curiosity and, therefore, teaches." Collectively called the "Words Are CATegorical" series, his humorous grammar-based titles have sold nearly two million copies. Additionally, Cleary has also written cartoon gags and humor essays, and has been a senior editor for American Greetings, a card company that is also one of the five largest creative companies in the world.

On his home page, Cleary described himself as a "frustrated student and reluctant learner." It was not until he was introduced to poetry as a third grader that he realized the power of words. He began writing on his own, usually funny bits, and by grade five he had sold a joke to a local radio station. "Discovering that I was good at something (writing quirky verse) gave me more confidence," he stated.

With his books, particularly in the "Words Are CATegorical" series, as well as with his school visits, Cleary's goal is "to kickstart a similar fascination with words among today's elementary schoolers" to the one he experienced. For *A Mink, a Fink, a Skating Rink: What Is a Noun?* he creates "humorous rhymes" that are combined with "silly illustrations," according to Lisa Gangemi in *School Library Journal.* Using his "witty zeal," Cleary concocts "certainly one of the least serious grammar lessons imaginable," a *Publishers Weekly* contributor noted of the same book. In *Hairy, Scary, Ordinary: What Is an Adjective?* cartoon cats play among an array of adjectives, in a book that *Booklist* reviewer Hazel Rochman predicted will "appeal to kids" because of its exaggeration, wordplay, and nonsensical situations. Writing in *School Library Journal*, Adele Greenlee called the work a "lighthearted, multifaceted illustration of the importance of adjectives." In keeping with its companion volumes, *To Root, to Toot, to Parachute: What Is a Verb?* reviews the definition and use of verbs with the help of slapstick cartoon cats. Together, according to Elaine Lesh Morgan in *School Library Journal*, rhymes and cartoons "painlessly teach a grammar lesson."

Under, Over, by the Clover: What Is a Preposition? sets each preposition in bright colors, making the part of speech obvious. Cleary's "humorous text does a solid but entertaining job of introducing different types of prepositions," wrote a contributor to *Kirkus Reviews*. In *Dearly, Nearly, Insincerely: What Is an Adverb?* the author tackles words that describe actions, putting the cartoonish cats that accompany each book in the series through a variety of stunts. In *Booklist*, Carolyn Phelan wrote that *I and You and Don't Forget Who: What Is a Pronoun?* explains that part of speech "with precision, brevity, and wit." Discussing *Pitch and Throw, Grasp and Know: What Is a Synonym?* Gloria Koster concluded in *School Library Journal* that Cleary's "excellent text goes a long way toward establishing the importance of synonyms." Another book in the popular series, *A Lime, a Mime, a Pool of Slime: More about Nouns*, was "recommended as an antidote to snooze-producing grammar texts" by Phelan.

Cleary's poetry book *Rainbow Soup: Adventures in Poetry* features the same puns and gags readers enjoy in his grammar books. Educational footnotes are provided that give readers literary definitions for parts and styles of poetry, and are "written in a tongue-in-cheek way that will engage young readers," according to Laura Reed in *School Library Journal*. Cleary's "verses are clever and comical," a *Publishers Weekly* critic noted, going on to suggest that young readers who find poetry unapproachable "may well warm up to its playful presentation here." *Rhyme and Punishment: Adventures in Wordplay* explains two of the basic structures involved in poetry and joke writing: rhymes and puns. Though noting that some of the puns might not be familiar to young readers, Grace Oliff noted in *School Library Journal* that the author's examples "are both amusing and get their point across." Despite his nickname of "word nerd," Cleary also tackles math basics in *The Mission of Addition, The Action of Subtraction,* and *How Long or How Wide?: A Measuring Guide*. The last-named title "measures up quite nicely," according to a contributor to *Kirkus Reviews*.

Cleary's picture book *Peanut Butter and Jellyfishes: A Very Silly Alphabet Book* "reads like a tongue twister,"

according to a *Kirkus Reviews* contributor. He is also the author of *Eight Wild Nights: A Family Hanukkah Tale*, a picture book that describes a loving but chaotic family full of pets and guests during the Jewish holiday. Though noting that the book is not a traditional or reverent holiday tale, Teri Markson wrote in *School Library Journal* that the author's "amusing rhythmic text carries the action along from one crazy night to the next."

Biographical and Critical Sources

PERIODICALS

Booklist, June 1, 2000, Hazel Rochman, review of *Hairy, Scary, Ordinary: What Is an Adjective?*, p. 1900; March 1, 2002, GraceAnne A. DeCandido, review of *Under, Over, by the Clover: What Is a Preposition?*, p. 1132; April 1, 2004, GraceAnne A. DeCandido, review of *Rainbow Soup: Adventures in Poetry*, p. 1361; May 1, 2004, Carolyn Phelan, review of *I and You and Don't Forget Who: What Is a Pronoun?*, p. 1560; February 1, 2005, Hazel Rochman, review of *Pitch and Throw, Grasp and Know: What Is a Synonym?*, p. 956; January 1, 2007, Carolyn Phelan, review of *A Lime, a Mime, a Pool of Slime: More about Nouns*, p. 112.

Childhood Education, winter, 2000, Jorie Borden, review of *Hairy, Scary, Ordinary*, p. 107.

Children's Bookwatch, April, 2005, review of *Pitch and Throw, Grasp and Know*.

Kirkus Reviews, September 1, 1999, review of *A Mink, a Fink, a Skating Rink: What Is a Noun?*, p. 1424; March 1, 2002, review of *Under, Over, by the Clover*, p. 331; February 1, 2003, review of *Dearly, Nearly, Insincerely: What Is an Adverb?*, p. 227; March 15, 2007, review of *Peanut Butter and Jellyfishes*; July 15, 2007, review of *How Long or How Wide?*

Publishers Weekly, February 26, 1996, review of *Jamaica Sandwich?*, p. 105; August 9, 1999, review of *A Mink, a Fink, a Skating Rink*, p. 352; February 26, 2001, "More Where That Came From," p. 88; February 16, 2004, review of *Rainbow Soup*, p. 172; March 13, 2006, "True Companions," p. 68; September 25, 2006, review of *Eight Wild Nights*, p. 68; April 9, 2007, review of *Peanut Butter and Jellyfishes*, p. 52.

Reading Teacher, May, 2007, Nancy Livingston and Catherine Kurkjian, "Summer Reading: Books Too Good to Miss," p. 794.

School Library Journal, June, 1996, Kathy Piehl, review of *Jamaica Sandwich?*, p. 120; June, 1996, Ellen M. Riordan, review of *It Looks a Lot like Reindeer*, p. 120; December, 1996, Elizabeth Trotter, review of *Give Me Bach My Schubert*, p. 91; November, 1999, Lisa Gangemi, review of *A Mink, a Fink, a Skating Rink*, pp. 135-136; July, 2000, Adele Greenlee, review of *Hairy, Scary, Ordinary*, p. 92; July, 2001, Elaine Lesh Morgan, review of *To Root, to Toot, to Parachute: What Is a Verb?*, p. 92; June, 2002, Wendy S. Carroll, review of *Under, Over, by the Clover*, p. 119; March, 2003, Dona Ratterree, review of *Dearly,*

Nearly, Insincerely, p. 216; June, 2004, Steven Engelfried, review of *Hair, Scary, Ordinary,* p. 56, and Laura Reed, review of *Rainbow Soup,* p. 125; July, 2004, Lisa Gangemi Kropp, review of *I and You and Don't Forget Who,* p. 91; March, 2005, Gloria Koster, review of *Pitch and Throw, Grasp and Know,* p. 191; October, 2005, Barbara Auerbach, review of *The Mission of Addition,* p. 136; November, 2005, Maura Bresnahan, review of *How Much Can a Bare Bear Bear?,* p. 112; June, 2006, Grace Oliff, review of *Rhyme and Punishment,* and Kathleen Muelen, review of *Stop and Go, Yes and No,* both p. 134; October, 2006, Teri Markson, review of *Eight Wild Nights,* p. 95; November, 2006, Jayne Damron, review of *A Lime, a Mime, a Pool of Slime,* and Erlene Bishop Killeen, review of *The Action of Subtraction,* both p. 118; May, 2007, June Wolfe, review of *Peanut Butter and Jellyfishes,* p. 114.

ONLINE

Authors Den Web site, http://www.authorsden.com/brian pcleary (December 3, 2007), "Brian P. Cleary."

Brian P. Cleary Home Page, www.brianpcleary.com (December 3, 2007).

Lakewood, Ohio Public Library Web site, http://www.lkw dpl.org/lfiles/cleary/ (December 3, 2007), "Brian P. Cleary."

D

DAVIES, Jacqueline 1962-

Personal

Born July 25, 1962, in Cleveland, OH; daughter of I. John (a physician) and Ann R. Davies; married John Bennett (a creative director); children: Sam, Henry, Mae. *Education:* Brown University, B.A., 1984.

Addresses

Home—MA. *E-mail*—jackie@jacquelinedavies.net.

Career

Children's book author.

Awards, Honors

Notable Social Studies Trade Book for Young People designation, National Council of Social Studies/ Children's Book Council (CBC), Children's Notable Book for Fiction Award, International Reading Association/CBC, and New York Public Library Books for the Teen Age selection, all 2003, all for *Where the Ground Meets the Sky;* John Burroughs List of Nature Books for Young Readers inclusion, and New York Public Library 100 Titles for Reading and Sharing selection, both 2004, and Outstanding Science Trade Book for Students K-12 designation, National Science Teachers Association/CBC, 2005, all for *The Boy Who Drew Birds;* Children's Book Sense Picks, 2007, for *The House Takes a Vacation.*

Jacqueline Davies (Reproduced by permission.)

Writings

Where the Ground Meets the Sky, Marshall Cavendish (New York, NY), 2002.
The Boy Who Drew Birds: A Story of John James Audubon, illustrated by Melissa Sweet, Houghton Mifflin (Boston, MA), 2004.
The Night Is Singing, illustrated by Kyrsten Brooker, Dial Books for Young Readers (New York, NY), 2006.

The House Takes a Vacation, illustrated by Lee White, Marshall Cavendish (New York, NY), 2007.
The Lemonade Stand (chapter book), Houghton Miffin (Boston, MA), 2007.

Sidelights

Jacqueline Davies is the author of a number of award-winning books for young readers, including the middle-grade novel *Where the Ground Meets the Sky* and the picture book *The House Takes a Vacation.* The author's debut title, *Where the Ground Meets the Sky,* is set in the 1940s and concerns twelve-year-old Hazel, who has recently moved with her family from New Jersey to a place in New Mexico known as the "Hill." The "Hill" is actually a remote military base on which her father works. While Hazel wonders what her father is working on in such secrecy, readers gradually realize that he is among the group of scientists creating the atomic bomb. The secrecy of such a job ultimately takes its toll on the family; Hazel's mother grows increasingly despondent due to her husband's secretive occupation, calling it "bad for the soul." Janet Gillen commented in a review for *School Library Journal* that Davies' "suspenseful story successfully captures the tensions of a volatile period in American history as the atomic bomb was being developed," and leaves young readers with "plenty to think about and no simple answers."

Davies' first picture book, *The Boy Who Drew Birds: A Story of John James Audubon,* tells the story of the French-born naturalist who, newly arrived in the United States when a young man, befriends a pair of nesting phoebe birds. When the birds leave in the fall, the young artist ponders their winter destination and decides to test the prevailing theories about migratory behavior. To determine if the creatures return to the same nests in the spring, he bands the young birds with silver thread before they fly south. In *Horn Book,* Joanna Rudge Long applauded Davies' "lively narration that illuminates Audubon's passion for observation and sets his pivotal insight into context," and Susan Scheps, writing in *School Library Journal,* called the work "a wonderful and accessible introduction to a man who made a great impact on the science of ornithology." In *Kirkus Reviews* a contributor praised *The Boy Who Drew Birds* as "winsomely imagined" and added that Davies' story sustains reader interest in the "bird-obsessed" artist "whose perfectionism led him to burn his artwork every year."

In Davies' *The Night Is Singing,* a bedtime tale told in verse, the author explores the sounds of a country evening. As a little girl prepares for bed, she notices the hissing of a radiator, the chiming of a hall clock, the squawking of a goose, the howling of a fierce wind, and, finally, the tip-tapping of her mother's feet as she comes to her daughter's room. According to Jennifer Mattson, writing in *Booklist,* Davies' text "conveys a vivid sense of cocooning safety, unpunctured even in the wake of a 'crashing' thunderstorm." Long observed that, "for addressing bedtime concerns," *The Night Is Singing* serves as "a welcome contrast to the monster-under-the-bed genre," and a contributor in *Kirkus Reviews* described the work as "gratifying and readable night after night."

With its owners gone, a home decides it could use a rest in Davies' offbeat title *The House Takes a Vacation.* After the Petersons drive off to enjoy their holiday, their residence develops a mind of its own and begins planning its escape. When the bedroom windows inquire about the destination, however, each part of the house offers its own suggestion. After much discussion, however, the roof, front door, chimney, and sun porch

Cover of Davies' middle-grade novel **Where the Ground Meets the Sky,** *featuring artwork by Peggy Dressell.* (Marshall Cavendish, 2002. Jacket illustration copyright © 2002 by Peggy Dressel. Reproduced by permission.)

agree to head to the beach. *School Library Journal* critic Judith Constantinides remarked that *The House Takes a Vacation* "is memorable mainly for its play on words," adding the book "is somewhat sophisticated in its humor." Writing in *Horn Book,* Kitty Flynn similarly noted that "some of the wordplay may not register with young readers . . ., but that doesn't detract from the story's absurd humor."

The Lemonade Stand, a chapter book, centers on Evan Treski and his younger sister, Jessie. Though the siblings generally get along well together, things change dramatically over the course of one summer. A bright and talented student, Jessie learns that she will skip a year of school and enter fourth grade with her brother. To make matters worse, in Evan's mind, they will be sitting in the same classroom. Soon misunderstandings abound, and as their rivalry grows, Evan and Jessie set up competing lemonade stands, each determined to outsell the other. "The plot rolls along smoothly," a contributor in *Kirkus Reviews* stated, and *Booklist* critic Carolyn Phelan observed that Davies "does a good job of showing the siblings' strengths, flaws, and points of view" in the work. *The Lemonade Stand* "is highly readable and engaging," remarked Maria B. Salvadore in *School Library Journal,* the critic going on to describe the book as "funny, fresh, and plausible."

Davies once told *SATA:* "The first book I ever wrote is called *The Sad Shape.* I wrote it when I was in kindergarten and I have it still. It's a modest opus, no more than one hundred words long, but I like to show *The Sad Shape* to students when I visit school because it proves two points: 1) anyone in the room can write a story as good as my early stuff, and 2) all stories have a shape (even if it is a sad one).

"I've been writing stories since I was five, but I turned to writing books for kids when I was thirty. Previously, I'd written nonfiction and short stories for adults, but honestly I couldn't quite figure out what the point was. Most of the adults I knew were pretty set in their ways. They'd figured out a lot of what makes the world tick, and they didn't get particularly worked up over the

Davies' picture book The Night Is Singing *is brought to life by Kyrsten Brooker's evocative paintings.* (Dial Books for Young Readers, 2006. Illustrations copyright © 2006 by Krysten Brooker. Reproduced by permission.)

books they read. But kids, kids are full of juice. They do get excited about the books they read—the ones that make them laugh, the ones that make them check under the bed before going to sleep, the ones that make them think and cry and think some more. Kids really get INTO a story, and that was the kind of audience I wanted for my books.

"When I talk to kids who've read my books, they often tell me their reactions. 'I was so sad when the cat died, I wished I could change that part.' 'Reading about John James Audubon made me go outside and start drawing birds myself. It's hard!' 'The character of Eleanor reminded me of my sister. I wish I was more like them because they're brave and have adventures.' I love these comments. They help me see inside the story that I wrote to the story that is actually experienced by the reader. I feel extraordinarily lucky to have such a collaborative experience with my readers."

Biographical and Critical Sources

PERIODICALS

Booklist, September 1, 2002, GraceAnne A. DeCandido, review of *Where the Ground Meets the Sky,* p. 112; November 1, 2004, Carolyn Phelan, review of *The Boy Who Drew Birds: A Story of John James Audubon,* p. 477; May 15, 2006, Jennifer Mattson, review of *The Night Is Singing,* p. 49; March 15, 2007, Carolyn Phelan, review of *The Lemonade War,* p. 46.

Bulletin of the Center for Children's Books, October, 2004, Deborah Stevenson, review of *The Boy Who Drew Birds,* p. 68; April, 2007, Deborah Stevenson, review of *The House Takes a Vacation,* p. 3327.

Horn Book, November-December, 2004, Joanna Rudge Long, review of *The Boy Who Drew Birds,* p. 726; July-August, 2006, Joanna Rudge Long, review of *The Night Is Singing,* p. 423; May-June, 2007, Kitty Flynn, review of *The House Takes a Vacation,* p. 263.

Kirkus Reviews, September 1, 2004, review of *The Boy Who Drew Birds;* April 15, 2006, review of *The Night Is Singing,* p. 404; February 15, 2007, review of review of *The House Takes a Vacation;* April 1, 2007, review of *The Lemonade War.*

Publishers Weekly, September 13, 2004, review of *The Boy Who Drew Birds,* p. 81.

School Library Journal, April, 2002, Janet Gillen, review of *Where the Ground Meets the Sky,* p. 146; December, 2004, Susan Scheps, review of *The Boy Who Drew Birds,* p. 128; June, 2006, Sally R. Dow, review of *The Night Is Singing,* p. 110; May, 2007, Judith Constantinides, review of *The House Takes a Vacation,* p. 90, and Maria B. Salvadore, review of *The Lemonade War,* p. 90.

U.S. News & World Report, September 27, 2004, Marc Silver, review of *The Boy Who Drew Birds,* p. 16.

Washington Post Book World, September 12, 2004, Elizabeth Ward, review of *The Boy Who Drew Birds,* p. 12.

ONLINE

Jacqueline Davies Web site, http://www.jacquelinedavies. net (December 20, 2007).*

*   *   *

DEBON, Nicolas 1968-

Personal

Born 1968, in Lorraine, France. *Education:* Attended École Nationale des Beaux-Arts (Nancy, France).

Addresses

Office—21 rue des Prés aux Bois, 78000 Versailles, France. *E-mail*—ndebon@yahoo.com.

Career

Author and illustrator. French Ministry of Culture, worked in contemporary visual arts department; French Ministry of Foreign Affairs, worked at French consulate, Toronto, Ontario, Canada; freelance illustrator, 1998—. Draftsman for a stained glass company in Toronto.

Awards, Honors

Governor General's Literary Award finalist, Canada Council, 2003, for *Four Pictures by Emily Carr; Boston Globe/Horn Book* Award, 2007, for *The Strongest Man in the World.*

Writings

SELF-ILLUSTRATED

A Brave Soldier, Groundwood Books/Douglas & McIntyre (Toronto, Ontario, Canada), 2002.

Four Pictures by Emily Carr, Groundwood Books/Douglas & McIntyre (Berkeley, CA), 2003.

The Strongest Man in the World: Louis Cyr, Groundwood Books (Toronto, Ontario, Canada), 2007.

Also author of *L'art contemporain en Ontario* (cultural guidebook).

ILLUSTRATOR

Virginia Walton Pilegard, *The Warlord's Puzzle,* Pelican (Gretna, LA), 2000.

Virginia Walton Pilegard, *The Warlord's Beads,* Pelican (Gretna, LA), 2001.

Virginia Walton Pilegard, *The Warlord's Fish,* Pelican (Gretna, LA), 2002.

Kris Hemphill, *Ambush in the Wilderness,* Silver Moon Press (New York, NY), 2003.

Stephanie Sammartino McPherson, *Liberty or Death: A Story about Patrick Henry,* Carolrhoda Books (Minneapolis, MN), 2003.

Shannon Zemlicka, *Florence Nightingale,* Carolrhoda Books (Minneapolis, MN), 2003.

Laura Scandiffio, *The Martial Arts Book,* Annick Press (Toronto, Ontario, Canada), 2003.

Jean E. Pendziwol, *Dawn Watch,* Groundwood Books/ Douglas & McIntyre (Toronto, Ontario, Canada), 2003.

Virginia Walton Pilegard, *The Warlord's Puppeteers,* Pelican (Gretna, LA), 2003.

Virginia Walton Pilegard, *The Warlord's Kites,* Pelican (Gretna, LA), 2004.

Virginia Walton Pilegard, *The Warlord's Messengers,* Pelican (Gretna, LA), 2005.

Jean E. Pendziwol, *The Red Sash,* Groundwood Books (Toronto, Ontario, Canada), 2005.

Virginia Walton Pilegard, *The Warlord's Alarm,* Pelican (Gretna, LA), 2006.

Dominique Demers, *Every Single Night,* English translation by Sarah Quinn. Groundwood Books (Toronto, Ontario, Canada), 2006.

Contributor of illustrations to textbooks.

Sidelights

French-born writer and illustrator Nicolas Debon began his career in children's books while working in the French consulate in Toronto, Ontario, Canada. Employed in the visual arts branch of the French Ministry of Culture, Debon was transferred to the French consulate in Toronto. After some time, he sought Canadian citizenship, left his government position, and found a job as a draughtsman for a stained glass company. At the same time, he began submitting work to Canadian publishers of children's books. Debon moved back to France in 2004, with plans to continue his illustration career with French publishers.

Debon's first work as an illustrator was creating art for Virginia Walton Pilegard's "Warlord" series, which includes such tales as *The Warlord's Puzzle, The Warlord's Beads,* and *The Warlord's Fish.* In these books, Pilegard relates legends about the inventors of various ancient Chinese innovations, including the compass and the abacus. Debon's illustrations for *The Warlord's Fish,* which discusses the invention of the compass, "convincingly visualize the historical setting and display a fine sense of color and composition," according to *Booklist* contributor Carolyn Phelan. In *School Library Journal* Laurie Edwards deemed the pictures "stunning" and complimented their "subtle shading and engaging design." Reviewing *The Warlord's Kites* for *School Library Journal,* Susan Scheps wrote that the illustrations feature "detailed scenes and stylized characters that bring the tale to life." Phelan noted that in *The Warlord's Alarm* "Debon's expressive paintings make dramatic use of the story, the characters, and the landscape."

Several other authors have had their texts paired with illustrations by Debon. In Jean E. Pendziwol's *Dawn Watch,* his art brings to life the seascape of the far north, with its Northern Lights, as well as the imaginary dragons introduced in the story. Gillian Engberg, writing in *Booklist,* felt that Debon's depiction of "the scenes' deep, shadowy blues and skewed angles, reminiscent of the sailboat's tilt, bring close the chilly wind, [and] the startling sky" of the polar setting. Of his work on Pendziwol's *The Red Sash,* a picture book set along the Great Lakes during the early nineteenth century, Victoria Pennell wrote in *Resource Links* that Debon's "bold illustrations add an authentic view of the landscape and the day-to-day life of the period." In Dominique Demers' bedtime tale *Every Single Night,* "Debon's handsome spreads of creatures wending their way to rest nicely counterpoint quieter scenes," according to Joanna Rudge Long in *Horn Book.*

In addition to his illustration work, Debon is also the author of three self-illustrated picture books dealing with Canadian history: *A Brave Soldier, Four Pictures by Emily Carr,* and *The Strongest Man in the World: Louis Cyr.* Described as a "well told, powerfully illustrated, and timely" anti-war tale by *School Library Journal* contributor Louise L. Sherman, *A Brave Soldier* is about a Canadian soldier named Frank who enlists to fight in France during World War I. He and his friend arrive at the front in high spirits, but they quickly become disillusioned. Before long, Frank's friend is killed, and in the same attack, Frank is wounded so badly that he is sent home. "While Debon does not gloss over the

Nicholas Debon pairs with author Dominique Demers to create the picture book **Every Single Night** *(Translated into English by Sarah Quinn. First published in English by Groundwood Books, 2005. Originally published by Gallimard/ Editions Imagine. Reproduced by permission of Groundwood Books.)*

brutal conditions experienced in World War I," Pennell wrote in *Resource Links* that "he does not dwell on the horror or glorify the fighting" either.

A finalist for Canada's Governor General's Literary Award, *Four Pictures by Emily Carr* offers a unique biography of the pioneering Canadian painter. Showing talent as a child, Carr abandoned her art as a young woman, not returning to the canvas until the age of fifty-six, when some of her early works finally received much-deserved critical attention. Debon drew on Carr's detailed journals in writing the book, and the words he gives Carr are drawn directly from the artist's own writings. Told in a format reminiscent of a comic book, *Four Pictures by Emily Carr* "distill[s] four periods in the Canadian artist's life . . . into enticing vignettes," Sophie R. Brookover wrote in *School Library Journal.* Finding Debon's approach "innovative," *Horn Book* critic Lolly Robinson recommended "this unusual and highly successful homage to Carr . . . for late bloomers of any age and vocation."

The Strongest Man in the World is a biography of the legendary Canadian circus performer who lived during the late nineteenth century. Told in illustrated panels from Louis Cyr's imagined perspective, the book recounts Cyr's early feats of strength, his business sensibility, and his eventual leadership of his own circus. "Through both artwork and text, Debon re-creates the world of the circus in the early 1900s," wrote *School Library Journal* contributor Alana Abbott. Martha V. Parravano, reviewing the work for *Horn Book,* felt that "Debon's approach is simultaneously unconventional and expert," and added that the paneled style of storytelling provided "immediacy and intimacy." A *Kirkus Reviews* contributor dubbed the book "a memorable glimpse into the life of a different sort of athlete," and a *Publishers Weekly* critic called *The Strongest Man in the World* "a thoroughly absorbing tale about a turn-of-the-20th-century celebrity." Karen Loch, in *Resource Links,* noted that Debon's book serves as "an excellent read for the struggling reader who is intimidated with books that contain a lot of text."

On the Groundwood Books Web site, Debon revealed his perspective on illustrating children's books. "I'm always amazed by the number of different ways a story can be illustrated," he noted. "Illustrating a story allows a considerable amount of freedom and this is probably what I like most about it. I believe there are still vast areas to explore in the creation of children's books."

Biographical and Critical Sources

PERIODICALS

Biography, summer, 2007, Susan Perren, review of *The Strongest Man in the World: Louis Cyr,* p. 421.

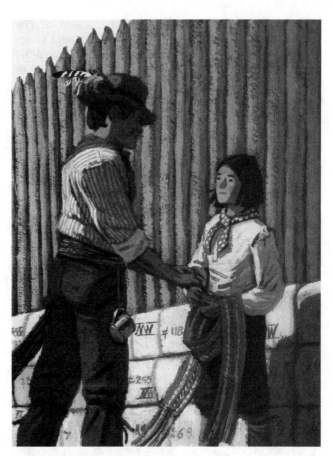

In **The Red Sash** *Jean E. Pendziwol's story about a canoeing family is the focus of Debon's brush.* (Groundwood Books, 2005. Illustrations copyright © 2005 by Nicolas Debon. Reproduced by permission of Groundwood Books.)

Booklist, November 1, 2002, Hazel Rochman, review of *A Brave Soldier,* p. 491; February 1, 2003, Carolyn Phelan, review of *The Warlord's Fish,* p. 1002; April 15, 2003, Carolyn Phelan, review of *The Martial Arts Book,* pp. 1468-1469; December 1, 2003, Hazel Rochman, review of *Four Pictures by Emily Carr,* p. 658; December 15, 2003, GraceAnne A. DeCandido, review of *The Warlord's Puppeteers,* p. 754; November 1, 2004, Gillian Engberg, review of *Dawn Watch,* p. 493; November 15, 2004, Carolyn Phelan, review of *The Warlord's Kites,* p. 591; June 1, 2005, Gillian Engberg, "A Day with Dad," p. 1819; November 15, 2005, Carolyn Phelan, review of *The Warlord's Messengers,* p. 52; December 1, 2005, Hazel Rochman, review of *The Red Sash,* p. 55; March 15, 2006, Carolyn Phelan, review of *Every Single Night,* p. 53; November 1, 2006, Carolyn Phelan, review of *The Warlord's Alarm,* p. 61; April 1, 2007, Ian Chipman, review of *The Strongest Man in the World,* p. 53.

Books in Canada, November, 2002, Deborah Wandal, review of *A Brave Soldier,* pp. 39-40.

Bulletin of the Center for Children's Books, May, 2007, Elizabeth Bush, review of *The Strongest Man in the World,* p. 365.

Children's Bookwatch, November, 2006, review of *The Warlord's Alarm.*

Horn Book, January-February, 2004, Lolly Robinson, review of *Four Pictures by Emily Carr,* p. 100; January-

February, 2006, Joanna Rudge Long, review of *The Red Sash*, p. 69; May-June, 2006, Joanna Rudge Long, review of *Every Single Night*, p. 293; May-June, 2007, Martha V. Parravano, review of *The Strongest Man in the World*, p. 299.

Kirkus Reviews, October 1, 2004, review of *Dawn Watch*, p. 966; September 1, 2005, review of *The Red Sash*, p. 980; March 1, 2006, review of *Every Single Night*, p. 228; March 15, 2007, review of *The Strongest Man in the World*.

Publishers Weekly, April 24, 2000, review of *The Warlord's Puzzle*, p. 90; April 10, 2006, review of *Every Single Night*, p. 71; May 7, 2007, review of *The Strongest Man in the World*, p. 59.

Resource Links, December, 2002, Victoria Pennell, review of *A Brave Soldier*, pp. 4-5; December, 2003, John Dryden, review of *Four Pictures of Emily Carr*, p. 24; December, 2005, Victoria Pennell, review of *The Red Sash*, p. 7; October, 2007, Karen Loch, review of *The Strongest Man in the World*, p. 23.

School Arts, April, 2004, Ken Marantz, review of *Four Pictures by Emily Carr*, p. 60.

School Library Journal, June, 2000, Margaret A. Chang, review of *The Warlord's Puzzle*, p. 124; February, 2002, Karen Land, review of *The Warlord's Beads*, p. 110; February, 2003, Louise L. Sherman, review of *A Brave Soldier*, p. 104, Laurie Edwards, review of *The Warlord's Fish*, p. 120; August, 2003, Lucinda Snyder Whitehurst, review of *Florence Nightingale*, p. 153; September, 2003, Donna Cardon, review of *Liberty or Death: A Story about Patrick Henry*, p. 203; November, 2003, Sophie R. Brookover, review of *Four Pictures by Emily Carr*, pp. 154-155; January, 2004, Lynda Ritterman, review of *The Warlord's Puppeteers*, p. 103; February, 2004, Edith Ching, review of *Ambush in the Wilderness*, p. 148; December, 2004, Shawn Brommer, review of *Dawn Watch*, p. 117; February, 2005, Susan Scheps, review of *The Warlord's Kites*, p. 108; December, 2005, Barbara Auerbach, review of *The Warlord's Messengers*, p. 120; January, 2006, Robyn Walker, review of *The Red Sash*, p. 111; May, 2006, Shelley B. Sutherland, review of *Every Single Night*, p. 86; November, 2006, Erlene Bishop Killeen, review of *The Warlord's Alarm*, p. 108; July, 2007, Alana Abbott, review of *The Strongest Man in the World*, p. 123.

Teaching Children Mathematics, February, 2003, Alison S. Claus, review of *The Warlord's Beads*, pp. 365-366; November, 2004, Carol Robitschek, review of *The Warlord's Puppeteers*, p. 239.

Tribune Books (Chicago, IL), June 23, 2007, Mary Harris Russell, review of *The Strongest Man in the World*, p. 7.

ONLINE

Annick Press Web site, http://www.annickpress.com/ (December 19, 2007), "Nicholas Debon."

Children's Literature Web site, http://www.childrenslit. com/ (February 29, 2006), "Nicholas Debon."

Groundwood Books Web site, http://www.groundwood books.com/ (December 19, 2007), "Nicholas Debon."

Nicolas Debon Home Page, http://ndebon.tripod.com (December 19, 2007).*

de MARCKEN, Gail

Personal

Born in MN; married Baudouin de Marcken (a Peace Corps administrator); children: three. *Education:* University of Minnesota, degree, c. 1965.

Addresses

Home and office—Ely, MN. *E-mail*—gail@demarcken. org.

Career

Illustrator. Peace Corps volunteer in Borneo, Malaysia, c. 1960; teacher of art while affiliated with Peace Corps, beginning 1965. Presenter at schools.

Illustrator

Bob Cary, *Born to Pull*, Pfeifer-Hamilton Publishers (Duluth, MN), 1999.

Jeff Brumbeau, *The Quiltmaker's Gift*, Pfeifer-Hamilton (Duluth, MN), 2000.

Jeff Brumbeau, *Miss Hunnicutt's Hat*, Orchard Books (New York, NY), 2003.

Joanne Larsen Line, *More Quilts from the Quiltmaker's Gift: Nineteen Traditional Patterns for a Generation of Generous Quiltmakers*, Orchard Books (New York, NY), 2003.

Tina Packer, *Tales from Shakespeare*, Scholastic Press (New York, NY), 2004.

Jeff Brumbeau, *The Quiltmaker's Journey*, Orchard Books (New York, NY), 2005.

Nancy Farmer, *Clever Ali*, Orchard Books (New York, NY), 2006.

Biographical and Critical Sources

PERIODICALS

Kirkus Reviews, February 15, 2003, review of *Miss Hunnicutt's Hat*, p. 301.

ONLINE

Gail de Marcken Home Page, http://www.demarcken.org (January 6, 2008).

Minnesota Sun Online, http://www.mnsun.com/ (December 19, 2002), John Klun, "Artist Finds Success in Retirement."

Peace Corps Online, http://peacecorpsonline.org/ (January 7, 2008), "Gail de Marcken."*

*   *   *

DENMAN, K.L. 1957-

Personal

Born 1957, in Calgary, Alberta, Canada. *Hobbies and other interests:* Horseback riding, gardening, nature study.

K.L. Denman (Reproduced by permission.)

Addresses

Home and office—Powell River, British Columbia, Canada. *E-mail*—write@shaw.ca.

Career

Children's author. Worked previously in environmental preservation, as a florist, as an occupational information advisor, and in various office jobs.

Member

Writers' Union of Canada, Children's Writers and Illustrators of British Columbia.

Awards, Honors

Quick Picks for Reluctant Readers nomination, American Library Association, 2006, for *Battle of the Bands*.

Writings

NOVELS

Battle of the Bands, Orca (Custer, WA), 2006.
Mirror Image, Orca (Custer, WA), 2007.
Rebel's Tag, Orca (Custer, WA), 2007.
The Shade, Orca (Custer, WA), 2008.
Spiral, Orca (Custer, WA), 2008.

Author's work has been translated into Spanish.

Sidelights

K.L. Denman was inspired to write for children and young adults when she began reading some marvelous young-adult fiction. Her teen children provided her with many story ideas, and her own teen experiences, including her time working on a ranch in Alberta, Canada, have also found their way into her fiction. Along with writing, Denman has held a variety of jobs, including being involved in environmental preservation and helping a local conservation group to create a butterfly garden at an elementary school.

Denman's first novel, *Battle of the Bands,* is geared toward reluctant readers. In the story, Jay fronts a punk band called the Lunar Ticks and he is determined to lead the band to greatness in an upcoming battle of the bands. He is disappointed when the Lunar Ticks are beaten by the Indigo Daze, because the Daze lyricist has incorporated a recent tragedy into the band's songs. The defeat prompts Jay to examine what it takes to be a great musician. Deciding that it is not the events that happen in a musician's life, but how the musician understands them, he and the Ticks find greater success in their performances. *Battle of the Bands* "is quite sweet in its depiction of budding teen romance and feels genuine in its portrayal of teen-parent relationships," wrote Emily Springer in her *Resource Links* review of the novel. In *School Library Journal,* Kristin Anderson noted that Denman's "characters are edgy but likable," and Lisa Carlson wrote in *Kliatt* that the novel is "a lively read with a strong theme that can lend itself to further discussion."

Mirror Image is the story of a relationship between two unlikely friends. Sable is a loner who has not gotten close to anyone since her father's death years before. Lacey, one of the most popular girls in school, is both beautiful and, in Sable's opinion, a bimbo. When the two teens team up for an art project, they start to see each other with new eyes. Lacey tries to teach Sable a bit about fitting in, and Sable becomes an ear for Lacey's concerns about her dark home life. Calling the novel's plot somewhat "contrived," Hazel Rochman wrote in *Booklist* that, nonetheless, Denman's "dialogue is fast and funny, and so is Sable's wry, honest first-person narrative." Wendy Hogan, writing in *Resource Links,* concluded of *Mirror Image* that "Denman has written from her heart and [the novel] . . . speaks the truth."

In Denman's third novel, *Rebel Tag,* another teen is dealing with the death of his father as well as with the loss of his grandfather, who left the family ten years earlier. When Sam receives a letter from his absent grandfather, who is hoping to build their relationship again through a mystical treasure hunt, he is not sure whether to forgive the man or remain angry. In *Canadian Review of Materials,* Marina Cohen wrote that *Rebel Tag* "will draw reluctant readers in from the get-go and hold them captive until the bittersweet end" due to Denman's "clean" prose and "brilliant" narrative voice.

On the *Author's Den* Web site, Denman explained that writing brings her both joy and peace. "Not that it's easy!" she admitted. "It isn't. It's a Tilt-a-wheel ride of blank lows, inspired highs, and spinning words into story."

Cover of Canadian writer Denman's young-adult novel Mirror Image. (Orca Book Publishers, 2007. Jupiterimages, cover photographer. Doug McCaffry, cover designer. Reproduced by permission.)

Biographical and Critical Sources

PERIODICALS

Booklist, March 15, 2007, Hazel Rochman, review of *Mirror Image,* p. 46.

Canadian Review of Materials, December 7, 2007, Marina Cohen, review of *Rebel's Tag.*

Kliatt, January, 2007, Lisa Carlson, review of *Battle of the Bands,* p. 21.

Resource Links, February, 2007, Emily Springer, review of *Battle of the Bands,* p. 31; April, 2007, Wendy Hogan, review of *Mirror Image,* p. 40.

School Library Journal, March, 2007, Kristin Anderson, review of *Battle of the Bands,* p. 208; November, 2007, Meredith Robbins, review of *Rebel's Tag,* p. 225.

ONLINE

Authors Den Web site, http://www.authorsden.com/ (December 3, 2007), "K.L. Denman."

K.L. Denman Blog site, http://kldenman.wordpress.com/ (November 28, 2007).

Orca Books Web site, http://www.orcabook.com/ (November 28, 2007), "K.L. Dedman."

Writers' Union of Canada Web site, http://www.writersunion.ca/ (December 3, 2007), "K.L. Denman."

*   *   *

DENTON, Terry 1950-

Personal

Born 1950, in Melbourne, Victoria, Australia; married; wife's name Kirsten; children: three. *Education:* Studied architecture at an Australian university. *Hobbies and other interests:* Bushwalking, ball sports, water sports, painting.

Addresses

Home—Mornington, Victoria, Australia. *Agent*—Booked Out Speakers Agency, P.O. Box 580, South Yarra, Victoria 3141, Australia. *E-mail*—terry@terrydenton.com.

Career

Author and illustrator. Co-creator and puppet designer for *Lift-Off,* Australian Children's Television Foundation, 1991-92. Has also worked in animation, painting, theater, etching, sculpture, and cartooning.

Awards, Honors

Children's Book Council of Australia (CBCA) Picture Book of the Year, 1986, for *Felix and Alexander;* American Family Choice Award, 1987, for *At the Café Splendid;* Australian Multicultural Book of the Year, 1993, for *Mr. Plunkett's Pool;* CBCA Honour designation, 1994, for *The Paw;* Best Designed Book of the Year, and Young Australian Best Book Award, 1994, for *Spooner or Later;* Young Australian Best Book Award, Kids Own Australian Literature Award (KOALA), and CBCA award shortlist, all 1995, all for *Duck for Cover;* KOALA award, 1996, Books I Love Best Yearly Award, 1998, and Young Australian Best Book Award, 1999, all for *Gasp!;* Young Australian Best Book Award, 1998, for *Zapt!,* and 2000, for both *Splat!* and *Just Stupid!;* Young Australian Best Book Award, and KOALA award, both 1999, both for *Just Annoying!;* Young Australian Best Book Award shortlist, and Books I Love Best Yearly Award, both 2002, both for *Just Crazy!;* Young Australian Best Book Award shortlist, and KOALA award, both 2002, both for *Just Tricking!;* KOALA award, 2003, for *Just Disgusting!;* Aurelis Award shortlist, 2003; Young Australian Best Book Award shortlist, 2006, for *The Worst Nurse.*

Writings

SELF-ILLUSTRATED

Felix and Alexander, Oxford University Press (Melbourne, Victoria, Australia), 1985.

Flying Man, Penguin (Ringwood, Victoria, Australia), 1985.

At the Café Splendid, Oxford University Press (Melbourne, Victoria, Australia), 1987.

Home Is the Sailor, Oxford University Press (Melbourne, Victoria, Australia), 1988.

The School for Laughter, Oxford University Press (Melbourne, Victoria, Australia), 1989.

Gasp!: The Breathtaking Adventures of a Fish Left Home Alone (also see below), Puffin Books (Melbourne, Victoria, Australia), 1995.

Zapt!: The Electrifying Adventures of a Fish Left Home Alone (also see below), Puffin Books (Melbourne, Victoria, Australia), 1997.

(With others) *Bedtime Stories* (includes *Felix and Alexander*), Hodder Children's Books (Sydney, New South Wales, Australia), 1997.

Splat!: The Explosive Adventures of a Fish Left Home Alone (also see below), Puffin Books (Ringwood, Victoria, Australia), 1998.

Crash!, Penguin (Camberwell, Victoria, Australia), 2003.

Gasp! Zapt! Splat!: The Explosive, Breathtaking and Electrifying Adventures of a Mad Fish on the Loose!, Claremont (Camberwell, Victoria, Australia), 2003.

It's True! Pigs Do Fly, Allen & Unwin (East Melbourne, Victoria, Australia), 2004.

Squish!, Penguin (Camberwell, Victoria, Australia), 2004.

Chomp!, Penguin (Camberwell, Victoria, Australia), 2006.

Wombat and Fox: Tales of the City, Allen & Unwin (Crows Nest, New South Wales, Australia), 2006.

Wombat and Fox: Summer in the City, Allen & Unwin (Crows Nest, New South Wales, Australia), 2007.

"STORYMAZE" GRAPHIC-NOVEL SERIES; SELF-ILLUSTRATED

The Ultimate Wave, Silverfish (Sydney, New South Wales, Australia), 1999, new edition, Allen & Unwin (Crows Nest, New South Wales, Australia), 2001.

The Eye of Ulam, Allen & Unwin (Crows Nest, New South Wales, Australia), 2001.

The Wooden Cow, Allen & Unwin (Crows Nest, New South Wales, Australia), 2002.

The Golden Udder, Allen & Unwin (Crows Nest, New South Wales, Australia), 2002.

The Minotaur's Maze, Allen & Unwin (Crows Nest, New South Wales, Australia), 2003.

The Obelisk of Eeeno, Allen & Unwin (Crows Nest, New South Wales, Australia), 2003.

ILLUSTRATOR

Max Dann, *Going Bananas,* Oxford University Press (Melbourne, Victoria, Australia), 1983.

Max Dann, *Mystery of the Haunted Theatre,* Oxford University Press (Melbourne, Victoria, Australia), 1983.

Heather Fidge, *The Monster Family,* Oxford University Press (Melbourne, Victoria, Australia), 1984.

Julie Knights and Helen Allen, *Ideas for Physical Education,* Primary Education (Blackburn, Victoria, Australia), 1984.

Morris Lurie, *The Story of Imelda, Who Was Small,* Oxford University Press (Melbourne, Victoria, Australia), 1984.

Keith Murray, *The Day the Grog Ran Out, and Other Stories from the Big Book,* Dove Communications (Blackburn, Victoria, Australia), 1985, tenth anniversary edition, 1995.

Joan Goodwin, *Mary MacKillop: A Great Australian,* Dove Communications (Melbourne, Victoria, Australia), 1985.

A Teddy Bear's Picnic: A Collection of Original Stories about Teddy Bears, Oxford University Press (Melbourne, Victoria, Australia), 1986.

Shirley Macdonald, *Pope John Paul II,* Collins Dove (Blackburn, Victoria, Australia), 1986.

Laurie Oakes and John Fitzgerald, *Australian Government,* Dove Communications (Blackburn, Victoria, Australia), 1986.

Maurice Saxby and Glenys Smith, *If Pigs Could Fly,* Methuen (North Ryde, New South Wales, Australia), 1987.

Rus Center, *If Wishes Were Tigers,* Macmillan Australia (South Melbourne, Victoria, Australia), 1987.

Robyn Green and Bronwen Scarffe, *'What a Day!,"* Collins Dove (Blackburn, Victoria, Australia), 1987.

Felicity M., *Manners for Kids,* Collins Dove (Blackburn, Victoria, Australia), 1987.

Doug MacLeod, *Ten Monster Islands,* Omnibus Books (Adelaide, South Australia, Australia), 1987.

Jeannie Rose, *Teresa Green,* Collins Dove (Blackburn, Victoria, Australia), 1987.

Pamela Shrapnel, *Meannie and the Min Min,* Angus & Robertson (North Ryde, New South Wales, Australia), 1987.

Peita Letchford, *Jimmy and His Fabulous Feathered Friends,* Angus & Robertson (North Ryde, New South Wales, Australia), 1988.

Pamela Shrapnel, *Freddie the Frightened and the Wondrous Ms. Wardrobe,* Angus & Robertson (North Ryde, New South Wales, Australia), 1988.

The Big Book of Christmas Carols: A Collection of Christmas Carols Chosen for Young Singers to Tell the Story of the Nativity, Oxford University Press (Melbourne, Victoria, Australia), 1989.

The Small Book of Christmas Carols, Oxford University Press (Melbourne, Victoria, Australia), 1989.

Dianne Bates, *When Melissa Ann Came to Dinner,* Harcourt Brace Jovanovich (Sydney, New South Wales, Australia), 1989.

Mem Fox, *Night Noises,* Omnibus Books (Adelaide, South Australia, Australia), 1989, reprinted, Penguin (Camberwell, Victoria, Australia, 2005.

Brenda Parkes, *Goodnight Goodnight,* Mimosa Publications (Hawthorn, Victoria, Australia), 1989.

Gordon Winch, *Thomas Torrington and the Fabulous Fire Suit,* Harcourt Brace Jovanovich (Sydney, New South Wales, Australia), 1989.

Jenny Wagner, *Amy's Monster,* Viking (New York, NY), 1990.

Max Dann, *Dusting in Love,* Oxford University Press (Melbourne, Victoria, Australia), 1990.

Morris Lurie, *What's That Noise? What's That Sound?*, Random House Australia (Milson Point, New South Wales, Australia), 1991.

(With Peter Gouldthorpe) David Drew, *The Paper Skyscraper: The Technology of Materials*, Rigby Heinemann (Port Melbourne, Victoria, Australia), 1992.

Jim Howes, *Rocky on Assignment*, Mammoth (Port Melbourne, Victoria, Australia), 1992.

Jim Howes, *The Rude Dictionary: A Dictionary of Words That Adults Never Tell You*, Omnibus Books (Norwood, South Australia, Australia), 1992.

Jim Howes, *The Wakadoo Cafe*, Mammoth (Port Melbourne, Victoria, Australia), 1992.

Paul Jennings and Ted Greenwood, *Spooner or Later*, Viking (Melbourne, Victoria, Australia), 1992.

Gillian Rubinstein, *Mr. Plunkett's Pool*, Random House Australia (Milsons Point, New South Wales, Australia), 1992.

Sandra McComb, *Lift-off ABC Book*, Mammoth (Port Melbourne, Victoria, Australia), 1993.

Sandra McComb, *Lift-off ABC Frieze*, Mammoth (Port Melbourne, Victoria, Australia), 1993.

Sandra McComb, *Nearly at the Wakadoo Cafe*, Mammoth (Port Melbourne, Victoria, Australia), 1993.

Natalie Jane Prior, *The Paw*, Allen & Unwin (St. Leonards, New South Wales, Australia), 1993.

Paul Jennings and Ted Greenwood, *Duck for Cover*, Viking (Ringwood, Victoria, Australia), 1994.

Jane Godwin, *Dreaming of Antarctica*, Puffin Books (Ringwood, Victoria, Australia), 1997.

Andy Griffiths, *Just Tricking*, Pan Macmillan Australia (Sydney, New South Wales, Australia), 1997, published as *Just Kidding!*, Macmillan Children's Books (London, England), 2001.

Jen McVeity, *The Frogs of Betts*, Addison Wesley Longman Australia (Melbourne, Victoria, Australia), 1997.

Gillian Rubinstein, *Jake and Pete and the Stray Dogs*, Random House Australia (Milsons Point, New South Wales, Australia), 1997.

Philip Adams and Patrice Newell, *What a Joke!: The Puffin Book of Australian Kids' Jokes*, Penguin (Ringwood, Victoria, Australia), 1998.

Bill Condon, *Chunderella*, Hodder Headline Australia (Rydalmere, New South Wales, Australia), 1998.

Bill Condon, *Jack and the Magic Baked Beans*, Hodder Headline Australia (Rydalmere, New South Wales, Australia), 1998.

Jackie French, *The Little Book of Big Questions*, Allen & Unwin (St. Leonards, New South Wales, Australia), 1998, Puffin Books (London, England), 1999.

Andy Griffiths, *Just Annoying*, Pan Macmillan Australia (Sydney, New South Wales, Australia), 1998, Macmillan Children's Books (London, England), 2001.

Steve Matthews, *Slugs' Revenge*, Longman (South Melbourne, Victoria, Australia), 1998.

Natalie Jane Prior, *The Paw in the Purple Diamond!*, Hodder Children's Books (Sydney, Victoria, Australia), 1998.

Moya Simons, *Whoppers*, Puffin Books (Ringwood, Victoria, Australia), 1998.

Phillip Adams and Patrice Newell, *What a Giggle!: More Kids' Jokes from Puffin*, Penguin (Ringwood, Victoria, Australia), 1999.

Margaret Clark, *Pop!*, Puffin Books (Ringwood, Victoria, Australia), 1999.

Bill Condon, *Bumplestiltskin*, Hodder Headline Australia (Sydney, New South Wales, Australia), 1999.

Bill Condon, *The Pop-eyed Piper*, Hodder Headline Australia (Sydney, New South Wales, Australia), 1999.

Michael Dugan, *The King Who Gobbled His Dinner*, Addison Wesley Longman Australia (South Melbourne, Victoria, Australia), 1999.

Andy Griffiths, *Just Stupid!*, Pan (Sydney, Victoria, Australia), 1999, new edition, Macmillan Children's Books (London, England), 2002.

Paul Jennings and Ted Greenwood, *Freeze a Crowd: Riddles, Puns, Conundrums*, Penguin (Ringwood, Victoria, Australia), 1999.

Gillian Rubinstein, *Ducky's Nest*, Random House Australia (Milsons Point, New South Wales, Australia), 1999.

Gillian Rubinstein, *Jake and Pete and the Catcrowbats*, Random House Australia (Milsons Point, New South Wales, Australia), 1999.

Trevor Todd, *Revenge of the Three Blind Mice*, Margaret Hamilton Books (Sydney, Victoria, Australia), 1999.

Paul Collins and Meredith Costain, editors, *Alien Encounters*, Pearson Education (South Melbourne, Victoria, Australia), 2000.

(With others) Margaret Clark, *Great Aussie Bites*, Puffin Books (Ringwood, Victoria, Australia), 2000.

Phil Cummings, *Lavinia Lavarr*, Lothian Books (Port Melbourne, Victoria, Australia), 2000.

Justin D'Ath, *Koala Fever*, Allen & Unwin (St. Leonards, New South Wales, Australia), 2000.

Justin D'Ath, *The Upside-down Girl*, Allen & Unwin (St. Leonards, New South Wales, Australia), 2000.

Andy Griffiths, *Just Crazy!*, Pan (Sydney, New South Wales, Australia), 2000, Macmillan Children's Books (London, England), 2001.

Christine Harris, *The Little Book of Elephants*, Hodder Headline Australia (Sydney, New South Wales, Australia), 2000.

Paul Jennings, *Sucked In*, Penguin (Ringwood, Victoria, Australia), 2000.

Gillian Rubinstein, *Jake and Pete and the Magpie's Wedding*, Random House Australia (Milsons Point, New South Wales, Australia), 2000.

Moya Simons, *Even Bigger Whoppers*, Penguin (Ringwood, Victoria, Australia), 2000.

Michael Wagner, *Ricardo Swaps His Lunch*, Pearson Education (South Melbourne, Victoria, Australia), 2000.

Andy Griffiths, *Just Wacky!*, Scholastic (New York, NY), 2000.

Philip Adams and Patrice Newell, *What a Laugh!: Heaps More Kids Jokes from Puffin*, Penguin (Ringwood, Victoria, Australia), 2001.

Margaret Clark, *S.N.A.G.: The Sensitive New-Age Gladiator*, Puffin Books (Ringwood, Victoria, Australia), 2001.

Andrew Daddo, *Sprung!*, Hodder Headline (Sydney, New South Wales, Australia), 2001.

Justin D'Ath, *Echidna Mania,* Allen & Unwin (Crows Nest, New South Wales, Australia), 2001.

Michael Dumbleton, *Passing On,* Random House Australia (Milsons Point, New South Wales, Australia), 2001.

Margaret Clark, *Mummy's Boy,* Puffin Books (Camberwell, Victoria, Australia), 2002.

Margaret Clark, *Silent Knight,* Puffin Books (Camberwell, Victoria, Australia), 2002.

Andrew Daddo, *Sprung Again!,* Mark Macleod Books (Sydney, New South Wales, Australia), 2002.

Justin D'Ath, *Astrid Spark, Fixologist,* Allen & Unwin (East Melbourne, Victoria, Australia), 2002.

Maureen Edwards, *Cooper Riley,* Word Weavers Press (Bulimba, Queensland, Australia), 2002.

Andy Griffiths, *Just Disgusting!,* Pan Macmillan Australia (Sydney, New South Wales, Australia), 2002, Scholastic (New York, NY), 2005.

Victor Kelleher, *Billy the Baked Bean Kid,* Lothian Books (South Melbourne, Victoria, Australia), 2002.

Andy Griffiths, *Just Joking!,* Scholastic (New York, NY), 2003.

Phillip Adams and Patrice Newell, *What a Hoot!: Kids' Jokes from the Net,* Puffin Books (Camberwell, Victoria, Australia), 2003.

Phillip Adams and Patrice Newell, *What a Joke! Collection,* Penguin (Camberwell, Victoria, Australia), 2003.

Margaret Clark, *Willie Tell or Won't He?,* Puffin Books (Camberwell, Victoria, Australia), 2003.

Andrew Daddo, *Dacked!,* Hodder Headline Australia (Sydney, New South Wales, Australia), 2003.

Paul Jennings and Ted Greenwood, *Spit It Out!,* Puffin Books (Camberwell, Victoria, Australia), 2003.

(With others) *Gigglers Green Set,* Blake Education (Glebe, New South Wales, Australia), 2003.

Phillip Adams and Patrice Newell, *What a Gag!: More Kids' Jokes from the Net,* Puffin Books (Camberwell, Victoria, Australia), 2004.

Margaret Clark, *Joan of Art,* Puffin Books (Camberwell, Victoria, Australia), 2004.

Andrew Daddo, *Flushed!,* Hodder Headline Australia (Sydney, New South Wales, Australia), 2004.

Andy Griffiths, *The Bad Book,* Pan (Sydney, New South Wales, Australia), 2004.

Victor Kelleher, *The Grimes Family,* Lothian Books (South Melbourne, Victoria, Australia), 2004.

Michael Wagner, *Bugged!,* Black Dog Books (Fitzroy, Victoria, Australia), 2004.

Michael Wagner, *Cheated!,* Black Dog Books (Fitzroy, Victoria, Australia), 2004.

Michael Wagner, *Crunched!,* Black Dog Books (Fitzroy, Victoria, Australia), 2004.

Michael Wagner, *Dogged!,* Black Dog Books (Fitzroy, Victoria, Australia), 2004.

Michael Wagner, *Flattened!,* Black Dog Books (Fitzroy, Victoria, Australia), 2004.

Michael Wagner, *Rattled!,* Black Dog Books (Fitzroy, Victoria, Australia), 2004.

Michael Wagner, *Slammed!,* Black Dog Books (Fitzroy, Victoria, Australia), 2004.

Michael Wagner, *Sledged!,* Black Dog Books (Fitzroy, Victoria, Australia), 2004.

Michael Wagner, *Smashed!,* Black Dog Books (Fitzroy, Victoria, Australia), 2004.

Michael Wagner, *Stretched!,* Black Dog Books (Fitzroy, Victoria, Australia), 2004.

Michael Wagner, *Twisted!,* Black Dog Books (Fitzroy, Victoria, Australia), 2004.

Margaret Clark, *The Worst Nurse,* Puffin Books (Camberwell, Victoria, Australia), 2005.

John Moreton, *The Adventures of Edgar Remington the Third,* Working Title Press (Kingswood, South Australia, Australia), 2005.

Michael Wagner, *Hammered!,* Black Dog Books (Fitzroy, Victoria, Australia), 2005.

Michael Wagner, *Spooked!,* Black Dog Books (Fitzroy, Victoria, Australia), 2005.

Michael Wagner, *Tricked!,* Black Dog Books (Fitzroy, Victoria, Australia), 2005.

Michael Wagner, *Whacked!,* Black Dog Books (Fitzroy, Victoria, Australia), 2005.

Mem Fox, *A Particular Cow,* Harcourt (Orlando, FL), 2006.

Richard Tulloch, *Beastly Tales,* Random House Australia (Milsons Point, New South Wales, Australia), 2006.

Archimede Fusillo, *Grandad's Phase,* Lothian Books (South Melbourne, Victoria, Australia), 2006.

Andy Griffiths, *The Cat on the Mat Is Flat,* Pan Macmillan Australia (Sydney, New South Wales, Australia), 2006.

Michael Wagner, *Grand Final Fever,* Black Dog Books (Fitzroy, Victoria, Australia), 2006.

Michael Wagner, *Maximum Maxx!,* Black Dog Books (Fitzroy, Victoria, Australia), 2006.

Margaret Clark, *Hester the Jester,* Puffin Books (Camberwell, Victoria, Australia), 2007.

Andrew Daddo, *That Aussie Christmas Book,* Scholastic Australia (Sydney, New South Wales, Australia), 2007.

Andy Griffiths, *Just Shocking!,* Pan Macmillan Australia (Sydney, New South Wales, Australia), 2007.

Andy Griffiths, *What Bumosaur Is That?,* Pan Macmillan Australia (Sydney, New South Wales, Australia), 2007.

Natalie Jane Prior, *The Paw Collection: Three Classic Stories in One Book,* Working Title Press (Kingswood, South Australia, Australia), 2007.

Michael Wagner, *Stacks of Maxx,* Black Dog Books (Fitzroy, Victoria, Australia), 2007.

Sidelights

Australian Terry Denton is a popular and prolific illustrator of books for young readers. Recognized for his playful, brightly colored, cartoon-style art, Denton has collaborated with such writers as Paul Jennings, Ted Greenwood, Gillian Rubinstein, Margaret Clark, and Andrew Daddo. In addition, he has published a number of self-illustrated titles, such as the books in the "Storymaze" series of graphic novels. Denton's works have won numerous awards, including the Children's Book Council of Australia Picture Book of the Year for *Felix and Alexander.*

Born in Melbourne, Victoria, Denton grew up in a large, raucous household that helped fuel his active imagination. "Trained from childhood in a home of five boys and a mad mother; humour was our ritual," he re-called to Children's Book Council of Australia Web site interviewer Anna McFarlane. "As a child I read hu-mour, watched humour and listened to humour: *Goons, Bugs Bunny Show, Daffy Duck.* This was the culture of my childhood." After studying architecture in college, Denton tried his hand at acting and animation before concentrating on illustration. He made his literary debut in 1983, providing the artwork for Max Dann's *Going Bananas.* When Denton illustrates a book, he enters a particular mindset that involves "playing, inventing, free association/lateral thinking . . . just the way I did as a kid . . . taking an idea and running with it," as he told McFarlane. "I have been lucky that I found a job that allowed me to use that seemingly useless skill to make a living."

Denton has enjoyed enduring partnerships with several authors, including fellow Australian Mem Fox. For the picture book *A Particular Cow,* Denton and Fox "worked . . . as a team, pulling the story apart and re-building it over a period of thirteen years," the illustra-tor recalled to McFarlane. "She kept simplifying the text until it was absolutely minimal." In the work, a bo-vine taking her customary Saturday stroll loses her way and wreaks havoc in her village. According to a critic in *Publishers Weekly,* Denton's "action-packed water-colors considerably amplify the book's comic delight." As *School Library Journal* critic Marge Loch-Wauters remarked, the book's "cartoon illustrations bounce with energy and are suffused with warm colors."

Denton has also teamed with writer Andy Griffiths on such works as *The Cat on the Mat Is Flat.* In his inter-view with McFarlane, Denton called this picture book "a true collaboration. We worked together in the same room, Andy on computer, me at a drawing desk. I would draw a character, [and] we would both look at it and work out ways to make it work better." Told in verse, *The Cat on the Mat Is Flat* features a number of wacky characters that survive hair-raising situations. "Denton's edgy, stick-figure-filled sketches enhance the zaniness factor and the offbeat, ironic humor," a *Publishers Weekly* critic noted.

Although Denton has found considerable success with Fox and Griffiths, the creative process he employs while working with those authors is not a typical one. "A lot of my collaborations have been with minimal input from the author, which I like," the illustrator told McFarlane. "A good writer shouldn't need to talk to the illustrator," he continued. "All they need to communi-cate should be in the text. The greatest skill of an illus-trator is to read the text and pick up the threads of what the writer is on about."

While beloved as an artist, Denton has also earned ac-claim for his self-illustrated works, including *The Ulti-mate Wave, The Eye of Ulam,* and other "Storymaze" titles, a series of "wacky adventures studded with puns and literary riffs that alternate between narrative and

Cover of Terry Denton's novel It's True! Pigs Do Fly, *featuring illus-trations by the author.* (Annick Press, 2006. Illustrations copyright © Terry Denton, 2006. Reproduced by permission.)

comics format," observed *Booklist* contributor Francisca Goldsmith. *Kliatt* reviewer Lynne Remick applauded Denton's efforts, stating that his "illustrations prove as wonderfully weird as his text."

In an essay on the Pan Macmillan Australia Web site, Denton stated: "In my writing and illustrating I suppose the two things that interest me most are human emo-tions and the wonderful, pointless detail of our existence. We're a weird race. Oh! . . . and colour . . . three things."

Biographical and Critical Sources

PERIODICALS

Booklist, May 15, 2003, Francisca Goldsmith, review of *The Ultimate Wave* and *The Eye of Ulam,* p. 1660.
Children's Digest, July-August, 2006, Emily Johnson, re-view of *It's True! Pigs Do Fly,* p. 13.
Kirkus Reviews, August 1, 2006, review of *A Particular Cow,* p. 786.

Kliatt, July, 2003, Lynne Remick, review of *The Ultimate Wave,* p. 30.

Publishers Weekly, May 31, 1991, review of *Amy's Monster,* p. 74; April 7, 2003, review of *The Ultimate Wave,* p. 67; March 1, 2004, reviews of *Just Joking!* and *Just Annoying!,* p. 72; July 17, 2006, review of *A Particular Cow,* p. 155; September 10, 2007, review of *The Cat on the Mat Is Flat,* p. 60.

Resource Links, April, 2006, Suzanne Finkelstein, review of *It's True! Pigs Do Fly,* p. 27.

School Library Journal, September, 2006, Marge Loch-Wouters, review of *A Particular Cow,* p. 171.

ONLINE

Allen & Unwin Web site, http://www.allenandunwin.com/ (December 1, 2007), "Terry Denton."

Booked Out Speakers Agency Web site, http://www. bookedout.com.au/ (December 1, 2007), "Terry Denton."

Children's Book Council of Australia Web site, http:// www.cbc.org.au/ (December 1, 2007), Anna McFarlane, "Andy Griffiths and Terry Denton: The Illustrator as Co-Author."

Pan Macmillan Australia Web site, http://www.panmacmillan.com.au/pandemonium/ (December 1, 2007), "Terry Denton."

Penguin Australia Web site, http://www.penguin.com.au/ (October 12, 2006), "Terry Denton."

Terry Denton Home Page, http://www.terrydenton.com/ (December 1, 2007).*

*   *   *

DRAGONWAGON, Crescent 1952-
(Ellen Parsons, Ellen Zolotow)

Personal

Born November 25, 1952, in New York, NY; daughter of Maurice (a writer, journalist, and biographer) and Charlotte (a publisher, children's book writer, and editor) Zolotow; married Crispin Dragonwagon (real name, Mark Parsons; an archaeologist), March 20, 1969 (divorced August 10, 1973); married Ned Shank (an architectural marketing consultant, innkeeper, writer and artist), October 20, 1978 (died November 30, 2000). *Education:* Educated in Hastings-on-Hudson, NY, and Stockbridge, MA. *Politics:* "Non-affiliated activist for environmental causes and social justice." *Religion:* "Spiritual, not religious." *Hobbies and other interests:* Gardening, reading, cooking, movies of the 1920s, 1930s, and 1940s, antiques, historic preservation, whitewater canoeing, environmentalism, fitness, theater.

Addresses

Home—Saxtons River, VT. *Agent*—Edite Kroll Literary Agency, 12 Grayhurst Park, Portland, ME 04102. *E-mail*—crescent@dragonwagon.com.

Crescent Dragonwagon (Photo courtesy of Crescent Dragonwagon.)

Career

Writer, novelist, chef, lecturer, public speaker, poet, journalist, and educator. Participant in artist-in-the-schools programs in Eureka Springs, AR, 1976-80, and Atlanta, GA, 1982-83; workshop presenter and/or lecturer at numerous conferences; developer and teacher of Fearless Writing workshops, 1990—. California Almond Board, spokesperson, 1993; Dairy Hollow House (bed-and-breakfast inn), Eureka Springs, co-owner and operator, until 1998; Writers' Colony at Dairy Hollow, Eureka Springs, co-founder, 1998, became Communication Arts Institute, 2005.

Member

Author's Guild, Authors League, Society of Children's Book Writers and Illustrators, Poets and Writers, International Association of Culinary Professionals, Archimedes Investment Management (president, 1999-2000), Eureka Group.

Awards, Honors

Outstanding Science Trade Book for Children, National Science Teachers Association/Children's Book Council (CBC), 1976, for *Wind Rose;* Notable Book citation, American Library Association, 1982, for *To Take a Dare;* Ossabaw Foundation fellow, 1982; Choice Book citation, National Council of Teachers of English, 1984, for *Jemima Remembers;* Parents' Choice Award, and Social Sciences Book of the Year, both 1984, both for *Always, Always;* Notable Book citation, *New York Times,* 1985, for *The Year It Rained;* Coretta Scott King Award,

1987, for *Half a Moon and One Whole Star;* Notable Children's Book in Social Studies, and Best Books citation, Wisconsin Children's Center, both 1987, both for *Diana, Maybe;* Ragdale Foundation fellow, 1990; Golden Kite Award, Society of Children's Book Writers, 1990, and Recommended Reading List for Children and Young Adults citation, National Conference of Christians and Jews, 1990-91, all for *Home Place;* Notable Children's Trade Book in Social Studies, National Council for the Social Studies/CBC, 1990, for *Home Place* and *Winter Holding Spring;* Porter Fund Award for Literary Excellence, 1991, for body of work; Porter Fund Prize, Arkansas Literary Society, fall, 1992, for body of work; Women on the Move award, Wyndham Hotels, 1997, for ideas for businesswomen travellers; Newman's Own Award, Paul Newman, 1997, for recipe using Newman's Own product, professional category; James Beard Award nomination, and Julia Child Award nomination, both for *Dairy Hollow House Soup and Bread.*

Writings

FOR CHILDREN

(Under name Ellen Parsons) *Rainy Day Together,* Harper (New York, NY), 1970.

Strawberry Dress Escape, illustrated by Lillian Hoban, Scribner (New York, NY), 1975.

When Light Turns into Night, illustrated by Robert A. Parker, Harper (New York, NY), 1975.

Wind Rose, illustrated by Ronald Himler, Harper (New York, NY), 1976.

Will It Be Okay?, illustrated by Ben Shecter, Harper (New York, NY), 1977.

Your Owl Friend, illustrated by Ruth Bornstein, Harper (New York, NY), 1977.

If You Call My Name, illustrated by David Palladini, Harper (New York, NY), 1981.

I Hate My Brother Harry, illustrated by Dick Gackenbach, Harper (New York, NY), 1983.

Katie in the Morning, illustrated by Betsy Day, Harper (New York, NY), 1983.

Coconut, illustrated by Nancy Tafuri, Harper (New York, NY), 1984.

Jemima Remembers, illustrated by Troy Howell, Macmillan (New York, NY), 1984.

Always, Always, illustrated by Arieh Zeldich, Macmillan (New York, NY), 1984.

Alligator Arrived with Apples: A Potluck Alphabet, illustrated by José Aruego and Ariane Dewey, Macmillan (New York, NY), 1985.

Half a Moon and One Whole Star, illustrated by Jerry Pinkney, Macmillan (New York, NY), 1986.

Diana, Maybe, illustrated by Deborah Kogan Ray, Macmillan (New York, NY), 1987.

Dear Miss Moshki, illustrated by Diane Palmisciano, Macmillan (New York, NY), 1988.

Margaret Ziegler Is Horse-Crazy, illustrated by Peter Elwell, Macmillan (New York, NY), 1988.

I Hate My Sister Maggie, illustrated by Leslie Morrill, Macmillan (New York, NY), 1989.

This Is the Bread I Baked for Ned, illustrated by Isadore Seltzer, Macmillan (New York, NY), 1989.

The Itch Book, illustrated by Joseph Mahler, Macmillan (New York, NY), 1990.

Winter Holding Spring, illustrated by Ronald Himler, Macmillan (New York, NY), 1990.

Home Place, illustrated by Jerry Pinkney, Macmillan (New York, NY), 1990.

Alligators and Others All Year Long: A Book of Months, illustrated by José Aruego and Ariane Dewey, Macmillan (New York, NY), 1992.

Annie Flies the Birthday Bike, illustrated by Emily Arnold McCully, Macmillan (New York, NY), 1992.

Brass Button, illustrated by Susan Paradise, Atheneum (New York, NY), 1997.

Bat in the Dining Room, illustrated by S.D. Schindler, Marshall Cavendish (New York, NY), 1997.

The Sun Begun, illustrated by Teresa Shaffer, Atheneum (New York, NY), 1999.

Is This a Sack of Potatoes?, illustrated by Catherine Stock, Marshall Cavendish (New York, NY), 2002.

And Then it Rained/And Then the Sun Came Out, illustrated by Diane Greenseid, Atheneum Books for Young Readers (New York, NY), 2003.

COOKBOOKS

The Commune Cookbook, Simon & Schuster (New York, NY), 1971.

The Bean Book, Workman (New York, NY), 1973.

Putting up Stuff for the Cold Time, Workman (New York, NY), 1973.

(With Jan Brown) *The Dairy Hollow House Cookbook,* illustrated by Jacquie Froelich, Macmillan (New York, NY), 1986.

Dairy Hollow House Soup and Bread: A Country Inn Cookbook, illustrated by Paul Hoffman, Workman (New York, NY), 1992.

Passionate Vegetarian, Workman (New York, NY), 2002.

The Cornbread Gospels, Workman (New York, NY), 2007.

OTHER

Stevie Wonder (biography), Flash Books, 1976.

Message from the Avocados (poetry), Edentata Press (Austin, TX), 1981.

(With Paul Zindel) *To Take a Dare* (young-adult novel), Harper (New York, NY), 1982.

The Year It Rained (novel), Macmillan (New York, NY), 1985.

Contributor to periodicals, including *Aphra, Cosmopolitan, Fine Cooking, Ingenue, Ladies' Home Journal, Lear's, McCall's, Mode, New Age, New York Times, New York Times Book Review, Nimrod, North American Review, Organic Gardening* and *Seventeen.*

Adaptations

Wind Rose was made into a motion picture by Phoenix Films in 1983.

Sidelights

The daughter of two noted authors, Crescent Dragonwagon has made writing a way of life since she was very young. The author of award-winning cookbooks, an acclaimed adult novel, and numerous books for children, Dragonwagon is a popular speaker and lecturer to both students and teachers alike. Among her most notable books for younger readers are *Half a Moon and One Whole Star, I Hate My Brother Harry,* and *Home Place,* while her young-adult novel *To Take a Dare* made her popular with teen readers after its 1982 publication. "From the time I learned the alphabet I wrote stories, beginning with drawing accompanied by a few words," Dragonwagon once commented, explaining her prolific output.

"Because my parents are writers," Dragonwagon once commented, "it seemed evident to me that when things happen to you in life, you write about them, and eventually they become books. Writing seemed natural, not esoteric or difficult." Born in 1952 to successful writers Charlotte and Maurice Zolotow, Dragonwagon quickly gained familiarity with the writing life. Her parents also gave her insight into the publishing process, and, undeterred by potential rejection, she submitted her first manuscript for publication before she was twenty years old. That first manuscript, published under the pseudonym Ellen Parsons, was *Rainy Day Together;* it was accepted for publication in 1969, the same year the sixteen-year-old author got married for the first time. "Most of life since has been focused in my writing: strong feelings and experiences, interesting people, overheard bits of conversation, almost everything that strikes me has a way of turning up in my work, sometimes surprising me greatly." One of Dragonwagon's favorite books continues to be one of her earliest, 1977's *When Light Turns into Night,* which she views as a personal attempt to understand what she has since described on her home page as "the balance between solitude and sociability. . . . one I think many of us struggle with our whole lives through."

An early book for children, *Wind Rose,* was dubbed by its creator as "typical of my writing process, beginning with an incident which sparked the idea." With no children of her own, Dragonwagon used her personal experiences of being in love and "attached them to the actual conception and birth of this child and wrote the book," which consists of a poem in which a mother explains to her child how and why she was conceived. The result is "a rather special children's book about conception and birth," according to reviewer Linda Wolfe in the *New York Times Book Review.* A *Publishers Weekly* contributor deemed the book "certainly one of the most attractive and beautiful introductions to the subject of birth," adding that "Dragonwagon's text is

honest and intensely personal." *Wind Rose* stands as an alternative to most books which focus on answering the question of where babies come from; it aims "to show the feeling side—*why* people have babies (under ideal circumstances) as opposed to simply *how*," Melinda Schroeder noted in *School Library Journal.* "Gentle and joyous, this celebrates the wonder of creation on a level young children will appreciate and find reassuring."

Many of Dragonwagon's children's books have also earned praise for their personal, gentle approach to childhood. *Diana, Maybe,* in which a little girl dreams of meeting her half-sister, has a "sensitive quality" that depicts the child's feelings "in a natural way," according to Lorraine Douglas in *School Library Journal.* Reviewer Jane Saliers similarly observed in *School Library Journal* that "children will recognize their own collisions between dream and reality" in *Margaret Ziegler Is Horse-Crazy.* Depicting a little girl's disillusionment when she discovers that horseback riding is not all she had imagined, the book is "a skillfully conveyed story of dreams, disappointment, and recovered pride," Saliers wrote in *School Library Journal.*

Other books by Dragonwagon are tender portraits of distinctive places. *The Itch Book,* for example, details a day in Arkansas that is so hot, even the animals itch. "Composed in poetic prose replete with descriptive phrasing, this glimpse into an Ozark day is modern American folklore at its best," Cathy Woodward commented in *School Library Journal.* Dragonwagon's sketch of local life is "a great book to share with children," the critic added. *Home Place* similarly conjures up a special images; while backpacking in a rural area, a family comes upon the abandoned ruins of an old house and wonders about the people who once lived there. With its imagined scenes of a loving family, "this mood piece captures that quiet, reflective feeling a country hike can prompt," Denise Wilms wrote in *Booklist.* *Home Place,* which earned Dragonwagon the Golden Kite Award from the Society of Children's Book Writers, was equally praised by a *Publishers Weekly* critic for its author's ability to imaginatively "limn . . . a forgotten family's day-to-day existence" with "striking craft."

While most of Dragonwagon's books for young people focus on somewhat serious topics, others are just plain fun. An off-track bat who finds his way into a busy hotel is saved from flying dinner forks by a young girl in *Bat in the Dining Room.* In *Alligators and Others All Year Long: A Book of Months* readers take a trip through the calendar along with a cavalcade of animals enjoying the special treats nature scatters throughout the twelve months of the year. From January, when cats sharpen their skates and hit the ice, through March, when lumbering moose lightheartedly frolic amid jaunty yellow daffodils, to December, when a tree is decorated and gifts are exchanged among the animals gathered together, Dragonwagon's book was described by *Booklist* contributor Deborah Abbott as an "ebullient celebration of the year" that "joyfully capture[s] highlights" of seasons and holidays in its "short, sprightly verses." Praising in particular the work of illustrators José Aruego and Ariane Dewey, a *Publishers Weekly* reviewer described *Alligators and Others All Year Long* as "bursting with splendid color and winsome animal characters" and ending "with a clever surprise and a sweet song." The successful collaboration among Aruego and Dewey and author Dragonwagon is mirrored in the equally upbeat *Alligator Arrived with Apples: A Potluck Alphabet Feast.*

Dragonwagon's first work of fiction for older readers, the novel *To Take a Dare,* was written with the aid and encouragement of Paul Zindel, himself famous for such young-adult books as *The Pigman.* "I had started a number of novels but never finished them," the author once related. "I knew that Paul worked with other writers. One day, I bit the bullet and wrote him a letter asking if he would work with me. He agreed. I wanted his assurance to finish my novel if I reached the point that I couldn't, and he gave it to me. As it turned out, ninety-eight percent of *To Take a Dare* is my writing, but I feel I couldn't have written it without his encouragement."

To Take a Dare was "sure to scandalize many parents at the same time that it hooks a large audience of worldly wise teens" reported Joyce Milton in her *New York Times Book Review* assessment. Narrated by Chrysta, a sixteen-year-old runaway, the book looks frankly at adolescent drinking, drug abuse, and sex and opens with this declaration: "On my thirteenth birthday my father called me a slut once too often, my dog was hit by a car, and I lost my virginity—what was left of it." After running away from home Chrysta develops a painful venereal disease that leaves her permanently sterile; she is also threatened with rape by her boss and with death by a twelve-year-old runaway she has mistakenly befriended. After living on the road for three years, Chrysta finds a job as a cook in a small resort town and begins to establish a more stable existence. She gains friends who stay with her through hard times, and begins a caring relationship with a young man. Her experiences, both good and bad, "somehow teach her she has a lot of strength, love, and other good qualities in spite of her unhappy childhood," Karen Ritter summarized in *School Library Journal.* As a *Publishers Weekly* critic concluded, *To Take a Dare* "is strong stuff but it is a voice that should be heard."

Dragonwagon's adult novel, *The Year It Rained,* provides similarly intense material in its account of a young woman struggling with mental illness, among other problems. In a narrative that ranges through past and present, seventeen-year-old Elizabeth Stein tells of her parents' bitter divorce, her father's alcoholism, her strained relationship with her mother, her hollow relationships with boyfriends, her conflicts at school, and her own suicide attempts. "Elizabeth takes the reader through, among, and around these situations, looking hard at every person and every detail from a bittersweet present perspective of comparative calm—calm brought about by successful treatment with vitamins of what has finally been diagnosed as biochemically based schizophrenia," Natalie Babbitt observed in a *New York Times Book Review* piece. Elizabeth's monologue "lends a decided cathartic impact" to this "affecting, introspective novel," a *Booklist* reviewer similarly commented.

While some critics praised *The Year It Rained,* others were less enthusiastic. Finding Elizabeth's character "insufferable," Roger Sutton wrote in *School Library Journal* that the protagonist never matures; by the end of *The Year It Rained* Elizabeth remains "as self-centered and self-important as [she was] to begin with." *New Statesman & Society* writer Nicci Gerrard, however, considered that an "often narcissistic self-questioning" is common to characters of this type, while Tim Wynne-Jones, writing in the Toronto *Globe & Mail,* remarked that Dragonwagon's protagonist "is better than most; she shows some compassion for those around her, and that in itself rescues *The Year It Rained* from formula." Gerrard likewise found "striking" how "well-written, discomforting, and entirely unpatronising" the novel is. While Dragonwagon's novel was marketed as "young adult," the critic maintained that "any adult might enjoy [it]." Babbitt remarked similarly that the book "would be ideal to read at age seventeen," she asserted, "but also at thirty, and again at forty-five when one's own children are circling seventeen—it faces so unflinchingly the anguished and so often unsuccessful attempts to get past all the precious but heavy baggage of love between mother and child and on into some kind of mutual understanding that can set both free."

Although Dragonwagon herself considers *The Year It Rained* more of an adult novel, "for the sensitive teenager, it's going to be a really good book," as she explained to Bo Emerson in the *Atlanta Journal-Constitution.* "The truth is," she added, "I think all of [these] categories are stupid." Indeed, Dragonwagon once explained: "I have always seen myself as a writer first. Not a children's book writer as such, or a novelist, or a poet, or a magazine writer, or a cookbook author—though I have done each of these types of writing. Writing is the lens through which I focus on the world and the things in it which trouble me, or interest me, or give me pleasure. The particular subject or feeling I am looking at through the lens determines what form the finished piece of writing will take." The only exception to this rule is in the case of longer works, where "the characters soon take over and do it *their* way, from *their* perspective—which may be very different from mine."

Charlie, the young main character of *Is This a Sack of Potatoes?,* is full of mischief and doesn't want to go to sleep. Instead, he hides beneath the covers as his mother pats the lump he makes and asks what it is under the bedclothes: a sack of potatoes, a ton of tomatoes, a peck of pears, or a cave of bears? Charlie's answer is always no until he finally pops out and reassures his mother that it is him beneath the covers. Shelle Rosenfeld, writing in *Booklist,* observed that "many children will like this sweet rendering of a familiar parent-child game."

Some of Dragonwagon's works deal with the unavoidable cycles of life, noting how loss and dark times are followed by recovery and brighter days. In *And Then it Rained/And Then the Sun Came Out* a flip-book featuring part of a whole story in each half of the book, she looks at what happens when a rainstorm drives people indoors. At first, they are happy to have the chance do things at home, such as read, listen to music, and dance. The cooling rain is a welcome relief from the hot weather. Soon, however, they begin to get irritable about being stuck inside because of the rain, and the weather becomes a nuisance. When a young boy wishes for the rain to stop, his father tells him that sun follows the rain just as rain always follows the sun. After flipping the book over, the story continues after the rain has stopped and the sun has started shining, and the cycle of the weather starts over again. A *Kirkus Reviews* critic called the book "good wet (or dry) fun for storytime." Sue Morgan, writing in *School Library Journal,* commented that the book's "fresh concept will intrigue children, and the stories, both of which are well-written, will amuse them."

Dragonwagon also continues to explore her interest in culinary arts with *Passionate Vegetarian,* a cookbook that encompasses the full range of vegetarian cooking. "This big, exuberant book marks [Dragonwagon's] foray into the cooking closest to her heart," remarked Judith Sutton in *Library Journal.* The author covers basic concepts and traditional staples of vegetarian cuisine, including beans, tofu, and pasta. She also looks at vegetable-based cooking from other cultures, in India and elsewhere. A *Publishers Weekly* critic noted that Dragonwagon is "passionate about her food," and concluded that her vegetarian cookbook is "vibrant and lively" and "seasoned with a large pinch of loving care."

Although Dragonwagon cultivates numerous other interests, such as cooking and teaching, she considers herself a professional, dedicated writer above all. "I feel lucky to have a profession which allows me to explore so many interests, while allowing me to stay true to the main and abiding interest in my life: writing. I have always known that this is what I wanted to do—and that, too, is lucky. It makes possible the persistent striving which underlies craft, talent, experience, gift, and good fortune." Dragonwagon sees the writer's colony she cofounded, which provides writers with uninterrupted time and space in which to work, an extension of this.

While personal tragedy—the loss of Ned Shank, her husband of twenty-three years, to a bicycling accident in late 2000—caused Dragonwagon to step away from some of her more lighthearted themes and deal with a major adjustment to her life, writing has continued to serve her, as it always has, as a means of understanding and coping with feelings and changing situations. "I also see writing as a highly utilitarian profession," she once noted. "To quote from a poem of mine called 'Looking for Bones in Her House,' 'She can write about anything that happens to her!'"

Biographical and Critical Sources

PERIODICALS

Atlanta Journal-Constitution, March 23, 1986, Bo Emerson, "*Year It Rained* Exposes Story of a Teen's Life."
Booklist, November 15, 1985, review of *The Year It Rained;* August, 1990, Denise Wilms, review of *Home Place,* p. 2171; March 1, 1993, Julie Corsaro, review of *Annie Flies the Birthday Bike,* p. 1234; October 15, 1993, Deborah Abbott, review of *Alligators and Others All Year Long: A Book of Months,* p. 445; June 1, 1997, Ilene Cooper, review of *Brass Button,* p. 86; October 1, 1997, J. Corsaro, review of *Bat in the Dining Room,* p. 335; December 15, 2002, Shelle Rosenfeld, review of *Is This a Sack of Potatoes?,* p. 766; June 1, 2003, Carolyn Phelan, review of *And Then it Rained/And Then the Sun Came Out,* p. 1784.
Globe & Mail (Toronto, Ontario, Canada), June 28, 1986, Tim Wynne-Jones, review of *The Year It Rained.*
Horn Book, March-April, 1985, review of *Jemima Remembers,* p. 175; November-December, 1990, Hanna B. Zeiger, review of *Home Place,* p. 725.
Instructor, May, 1984, Allan Yeager, review of *Coconut,* p. 87.
Kirkus Reviews, April 15, 2003, review of *And Then It Rained/And then the Sun Came Out,* p. 606.
Library Journal, August, 1986, Ruth Diebold, review of *Dairy Hollow House Cookbook,* p. 149; November 15, 2002, Judith Sutton, review of *Passionate Vegetarian,* p. 94.
New Statesman & Society, July 7, 1989, Nicci Gerrard, "Rites of Passage," review of *The Year It Rained,* p. 38.
New York Times Book Review, May 23, 1976, Linda Wolfe, review of *Wind Rose,* p. 16; April 25, 1982, Joyce Milton, "Three for the Road," review of *To Take a Dare,* p. 49; November 10, 1985, Natalie Babbitt, "Love, and Learn to Bear It," review of *The Year It Rained,* p. 35; October 26, 1986, Rollene W. Saal, review of *Half a Moon and One Whole Star,* p. 48; May 10, 1987, review of *Diana, Maybe,* p. 26.
Publishers Weekly, January 19, 1976, review of *Wind Rose,* p. 102; October 2, 1981, Jean F. Mercier, review of *If You Call My Name,* p. 111; March 19, 1982, review of *To Take a Dare,* p. 71; May 11, 1984, review of *Coconut,* p. 272; June 29, 1984, review of *Always, Always,* p. 105; May 30, 1986, review of *Half a Moon and One Whole Star,* p. 64; July 18, 1986, review of *Dairy Hollow House Cookbook,* p. 77; September 11, 1987, review of *Alligator Arrived with Apples: A Potluck Alphabet,* p. 94; August 31, 1990, review of *Home Place,* p. 65; August 23, 1993, review of *Alligators and Oth-*

ers All Year Long, p. 72; May 5, 1997, review of *Brass Button,* p. 209; February 15, 1999, review of *This Is the Bread I Baked for Ned,* p. 109; October 7, 2002, review of *Passionate Vegetarian,* p. 69.

School Library Journal, April, 1976, Melinda Schroeder, review of *Wind Rose,* p. 60; April, 1981, Patricia Dooley, review of *If You Call My Name,* p. 106; May, 1982, Karen Ritter, review of *To Take a Dare,* p. 68; November, 1983, Helen E. Williams, review of *Katie in the Morning,* p. 61; May, 1984, Dana Whitney Pinizzotto, review of *Coconut,* p. 64; May, 1984, Connie Weber, review of *Always, Always,* p. 63; February, 1985, Reva S. Kern, review of *Jemima Remembers,* p. 63; November, 1985, Trev Jones, review of *The Year It Rained,* p. 95; December, 1985, Roger Sutton, "High School Confidential," review of *The Year It Rained,* p. 43; March, 1987, Laura McCutcheon, review of *Dear Miss Moshki,* p. 25; November, 1987, Jane Saliers, review of *Alligator Arrived with Apples,* p. 88; January, 1988, Lorraine Douglas, review of *Diana, Maybe,* p. 64; June-July, 1988, Jane Saliers, review of *Margaret Ziegler Is Horse-Crazy,* p. 90; December, 1989, Ruth Semrau, review of *This Is the Bread I Baked for Ned,* p. 78; March, 1990, Nancy A. Gifford, review of *I Hate My Sister Maggie,* p. 190; June, 1990, Cathy Woodward, review of *The Itch Book,* and Joanne Aswell, review of *Winter Holding Spring,* p. 99; February, 1991, Carey Ayers, review of *Home Place,* p. 725; July, 1993, Nancy Seiner, review of *Annie Flies the Birthday Book,* p. 59; January, 1994, review of *Alligators and Others All Year Long,* p. 106; June, 1997, Virginia Golodetz, review of *Brass Button,* p. 86; September, 1997, Martha Rosen, review of *Bat in the Dining Room,* p. 179; November 1, 2002, Rosalyn Pierini, review of *Is This a Sack of Potatoes?,* p. 122; May 1, 2003, Sue Morgan, review of *And Then It Rained/And Then the Sun Came Out,* p. 112.

ONLINE

Crescent Dragonwagon Web site, http://www.dragon wagon.com (September 23, 2001).

Passionate Vegetarian Web site, http://www.passion atevegetarian.com/ (July 25, 2007), biography of Crescent Dragonwagon.

Writers' Colony at Dairy Hollow Web site, http://www. writerscolony.org/ (July 25, 2007).

Autobiography Feature

Crescent Dragonwagon

Crescent Dragonwagon contributed the following autobiographical essay to *SATA:*

A LIFE SO FAR

The Former Ellen Zolotow

Before I became Crescent Dragonwagon, I was named Ellen Zolotow, a name no one—and I mean no one, not my mother, not my Aunt Dot—has called me for more than twenty years. It is not a name I associate with a happy period of my life, although there were happy moments from time to time in it, particularly in its earliest years. But then, happiness, especially when one is young, does not always serve writers well. I think it is almost universally true that writers, at least at some point during their growing-up years, are lonely, and feel themselves to be in some ways outsiders. Being outsiders, they develop those habits of observation, thinking, and questioning which eventually inform their writing.

I remember being quite exuberant, outgoing, friendly, at times very talkative and at ease when I was a very little girl; when we drove on tollway roads, I always asked the toll-takers, "What's your name?" (Some of them told me.) I especially loved to make or hear jokes. My mother says that once, when I was about three, she caught me leaning out the upstairs window, talking to some housepainters at work on our house. "Painters," I was calling to them, "Please give us a nice polka-dot trim!" Once my Grandpa Louis sent me a letter in which he complained that in his new California apartment, all the ladies liked to exchange recipes. "Oh, well," he wrote me, "what do I care how they fry their ice cream?" I thought this was hysterically funny. (As an adult, I also wonder at the amazing ability he must have had to know what a five-or six-year-old grandchild he saw only occasionally would find so funny, and I regret that I did not know him better.)

But at times I was also quite content to play by myself for hours. I had an elaborate, novelistic kingdom of dolls, centered around an orphanage. Each doll had a distinct personality; loyalties and friendships changed and developed from day to day. (I was aghast when I learned that other girls "played dolls" with each other. How could that be? It was so private and internal; how could you ever explain to someone else all you knew about your dolls' lives? What if they wanted to make your dolls behave in ways foreign to their personalities?) Once I learned to read and write, I gladly spent hours by myself doing these things. (I even made books for my dolls, little tiny stapled-together books, written in the most miniscule handwriting; my mother still has a few of them.) From the first it seems to me that I either interacted intensely with other people, or quietly (and equally happily) went my own way into a dreamy, thoughtful, private, quiet world. There was little middle ground. I still have these two, completely opposite, tendencies today.

My parents, both writers, were also both continual readers. Books permeated the house. There were bookshelves, filled, on almost every wall, in every room. There were books lying open on the coffee table in the living room, books by the beds, books in the bathroom, more books in boxes in the attic.

My parents loved me in entirely different ways. My mother's way was quiet, steady, thoughtful, deeply compassionate and sensitive; she seemed willing to enter my world, eager to know what I felt, almost too curious about the details of my inner life (which often made me clam up). My tall, very-funny father, a bonafide Character-with-a-capital-C, was the opposite. He was (when not depressed or angry) loud, outgoing, enthusiastic, and not in the least sensitive in the way my mother was; he would never in a million years say something like, "You seem quiet. Are you sad about something?" as my mother might. If my mother seemed to want me to let her in on the secret world of my private thoughts and feelings and activities, my father seemed to make room for me in his (at least sometimes). Sometimes he literally would take me into it, as when, during the period he was a Broadway critic, I sometimes accompanied him to plays and musicals. He seemed more interested in ideas, thoughts, and happenings than feelings, and, although almost always interested if I volunteered something, rarely questioned and drew me out the way my mother did.

Both of them, however, had an enormous respect for not just the written word but originality and creativity. They encouraged these things—perhaps without even meaning to—in the very sorts of conversations they had with me and each other and my brother Stephen. Things were open-ended, not right or wrong; a person had to figure out what he or she thought. "Whose white dog is that?" I might say, glancing out the window at a stray trotting by. "I don't know," either of them might reply. "Who do you think it belongs to, what kind of family?" and we might, together, make up an imaginary family to whom the dog belonged. This sort of open-endedness went into a lot of my discussions with either or both parents. "Well, what do you think?" "Why, what would you do?" Once, when I was very little, I told them at breakfast that I had dreamed I'd seen God sitting in the mulberry tree in the backyard. "What did he look like?" they quickly asked me. I explained that he was an old man with a long beard. They did not tell me this was correct, incorrect, sacrilegious; they did not laugh at me (though I am sure they laughed about it later with their friends). They merely nodded thoughtfully. (I can still see them, that morning, in my mind, clearly, as I can see the long, sad face of the God I dreamed of in the mulberry tree.)

As I grew older and went to school, I realized quickly that the kind of open-endedness and self-reliance on your own thoughts and feelings about things, which I had grown up with, was not how it was done in the outside world. At school, there were many more precise rules about what a person—a child, especially—should and should not do, and why. Questions were not open-ended; there were right and wrong answers, period. Worse, you got graded on them and if you did not agree with the so-called correct answer, you got poor grades and were thought stupid, weird, or deliberately recalcitrant. This was an overwhelming difference—the freedom of thought that existed within, but not outside, my family as I grew up.

All this was in the town of Hastings-on-Hudson, about an hour outside of New York City. This sense of difference made me feel uncomfortable, and wary. It made me an outsider, an observer—and, I think, made me begin thinking like a writer.

In addition to this main difference, there were four other factors that made me an outsider in Hastings:

1. Ours was the only Jewish family in a predominantly Catholic town.

2. My father and mother were both writers, in a town where half the kids' fathers commuted to New York where they were executives, and the other half of the kids' fathers worked in a local copper-wire manufacturing company, Anaconda, which everyone called "the Factory." (Few mothers worked.)

3. I was just different in and of myself—a different kind of kid.

4. Our family, besides being oddball, was—as they say now—somewhat "dysfunctional," and grew more so as the years went on.

I will tell you some stories about being different.

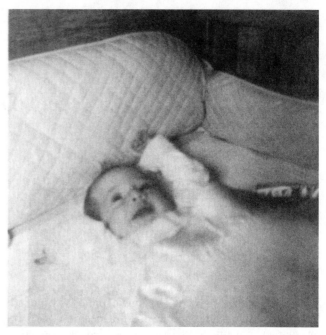

Baby Ellen (Photo courtesy of Crescent Dragonwagon.)

Vera Zupnik Raises Some Big Questions

I knew we were missing something in the religious area, but it was not clear what, at first. Because my parents were not practicing, religious Jews, at first I understood being a Jew to simply mean not being a Catholic. For example, we did not have Christmas, evidence of which I could see each December, in every lit, tree-filled window in the town. But, we also did not have Chanukah—however, since I had never seen a menorah, I was at first unaware that something was lacking on the Jewish side, too. But it was.

I gradually gathered that in addition to being a religion, which a person might or might not practice, being Jewish was also a vague racial and cultural thing. It was eating corned-beef sandwiches on rye bread; it was a certain kind of humor, of speech. I understood, vaguely, that we were this kind of Jew, but not the religious kind. Being Jewish was also, I came to realize as I grew a little older, being part of the group of people a terrible man named Hitler and his army, the Nazis, had killed millions of, again for no reason I could understand (and still can't). I cannot remember where I heard of World War II, concentration camps, and so on, but almost as far back as memory goes I remember knowing about them, and brooding about why and how such a thing could be, and what, if anything, one person could have done about it.

Hastings-on-Hudson, being a suburb, had a train station, through which traveled the commuter trains which carried the fathers swiftly into New York for work in the morning, and back home in the evening. Long, long, slow freight trains also passed through the Hastings train station. The freight trains mostly traveled at night. I remember, as a quite young girl, lying in bed at night, hearing the sound of the freight trains, the repetitive rhythm of their wheels on the track pierced from time to time by that sad, high whistle. I remember lying awake and wondering at the idea of people—families, little children, people like me—being loaded into such trains and shipped away to be murdered, crowded together, and my stomach would turn over in fear, imagining the fear they must have felt, even while I knew it must have been unimaginably worse than what I could imagine. Again and again, I thought, "Why? How?"

In fourth grade, I met Karen, my best friend for several years. One Saturday, when we were in about fifth grade, we were walking in the Village, as everyone referred to the downtown area of Hastings-on-Hudson. We passed the recently put-in pizza parlour, where you could buy pizza by the slice for a quarter, and in front of which older, slightly dangerous-looking teenagers hung out.

And one, a much-older girl of sixteen or seventeen, stepped out in front of Karen and me and blocked the sidewalk. She was big, and on the heavy side.

"Hey, Jew," she said. "Dirty Jew, ya dirty Jew."

I remember vividly her eye makeup; iridescent blue eye shadow over dark hostile eyes, long black lines drawn along the base of her eyelashes, going up to a long sharp point at the end.

I said, looking at her, "I'm not dirty. I take a bath every night."

She said, "Yeah, you're dirty. A dirty, dirty Jew." And then, in tones of deepest contempt, "Your mother written any more kiddie books lately?"

If I answered that question, I do not remember with what. My heart was pounding, I was frightened, shocked, outraged, and simply astonished that an unknown teenager should say such things, should in the first place know that I was a Jew (when in some ways I barely knew it myself) and even that my mother wrote children's books! Were these things in some way connected? And why should writing children's books be a matter of scorn? My thoughts whirled and crashed into each other as I stood frozen, staring at that iridescent blue, those black slashes of lines, stunned.

We walked half a block in silence, then I said, "I can't believe that just happened." As I said it, I realized I was shaking, trembling all over.

"I can't believe it either," said Karen. Then she said, "That was really good, what you said back."

"It was?"

"Yeah. 'I take a bath every night.' That was good."

"Well, I do take a bath every night," I said.

"I *know* that," said Karen. "Gah, I'm your best friend, I *know* that."

So there I was: a clean little Jew girl whose mother wrote children's books, who had a good friend named Karen, who lived in a town—in a world—where all at once, when you were least expecting it, where you were walking downtown with your friend, a stranger who turned out to be named Vera Zupnik could step out of the doorway of Hastings Pizza and say awful and intimate things to you.

I don't remember anyone else saying anything anti-Semitic to me, in all the years I lived in Hastings (which was more or less from birth—though I was born in New York City proper, on November 25, 1952—till age fourteen). But the freight trains, and Vera Zupnik, and her black-lined eyes, and the questions she raised for me about life, have stayed with me forever.

"You Must Come By It Naturally"

My mother wrote "kiddie books," as Vera had said with such scorn, and my father wrote books and articles about show-business personalities. However, what they did tells only the smallest part of who and what they were, and were to me.

I wondered, even as a little girl, what on *earth* two such people were doing in Hastings-on-Hudson.

What they were doing there was this: my mother wanted to live in the country. My father wanted to live in the city. Hastings-on-Hudson was their compromise, but I think both of them felt that they had been cheated out of what they *really* wanted, and I think I felt and was made increasingly restless and unhappy by *their* unhappiness (I believe children always feel whatever is going on with the parents, whether or not something is said about it). I also had a growing sense that things were very different from what they appeared—that much was going on that was somehow not normal, usually in ways I could not articulate to myself. From the exuberant little girl I had been, I gradually became quieter, shyer, more frightened to express myself. Some of this was the pressure of school, where (from the first day) I saw that there was a pressure to conform that I had simply not been brought up to yield to, nor was I temperamentally inclined that way. But some of this was also change within our family, gradual, subtle, and not articulated, as my father's mood swings became more marked, and as my mother seemed to grow unhappier, more quiet.

Now everything certainly *looked* normal enough on Elm Place. The street, the town, had its ordinary seasons and cycles, bounded and predictable, unoriginal, safe. There were daily patterns, weekly, seasonal. On Mondays the garbageman picked up the trash, causing the dogs on the street to bark more wildly than they did at any other time. In the summer, weekend mornings began with the predictable sound of lawn mowers droning up and down the block, and the scent of fresh-cut grass, which would be replaced, in the late afternoon, by the smell of sizzling meat being cooked over charcoal grills in backyards up and down the street, the fragrant smoke funneling up and out into the dusky summer sky. In the fall the smoke was of burning leaves, a sweet, predictable, evocative odor, which can still (like the charcoal grill smell of summer) take me back to childhood.

Elm Place sloped up a mild hill. One day I quit practice-riding my bike back and forth along our driveway and ventured to the top of the street. Looking down before this first momentous ride (I had told no one I was about to undertake it), this gentle hill became an enormous mountain. It's still vivid to me, the terrifying exhilaration of the first trip down, going so fast my hair was blown back, then suddenly panicking, braking, half-falling, half-jumping off the bike, and ending up on the very hard pavement, bike on top of me, bleeding in several places, scared and hurt and screaming bloody murder to Sidney Fields, the across-the-street neighbor and father of two boys about my age, who was innocently raking his yard as I flew by and crashed. But at the same time, even as I was led, snuffling and crying, by Sidney Fields back to our house to be Mercurochromed (more screams) and Band-aided, remembering the sensation of speed, my hair being blown back—and resolving to try again soon. Small vivid memories like this one, which is the basis of my book *Annie Flies the Birthday Bike,* permeate my children's books.

Besides going on bike rides, reading, playing with dolls, and writing stories, I loved cooking. I kept my mother company and often, happily, helped her make dinner; I was befriended by an old lady around the corner, Miss Kay, who proved to be my culinary soul mate. She taught me how to make orange sponge cake, brownies, and many other baked things, leveling off cups of flour carefully with a flat-bladed knife. My love of cooking has stayed with me all my life, and I write cookbooks, such as *The Dairy Hollow House Cookbook* and *Dairy Hollow House Soup and Bread: A Country Inn Cookbook,* along with my other kinds of books. (The kind of cookbooks I write always have not only recipes, but stories; stories about the people who gave me the recipes or who loved that particular dish, stories about ingredients, farmers, the place where something is grown or where I first learned about it . . . People are always telling me, "I read your cookbook like a novel!") I have also, at various times, had a second profession as a chef alongside writing, which is handy since 1) I love to cook and 2) writing is not the best way in the world to make a living. People may not always wish to read what you write, but if they are hungry and you are a good cook, they will *always* want to eat what you prepare.

At the top of Elm Place ran a long, flat, wide tree-lined path called the aqueduct. Water pipes ran under it. The aqueduct was one of the main borders of my childhood. As a little girl I walked it often with my parents. I gathered violets there in the spring (once Tony Fields and I

tried to sell bunches of them, but with little success), and orange-and-yellow bittersweet vines in the fall. Once, someone (my mother? a neighbor?) pointed out a vine with small purple flowers, saying that it was deadly nightshade, terribly poisonous; passing the tree where the deadly nightshade grew always gave me a pleasantly creepy shiver.

The aqueduct was where we walked the family dog, a large black poodle named Cleo. Although many dog-walkers and dogs used the aqueduct, Cleo had a love of eating crayons. Long after she had visited, you could identify which piles of dog excrement were hers by their splotches of bright yellow, red, or purple.

The aqueduct was the route to my much-hated school; a right turn on the aqueduct and a mile walk took me there. I turned left, often, after school, when I rode on my bike or took long solitary walks, a Macintosh apple in my pocket for a snack. An elegant, sinister old mansion known as the Zinnser Estate was set on several acres of land adjacent to and visible from the aqueduct perhaps a half a mile away from Elm Place. Who the Zinnsers were or how they had made their money I never knew. What I do know is that in my early teens, it was torn down, without preliminary warning or notification of any kind. One day it was there, the next gone. A ball field was put in its place. But it was shocking then, a violent dislocation, and it still looks wrong to me today, though I see people playing happily on the field that replaced it when I go back to Hastings to visit my mother, who still lives on Elm Place. Do those people who play there know that a large, mysterious house once stood where they catch fly balls and steal bases? Who were the Zinnsers? Why was the home torn down, and does anyone remember it? These are the kind of what-if and why questions that have been part of me for as long as I can remember, like the Vera Zupnik questions, and which certainly go into my writing, as in *Home Place,* though that book was written about a different kind of old and long-gone home, one in Arkansas, where I live now as an adult, rather than Hastings, my childhood home.

I had one brother, Stephen, who was quite a bit older than me. We fought a lot—the story of which is told in my book *I Hate My Brother Harry.* But he went to college and moved out of the house when I was about seven, so that for many of my growing-up years I felt like an only child, which was, I have to say, an enormous relief.

Besides Hastings, my childhood was also permeated by summer and fall visits to my Aunt Dot's farmhouse in Vermont. It was not a working farm with pigs and chickens, but rather a retreat, a rambly old house, barn-red, with comfortable porches and lazy wasps, and a view out to the mountains and down to the pond, and indoors a faint, pleasantly mildewy odor of old wood and old paper, and outdoors, a delicious smell of cold and pine and fern so good it was almost painful. Visits to the

"In later years, about 1989, with mother, Charlotte Zolotow" (Photo courtesy of Crescent Dragonwagon.)

farm became part of my book *Jemima Remembers,* and I vowed, quite early in my life, that as an adult I would live at least part of each year in the country.

Another part of my life was spent in writing. Even before I knew the alphabet, I used to *tell* stories. For example, I would draw pictures, then tug on the sleeve of any available adult and explain the picture. Sometimes my mother would write down the stories I told her, and a few of the drawings still exist, her rounded handwriting in one corner. "This girl lives over here. She has no neighbors. One day a horse comes to her fence, over here by the garden."

Later, I also remember telling stories to several other little girls in the bathroom at the Hastings Elementary School, where the tiles gave a nice satisfying echo to the voice, and where, in addition, the radiator was so hot that (at dramatic and appropriate points in the story) it could be sprinkled amply with water from the sink. Upon hitting the radiator, the water would evaporate almost immediately with a loud, hissing sizzle—very handy for sound effects of snakes, witches, or whatever else I might work into the story.

But once I knew how to write, I did. Stories, poems—not for school, but for my own pleasure. But pleasure is

too weak a word for the blissful self-absorption, so deep one is almost absent from oneself. Writing has worked this spell on me from my earliest days, and the act of writing in itself continues to do so. Somehow, sitting down to write harnesses mysterious forces of creation, and the way it honestly feels is that those forces themselves do the writing. (When it doesn't go well, it feels as if the forces have just gone off to do something else that day; possibly help another writer, or go on a picnic, or nap, or who knows what.) The writer may not, often does not, know where the story is coming from or where it is going, which is why I think we speak of writing, or other artistic talents, as a "gift." I have known since childhood, since long before I could articulate it, that these things are literally "given" to the artist or writer by some power greater than him or herself.

So, I wrote from the first, and sometimes it came easily, and sometimes it didn't, but it was always an engrossing, transcending experience; "a sheer act of consummation in itself," as my father once put it. Sometimes I showed what I wrote to one of my parents, sometimes not. I do remember my first publication, in a xeroxed summer-camp newsletter around 1964 or '65. I had two poems in it; one about jumping into very cold water, the other about watching the sleeping golden retriever of the camp director. The dog, asleep, would sometimes twitch violently or growl. In my poem I took up what he might be dreaming of.

Sometimes when people find out that my mother is Charlotte Zolotow and my father (who died this year, 1991) was Maurice Zolotow, they say something like "Writing must be in your genes," or "Oh, I guess writing just comes naturally to you." This always irritates me, since a writer, no matter who his or her parents are, is always alone when he or she sits down at the computer or typewriter to do work that sometimes comes easily, but often does not. When people say I write because of my genes or "naturally," it's as if it doesn't take any effort of my own, which is absolutely not true. Too, people have been saying this to me in one way or another since I was a girl. At school I used to get a lot of "Which of your parents helped you write this, your mother or your father?" This is discouraging if you yourself worked for hours writing or rewriting a story or poem until it sounded just right. (I sometimes wonder if maybe part of the reason I changed my name, besides the reasons I will tell you about shortly, was because I was tired of having my own writing attributed to my parents.)

But, while I feel right down to the marrow of my bones that I would have been a writer even had I been born into a family of shoemakers in Ohio or surfers in Hawaii, there is no doubt that Maurice and Charlotte's writing was an influence—not in making me *want* to be a writer, but in making the whole process of writing *as a profession* seem very unmysterious and matter-of-fact to me. If your father is a carpenter and you grow up around his shop, you know what dovetail joints and Phillips head screws are, and the way a box or a window frame goes together seems normal to you. It was the same way for me with the profession of writing.

One day, when I was quite young, I came downstairs. My mother was seated in the living room with a notebook in which she was writing balanced on her knee. She looked up and said, "What are some of the terrible things Stephen does to you?"

Stephen was my big brother, hated and feared, whose side I always thought my parents took. Aha, I thought! At last! A chance to tell the *truth*! Justice!

I told my mother about Stephen pretending to call snakes into the room at night and convincing me they were hidden under the pillows. I told her about the names he called me, the time he threw my doll out the window, and much more. It was very satisfying. Surely, I thought, fairness would now prevail.

It did not. Instead, a year or so later, the book that my mother had been working on that morning was published. It was called *Big Brother, Little Sister.* (I thought she soft-pedaled the antagonism that existed between Stephen and me, and I wrote my own version of these events later in *I Hate My Brother Harry* and *I Hate My Sister Maggie.*)

I learned the same lesson in a different way from my father, a nonfiction magazine and book writer, and a critic, of insatiable and far-reaching curiosity. One night I went with him as he drove out to the town of Tarrytown to pick up fried chicken from a take-out place, a chain that to my knowledge no longer exists, Chicken Delight, whose slogan was "Don't cook tonight, call Chicken Delight." The chicken was not quite ready, and so my father engaged the man behind the counter in conversation; interviewing him, really. My father grew more and more fascinated by the chicken man's answers, exclaiming "Really!" and "Of course!" with great excitement, and asking more and more questions. (As I recall, the Chicken Delight chain was owned not by a chicken company but by a paper manufacturer—since of course the chicken was wrapped, bagged, napkined, etc., in great quantities of paper, in those pre-environmentally aware days.)

Although my father never wrote about Chicken Delight, some awareness dawned on me as I watched him, seeing clearly something which I realized I had witnessed my father doing many times—interviewing, probing, observing. Through him, I saw that certain kinds of writing—most, really—rely on a tremendous curiosity, observation, and probing of the world around the writer, for anything may find its way into the work. Even if it doesn't—as in the Chicken Delight—the habits of observation and vast interest in the world around the writer must stay sharp.

So, while I knew from direct experience the "art" side of writing, I saw, through my parents' examples, the "profession" side. I saw that things happened to you or you saw them happen to others, that when they interested you you wrote about them. You then sent this writing off to a publishing house, and either it was accepted (in which case you got paid for it and it was published as a book or magazine article) or rejected (in which case it did not get paid for and published—but you could send it somewhere else where it might get accepted). I saw also that writing was work—my father disappeared upstairs to his office in the attic every day, my mother to her desk in a corner of the bedroom. If my brother or I happened to see my father when he came downstairs to make himself lunch, we had been well instructed not to talk to him or interrupt him in any way, but to "play invisible daddy" because otherwise we might "interrupt his train of thought." We were allowed, but not encouraged to interrupt my mother—though we did all the time anyway. (It was a very sexist time, the 1950s, when all this took place. No one questioned that a woman's work might be as important as a man's; of course we could interrupt her, she was our mother. Nowadays, at least I hope, these assumptions would not be made.)

At any rate, in the sense of seeing writing as a way to make a living, my parents certainly influenced me. It never seemed scary to me to send writing out, nor did I have any fear of rejection. I knew that came with the territory.

But long before I became a writer in the sense of writing my own stories, sending them off, being paid money for them, and getting paid to do it, I was not only actually writing, I was a writer mentally—observing, probing, noticing. This sense was heightened by my mother having read me the Laura Ingalls Wilder books when I was very small, in which Laura tells of her own life in great detail, but never as "I," always as "Laura." Since I already felt so much an outsider in Hastings-on-Hudson, I frequently thought of myself not as "I" but as "she" or "Ellen," and I seemed, for years as I remember, to have observed my life as if it were a book I was reading, even as I lived it. "Ellen walked into the gym class late. Mrs. Jensen grew angry at her." (1 should probably add here that I *hated* school, and always regarded going as something like a prison sentence that had to be served. When I remember school, both in Hastings and later, briefly, at a boarding school in Massachusetts, described somewhat in my novel *The Year It Rained,* I remember, mostly, endless boredom, and waiting for it to be over, and feeling different from the other children. I also remember being told by probably well-meaning adults, who seemed to me as strange and distant as if they inhabited another planet (and to whom I no doubt also seemed quite strange), "Now, Ellen . . . if we make an exception for you. . . ." I got terrible marks in everything except English.)

Possibly I thought of myself as "she" and "Ellen" not only because my writer's temperament was beginning to crystallize and form, but because I wanted, or needed, in some way to distance myself from my life and the life of our family, which was growing increasingly unhappy for reasons I could not put my finger on. A lot was going on, which was painful in some undefined way, unclear and mysterious as to the why and what and how. My mother quit staying at home to go back to work in the city, at the publishing company she had worked at before she and my father had children, my parents fought increasingly, my father became more— well, when I learned the word "inconsistent" I thought "That's Maurice!" (I always called my parents by their first names). He would be cheerfully happy, talkative one day, enraged and breaking furniture the next, frequently withdrawn. Gradually, he seemed less and less interested in inviting me, or anyone, into his world in the way he had when I was a young child.

I could not put a name to it, but something was wrong. Although I had been an outgoing little girl, I grew quieter and quieter.

My father was, eventually, the first one to name the problem and begin fixing it, years later.

"I Have Found It!"

We will cut, now, from my childhood to the beginning of my adulthood; to a cold, grey January day in 1972 when I arrived in a little tiny Ozark mountain town called Eureka Springs, Arkansas. Eureka is Greek for "I have found it," and, indeed, I thought that day, and think still, that I had. I simply fell in love with Eureka Springs that day. I fell in love with this funny, quirky, lovely little town in precisely the same way most people (if they're lucky) fall in love with another person. This love of the town would find its way into much of my writing from this time on: *The Itch Book, Katie in the Morning, Home Place,* many articles, and the two "Dairy Hollow" cookbooks.

Founded in the 1880s, a time when people believed that pure mineral water could cure many diseases, Eureka Springs boomed, growing up around sixty-some springs, in a hilly, isolated, forested corner of Arkansas. Indians had used those same springs for centuries, and considered the area sacred; whites, too, felt a magic about the place. I can attest that from the very first time I came to Eureka Springs, on a day so misty I could feel the tiny droplets of water moistening my face and curling my hair, I too felt an indefinable something. I would discover that people had been trying to describe that something for a century, and I joined a long line of refugees to Eureka Springs, expatriates from all over America and indeed the world, restless people who somehow found what they were looking for in the tiny city. Walking up its hills, seeing its peculiar Victorian architecture tucked improbably onto rock ledges and bluffs and in valleys, I felt I had come home.

Only later did I learn that the town's motto, since the 1880s, had been "Where the Misfit Fits," and that about ten percent of the population were artists and writers, and that, historically, this had always been so. And, because I arrived in the deepest off-season, only later did I learn that the town's sole industry was tourism, and that during the summer there was a different Eureka: noisy, crowded, carefree, happy-go-lucky, part carnival, part tacky, part friends and family having a good time together.

I have never been able to stay with keeping a diary very long, but it happened that I was keeping one at the time I arrived in Eureka Springs. The journal entry on the day of my arrival in town reads, "Not going to go to California. Found a place. Home at last. 'Bout time."

It *was* time. I was about a month past my nineteenth birthday that January day and I had been through a lot. I had dropped out of school. I was quite desperate to get out of school and to leave home, be on my own, and begin writing. Elm Place and Hastings had never been happy places for me, and seemed steadily to be growing worse, simply oppressive with unhappiness. My parents had divorced, and my father, who had been suffering from severe depression had under gone a series of shock treatments. Eventually he stopped having them, moved to California, and realized that his real problem was drinking. He joined Alcoholics Anonymous, stopped drinking, and started the long journey of becoming a new person and regaining his writing career, which had more or less gone down the tubes. His drinking was the thing, or at least one of the central things, that, it turned out, had made our family life go wrong. In time, I came to feel such love and respect for him, for his having the courage to name the problem, admit it, and begin fixing it.

While this was going on, I married a very nice man named Mark Parsons, a.k.a. Crispin Dragonwagon, a tall, bearded, curly-headed Texan with a background in archeology. Like me, he seemed to have always been involved in thinking about the big why-is-the-world-this-way questions. He was much older than me, twenty-eight to my sixteen (of course, now seems young to me. Then it seemed like the height of maturity and sophistication.)

Crispin/Mark and I lived together with a number of housemates in a wonderful rambly old brownstone in Brooklyn, near Fort Greene Park. I dearly loved that year, the year I was sixteen, 1969, in New York with Crispin and the others. For the first time I could remember I felt *not* different, *not* alone or lonely. There were lots of late-night talks and jokes, lots of reading and discussion about books, lots of friendly argument about the big, Vera Zupnik-kind of questions. There was good food, and a lot of it, and I learned about cooking along with everything else.

As for my writing career, it began that year. Although I'd been writing stories virtually since I learned the al-

Teaching, about 1979 (Photo courtesy of Crescent Dragonwagon.)

phabet, my first year after dropping out of tenth grade I became a professional. I sold my first children's book, *Rainy Day Together,* and a cookbook. I was elated, giddy with joy, astonished and yet, at the same time, not surprised at all, for I had always known I was a writer. Not "would become," but *was*; now, though, I was getting paid for it, and other people would know, too.

Being out of school, writing and actually getting paid for it, making my own decisions, being away from my family, being in a congenial household with a group of friendly, intelligent people, being in love with a handsome and original man who loved me back—for the first time in my life I felt I was doing exactly what I was meant to do.

I must digress here to tell you the story of my weird name.

Dr. Agonwagon

"Is that your real name?"

"How did you get that name?"

I get asked a lot of questions, but these are my two least favorite, because, as you can imagine, I get asked them *all the time*. The story of how I became Crescent Dragonwagon is one I could very happily live the rest of my life without ever, ever, ever telling again. But, to be fair, when I know very well I would ask someone whose name was Paintbrush Hogbottom or Pickle Sycamore if that was their real name, how can I blame anyone for asking? Besides, becoming Crescent Dragonwagon is my own fault.

So, hoping that repeating the story here in writing one more time will spare me a few dozen retellings in person, here goes:

Lots of people do unusual things when they are teenagers, but most have the common sense not to cast them in concrete, as I did, by choosing a weird name when I was sixteen. Here is how it happened.

When I got married for the first time, my then-husband-to-be and I thought the woman should not take the man's last name. So, we decided to choose a new last name. We discovered, on the way to doing this, that our old first names had meanings we did not agree with (it was the late sixties, a time when lots of people my age and his wanted to change the world; we did not agree with much).

His old first name, which was Mark, meant "the warrior"; we were anti-war. My old first name, Ellen, meant "the queen"; we were anti-authoritarian. He came up with new first names; Crispin, for him, meaning "curly-headed one," and Crescent for me, meaning "the growing" (once mistakenly reported in a newspaper article as meaning "the growth"!).

The wedding drew nearer and nearer. We still hadn't come up with a new last name. One day, after discussing and discarding several possibilities, I said, "Maybe we're taking ourselves too seriously, maybe we should pick something completely frivolous." He said, "Like what?" I said, "Like, oh, urn, like Dragonwagon."

Thus we became Crescent and Crispin Dragonwagon. If I had had any idea how many countless thousands of times I would have to explain this ridiculous name, I would have picked something a lot less flashy—like Jane Smith, say. (People don't think I mean this; I do.) But by the time I realized how long the rest of my life would be, and how many times I'd explain the name, I had a few books out and the start of a professional reputation. At one time, on my first solo novel, *The Year It Rained,* I begged and pleaded with my editor to let it be published under the name C.D. Shank (C.D. being a carry-over from Crescent Dragonwagon, and also what many of my friends call me, and Shank being the last name of my second husband, Ned). Well, my editor refused very heatedly, over a year's time, saying that readers knew me as Crescent Dragonwagon, no one would have any reason to pick up a book by C.D. Shank, and so on. Eventually I gave up. (People also sometimes don't believe that I couldn't get my own way on being called C.D. Shank on my own book if I *really* wanted to; but it is true.) So, I am stuck with the name Crescent Dragonwagon, and explaining it all the time, and, as I said, I really have no one but myself to blame.

But, there are one or two good things about it. It is fun to see how computers chew up the name. I get mail addressed to Dargonwoodren, Dragonmudgeon, Crescent O'Wagon (the Irish branch of the family), and (my favorite) Dr. Agonwagon. I get letters from American Express that begin "Dear Mr. Wagon." And once, Ned and I were grocery shopping in Fayetteville, Arkansas. Ned handed the checkout girl one of our checks, which have both of our names on them.

The checkout girl looked at the check. Then she looked up at Ned.

"What," she asked him curiously, sounding it out syllable by syllable, "is a Cre-scent-Drag-on-wagon?"

Ned gestured toward me, browsing amidst the magazines. "It's my wife," he said.

The checkout girl gasped, then put her hands on her hips. She turned to me and said, "I'd slap him for that!"

The Road Home to Arkansas

How did you get from New York to Arkansas?" is something else I get asked a lot, almost as often as I get asked about my name. Mark/Crispin was from West Texas originally, and, as I always had, wanted to live in the country. We spent the year we lived in Brooklyn together dreaming over real estate catalogs. I wanted to move to Vermont, which I knew and loved, but land was very expensive there. He wanted to move to the hill country of Texas, but land was expensive there, too. Gradually, we narrowed the choice down to the Ozarks: pretty, mountainous, isolated, affordable.

With the money from my first books and a $2,000 inheritance from my Grandpa Louis, Crispin Dragonwagon and I headed south to buy land. Just as we were about to pull out to begin our new life, one of the kids on the block we were leaving in Brooklyn gave us a gift. This boy, Dennis, had wanted to be a veterinarian, and had been given a fuzzy baby duckling for Easter. It had grown up, and his mom was threatening to make it into soup if Dennis didn't find a home for it. On the day we left, with the car packed to the gills, Dennis appeared with the duck. "Would you take him to the country?" he asked us. Crispin rearranged the car and made an improvised cage out of two plastic milk crates and some mesh. He and I drove over a thousand miles with that duck in the backseat. Every time the car went around a curve, the duck protested with a loud and irritable "ack, ack, ack." Perhaps that duck's descendents still live on the farm in Missouri that Crispin and I bought all those years ago.

Most people would say sixteen is too young to get married. They would certainly have been right in my case. I moved out after a year of living with Crispin on the farm, and went to St. Louis, the biggest city close (three or four hours' drive) to the farm. I chose to go there rather than back to New York; I wanted to move to somewhere where I knew no one and see if I could make a life for myself from scratch, without a husband, or a parent, or a parent's reputation. I wanted to make my own way, to prove to myself I could be independent. In St. Louis I wrote for an underground paper called the *Outlaw,* and I cooked at a restaurant called Our Daily Bread, and I took yoga classes. I thought about the big questions which I felt no closer to having answered than I ever had, and I wondered what to do with the rest of my life. I knew I wanted to be, indeed *had* to be, a writer; I knew I loved the Ozarks; I knew the farm had been too isolated for me; beyond this, I was not certain of much. I missed, very much, that year in Brooklyn, the one year of which I could say, unequivocally, "I was happy."

By this time, the St. Louis period, I was growing closer and closer to my parents, even though they lived far away. I was beginning to look at them as friends and colleagues, and to love and enjoy them in this way, not just because they were parents and it was my duty to love them. I had a very special relationship with my father, since he had joined AA. It was as if we had started over again the year I was eighteen and he was fifty-seven, and in a funny way, because we were both starting over, it was as if we were growing up together, were running buddies, pals the same age.

One of the most powerful influences in my life was undoubtedly watching my father remake himself. At a time when most people are retiring, he was becoming a new human being: a kind and reasonably happy person, one who did not break chairs one day and bring home roses the next, one who was level, hard-working, but an enormous amount of pure, exuberant, irrepressible fun. He seemed filled with wonder at the way his life had been returned to him, and I was powerfully inspired by his example as I saw him contend with each messy piece of his old life, and try to clean it up, make it better. For instance, when he first joined AA, about the time I left Crispin and the farm, I hitchhiked out to see him with $20 in my pocket. He was living on Master-Charge, and was so broke he borrowed $2 from me to get a haircut (which he could not put on Mastercharge). I learned later that he was $30,000 in debt. But slowly, methodically, carefully, he paid back every cent. Ten years after he joined AA he was debt free.

Through his example, I began learning. Be responsible. Be kind. You can still be different, be crazy, be creative—but it does not have to isolate you or make you lonely. You choose the colors, you stretch the canvas. It's your painting, so paint it. It's your life.

To this lesson was added a second powerful lesson, which also certainly shaped the rest of my life. During the time in St. Louis, I was the victim of a violent crime. At one point, in a cornfield outside the city, a gun was held to my head, and I thought, "This is it. I will never get out of this alive." And in those moments I thought: I thought about how much I loved my parents and friends, I thought about poems I had never finished and work I had left undone, and how much time I had wasted, and the world—right at the moment I was about, I thought, to leave it—suddenly appeared intensely beautiful to me. I became conscious of everything around me; conscious of the fact that everything—the wind rustling the corn, the blue sky, the smell of the earth, myself, even the man holding the small pearl-handled revolver—was in some mysterious way linked . . . so linked that they were one thing. And with this sense, fear left me, and I grew very peaceful.

When I did survive this experience, my life was changed. It had, like my father's life, been given back to me, on very different terms from the first time around. I felt keenly that it was important not to waste time; it was important to pursue what you wanted to do unapologetically and wholeheartedly, and essential to tell

and show people whom you loved, that you loved them. Most of all, I felt that I must learn a way to return to that transcendent peace (which probably saved my life, since it also helped me deal with the criminals calmly) and live with it on a daily basis. Some people call an experience like this a spiritual awakening, and it was—not in a way that has to do with religion, or church, or synagogue, or anything you believe, but with an *experience.*

Starting with this experience, which I believe now to have been grace, I began in earnest the search to return to what had been shown me in that cornfield; a spiritual search. Step by step, I was led slowly and inexorably to that way by which I might indeed live in inner peace—a kind of peace and happiness and certainty which stayed strong within me, regardless of what happened, good or bad, on the outside. In retrospect, I think I had been searching all my life, yet I had to awaken to it, and with a certain desperation. I also believe that spiritual matters are the most personal and private known to human beings; they are written in that language of the heart exclusive to a person and what AA calls his or her Higher Power. Discussion of such matters diminishes them by bringing them down to our clumsier human language. I can only say that, having found Someone who answers all my questions, I have been given an unchanging and permanent background against which all other happenings of my life come and go. Gratitude and amazement for this gift, awe for that Someone, permeates me down to the marrow of my bones. It is the basis of everything else.

During the year I had lived in St. Louis, several people—at the yoga center and elsewhere—had said to me, "You know, there's this little town in Arkansas called Eureka Springs. You should go there, it would be your kind of place." After the violent crime, I listened closely to everything I heard, and I kept hearing this, from different people, most of whom did not know each other. Finally, I did go.

And that is how I found my way, starting on that misty grey January day, to the place in which I have more or less lived, more or less happily, ever after.

Professional Fairy Godmother

I met my second husband, Ned Shank, in 1977, in Little Rock, Arkansas, at a potluck dinner. He likes to say, "I came with a kipper salad and left with you." It did not happen quite that fast, but it was pretty fast—almost as fast as my falling in love with Eureka Springs. Ned is tall and friendly and blue-eyed and smart. He is from Iowa. He is kind, handsome, and likes to make jokes, and when we play Scrabble, he beats me almost exactly half the time (we keep a lifetime Scrabble score tally in our Scrabble dictionary, so we know). His background is in historic preservation; that is, protecting and preserving old buildings, keeping them from being torn down or added onto in a way that fakes or obscures their true architectural history. Naturally, he loves Eureka Springs. He also loves to eat (especially pancakes), and he never minds washing the dishes when I cook. We have two cats, Catullus, a huge tabby, and Z-Cat, a small, hyperactive calico. We like to stay at country inns, buy antiques, and canoe. We both like to read, and talk about what we read, and we go on long walks together.

Two years after Ned and I married, a tiny farmhouse across the road from the little house I have lived in since I first moved to Eureka came up for sale. These two houses are in a valley called Dairy Hollow, because there were many dairies in Eureka's old days. The last one, the Rhiel Dairy, was still in existence when I moved here in 1972. There, Ethel Rhiel, a kind and feisty blue-eyed lady in her seventies, milked eight jersey cows by hand every morning and night.

With a friend, Bill Haymes, Ned and I bought that next-door farmhouse and began one of the great adventures of our life together: Dairy Hollow House, a country inn and restaurant. Ten years later, Dairy Hollow House is three houses: the original farmhouse, which has three guest rooms; the innkeeper's house, where Ned and I still live; and a newer, larger house, the Main House, which is close by and has three suites, a check-in area, a great big kitchen, and a really pretty restaurant dining room, with lots of windows, and a fireplace, and lace curtains, and white tablecloths, and a lattice made of twigs, and a stencil of ivy cut from a spray of ivy on the oak tree just outside one window. Every morning, breakfast is brought to each room in a big, split-oak basket; every evening, dinner is served at the restaurant at 7:00. Each guest room has a fireplace and a vase or two of fresh flowers, usually wildflowers and garden flowers mixed together.

The inn has grown and grown and will probably grow just a little more. We now hire quite a few people to help us run the inn, and these people—like Paula Martin, who manages the front desk, knows everything there is to know about quilts and bookkeeping, and moved here from Oklahoma City; or Sandy Allison, a big-hearted blonde from Texas, who is a great cook and manages our kitchen; or Mark Wayne Clark, our dish-washer, a local young man who is a mechanical/automotive genius and lives so far out in the country that there's a black bear living in the woods near his family home—these people and their families have become in a way part of our family.

Another part of our family is our friends—friends like Bill Haymes, a musician, who wrote the music at the end of *Alligators and Others, All Year Long,* and started Dairy Hollow House with us. Crow Johnson, another musician, is also a close friend, and so is Chou-Chou Yearsley, who owns a shop here in Eureka, and Jane Maas, who runs an advertising agency in New York,

ers, and many others who add much to our lives, and, I hope, we to theirs. This "family" is especially important to us because we don't have children. I'm not able to, physically, and we probably will not adopt. (Sometimes people think it is strange that someone who writes for children does not have children of her own, but I write mostly out of remembering my own childhood, overlaid with emotions I may be feeling now, as an adult. Emotions, after all, have no age. The causes may change, but "sad" feels like "sad" whether you are six or sixty-five.)

Besides our friends and the people who work at the inn, our lives are filled with the people who come and stay or dine at the inn. In a way, having an inn is like sending out a party invitation to the world, and then seeing who comes. The loveliest people end up at our door: computer programmers and district attorneys, doctors and actresses, wildflower experts and chefs, writers and hatmakers, musicians, historians, secretaries, politicians, teachers, bankers. Some come year after year. Some send us recipes, or write us letters. At least five or six couples have told us that they conceived their babies at the inn, and people leave long notes in the books we put in the rooms, which we call "room diaries." Mostly they tell us how much they loved staying here, how good it was to get away from their too-busy regular life, how much they loved Eureka Springs, our staff, and getting to curl up by the fireplace in their room on cold days and sip the hot apple cider we had waiting

"With Maurice after a murder-mystery weekend at Dairy Hollow. I'm still in costume" (Photo courtesy of Crescent Dragonwagon.)

"The dining room at Dairy Hollow House, Eureka Springs, Arkansas"
(Photo courtesy of Crescent Dragonwagon.)

for them when they checked in. We did find one entry that said, "Thank you Ned and Crescent for sharing your home and lives with us; thank you Z-Cat for sharing your mouse with us at three a.m."

In all, being an innkeeper is much like being a professional fairy godmother. You try to make people happy; to grant their wishes, including those they had but didn't know they had. I can't say we make everybody happy, but we come pretty close. It is quite an intimate way to be involved in other peoples' lives. Feeding and housing them, perhaps making their wedding cake or helping them celebrate their thirty-third anniversary, brings us in contact in so different a way from the way I come in contact with people through my books. Both ways are deeply satisfying; each, perhaps, more so, because the other is so different. In a funny way, it balances.

We do lots of off-the-wall kinds of things here, like our quarterly mystery weekends, which I write. Ned and I play parts in them. For example, I sometimes bleach my hair blonde and become Mrs. Mary Jo Louise Umbecker, an Atlanta matron; Ned is brilliant as Lord "Figgie" Chillington-Worcestershire III, a British detective, or the Reverend Billy Joe-Bob Clayton, a scurrilous preacher. One year my father, Maurice, came from California and played the part of Digby Crumley, a corrupt Southern attorney. On mystery weekends our guests play roles, too.

But I think the real reasons our guests love coming here is not so much the fresh flowers and quilts and deli-

cious food and fireplaces and pictures on the wall and the hot tub in the woods. Although these things play a part, they are still just background. It's that we, the innkeepers, have fun and love our lives here in Eureka, and feel grateful to have found each other, our professions, and the town. We welcome our guests from the heart. I think most of our staff, too, feels this way. These sorts of feelings create an atmosphere that goes beyond the physical stuff, though the stuff we have is also very nice indeed. The guests might see us only when they check in, check out, and at dinner—but they can feel this atmosphere. It makes a difference.

These days, Ned is full-time innkeeper; he's also chairman of the Eureka Springs Historic District Commission. As for me, I write most mornings and cook in our restaurant about three or four nights a week. (Although I cook rabbit, pork, game hen, etc., and, I am told, cook them quite well, I have been a vegetarian since 1976; Ned's also a non-meat eater.) I also plan all the menus for the restaurant, try to keep up with the garden, do the inn's "Moo's-Letter" and occasionally arrange the room flowers. I go on walks three times a week (sometimes with Ned or close friends from around here), and I work out hard (push-ups, sit-ups, lifting weights for an hour or so) three times a week.

Eureka Springs, too, is very much a part of my life. I simply felt unrooted until I found it. I love "being a good citizen"—voting, expressing my opinion, employing other people and being part of the local economy, caring, doing my turn at jury duty, feeling that what I do makes a difference. I read a lot about the city's history, and I still love looking at its architecture and thinking about its people, the beloved "misfits" of the town, past, present, and future.

Nonetheless, I am in and out of town. I go off to teach and lecture at regular intervals, too. (Sometimes I quilt or embroider things for Dairy Hollow on the plane or in strange hotels—it makes me feel happy and at home wherever I am.) In January, February, and early March, the off-season, when the inn is very slow, I usually disappear for two or three months. I dump Ned, the inn, the cats, and my friends, and I hightail it to somewhere remote and isolated (last year, a cabin in Tennessee; this year, a summer cottage in Sag Harbor, New York). This is a very important part of each year for me. While I'm there, I just write, write, write, write, write. This writing time by myself is all the more precious because it is rare and in total contrast to the frenetic though happy busyness of the rest of my life.

I remain close to my mother, Charlotte; we have long visits a couple of times a year, and talk on the phone all the time and dash off letters frequently. Often, if I finish a poem or a children's book, I call her up and read it to her. Sometimes, she does the same with me.

I'm busy, too busy, extremely busy all the time, and I would be lying if I said that it is not sometimes difficult and stressful to be so busy, in so many areas; it is like choreographing a very complicated ballet, and sometimes the dancers crash into each other instead of exiting, entering, and jeté-ing gracefully. However, given that I like to do so many different things, it's a pretty good fit—even if it is too busy. And I think this life could have been prophesied for me almost from childhood—times of being alone balanced by times of being intensely with others—the physical, present-time, for-others work of cooking balanced by the private, go-inside-yourself, cerebral work of writing, living in the country balanced by visits to other cities and countries to teach, study, or write.

But I also, in the midst of the busyness, try to stay peaceful *inside*. I have never forgotten the moment of peace which was given to me at the very instance I thought I would be killed, and the spiritual sustenance that grew out of the seeking that followed that experience. I try to live in *that* light—live in a sense beyond the happenings of life. My father, after he sobered up, used to often quote the Latin phrase *Laborare est orare*—to work is to pray.

I think an awful lot about my father, who died this year, and who, as I mentioned earlier, I feel I "grew up" with. I miss him very much, and I don't know that I will ever get over missing him. Not long ago I dreamed he came back to life. In my dream, he stood at the back of the kitchen in our restaurant, next to the storage bins of apples, potatoes, and onions. I hugged him, told him how much I had missed him, and asked him why it had taken him so long to return. He paused and said, "Well, it's not like going to Mexico, you know."

Because death is not like going to Mexico—because it is not a place you can come back from—I feel all the more keenly than ever that life is to be lived to the utmost degree, with purpose and clear destination in the highest spiritual sense, and, growing out of that, a natural and grateful joy and enthusiasm for everything one does, touches, tastes, smells. Once, at the restaurant, I served Maurice, my father, a scoop of our chocolate bread pudding with raspberry sauce and whipped cream. He took a bite and said, "Wow." He took another bite and shook his head in wonder. He took a third bite and said, "On a scale of one to ten, I give this dessert 5,000." That is the way I would like to live . . . clear off the scale, ringing in at least 5,000.

To me, this means shaping your life in such a way that you never have to say "Oh, I wish I had . . .," and instead doing the things you wish to do. To be part of a community, to pursue your interests and passions, even if no one else believes they can be incorporated into one life; to have work that is meaningful, even blissful, in the doing itself, work that is much more than just a

With Ned and Z-Cat, 2000 (Photo courtesy of Crescent Dragonwagon.)

way to make money. These are what, to me, give meaning, satisfaction, and joy.

But perhaps most of all, living fully means loving other people and letting them love you back and making sure both of you know it. Loving others, along with work and community; loving with passion and enthusiasm, and, first and last, loving God or your Higher Power or whatever name you choose to give to That. It is this latter love which confers a secret, detached, private part of yourself which stays peaceful and certain, as everything else comes and goes.

And the countless thousands of ways we find to do this make the best stories, and the most interesting lives, of all.

Crescent Dragonwagon contributed the following update to *SATA* in 2007:

I flip open the red hardcover copy of *Something about the Author Autobiography Series* not just to reread what I last wrote, but to check the date of its publication— 1992. Fifteen years ago, as of this writing, which takes place on a hot June day, in Vermont, in 2007.

Vermont is where I live now, in what I alluded to in my earlier entry as "my Aunt Dot's farmhouse . . . a retreat, a rambly old house, barn-red, with comfortable porches and lazy wasps and a view out to the mountains and down to the pond." It is still all those things, but it is not Aunt Dot's house any longer: it is mine.

Aunt Dot just turned ninety-seven, and she lives in what was then (and still is) her other home, an apartment in New York a block away from the East River, which she shares with a caregiver. Sometimes, though, she *thinks* she lives, thinks she actually *is,* here at the farm. She also thinks that Jim Cherry, her boyfriend/ companion for the last twenty years of his life, is not only still alive, but due to arrive for dinner, along with "Mother and Dad." Those are her parents, my grandparents, dead forty-some years now, as Jim has been, oh, a good ten or twelve years.

Although my aunt's state of mind is sometimes called dementia or senility, I prefer to think of it just as different, other, not as diseased or sad—just on an emotional rather than literal continuum of time and space as we usually conceive of it. What is and was important to her remains, just rearranged, sometimes almost poetically, and seasoned with a certitude and sass she always had. This is comforting to me.

When I last wrote here, my life was different, in almost every way, with the exception of writing and a state I then called "in the midst of the busyness, try(ing) to stay peaceful inside . . . in a sense beyond the happenings of life." I think the operative word here may be *inside,* because the differences in my life then and now are all outside. While I can say that writing and living

beyond the occurrences remain the background against which everything else, and I mean, sadly, *everything* else, and *everyone* else, comes and goes, that is inside. Outside, it's another story.

When I last wrote I was grieving the death of my father, trying to make sense out of and peace with his loss, trying to figure out how to keep alive in me those parts of him which I missed so deeply. And now I find myself slowly doing the same with another loss.

My father was seventy-six when he died. Though I grieved him, his death was not a difficult or painful one for him, nor was it out of sequence. It had followed the human equivalent of the track of the seasons: spring, summer, fall, winter, the track that, today, at least, we think of as the natural one: he was born, then was a baby, a child, a teenager, a young man, a middle-aged man, an old man, and only then passed beyond life in a particular body, as a particular person, to whatever is next.

But Ned, my husband, who is woven all through the account of my life I gave here then, and is still woven throughout my life (though in an entirely different way now), was only forty-four when he exited life.

This was on an unusually warm and sunny November afternoon back in Arkansas in 2000. He'd gone out to take his typical two-or-three-times-a-week bicycle ride and though the days were short, and it was around 4:00 P.M., it was still very light out.

His usual ride took him out to the Conoco station near where Beaver Lake and the White River intersect. They rent canoes there, so Ned always called it "Canoe-co." He'd stop there and turn around. It was about twelve miles there (mostly uphill) and twelve miles back (mostly downhill). How exhilarated he always was when he came back from these rides! A tall man, on an extra-large yellow mountain bicycle I gave him for, I think, his thirty-fifth birthday, he wore a very shiny helmet with a teeny rear-view mirror attached to it. His favorite biking shorts were black, with a stripe of turquoise down the sides and inside, a thick padded crotch of beige, to help him pad his butt on the narrow bicycle seat. He had special rainbow type sunglasses, and purple and black felt gloves with turquoise fingers, and a sports watch so he could time himself. When he returned home—even if he'd had to bicycle in the rain (he had a whole different outfit for that, yellow waterproof rain pants and a yellow hooded windbreaker)—he was always happy, calm, and dripping with sweat.

Only, this time he didn't come home. A red Chevy pickup; a sharp curve; an obscuring rock outcropping that cut off vision both ways for six seconds; dusk; a steep drop-off—his one-way journey. Sometime this is called "an act of God," though I can't tell you whether it was or not (nor, in my view, can anyone else—though there are certainly many people out there who will tell you definitively one way or another).

Ned died about four hours after he and the pick-up collided, in a hospital emergency room in Springdale, Arkansas, having lost consciousness sometime on the Medi-Vac helicopter that took him there. I had kissed him goodbye that morning; I had called him at noon that afternoon: I was going off to audit a survey of poetry class at the University of Arkansas and that was its last session; it was just a quick goodbye-I-love-you-I'll-see-you-later call.

In the "family waiting room" at the hospital, the emergency-room doctor, who for some reason was wearing scrubs with a ridiculous print, a black background with bright red-and-yellow fruit on it, came out to talk to me. "He's critical," he said.

"But he will live," I said. I didn't say it as a question

When my friend Chou-Chou and I had driven over to Springdale, we had talked about where we'd put the hospital bed; probably her living room, too many steps at our home. I'd been told by the EMT people that Ned had broken several bones. I'd broken a leg once (Ned had cared for me tenderly) and I knew how much that had hurt; I could only imagine how much he must be hurting. In the car I'd thought about helping him, the encouragement he would need, my saying to him over and over, "I know you don't believe it now, but you *will* be able to ride a bicycle again, you will, I promise."

The doctor said to me, "Well, it's very serious."

I repeated, again as a statement, "But he *will* live."

The doctor said, "Well, his heart's already stopped three times."

They wouldn't let me in to ER while he was still alive. I wanted to be in there, badly, to talk to him, maybe to have my voice or presence reach him somehow, reassure him, maybe give him the strength to somehow come back into life fully one more time, or else have sent him on his way with some measure more or peace or comfort. But I didn't argue, sensing, perhaps, that I couldn't win anyway, and that it was better that the doctor get back to him than be talking to me. So I waited. I stared at the floor, hard, scrubbable vinyl tile, seamless, beige background with tiny flecks of grey and mustard yellow.

A few minutes later the doctor came back in again.

"We lost him," he said.

I said, "No."

Chou-Chou said, "We were not even told this was a possibility!" and then burst into tears.

I said "No," again.

I have ever since distrusted the scenes on TV and in movies where someone is informed of a sudden death: a wife of a husband's death, parents of their child's, and screaming begins. It's too big, too much to take in, and too unreal for screaming.

"May I see him?" I asked. "I want to see him."

"Let us just get him cleaned up a little."

It seemed like an extremely long time until they let came to get me, though it was probably only ten or fifteen minutes. When I went in he was swaddled in sheets up to his neck. Nurses were still mopping up blood from the floor. In the haze of hyper-reality and unreality, disbelievingly seeing something I knew I would remember forever, along with the thousands of other pictures of Ned I had in my mind, I leaned down and kissed his broken face, touched his reddish beard, put my hands on his sternum. I told him I loved him, I said some special private words that we had many times said to each other and said together, during the course of the twenty-three years on which we had traveled the globe as partners, mates, husband and wife, friends, committed selfless acts and acts of betrayal, had made each other laugh and cry.

They told me they were going to move his body from the emergency room to a room down the hall but I could see him there if I wanted to. Instead I walked back into the family waiting room, accompanied by a chaplain who seemed as strange to me as a giant grasshopper. I called people—family, friends—to tell them what had happened. People from organ recovery came and asked me if I wanted Ned's organs (those which hadn't been damaged) "harvested" for donation to others who might use them. Yes, I said. People from the funeral home came. Cremation, I said.

"Do you want to see him again?" a nurse asked me, "because we're going to have to move him again pretty soon." I said yes and I went down to that second room. In the few minutes that had passed since ER, he had somehow left, completely. There was no sense of Ned anymore. No longer him, it was an "it," a body. I returned to the family waiting room, the vinyl under my feet, treading this strange unreal night. About another fifteen minutes passed. "We're getting ready to move him," the nurse said, "Do you want to see him one more time?" And this time I felt he was really, really no longer present—utterly vanished, gone. With every corpuscle of my being, I wished him, wherever he was, if he was somewhere (and he had to be, didn't he?), well.

That was almost seven years ago. I have a good life now, though almost wholly not the one I had imagined. I think, by now, the grief at Ned's sudden loss has been mostly composted. I understand, now, that you don't "get over" or resolve grief. Rather, you just let it rest in you because you have no other choice; you cannot alter a death. Grief just slowly decomposes, the way leaves and banana peels and egg shells and grass clippings in a compost pile slowly turn back into newly rich earth. And this is where you have a choice: you can then, if you wish, apply the composted sorrow and grief and learning to your garden and your life, the better to nourish your tomatoes and peppers and beans, and, again, your life and how you live it. The emotions are so intense that not to use them somehow would, it seems to me, be a double tragedy. I would not wish grief on anyone, yet I know that there is no human being who is immune to it, who will not experience it eventually but, until he or she gets there, no matter how empathetic he or she is, will realize that this place was unimaginable beforehand. And I also know that grief, because it is so full, so overwhelming, so non-negotiable, so frightening, and because it is the price-tag of having loved and been loved, is extraordinarily rich as it decomposes. As it breaks down, so does the old you. The old you becomes a new you—here is where the choice comes in. The new you, if you so chose, is recognizable, but enriched, changed, sobered, humbled by the mysterious unknowableness of why things happen as they do. Of course, you can choose other new yous: bitter, angry, closed off, perceiving yourself as a victim of fate. I slowly, slowly chose and developed the first kind of new self, and am still doing so.

It was not until six years after Ned's death, fall of 2006—fall, which had once been my favorite season, but had become the season that was Ned's last on earth—that I felt able to love the colors of the trees and sky, the air, the coming change. I am not "over" Ned's death—I never will be, and I cried just now over the computer writing about it, cried for what must be the millionth or two millionth time. But I think I have composted it. Rather than "over" it, it is under and in me, a large part of the very soil from which grows who I am today, now. And not only his death, but his life, and our shared life.

*

Ned's death was the domino that knocked over a lot of other dominos that had been fixed and certain points in my life. As much as I loved Eureka Springs, once I understood fully that not only could I not get my whole old life back (which of course I couldn't), I came to realize that having it partially was worse than not having it at all. I would have to begin again.

By the time of Ned's collision with the red pick-up, we had already transformed what had been our inn into a nonprofit organization which served writers, and, after two years of fundraising, were joyfully functioning with a terrific board of directors and Ned as executive director.

My second grief, and one which lacked the clean purity that I had with Ned's loss, was over what happened to this nonprofit that had been Ned's and my last, and perhaps best, joint project. I have since learned there is a name for the series of betrayals that took place: what happened to me is called "Founder's Syndrome." It is when an organization started originally by a person or people, undergoes change, and, in its next generation, those who are responsible for it feel the need, in putting their own stamp on it, to wipe out as much as possible

of the founders' spirit and touch and style and even historical presence. It is also common for the new incoming regime to speak words that do not align with actions; for the founder or founders to be told, "Yes, we want you, we need you, we value you," while undermining every contribution the founder(s) makes. This, not to put too fine a point on it, is what happened to me; I was made, as I like to say, "dragona non grata." I am usually not a pansy or push-over, usually pretty good at reading people, but, no doubt because it was taking every resource I possessed emotionally to merely get up each day in the unchanging permanent face of Ned's death, I just didn't understand this gap between what was being said and what was being done. The mysterious disappearing receipts, the objects borrowed for "just a day or two" and never returned, the asked-for-and-then-discarded photo albums, the packages for those I was to present donation proposals to which mysteriously never got mailed. So I walked into Ms. X's office, the appointment I had worked and pulled strings for four months, only to discover that she had never received what we were supposed to go over (not only looking a complete idiot but losing some $120,000 a year that would have flowed to the organization). The events planned, my offers to assist, the curt "No, we won't need you on this one," statements, which were followed, at the last minute, when there was no possible time to do whatever I had offered and been rebuffed for in the right way, the panicked, urgent requests: "Stop everything, come help us, we need you now!"

It took a therapist, who worked with me as I treaded my way through the terrible months after Ned's loss, to say, "Look at the actions, not the words here. If the actions were words, you'd be saying something like 'What's my job description here now, what exactly is it that you want me to do?' and they would be saying, 'Get the f— out of here!'"

To say all this was hard is as vast an understatement as I have ever made. For the last six months I lived in Eureka Springs, I traveled the bumpy back-roads to get to my studio and home rather than drive past the buildings into which Ned and I had poured almost twenty years of life and love and vision and hope and good cheer, first as our inn, then as the nonprofit. In retrospect, I wonder if it took this—took in effect being hit over the head repeatedly with a two-by-four—to get me to leave Eureka Springs and begin a new life. Maybe it did.

Many times I would hear my father's aphorisms in the back of my mind during this period. "Nothing is wasted on the writer," he would say. Would I someday write about the razor-sharp clean cut of grief, amputating Ned from life and from my life, as opposed to the dirty, oozing infected series of lacerations that was the end of my involvement with the nonprofit? I don't know the answer to that; though, of course, here I am, writing about it. And I would also hear Maurice, my father, saying "God sees the truth, but waits." Friends and colleagues who have lived through "Founder's Syndrome," tell me

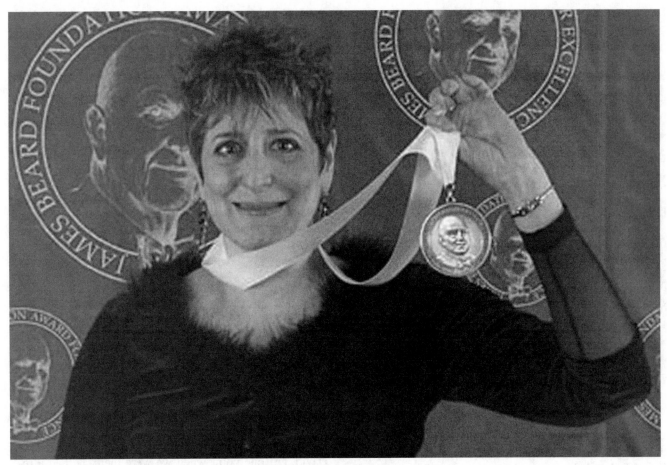

Crescent with her James Beard Award prize medallion, 2003 (Photo courtesy of Crescent Dragonwagon.)

that I, too, must wait; that someday, "Two or three generations of directors away, someone will come and find you and want to know what really happened, and get the pieces of history and artifacts they discarded. You might be really old when it happens, but it will happen. Someday, that betrayal will be made right." And though that hasn't happened outside yet, I can feel it beginning to happen inside. If it's a syndrome after all, that means that no matter how it felt at the time, it was not entirely personal. And maybe I did make the right choice, in finally bowing out completely: for in altered form, that nonprofit does still exist and still serves writers.

Creating a new life, is an odd thing. In one sense, you have to take action, you have to move towards it. In another; you have to stay still and let that new life reveal itself to you. But that stillness is not passivity. It's also action: to be that receptive, that permeable and open, that patient—this is a lot of work. Work of a kind that did not and does not come naturally to me, Ms. Let's-Get-the-Show-on-the-Road.

But eventually, and gradually, it happened and continues to happen. I moved to my aunt's old farmhouse. First part-time, then full-time; first as a guest, and then, when my aunt was unable to afford to keep the place and it was to be sold to make money for her to live on, buying it, a process I am still doing, and not without

difficulty. At times I wonder, do I own the place, or does it own me? But then I step outside, on the blue-stone step beyond the front door, and I look east. I can see for twenty miles, clear into New Hampshire. The sky is always changing, and ranges of mountains begin at the very edge of a long, beautiful sloping field in front of the house. Sometimes I can see just the first range, deep green with evergreens. The second is blue; the third gray, and the fourth and fifth paler gray. I have many times seen rainbows, double rainbows, arching over those mountains. I have never lived somewhere so intensely green in the summer, punctuated by the white of birches, a tree Arkansas could not have been home to as it was too hot. And the New England winters, which I had dreaded and feared, have turned out to be luscious and pristine. Snow, where there is little traffic and everyone is prepared for it, is quite extraordinary. One day, for instance, I was out snow-shoeing just before dusk, and the way the light hit the particularly crystal-line snow made each flake a prism. Just by turning my head, I could see countless spangled tiny rainbows glinting, like tiny, intricate sequins.

"But what about the winters?" ask my friends in Arkansas—and yes, despite the emotional violence of the separation with the nonprofit, I do indeed still have many friends there. Indeed some I mentioned here fifteen years ago—Bill Haymes, Chou-Chou, the Mitchell-

"My Aunt Dot's farmhouse," Vermont (Photo courtesy of Crescent Dragonwagon.)

West family—come to visit me here periodically. Ah, the winters. I tell them two things: I quote my Vermont friend Deborah Krasner, who says, tongue in cheek, of winter, "It keeps the riffraff out," and I tell them (and this is original), "Well, my friend, once I too suffered from claustrosnowbia. But it can be overcome very easily!"

Back on the first go-round of writing this entry, I talked about what seems to have been my lifelong tendency towards either interacting intensely with other people or spending time in happy solitude, with little middle ground. This is still true. If thirty-five acres on the top of a hill in Southeastern Vermont sounds like the perfect place for solitude, well, it is. But if solitude sounds like loneliness, it isn't. In addition to my old Arkansas friends and my new Vermont friends, I share my life and often my home with my boyfriend, David, a filmmaker who divides his time between Vermont and California. An active, handsome, funny, erudite, and really smart guy, far more politically active than I am or will ever be, he met me not at a potluck dinner (as I did Ned) but in a manner that couldn't possibly have worked all those years ago, as it didn't exist: the Internet.

The picture of David that he posted on the Internet (with his toned bicep visible and a truly "Come hither, baby!" look in his eye) hangs in my hallway now, along with pictures of my father and mother, of many Eureka friends, of me at dinner at the White House with two former Dairy Hollow guests, Bill and Hillary Clinton, and of course, many photographs of Ned. But when I

think about what made me answer to David's ad, it wasn't his biceps. It was a line about ". . . the journey two people may take, from strangers, to friends, perhaps to becoming intimate partners . . . all without knowing if they will get there." It was the "all without knowing if they will get there" that spoke to me so clearly, grappling, as I was, with impermanence, mystery and becoming comfortable with the unknown and the unknowable.

My writing now? Of course I continue to write. My book *Passionate Vegetarian,* which I wrote when Ned was alive but which was published after his death, and which is dedicated to him, is 1,208 pages long and won the James Beard Award. My new cookbook, *The Cornbread Gospels,* will be in stores about two months from the date on which I'm writing these words. Several children's books, including *Bat in the Dining Room, Brass Button, And Then It Rained/And Then the Sun Came Out,* and *Is This a Sack of Potatoes?,* have all been published. Each of them has its own story and reason for being. I keep up with Web sites on individual books as well as my home page, www.dragonwagon. com. I also write poetry intermittently and memoir, as I always have, and I teach a course I developed, called Fearless Writing™—I've even taught it as far away as in Italy (though in English, not Italian).

Italy—a place Ned and I always talked about visiting together, but never had the chance to. It was surpassingly strange, and sad, and sweet, to be there with David. (At one point when we were there, he had a really bad flu. One night, when he awoke burning with fever, I said, "Oh, darling D, I'm so sorry you got sick while we were here!" I got up and got a cold washcloth to put on his forehead. As I did, he replied, feverishly, earnestly, with this absolutely nonsensical loving response: "Well, if I had to have this flu, anywhere, with anyone, I would rather have had it in Italy, with you!" He fell back asleep immediately; I lay there laughing in the dark.)

And yes, I think Ned and David would like each other. Logan West is the now-grown-up son of my Arkansas friends George and Starr (it was at Starr's home that the fateful potluck where I met Ned took place). Logan, who'd known Ned all his life, met David here in Vermont one Thanksgiving. "It's scary how much they would like each other," Logan said. "In fact; I think they might just ignore you!"

In addition to sharing my home with David much of the time, I share it, as always, with a cat or cats. Z-Cat moved up here with me from Arkansas, but died about two years ago; two young tabbies, Cattywhompus (which means sideways or crooked in Arkansas slang) and his sister Gordita (Spanish for Little Fat One, which she is) have taken her place. Or rather, not her place; every cat, like every person one loves, is irreplaceable. Rather, the two cats have created their own place, in my home and life and heart.

*

Crescent and David (Photo courtesy of Crescent Dragonwagon.)

Of course when I wrote about "a life so far" for this series earlier, I had no idea of what lay ahead of me. None of us do. Drawn between the present and the future is an opaque curtain, absolutely impenetrable, and for that, I must say, at this remove, I am thankful. I think of the dedication in *Passionate Vegetarian:* "To Ned Shank—what a feast we had!" I am still feasting, in this life, as rich and bittersweet and dark and melting as really good chocolate. I feast with others sometimes and alone sometimes; inside by the woodstove in the winter, outside on the screen porch in the summer, looking out into the bright flower bed my aunt had put in and which I keep more or less weeded.

My aunt. Having started this telling with her, I think I will end with her. David and I visited her about a year ago, then he left to run some errands and it was just her and me, sitting in her bedroom. There was some noise from the kitchen.

"What's that sound?" she asked me.

"I think it's Zorina, fixing your dinner," I said, "Would you like me to go see?"

"Yes," she said, decisively. So I got up and went to the tiny kitchen, where Zorina was indeed making dinner, stir-frying red pepper strips. I came back and informed Aunt Dot of this.

"Will there be enough for Jim when he comes by?" she asked me, meaning Jim Cherry, the last love of her life, long dead.

I paused and thought about it. "Well, I don't think he'll be coming by, Aunt Dot, but if he did there would be enough for him."

Aunt Dot sighed and looked thoughtful. "Where *do* all our Jims get to?" she asked.

"That," I said, "is a very good question."

"I know!" said Aunt Dot suddenly, with the air of having had a brainstorm. "In that big house of mine—where is it again, New Hampshire?"

"Vermont," I said.

"Vermont," she repeated, a little dreamily. "Why don't we all have dinner there? A good, big dinner. I'll be there, and you. And Jim can come, and Mother and Dad, and Charlotte, and your husband, and that nice man who was here before, with the ponytail" (she meant David) "—we can all have dinner together. Won't that be nice?"

"Yes, Aunt Dot," I said. "It will be."

F

FAGAN, Cary 1957-

Personal

Born 1957, in Toronto, Ontario, Canada; children: two daughters.

Addresses

Home and office—Toronto, Ontario, Canada.

Career

Writers of novels for adults and picture books for young readers.

Awards, Honors

City of Toronto Book Award; Jewish Book Committee Prize for Fiction, 1994, for *The Animals' Waltz*; Sydney Taylor Honor Book, Jewish Book Award, and World Storytelling Award, all 2000, all for *The Market Wedding*; Mr. Christie Silver Medal, 2001, for *Daughter of the Great Zandini*; Norma Fleck Award shortlist for children's nonfiction, 2002, for *Beyond the Dance*.

Writings

FOR CHILDREN

Gogol's Coat, illustrated by Regolo Ricci, Tundra (Plattsburgh, NY), 1998.

The Market Wedding, illustrated by Regolo Ricci, Tundra (Plattsburgh, NY), 2000.

Daughter of the Great Zandini, illustrated by Cybèle Young, Tundra (Plattsburgh, NY), 2001.

(With Chan Hon Goh) *Beyond the Dance* (biography), Tundra (Plattsburgh, NY), 2002.

The Fortress of Kaspar Snit, Tundra (Plattsburgh, NY), 2004.

Directed by Kaspar Snit, Tundra (Plattsburgh, NY), 2007.

Ten Old Men and a Mouse, illustrated by Gary Clement, Tundra (Plattsburgh, NY), 2007.

My New Shirt, illustrated by Dusân Petriĉiĉ, Tundra (Plattsburgh, NY), 2007.

Ten Lessons of Kaspar Snit, Tundra (Plattsburgh, NY), 2008.

FOR ADULTS

History Lessons, Hounslow, 1990.

City Hall and Mrs. God, Mercury (Stratford, Ontario, Canada), 1990.

The Little Black Dress: Tales from France, Mercury (Stratford, Ontario, Canada), 1993.

A Walk by the Seine: Canadian Poets on Paris, Black Moss Press (Windsor, Ontario, Canada), 1995.

The Animals' Waltz, St. Martin's Press (New York, NY), 1996.

The Doctor's House, Paperplates (Toronto, Ontario, Canada), 1996, published as *The Doctor's House and Other Fiction,* Stoddart (Toronto, Ontario, Canada), 2000.

Sleeping Weather, Porcupine's Quill (Erin, Ontario, Canada), 1997.

Felix Roth, Stoddart (Toronto, Ontario, Canada), 1998.

The Mermaid of Paris, Key Porter (Toronto, Ontario, Canada), 2003.

The Little Underworld of Edison Wiese, Hungry I Books (Montreal, Quebec, Canada), 2003.

Contributor to periodicals, including Toronto *Globe and Mail, Montreal Gazette,* and *Books in Canada.*

Sidelights

Cary Fagan's desire to write may have been partially inspired by sibling rivalry. "My two older brothers, my childhood companions, were always better than me in math, geography, history, and most other subjects," the Canadian author recalled on his home page. "The one thing I seemed better at was writing stories and poems." At first, Fagan wrote marionette shows to perform with his cousin at birthday parties, and although he had not been an avid reader as a child, by his teens he was reading the work of Charles Dickens and other literary classics. During college, he won eight student writing awards, and these successes encouraged Fagan to submit stories and poems to small literary magazines. Now a writer for both children and adults, Fagan has published nearly twenty books, from picture books to novels to volumes of poetry. He has also continued to win awards for his work, among them the City of Toronto Book Award and the Jewish Book Committee Prize for Fiction.

Fagan's books for adults include *The Animals' Waltz,* which a *Publishers Weekly* critic considered an "engaging and haunting novel." His first book for younger readers, the picture book *Gogol's Coat,* is loosely based on the tale "The Overcoat" by Nikolai Gogol. Gogol is the youngest but most talented copier working at Office of Alphabet Copiers, where he does not make a lot of money. When cold weather arrives and his old coat is beyond repair, Gogol must buy a new one. This new coat fuels the jealousy of one of his coworkers, and the man steals it, but in the end the young copier discovers the thief. "Fagan's characteristic humor, subtle and keen, also shines," wrote a critic for *Resource Links,* adding that in *Gogol's Coat* "the writing is remarkably childlike and light" and "the story, optimistic." Carolyn Phelan, reviewing the same book in *Booklist,* considered *Gogol's Coat* to be "a distinctive Canadian picture book."

In *The Market Wedding* Fagan takes another popular tale, "A Ghetto Wedding" by Abraham Cahan, and adapts it for young readers. In his story, Morris and Minnie both work in the marketplace; they fall in love and decide to get married. Worried about not having enough money, Morris hatches a plan to make sure Minnie can have the ideal wedding, "which leads to enough complications for a Hollywood cliffhanger," according to Michael Cart in *Booklist.* A *Resource Links* contributor noted that not only would young readers appreciate the book, but *The Market Wedding* will "be a marvelous book for high school students to read and compare with other love stories." Stephanie Zvirin, reviewing the title for *Booklist,* complimented Fagan's "witty text," and in *School Library Journal* Susan Scheps concluded that Fagan's "ironic humor socks home one of life's basic lessons."

Ten Old Men and a Mouse is an original tale of ten lonely men who are the only people left attending their synagogue. When a mouse arrives, they plot to get rid of her, but soon, they begin to identify with her. One notes that he gets an itch in a similar place, while another identifies with the mouse's elaborate yawns. When the mouse has a litter, however, they take them out to the countryside. A year later the mouse returns; like the old men, his children have grown up and moved away. "The witty dialogue and comedic pacing make this book

Cary Fagan's humorous picture book **Ten Old Men and a Mouse** *features Gary Clement's engaging painted illustrations.* (Tundra Books, 2007. Illustration © 2007 by Gary Clement. Reproduced by permission.)

a fun read aloud choice," wrote Linda Ludke in her review of *Ten Old Men and a Mouse* for *Resource Links.*

Fagan's first novel for young readers, *Daughter of the Great Zandini,* recounts the story of Fanny, who is gifted at magic but, because she is a girl, is not expected to follow her father's profession. Instead Fanny's brother, Theodore, who is completely uninterested in magic, is being trained as the Great Zandini's apprentice. Set in Quebec and burnished with a slight French lilt due to Fanny's narration, the story escalates to a confrontation: a challenge to the Great Zandini from a mysterious boy who turns out to be Fanny herself, in disguise. "Fagan's prose is engaging and appears well researched, from the exotic magic tricks to the portrayal of the place of girls" in the early 1800s, wrote Linda Ludke in *School Library Journal.* Connie Frost, reviewing the book for *Resource Links,* deemed *Daughter of the Great Zandini* "a wonderful tale of magic and mystery wrapped into one."

Kaspar Snit, the star of three novels Fagan has written for young readers, is desperate to become the most evil person in the world. In *The Fortress of Kaspar Snit* the Blande family is called in to help solve the mystery of disappearing fountains, a mystery that has Snit at its core. Because Mr. Blande is an expert, the police think he may be able to help solve the crimes, but soon, the Blandes also become a target. Lucky for them, they also moonlight as superheroes. "Fagan's comic novel

Cover of Fagan's novel Directed by Kaspar Snit, *featuring artwork by Marilyn Kovalski.* (Tundra Books, 2007. Reproduced by permission.)

has many enjoyable moments in its highly implausible plot," wrote Jill McClay in *Resource Links,* the critic adding that some "passages are evocative and beautifully written." Snit's diabolical plans continue in *Directed by Kaspar Snit,* as the villain takes over the Blandes' favorite television show. Eva Wilson, reviewing the book for *Resource Links,* considered the tale "an excellent launching pad for discussions on morality, good and evil and the artificial world of television."

Along with his fiction, Fagan has also coauthored Chan Hon Goh's autobiography, *Beyond the Dance: A Ballerina's Life.* The book follows Goh's life, from her immigration from Beijing, China to Vancouver, British Columbia, Canada to her parents' work establishing the Goh Ballet Company. Fagan and Goh discuss both the hardships of Goh's early life and her successes as a member of the National Ballet of Canada. Cheri Estes, writing in *School Library Journal,* considered the book "highly readable."

Discussing his books on his home page, Fagan wrote that "I write for children as much as I write for adults. In fact, I'm usually working on both a kids' book and an adult book, and I think each one influences the other."

Biographical and Critical Sources

PERIODICALS

Booklist, February 1, 1999, review of *Gogol's Coat,* p. 979; December 1, 2000, Michael Cart, review of *The Market Wedding,* p. 706; September 15, 2001, Stephanie Zvirin, review of *The Market Wedding,* p. 225.

Christian Science Monitor, May 8, 1996, Merle Rubin, review of *The Animals' Waltz,* p. 15.

Publishers Weekly, December 18, 1995, review of *The Animals' Waltz,* p. 42.

Resource Links, December, 1998, review of *Gogol's Coat,* p. 3; October, 2000, review of *The Market Wedding,* pp. 1-2; December, 2001, Connie Forst, review of *Daughter of the Great Zandini,* p. 13; April, 2004, Eva Wilson, review of *Directed by Kaspar Snit,* p. 14; June, 2004, Jill McClay, review of *The Fortress of Kaspar Snit,* p. 6; April, 2007, Linda Ludke, review of *Ten Old Men and a Mouse,* p. 2.

School Library Journal, March, 2001, Susan Scheps, review of *The Market Wedding,* p. 208; April, 2002, Linda Ludke, review of *Daughter of the Great Zandini,* p. 109; April, 2003, Cheri Estes, review of *Beyond the Dance,* p. 182; August, 2004, Tim Wadham, review of *The Fortress of Kaspar Snit,* p. 121; March, 2007, Heidi Estrin, review of *Ten Old Men and a Mouse,* p. 160; June, 2007, Elaine E. Knight, review of *Directed by Kaspar Snit,* p. 144.

ONLINE

Canadian Children's Book Centre Web site, http://www.bookcentre.ca/ (December 18, 2007), "Cary Fagan."

Cary Fagan Home Page, http://www.caryfagan.com (December 18, 2007).

Random House Web site, http://www.randomhouse.com/ (December 18, 2007), profile of Fagan.

Transatlantic Literary Agency Web site, http://www.tla1.com/ (December 18, 2007), "Cary Fagan."*

*   *   *

FARNSWORTH, Bill 1958-

Personal

Born October 11, 1958, in Norwalk, CT; son of John M. and Gloria Farnsworth; married Deborah M. Jajer (a school teacher), October 6, 1984; children: Allison Marie, Caitlin Elizabeth. *Education:* Ringling School of Art, degree (with honors), 1980.

Addresses

Office—99 Merryall Rd., New Milford, CT 06776. *E-mail*—bill@billfarnsworth.com.

Career

Illustrator, beginning 1980.

Bill Farnsworth (Reproduced by permission.)

Illustrator

The Illustrated Children's Bible, Harcourt (San Diego, CA), 1993, portion published as *The Illustrated Children's Old Testament,* 1993.

Dorothy and Thomas Hoobler, *French Portraits,* Raintree Steck-Vaughn (Austin, TX), 1994.

Sanna Baker, *Grandpa Is a Flyer,* Albert Whitman (Morton Grove, IL), 1994.

Cheryl Ryan, *Sally Arnold,* Cobblehill Books/Dutton (New York, NY), 1995.

Janice Cohn, *The Christmas Menorahs: How a Town Fought Hate,* Albert Whitman (Morton Grove, IL), 1995.

Ronald Kidd, *Grandpa's Hammer,* Habitat for Humanity International (Americus, GA), 1995.

Mary Quattlebaum, reteller, *Jesus and the Children,* Time-Life Kids (Alexandria, VA), 1995.

Darice Bailer, *The Last Rail: The Building of the First Transcontinental Railroad,* Soundprints (Norwalk, CT), 1996.

Sanna Anderson Baker, *Mississippi Going North,* Albert Whitman (Morton Grove, IL), 1996.

Andrew Gutelle, reteller, *David and Goliath,* Time-Life Kids (Alexandria, VA), 1996.

Nan Ferring Nelson, *My Days with Anica,* Lothrop (New York, NY), 1996.

Kathleen V. Kudlinski, *Shannon: A Chinatown Adventure, San Francisco, 1880,* Aladdin (New York, NY), 1997.

Kathleen V. Kudlinski, *Shannon, Lost and Found: San Francisco, 1880,* Aladdin (New York, NY), 1997.

Kathleen V. Kudlinski, *Shannon: The Schoolmarm Mysteries, San Francisco, 1880,* Aladdin (New York, NY), 1997.

Elizabeth Van Steenwyk, *My Name Is York,* Rising Moon (Flagstaff, AZ), 1997.

Susan Korman, *Horse Raid: An Arapaho Camp in the 1800s,* Soundprints (Norwalk, CT), 1998.

Steven Kroll, *Robert Fulton: From Submarine to Steamboat,* Holiday House (New York, NY), 1999.

Marcia K. Vaughan, *Abbie against the Storm: The True Story of a Young Heroine and a Lighthouse,* Beyond Words (Portland, OR), 1999.

Claire Sidhom Matze, *The Stars in My Geddoh's Sky,* Albert Whitman (Morton Grove, IL), 1999.

Richard Ammon, *Conestoga Wagons,* Holiday House (New York, NY), 2000.

Elizabeth Van Steenwyk, *When Abraham Talked to the Trees,* Eerdmans (Grand Rapids, MI), 2000.

Avi, *Prairie School: A Story,* HarperCollins (New York, NY), 2001.

Linda Oatman High, *A Humble Life: Plain Poems,* Eerdmans (Grand Rapids, MI), 2001.

Nan Gurley, *Twice Yours: A Parable of God's Gift,* Zonderkidz (Grand Rapids, MI), 2001.

Janet Beeler Shaw, *Meet Kaya: An American Girl,* Pleasant Company (Middleton, WI), 2002.

Janet Beeler Shaw, *Kaya and Lone Dog: A Friendship Story,* Pleasant Company (Middleton, WI), 2002.

Janet Beeler Shaw, *Kaya Shows the Way: A Sister Story,* Pleasant Company (Middleton, WI), 2002.

Janet Beeler Shaw, *Kaya's Hero: A Story of Giving,* Pleasant Company (Middleton, WI), 2002.

Janet Beeler Shaw, *Changes for Kaya: A Story of Courage,* Pleasant Company (Middleton, WI), 2002.

Janet Beeler Shaw, *Kaya's Escape: A Survival Story,* Pleasant Company (Middleton, WI), 2002.

David A. Adler, *A Hero and the Holocaust; The Story of Janusz Korczak and His Children,* Holiday House (New York, NY), 2002.

Gary D. Schmidt, *The Great Stone Face: A Retelling of a Tale by Nathaniel Hawthorne,* Eerdmans (Grand Rapids, MI), 2002.

Lenice Strohmeier, *Mingo,* Marshall Cavendish (New York, NY), 2002.

Darice Bailer, *Railroad!: A Story of the Transcontinental Railroad,* Soundprints (Norwalk, CT), 2003.

Pam Flowers, *Big-enough Anna: The Little Sled Dog Who Braved the Arctic,* Alaska Northwest (Anchorage, AK), 2003.

Karyn Henley, *Gram's Song,* Tyndale House (Wheaton, IL), 2003.

Nancy LeSourd, *Christy: Christmastime at Cutter Gap* (based on a novel by Catherine Marshall), Zonderkidz (Grand Rapids, MI), 2003.

Janet Beeler Shaw, *Kaya and the River Girl,* Pleasant Company (Middletown, WI), 2003.

Janet Beeler Shaw, *Kaya's Story Collection,* Pleasant Company (Middletown, WI), 2003.

Elizabeth Van Steenwyk, *One Fine Day: A Radio Play,* Eerdmans (Grand Rapids, MI), 2003.

Richard Ammon, *Valley Forge,* Holiday House (New York, NY), 2004.

Tracy Leininger Craven, *Our Flag Was Still There: The Story of the Star-spangled Banner,* His Seasons (San Antonio, TX), 2004.

Julie Dunlap, *John Muir and Stickeen: An Icy Adventure with a No-Good Dog,* NorthWord (Chanhassen, MN), 2004.

Deborah Hopkinson, *Adventure in Gold Town,* Aladdin (New York, NY), 2004.

Deborah Hopkinson, *The Long Trail,* Aladdin (New York, NY), 2004.

Deborah Hopkinson, *Sailing for Gold,* Aladdin (New York, NY), 2004.

Nan Gurley, *What Color Is Love?: A Parable of God's Gifts,* Zonderkidz (Grand Rapids, MI), 2005.

Laurie Lears, *Megan's Birthday Tree: A Story about Open Adoption,* Albert Whitman (Morton Grove, IL), 2005.

Virginia Driving Hawk Sneve, *Bad River Boys: A Meeting of the Lakota Sioux with Lewis and Clark,* Holiday House (New York, NY), 2005.

Susan Goldman Rubin, *The Flag with Fifty-six Stars: A Gift from the Survivors of Mauthausen,* Holiday House (New York, NY), 2005.

Janet Beeler Shaw, *Kaya's Short Story Collection,* Pleasant Company (Middleton, WI), 2006.

David A. Adler, *Heroes for Civil Rights,* Holiday House (New York, NY), 2007.

Ruth Vander Zee, *Eli Remembers,* Eerdmans (Grand Rapids, MI), 2007.

Bill Wise, *Louis Sockalexis: Native American Baseball Pioneer,* Lee & Low (New York, NY), 2007.

Joseph Bruchac, *Buffalo Song,* Lee & Low (New York, NY), 2008.

Linda Oatman High, *Tenth Avenue Cowboy,* Eerdmans (Grand Rapids, MI), 2008.

Susan Goldman Rubin, *Simon Wiesenthal: He Never Forgot,* Holiday House (New York, NY), 2009.

Sidelights

A painter, Bill Farnsworth has contributed illustrations to numerous works for children written by prominent authors such as Avi, Steven Kroll, and David A. Adler. Farnsworth often receives high marks from reviewers for his oil paintings, which are recognized for their ability to harmonize with the author's text. "The artist excels at landscapes, but his faces are also wonderfully impressive," wrote Kay Weisman in reviewing Farnsworth's work for Gary D. Schmidt's *The Great Stone Face: A Retelling of a Tale by Nathaniel Hawthorne.* Interestingly, Farnsworth did not begin his career as a painter in oils. "I started out drawing cartoons," he explained to James Roland for the *Sarasota Herald Tribune.* "I would draw Donald Duck really well. I'd sell them to other kids for a nickel a piece until the teacher caught me and made me sit in the back of the class and give all the money back."

In his work for Cheryl Ryan's *Sally Arnold,* Farnsworth brings to life the book's story about young Jenny Fox and Sally Arnold, a garbage-collecting town eccentric, as the two develop a friendship. "Farnsworth's beautiful, light-filled paintings steal the show," observed *Booklist* critic Lauren Peterson, while a *Publishers Weekly* critic described Farnsworth's paintings as "hazy, nostalgic affairs" that reflect the story's "genial use of familiar conventions." Several of Farnsworth's illustration projects depict unconventional friendships. With a story by Lenice Strohmeier, *Mingo* is a tale about a slave who is given his freedom, and the little girl who has considered him her friend and now does not want him to leave. The book's "dramatic oil paintings focus on the tender relationship," concluded Linda Perkins in her *Booklist* review of the book.

A traditional Native-American event is captured in Farnsworth's illustrations for Peter Roop's *The Buffalo Jump.* According to *School Library Journal* critic Celia A. Huffman, the illustrator's "oil representations depict the culture, setting, and lifestyle of the Blackfeet nation." Also referring to Farnsworth's art, a *Publishers Weekly* critic commented that "his dramatic scenes of stampeding buffalo churning up clouds of dust add suspense." Farnsworth has illustrated several other tales with Native-American themes, including Janet Beeler Shaw's "American Girl" series books featuring Kaya, a Nez Perce girl living in 1764. Farnsworth traveled to Nez Perce communities in Idaho and Washington state to gather the details he incorporates into his drawings for the "Kaya" books, and his work has received the support of the Nez Perce tribe's executive committee.

Another Native-American perspective is explored in his work for Virginia Driving Hawk Sneve's *Bad River Boys: A Meeting of the Lakota Sioux with Lewis and Clark.* Discussing this book, a *Kirkus Reviews* contributor wrote that "Farnsworth's oil paintings put the setting in the early 1800s and depict the landscape, the Native Americans and the explorers in an accurate and respectful manner." *Louis Sockalexis: Native American Baseball Pioneer,* Bill Wise's biography of a notable Native American, features "color-drenched paintings [that] do an excellent job of bringing this period to life and capturing the intense emotion of the ballpark drama," according to Marilyn Taniguchi in *School Library Journal.*

Farnsworth contributed art to *Abbie against the Storm,* a book written by Marcia K. Vaughan. Based on a true-life story, the work follows a young girl who struggles to keep two important lighthouses lit during a stretch of forbidding weather. The events are depicted in pictures that "make the violently changing moods of the sea so palpable that readers can feel her danger and celebrate her courage," claimed *School Library Journal* critic Margaret A. Chang. Writing in *Publishers Weekly,* a contributor credited Farnsworth's artwork for adding to the story's suspense, writing that his "resplendent paintings of the turbulent seas heighten the drama and lend the tale immediacy." Moving to quieter terrain, Farnsworth's illustrations also appear in *A Humble Life: Plain Poems,* a book of verse written by Linda Oatman High. *Booklist* reviewer Susan Dove Lempke remarked that "the poems and the paintings offer a quiet, pleasurable reading experience," and Sharon Korbeck wrote in *School Library Journal* that "the seamless meshing of words and illustrations creates anything but 'plain poems.'"

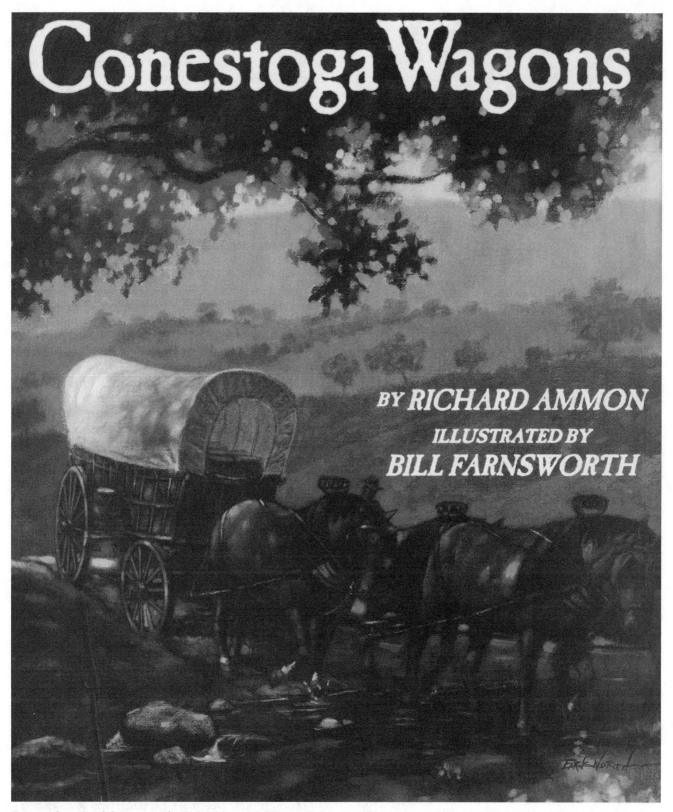

Farnsworth produced the cover art for Richard Ammon's 2000 novel, Conestoga Wagons. (Holiday House, Inc., 2000. Illustration copyright © by Bill Farnsworth. Reproduced by permission of Holiday House, Inc.)

From parables to biographies to historical fiction, Farnsworth's illustrations work to enhance the mood of the text. In Nan Gurley's *Twice Yours: A Parable of God's Gift,* his "lovely, sun-dappled paintings lighten the tale," according to Shelley Townsend-Hudson in *Booklist. A Hero and the Holocaust: The Story of Janusz Korczak and His Children,* with a text by David A. Adler, is accompanied by "somber and atmospheric watercolors,"

Farnsworth contributes his detailed, well-researched art to Janet Shaw's middle-grade novel Kaya's Hero, *part of the "American Girl" series.* (American Girl, 2002. Copyright © 2002 by American Girl, LLC. Reproduced by permission of American Girl Publishing.)

wrote a contributor to *Kirkus Reviews.* Hazel Rochman, writing about the same book in *Booklist,* proclaimed that Farnsworth's "illustrations, oil paintings on linen in sepia tones, are unforgettable." Of Pam Flowers' action-oriented *Big Enough Anna: The Little Sled Dog Who Braved the Arctic,* Maryann H. Owen wrote in *School Library Journal* that "Farnsworth's soft, sunlit oil paintings convey the cold and vast expanse of the northern climes while deftly depicting the action."

Some of Farnsworth's illustration projects require him to depict specific historic events. Of his depiction of the Wright Brothers' flight at Kitty Hawk, North Carolina in Elizabeth Van Steenwyk's *One Fine Day: A Radio Play,* a *Publishers Weekly* critic wrote that "Farnsworth's oil on linen portraits strike just the right balance between realism and fancy." Nancy Menaldi-Scanlan, in *School Library Journal,* wrote of the same book that the "paintings . . . not only elucidate but also expand upon the text." In *Valley Forge,* an introduction to the life of General George Washington and the Revolutionary War written by Richard Ammon, Farnsworth's "solid oil paintings effectively portray the soldiers in action and in reflection," according to Carolyn Phelan in *Booklist.* Naturalist John Muir's travels in Alaska are the subject of Julie Dunlop's *John Muir and Stickeen:*

An Icy Adventure with a No-Good Dog, and here "Farnsworth's painterly oils capture the grandeur of the landscape," in the opinion of *Booklist* contributor Jennifer Mattson. Sean George reviewed the same title in *School Library Journal,* writing that "Farnsworth's illustrations are as majestic as the setting and as personable as the characters." A story about the prisoners of Mauthausen, a Nazi slave labor camp that was ultimately liberated by Allied forces during World War II, is the focus of Susan Goldman Rubin's *The Flag with Fifty-six Stars: A Gift from the Survivors of Mauthausen.* "Farnsworth's realistic oil-on-linen paintings" for this book were judged as "nothing short of extraordinary" by a *Publishers Weekly* contributor.

Farnsworth once told *SATA:* "Real people and events that have in some way influenced our lives are the core of what I paint. From book jackets, children's books, and magazine illustration to private portrait commissions and limited-edition prints and plates, the research involved with a particular painting can be quite extensive, especially if it is some kind of historical matter. Whatever the wide variety of subject matter might be, my personal goal is to give the client more than what they asked for and aim for the very best painting I've ever done. The whole process of reading a manuscript, doing the research, and producing the finished art is very exciting and fun. An artist must continually grow with every project in order to improve and sharpen his skills as a draftsman. And what will ultimately make your personal view unique is what you have to say from your heart."

Biographical and Critical Sources

PERIODICALS

Booklist, April 1, 1995, Hazel Rochman, review of *Grandpa Is a Flyer,* p. 1422; May 1, 1996, Lauren Peterson, review of *Sally Arnold,* p. 1513; September 15, 1996, Leone McDermott, review of *My Day with Anka,* p. 249; October 15, 1996, Hazel Rochman, review of *The Last Rail: The Building of the First Transcontinental Railroad,* p. 46; May 15, 1999, Hazel Rochman, review of *The Stars in My Geddoh's Sky,* p. 1702; December 15, 2001, Susan Dove Lempke, review of *A Humble Life: Plain Poems,* p. 734; February 1, 2002, Shelley Townsend-Hudson, review of *Twice Yours: A Parable of God's Gift,* p. 946; October 1, 2002, Kay Weisman, review of *The Great Stone Face,* p. 327; December 1, 2002, Hazel Rochman, review of *A Hero and the Holocaust: The Story of Janusz Korczak and His Children,* p. 658; January 1, 2003, Julie Cummins, review of *One Fine Day: A Radio Play,* p. 886; January 1, 2003, Karen Hutt, review of *Kaya's Escape!,* p. 893; June 1, 2003, Linda Perkins, review of *Mingo,* p. 1779; January 1, 2004, Hazel Rochman, review of *Sailing for Gold,* p. 856; September 15, 2004, Carolyn Phelan, review of *Valley*

Forge, p. 236; November 15, 2004, Jennifer Mattson, review of *John Muir and Stickeen: An Icy Adventure with a No-Good Dog,* p. 588; March 1, 2005, Jennifer Mattson, review of *Megan's Birthday Tree: A Story about Open Adoption,* p. 1204; March 15, 2005, Hazel Rochman, review of *The Flag with Fifty-six Stars: A Gift from the Survivors of Mauthausen,* p. 1292; November 15, 2005, Gillian Engberg, review of *Bad River Boys: A Meeting of the Lakota Sioux with Lewis and Clark,* p. 53; February 15, 2007, Ian Chipman, review of *By the Sword: A Young Man Meets War,* p. 74; July 1, 2007, GraceAnne A. DeCandido, review of *Louis Sockalexis: Native American Baseball Pioneer,* p. 53; July 1, 2007, Hazel Rochman, review of *Eli Remembers,* p. 59.

Bulletin of the Center for Children's Books, April, 2005, Hope Morrison, review of *The Flag with Fifty-six Stars,* p. 356.

Childhood Education, fall, 2007, Connie Green, review of *By the Sword,* p. 48.

Children's Bookwatch, December, 2004, review of *John Muir and Stickeen.*

Kirkus Reviews, September 15, 2002, review of *A Hero and the Holocaust,* p. 1382; January 1, 2003, review of *One Fine Day,* p. 67; March 1, 2003, review of *Mingo,* p. 399; February 1, 2004, review of *Sailing for Gold,* p. 134; June 15, 2004, review of *The Long*

Farnsworth deals with an inspiring topic in his paintings for Susan Goldman Rubin's **The Flag with Fifty-six Stars.** (Holiday House, Inc., 2006. Illustrations copyright © by Bill Farnsworth. Reproduced by permission of Holiday House, Inc.)

Trail, p. 577; August 1, 2004, review of *Valley Forge,* p. 737; October 15, 2004, review of *John Muir and Stickeen,* p. 1005; April 1, 2005, review of *The Flag of Fifty-six Stars,* p. 423; September 1, 2005, review of *Bad River Boys,* p. 983.

Publishers Weekly, September 18, 1995, review of *The Christmas Menorahs: How a Town Fought Hate,* p. 103; May 13, 1996, review of *Sally Arnold,* p. 76; August 19, 1996, review of *The Buffalo Jump,* p. 67; February 3, 1997, review of *The Last Rail,* p. 46; February 7, 2000, review of *Abbie against the Storm: The True Story of a Young Heroine and a Lighthouse,* p. 85; June 24, 2002, "Native American Girl," p. 59; November 4, 2002, review of *The Great Stone Face,* p. 87; January 20, 2003, "First in Flight," p. 85; March 21, 2005, review of *The Flag with Fifty-six Stars,* p. 51; September 24, 2007, review of *Eli Remembers,* p. 71.

Reading Teacher, March, 2003, review of *A Hero and the Holocaust,* p. 585.

Sarasota Herald Tribune, November 25, 2003, James Roland, "Illustrator's Artistic Adventures: Bill Farnsworth Talks to Students about a Nez Perce Indian Character He Drew for a Book," p. BV1.

School Library Journal, July, 1995, Carole D. Fiore, review of *Grandpa Is a Flyer,* p. 54; October, 1995, Jane Marino, review of *The Christmas Menorahs,* p. 103; April, 1996, Jane Marino, review of *Sally Arnold,* p. 116; September, 1996, Leda Schubert, review of *My Day with Anka,* p. 186; October, 1996, Melissa Hudak, review of *Mississippi Going North,* p. 111; February, 1997, Celia A. Huffman, review of *The Buffalo Jump;* April, 1999, Rosie Peasley, review of *Robert Fulton: From Submarine to Steamboat,* p. 115; May, 1999, Diane S. Marton, review of *The Stars in My Geddoh's Sky,* p. 93; July, 2000, Margaret A. Chang, review of *Abbie against the Storm,* p. 89; September, 2000, Anne Chapman, review of *Conestoga Wagons,* p. 213; December, 2000, Marlene Gawron, review of *When Abraham Talked to the Trees,* p. 137; May, 2001, Carol Schene, review of *Prairie School,* p. 108; October, 2001, Sharon Korbeck, review of *A Humble Life,* p. 140; November, 2002, Grace Oliff, review of *The Great Stone Face,* p. 135; January, 2003, Alicia Eames, review of *The Stars in My Geddoh's Sky,* p. 84; March, 2003, Martha Link, review of *A Hero and the Holocaust,* p. 212; April, 2003, Nancy Menaldi-Scanlan, review of *One Fine Day,* p. 193; June, 2003, Susan Scheps, review of *Mingo,* p. 120; January, 2004, Maryann H. Owen, review of *Big-enough Anna: The Little Sled Dog Who Braved the Arctic,* p. 114; March, 2004, Sandra Kitain, review of *Gram's Song,* p. 170; July, 2004, Anne Knickerbocker, review of *Sailing for Gold,* p. 77; October, 2004, Lynda Ritterman, review of *Valley Forge,* p. 184; November, 2004, Anne Knickerbocker, review of *The Long Trail,* p. 107; December, 2004, Sean George, review of *John Muir and Stickeen,* p. 106; May, 2005, Anne Chapman Callaghan, review of *The Flag with Fifty-six Stars,* p. 116; June, 2005, Deborah Vose, review of *Megan's Birthday Tree,* p. 120; November, 2005, Marilyn Taniguchi, review of *Bad River Boys,* p. 108; March, 2007, Ann Welton, review of *By the*

Sword, p. 225; May, 2007, Marilyn Taniguchi, review of *Louis Sockalexis,* p. 127.

Tribune Books (Chicago, IL), April 22, 2007, Mary Harris Russell, review of *Louis Sockalexis,* p. 9.

ONLINE

Bill Farnsworth Home Page, http://www.billfarnsworth. com (December 21, 2007).

Houghton Mifflin Web site, http://www.eduplace.com/kids/ (December 21, 2007), "Bill Farnsworth."

HarperCollins Web site, http://www.harpercollinschildrens. com/ (December 21, 2007), "Bill Farnsworth."

*   *   *

FLORES-GALBIS, Enrique 1952-

Personal

Born 1952, in Havana, Cuba; immigrated to United States, 1961; naturalized citizen; son of an architect and an educator; married Laurel Ives (a graphic artist); children: two daughters. *Education:* Central Connecticut State University, B.S. (art education); studied at New York University; Parsons School of Design, M.F.A., 1992; also studied at Art Students' League, National Academy of Design, and Pratt Institute.

Addresses

Home—Forest Hills, NY. *Agent*—Stimola Literary Studio, 306 Chase Ct., Edgewater, NJ 07020. *E-mail*— efg@efgportraits.com.

Career

Portrait and landscape painter, art teacher, and author. Member of faculty of Visual Arts Center of New Jersey, Summit, for twenty years, and Parsons School of Design for sixteen years; also teaches at Morris Museum and Montclair Museum; teaches private landscape-painting workshops in United States and Europe. *Exhibitions:* Work exhibited at Museum of Contemporary Hispanic Art and National Arts Club.

Awards, Honors

Cintas Foundation fellowship, 1980-81, 1985-86; Helena Rubenstein fellowship; Phillip Lehrman Award.

Writings

Raining Sardines (young-adult novel), Roaring Brook Press (New Milford, CT), 2007.

Sugar in the Rain (young-adult novel), Roaring Brook Press (New Milford, CT), 2008.

Sidelights

Painter and educator Enrique Flores-Galbis is the author of *Raining Sardines,* a critically acclaimed novel for young adults. A native of Cuba, Flores-Galbis and his two older brothers immigrated to the United States during "Operation Pedro Pan," a mass exodus of 14,000 children that left Cuba in 1961. "At the time I didn't know how disillusioned my family was becoming with [Communist dictator Fidel] Castro, even though he and my father had been friends at the University of Havana," Flores-Galbis told Marian H. Mundy in the Newark *Star-Ledger.* After Flores-Galbis arrived in Florida, he was placed in a refugee camp for several months. "I didn't know what would become of me," he recalled to Mundy. "All I had from Cuba was memories. I hugged them tight for comfort." With the help of relatives, his parents eventually made their way to the United States, and the family settled in southern New England. Flores-Galbis's second novel, *Sugar in the Rain,* centers around this cross-cultural journey.

Flores-Galbis attended Central Connecticut State University, earning a bachelor's degree in art education, and then studied painting at New York University with photo-realist Adelle Weber. He also studied at the Art Students' League with portraitist Daniel Greene and at the National Academy of Design with Raymond Everett Kinstler. In 1992, Flores-Galbis received a master of fine arts degree from Parsons School of Design. He lectures at the Visual Art Center of New Jersey and the Metropolitan Museum of Art in New York City. He also teaches private landscape painting workshops in the United States and Europe.

Raining Sardines, Flores-Galbis's debut work of fiction, was inspired by his return trip to his Cuban homeland in 1996. "I felt I was home geographically," the artist and author related to Mundy. "The place, not historical facts, made me feel tied to it. The earth, the sand, the sea all remembered me, and I belonged to them."

In *Raining Sardines* Flores-Galbis introduces nine-year-old Enriquito, a logical thinker with a gift for engineering solutions to problems, and eleven-year-old Ernestina, an emotional and imaginative artist. The two friends live in a small fishing village in pre-revolutionary Cuba, in the shadow of a jungle-covered mountain that overlooks the bay where pirates once looted Spanish galleons filled with gold. According to local legend, the mountain is inhabited by the spirit of Hatuey, the leader of the Taino. Native to the region, the Taino thwarted the invading Spaniards by following Hatuey's command and tossing their gold into a lake in a hidden valley. When Don Rigol, a wealthy and powerful Spanish-born landowner, lays claim to a nearby mountain and begins clearing the jungle to make room for his coffee plantation, he endangers the herd of wild Paso Fino ponies living in the mountain wilderness. Enriquito and Ernestina oppose Rigol's efforts, and they eventually learn that the Don is actually searching for the missing treasure. According to *School Library Journal* reviewer Kathy Piehl, Flores-Galbis's "story intersperses episodes of magical realism with . . . adventure sequences" such as Enriquito's dramatic escape from jail and Ernestina's encounter with a Cayman. Although a contributor in *Kirkus Reviews* stated that the story's "happy ending is never in doubt," the critic noted that "the Cuban cultural elements add flavor and spice" to Flores-Galbis's novel. Writing in *Booklist,* Hazel Rochman predicted that the author's effort to address "urgent conservation issues will strike a chord with kids everywhere."

Biographical and Critical Sources

PERIODICALS

Booklist, April 1, 2007, Hazel Rochman, review of *Raining Sardines,* p. 40.

Bulletin of the Center for Children's Books, June, 2007, Hope Morrison, review of *Raining Sardines,* p. 413.

Kirkus Reviews, February 15, 2007, review of *Raining Sardines.*

New York Times, May 28, 1989, Vivien Raynor, "Duality of Existence in Latin Works."

School Library Journal, April, 2007, Kathy Piehl, review of *Raining Sardines,* p. 134.

Star-Ledger (Newark, NJ), May 15, 1997, Marian H. Mundy, "Cuban-American Artist Goes Home Again to Refresh Memory," p. 1, and "At One with the Land, Not the People," p. 6.

ONLINE

Enrique Flores-Galbis Home Page, http://www.efgportraits.com (December 1, 2007).

* * *

FORMAN, Ruth 1970-

Personal

Born 1970. *Education:* University of California—Berkeley, B.A.

Addresses

Home and office—Los Angeles, CA.

Career

Poet, filmmaker, and teacher. Voices of Our Nation Arts Foundation, teacher. Presenter at workshops and poetry performances, including for Public Broadcasting System television series *The United States of Poetry,* National Black Arts Festival, and National Public Radio. Judge for poetry competitions, including PEN USA West awards, 2001. Actor on stage for *For an End to the Judgment of God/Kissing God Goodbye.*

Member

PEN USA West.

Awards, Honors

Barnard New Women Poets Prize, 1993, and Popular Paperback citation, American Library Association, 2001, both for *We Are the Young Musicians*; Josephine Miles Award for Poetry, PEN Oakland, 1999, for *Renaissance*; Durfee artist fellowship, 2001.

Writings

We Are the Young Magicians, Beacon (Boston, MA), 1993.
Renaissance, Beacon (Boston, MA), 1997.
Young Cornrows Callin out the Moon, illustrated by Cbabi Bayoc, Children's Book Press (San Francisco, CA), 2007.

Sidelights

When poet and filmmaker Ruth Forman was growing up, she spent many summers on the brownstone steps of her aunts' and uncles' homes in Philadelphia. Forman drew on these memories in her poetry picture book *Young Cornrows Callin out the Moon.* In addition to her writing, Forman participates as a teacher in poetry workshops and as a performer both on stage and on the radio, sharing her poetry orally.

Young Cornrows Callin out the Moon draws readers into a summer day in South Philadelphia where children's days are rich with the promise of lemonade and the sound of the ice-cream truck, and time is spent dancing in the streets. Forman's young characters play double Dutch and freeze tag, and mothers bake corn bread. The author's rhyming text "is sweet and evocative of a blissful childhood filled with tastes and sights and sounds that seem idyllic," noted Mary Hazelton in *School Library Journal.* In *Booklist,* Hazel Rochman wrote that "every page of this book shows the fun they have in the lively urban community."

In addition to her picture book, Forman is the author of poetry collections that include *We Are the Young Magicians,* which won the Barnard New Women Poets Prize. "What a reader of poetry looks for in a poet is the clear eye, the telling word, the communicating heart. Each is found in effortless abundance in the four generous sections that comprise this book," wrote Gloria Oden in a review of Forman's debut for *MELUS.* Donna Seaman, reviewing the work for *Booklist* described *We Are the Young Magicians* as "dazzling, [with] each poem a veritable fireworks display." According to Seaman, Forman's collection titled *Renaissance* includes poems that read "like carefully banked embers." Ann K. van Buren, reviewing *Renaissance* for *Library Journal,* noted that, here, the collected verses "celebrate language and cultural roots," and a *Publishers Weekly* critic observed that Forman "demonstrates a strong rhythmic sense in her musical repetitions and in her keen use of black vernacular."

Biographical and Critical Sources

PERIODICALS

Booklist, March 15, 1993, Donna Seaman, review of *We Are the Young Magicians,* p. 1292; February 15, 1998, Donna Seaman, review of *Renaissance,* p. 970; February 1, 2007, Hazel Rochman, review of *Young Cornrows Callin out the Moon,* p. 60.

Bulletin of the Center for Children's Books, June, 2007, Deborah Stevenson, review of *Young Cornrows Callin out the Moon,* p. 414.

Library Journal, January, 1998, Ann K. van Buren, review of *Renaissance,* p. 104.

MELUS, fall, 1993, Gloria Oden, review of *We Are the Young Magicians,* p. 111.

Publishers Weekly, March 22, 1993, review of *We Are the Young Magicians,* p. 75; January 26, 1998, review of *Renaissance,* p. 88.

School Library Journal, March, 2007, Mary Hazelton, review of *Young Cornrows Callin out the Moon,* p. 195.

Women's Review of Books, October, 1993, Adrian Oktenberg, review of *We Are the Young Magicians,* p. 23.

ONLINE

Montalvo Arts Center Web site, http://montalvoarts.org/ (December 21, 2007), profile of Forman.

Poetry for the People Web site, http://poetryforthepeople.org/ (December 21, 2007), profile of Forman.

World of Poetry Web site, http://www.worldofpoetry.org/ (December 21, 2007), profile of Forman.*

*   *   *

FRANKLIN, Madeleine
See L'ENGLE, Madeleine

*   *   *

FRANKLIN, Madeleine L'Engle
See L'ENGLE, Madeleine

*   *   *

FRANKLIN, Madeleine L'Engle Camp
See L'ENGLE, Madeleine

*   *   *

FRENCH, Jackie 1953-
(Jackie Anne French)

Personal

Born November 30, 1953, in Sydney, New South Wales, Australia; daughter of Barrie (a management consultant) and Valerie (a social reformer) French; married David Dumaresq (divorced); married Bryan Sullivan, January 20, 1988; children: (first marriage) Edward. *Education:* University of Queensland, B.A. *Politics:* "Fluctuating." *Religion:* "Nonspecific."

Addresses

Home—P.O. Box 63, Braidwood, New South Wales 2622, Australia. *E-mail*—jackief@dragnet.com.au.

Career

Author. Worked variously as a sugar packer, cook, journalist, chambermaid, and as a gopher for a private detective; public servant, 1973-75; farmer, 1975-85; writer, 1985—. Director, Wombat Foundation.

Member

Australian Society of Authors, Braidwood Historical Society, Araluen Bush Fire Brigade.

Awards, Honors

New South Wales Premier's Award, 1991; Children's Book Award shortlist, New South Wales Premier's Literary Awards, 1991, Children's Book Council of Australia (CBCA) Award shortlist, 1992, and West Australian Young Readers Book Award (WAYRBA) shortlist, Primary Age Readers, 1993, all for *Rainstones;* Notable Book designation, CBCA, 1992, for *The Roo That Won the Melbourne Cup;* Wilderness Society Award, 1993; Royal Blind Society Talking Book of the Year designation, 1994; Human Rights Award, Talking Book of the Year shortlist, Australian Multicultural Children's Literature Award shortlist, and Notable Book designation, CBCA, all 1994, all for *Walking the Boundaries;* Family Award high commendation, New South Wales Family Therapy Association/Victorian Association of Family Therapists, and Honor Book designation, CBCA, both 1995, both for *Somewhere around the Corner;* Book of the Year designation, CBCA, 1999, for *Daughter of the Regiment;* Eve Pownall Award for Information shortlist, CBCA, 2000, for *How to Guzzle Your Garden;* Book of the Year Award, CBCA, and Sanderson Young Adult Audio Book of the Year shortlist, Vision Australia Library, both 2000, WAYRBA shortlist, Young Australian's Best Book Award (YABBA) shortlist, and Books I Love Best Yearly Award (BILBY) shortlist, all 2001, and KOALA shortlist, Children Choice Book Awards (Sweden) shortlist, and UK National Literacy Association WOW! Award, all 2002, all for *Hitler's Daughter;* Notable Book citations, CBCA, 2001, for *Lady Dance, Stamp, Stomp, Whomp,* and *Missing You, Love Sara;* WAYRBA shortlist, 2001, and KOALA shortlist and YABBA shortlist, both 2002, all for *Missing You, Love Sara;* Notable Book designation, CBCA, for *Felix Smith Has Every Right to Be a Crocodile, Little Book of Big Questions, The Fascinating History of Your Lunch,* and *How the Finnegans Saved the Ship;* Wilderness Society Book of the Year shortlist, for *Hairy Charlie and the Frog;* Book of the Year award,

Australian Capital Territory, 2002, for *In the Blood;* Aurealis Award, Australian Science Fiction, 2002, for *The Café on Callisto;* ABA/Neilson Data Book of the Year award, and Honor Book designation, CBCA, KOALA Award for Best Picture Book, YABBA shortlist, Lemmee Award, Notable Children's Book designation, American Library Association, and Favorite Picture Book of the Year award, Cuffie Awards, all 2003, Benjamin Franklin Award, and Humpty Dumpty Picture Book of the Year honor, Mid-South Independent Booksellers Association, both 2004, and BILBY Award shortlist, 2007, all for *Diary of a Wombat;* Notable Book designation, CBCA, and Patricia Wrightson Award shortlist, both 2003, both for *Ride the Wild Wind;* Notable Book designation, and KOALA shortlist, both 2004, both for *Too Many Pears;* Notable Book designation, CBCA, 2004, for *Valley of Gold;* Aurealis Award for Best Young Adult Novel shortlist, 2004, for *Flesh and Blood;* KOALA award shortlist, 2005, for *Pete the Sheep;* Eve Pownall Award, 2005, for *To the Moon and Back;* Young People's History Prize shortlist, New South Wales Premier's History Awards, 2006, and WAY-BRA shortlist, 2007, both for *They Came on Viking Ships;* New South Wales Premier's Literary Awards shortlist, 2006, for *The Secret World of Wombats;* YABBA shortlist, Australian Book Industry Award in Younger-Reader category, and Notable Book designations, CBCA, all 2007, all for *Josephine Wants to Dance;* YABBA shortlist and Notable Book designation, CBCA, both 2007, both for *The Goat Who Sailed the World;* CBCA Award shortlist in Younger Readers category, 2007, for *Macbeth and Son;* Australian nominee for Hans Christian Andersen Award, 2008; numerous child-selected awards; named Australian Capital Territory Children's Ambassador.

Writings

FOR YOUNG READERS

(Self-illustrated) *Smudge,* Childerset (Australia), 1988.

Rainstones (short stories), Angus & Robertson (Pymble, New South Wales, Australia), 1991.

The Roo That Won the Melbourne Cup, illustrated by Carol McLean-Carr, HarperCollins (Pymble, New South Wales, Australia), 1991.

The Boy Who Had Wings, HarperCollins (Pymble, New South Wales, Australia), 1992.

Walking the Boundaries, illustrated by Bronwyn Bancroft, Angus & Robertson (Pymble, New South Wales, Australia), 1993.

Hairy Charlie and the Frog, illustrated by Dee Huxley, CIS (Carlton, Victoria, Australia), 1994.

Hairy Charlie and the Pumpkin, illustrated by Dee Huxley, CIS (Carlton, Victoria, Australia), 1994.

Twelve Bottles Popping, CIS (Carlton, Victoria, Australia), 1994.

The Secret Beach, Angus & Roberson (Pymble, New South Wales, Australia), 1995.

Alien Games, Angus & Roberson (Pymble, New South Wales, Australia), 1995.

Annie's Pouch, illustrated by Bettina Guthridge, Angus & Robertson (Pymble, New South Wales, Australia), 1995.

Mermaids, photographs by Bernard Rosa, Angus & Robertson (Pymble, New South Wales, Australia), 1995.

Somewhere around the Corner, HarperCollins (Pymble, New South Wales, Australia), 1996.

Mind's Eye, Angus & Robertson (Pymble, New South Wales, Australia), 1996.

Summerland, Angus & Robertson (Pymble, New South Wales, Australia), 1996.

A Wombat Called Bosco, illustrated by Bettina Guthridge, Angus & Robertson (Pymble, New South Wales, Australia), 1996.

Beyond the Boundaries, Angus & Robertson (Pymble, New South Wales, Australia), 1996.

The Warrior: The Story of a Wombat, illustrated by Bettina Guthridge, Angus & Robertson (Pymble, New South Wales, Australia), 1996.

The Book of Unicorns, HarperCollins (Pymble, New South Wales, Australia), 1997.

Dancing with Ben Hall and Other Yarns, illustrated by Gwen Harrison, Angus & Robertson (Pymble, New South Wales, Australia), 1997.

The Boy with Silver Eyes, illustrated by David Miller, Lothian (Port Melbourne, Victoria, Australia), 1997.

There's a Wallaby at the Bottom of My Garden, illustrated by Bettina Gutheridge, Koala Books (Redfern, New South Wales, Australia), 1997.

There's an Echidna at the Bottom of My Garden, illustrated by David Stanley, Koala Books (Redfern, New South Wales, Australia), 1998.

Soldier on the Hill, HarperCollins (Pymble, New South Wales, Australia), 1998.

The Little Book of Big Questions, illustrated by Terry Denton, Allen & Unwin (Sydney, New South Wales, Australia), 1998.

Felix Smith Has Every Right to Be a Crocodile, illustrated by David Stanley, Koala Books (Redfern, New South Wales, Australia), 1998.

How the Aliens from Alpha Centauri Invaded My Math Class and Turned Me into a Writer . . . and How You Can Be One Too, HarperCollins (Pymble, New South Wales, Australia), 1998.

Daughter of the Regiment, Angus & Robertson (Pymble, New South Wales, Australia), 1999.

Tajore Arkle, HarperCollins (Pymble, New South Wales, Australia), 1999.

Hitler's Daughter, HarperCollins (Pymble, New South Wales, Australia), 1999, HarperCollins (New York, NY), 2003.

Charlie's Gold, Koala Books (Redfern, New South Wales, Australia), 1999.

Bert and the Band, Koala (Mascot, New South Wales, Australia), 2000.

Captain Purrfect (reader), illustrated by Gus Gordon, Koala Books (Mascot, New South Wales, Australia), 2000.

The Little Book of Big Questions, illustrated by Martha Newbigging, Annick (Toronto, Ontario, Canada), 2000.

Missing You, Love Sarah, HarperCollins (Pymble, New South Wales, Australia), 2000.

Dark Wind Blowing (middle-grade novel), HarperCollins (Pymble, New South Wales, Australia), 2000.

Lady Dance, HarperCollins (Pymble, New South Wales, Australia), 2000.

The Book of Challenges, HarperCollins (Pymble, New South Wales, Australia), 2000.

Stamp Stomp Whomp and Other Interesting Ways to Kill Pests, HarperCollins (Pymble, New South Wales, Australia), 2001.

The Café on Callisto (chapter book), illustrated by Sarah Baron, Koala (Mascot, New South Wales, Australia), 2001.

Ride the Wild Wind: The Golden Pony and Other Stories, Angus & Robertson (Pymble, New South Wales, Australia), 2001.

How the Finnegans Saved the Ship, HarperCollins (Pymble, New South Wales, Australia), 2001.

In the Blood (young-adult novel), HarperCollins (Pymble, New South Wales, Australia), 2001.

The Fascinating History of Your Lunch, HarperCollins (Pymble, New South Wales, Australia), 2002.

The Space Bug (reader), illustrated by Mitch Vane, Koala (Mascot, New South Wales, Australia), 2002.

Diary of a Wombat, illustrated by Bruce Whatley, Harper-Collins (Pymble, New South Wales, Australia), 2002, HarperCollins (New York, NY), 2005.

Space Pirates on Callisto (chapter book), illustrated by Sarah Baron, Koala (Mascot, New South Wales, Australia), 2002.

The White Ship (historical novel), HarperCollins (Pymble, New South Wales, Australia), 2002.

Blood Moon ("Outlands" trilogy; young-adult novel), HarperCollins (Pymble, New South Wales, Australia), 2002.

Blood Will Tell ("Outlands" trilogy; young-adult novel), HarperCollins (Pymble, New South Wales, Australia), 2003.

Valley of Gold, HarperCollins (Pymble, New South Wales, Australia), 2003.

Vampire Slugs on Callisto (chapter book), illustrated by Sarah Baron, Koala (Mascot, New South Wales, Australia), 2003.

Big Burps, Bare Bums, and Other Bad Mannered Blunders: Aunti Jackie's Guide to Behaving Almost Perfectly, HarperCollins (Pymble, New South Wales, Australia), 2003, published as *Big Burps, Bare Bums, and Other Bad-Mannered Blunders: Over 180 Tips on How to Behave,* Angus & Robertson (Pymble, New South Wales, Australia), 2003.

Bears Don't Bounce! (lift-the-flap book), illustrated by Matt Cosgrove, Koala (Mascot, New South Wales, Australia), 2003.

Pigs Don't Fly!, illustrated by Matt Cosgrove, Koala (Mascot, New South Wales, Australia), 2003.

Pear Pinching Pamela, illustrated by Bruce Whatley, Koala (Mascot, New South Wales, Australia), 2003, pub-

lished as *Too Many Pears!,* Star Bright Books (New York, NY), 2003.

The Black House (middle-grade novel), Koala (Mascot, New South Wales, Australia), 2003.

(With Bryan Sullivan) *To the Moon and Back: The Amazing Australians at the Forefront of Space Travel,* illustrated by Gus Gordon, HarperCollins (Pymble, New South Wales, Australia), 2004.

Tom Appleby: Convict Boy, Angus & Robertson (Pymble, New South Wales, Australia), 2004.

Flesh and Blood ("Outlands" trilogy; young-adult novel), HarperCollins (Pymble, New South Wales, Australia), 2004.

Pete the Sheep, illustrated by Bruce Whatley, HarperCollins (Pymble, New South Wales, Australia), 2004, published as *Pete the Sheep-Sheep,* Clarion (New York, NY), 2005.

The Secret World of Wombats, illustrated by Bruce Whatley, Angus & Robertson (Pymble, New South Wales, Australia), 2005.

They Came on Viking Ships, Angus & Robertson (Pymble, New South Wales, Australia), 2005, published as *Rover,* HarperCollins (New York, NY), 2007.

One Perfect Day, illustrated by Peter Bray, National Museum of Australia Press (Canberra, Australia Capital Territory, Australia), 2006.

Macbeth and Son, Angus & Robertson (Pymble, New South Wales, Australia), 2006.

Josephine Wants to Dance, illustrated by Bruce Whatley, Angus & Robertson (Pymble, New South Wales, Australia), 2006, published as *Josephine Loves to Dance,* Harry Abrams (New York, NY), 2007.

The Shaggy Gully Times: The Punniest Newspaper You'll Ever Read, illustrated by Bruce Whatley, Angus & Robertson (Pymble, New South Wales, Australia), 2007.

Pharaoh: The Boy Who Conquered the Nile, HarperCollins (Pymble, New South Wales, Australia), 2007.

The Day I Was History, illustrated by Christina Booth, National Museum of Australia Press (Canberra, Australia Capital Territory, Australia), 2007.

The Wonderful World of Wallabies and Kangaroos, illustrated by Bruce Whatley, HarperCollins (Pymble, New South Wales, Australia), 2008.

A Rose for the Anzac Boys (historical novel), HarperCollins (Pymble, New South Wales, Australia), 2008.

"CHILDREN OF THE VALLEY" SERIES

The Music from the Sea, illustrated by Victoria Clutterbuck, Aird Books (Melbourne, Victoria, Australia), 1992.

City in the Sand, illustrated by Victoria Clutterbuck, Aird Books (Melbourne, Victoria, Australia), 1993.

House of a Hundred Animals, illustrated by Victoria Clutterbuck, Aird Books (Melbourne, Victoria, Australia), 1993.

The Metal Men, illustrated by Victoria Clutterbuck, Aird Books (Melbourne, Victoria, Australia), 1994.

The Tribe That Sang to Trees, illustrated by Victoria Clutterbuck, Aird Books (Melbourne, Victoria, Australia), 1996.

French's children's books have been translated into nine languages.

"PHREDDE" NOVEL SERIES

A Phaery Named Phredde: Stories to Eat with a Banana, HarperCollins (Pymble, New South Wales, Australia), 1998.

Phredde and a Frog Named Bruce: Stories to Eat with a Watermelon, Angus & Robertson (Pymble, New South Wales, Australia), 1999.

Predde and the Zombie Librarian: Stories to Eat with a Blood Plum, Angus & Robertson (Pymble, New South Wales, Australia), 2000.

Phredde and the Temple of Gloom: A Story to Eat with a Mandarin, Angus & Robertson (Pymble, New South Wales, Australia), 2001.

Phredde and the Leopard-skin Librarian: A Story to Eat with a Dinosaur Apple, HarperCollins (Pymble, New South Wales, Australia), 2002.

Phredde and the Purple Pyramid: A Story to Eat with a Passionfruit, HarperCollins (Pymble, New South Wales, Australia), 2003.

A Box Full of Phaeries, Phreddes, and Fruit (includes *Stories to Eat with a Banana,* *Stories to Eat with a Watermelon,* and *Stories to Eat with a Blood Plum*), Angus & Robertson (Pymble, New South Wales, Australia), 2003.

Phredde and the Vampire Footy Team, Angus & Robertson (Pymble, New South Wales, Australia), 2004.

Phredde and the Ghostly Underpants: A Story to Eat with a Mango, Angus & Robertson (Pymble, New South Wales, Australia), 2005.

"WACKY FAMILIES" SERIES

My Mum the Pirate, illustrated by Stephen Michael King, Angus & Robertson (Pymble, New South Wales, Australia), 2003, published as *My Mom the Pirate,* Stone Arch Books (Minneapolis, MN), 2007.

My Dog the Dinosaur, illustrated by Stephen Michael King, Angus & Robertson (Pymble, New South Wales, Australia), 2003, Stone Arch Books (Minneapolis, MN), 2007.

My Dad the Dragon, illustrated by Stephen Michael King, Angus & Robertson (Pymble, New South Wales, Australia), 2004, Stone Arch Books (Minneapolis, MN), 2007.

My Uncle Gus the Garden Gnome, illustrated by Stephen Michael King, Angus & Robertson (Pymble, New South Wales, Australia), 2004.

My Uncle Wal the Werewolf, illustrated by Stephen Michael King, Angus & Robertson (Pymble, New South Wales, Australia), 2005, published as *My Uncle the Werewolf,* Stone Arch Books (Minneapolis, MN), 2007.

My Gran the Gorilla, illustrated by Stephen Michael King, Angus & Robertson (Pymble, New South Wales, Australia), 2006.

My Auntie Chook the Vampire Chicken, illustrated by Stephen Michael King, Angus & Robertson (Pymble, New South Wales, Australia), 2006.

My Pa the Polar Bear, illustrated by Stephen Michael King, Angus & Robertson (Pymble, New South Wales, Australia), 2007.

One Big Wacky Family, illustrated by Stephen Michael King, Angus & Robertson (Pymble, New South Wales, Australia), 2008.

"FAIR DINKUM HISTORY" SERIES; NONFICTION

Grim Crims and Convicts, 1788-1820, illustrated by Peter Sheehan, Scholastic (Linfield, New South Wales, Australia), 2005.

Shipwreck, Sailors, and 60,000 Years: 1770 and All That Happened before Then, illustrated by Peter Sheehan, Scholastic (Linfield, New South Wales, Australia), 2006.

Rotters and Squatters, illustrated by Peter Sheehan, Scholastic (Gosford, New South Wales, Australia), 2007.

Gold, Graves, and Glory, illustrated by Peter Sheehan, Scholastic (Gosford, New South Wales, Australia), 2007.

A Nation of Swaggies and Diggers, illustrated by Peter Sheehan, Scholastic (Gosford, New South Wales, Australia), 2008.

"ANIMAL STARS" SERIES

The Goat Who Sailed the World, HarperCollins (Pymble, New South Wales, Australia), 2006.

The Dog Who Loved a Queen, HarperCollins (Pymble, New South Wales, Australia), 2007.

The Camel Who Crossed Australia, HarperCollins (Pymble, New South Wales, Australia), 2008.

OTHER

Organic Gardening in Australia, Reed Books (Australia), 1987.

Natural Rose Growing: An Organic Approach to Gardening, Angus & Robertson (Pymble, New South Wales, Australia), 1988.

The Organic Garden Doctor, Harper Collins (Pymble, New South Wales, Australia), 1988.

Natural Control of Household Pests, Aird Books (Melbourne, Victoria, Australia), 1990, 2nd edition, 2002.

The Wilderness Garden: A Radical New View of Australian Growing Methods, Aird Books (Melbourne, Victoria, Australia), 1993, 2nd edition published as *The Wilderness Garden: Beyond Organic Gardening,* 2007.

The Salad Garden, Reed Books (Australia), 1993.

Organic Control of Household Pests, Aird Books (Melbourne, Victoria, Australia), 1993.

Organic Control of Common Weeds, Aird Books (Melbourne, Victoria, Australia), 1993, revised, 1997.

The Earth Gardeners Companion: A Month-by-Month Guide, Earth Garden (Trentham, Victoria, Australia), 1993.

The Chook Book, Aird Books (Melbourne, Victoria, Australia), 1993.

Jackie French introduces youngsters to life in her native Australia in **Annie's Pouch,** *featuring artwork by Bettina Guthridge.* (Angus & Robertson, 1995. Cover and internal illustrations copyright © Bettina Guthridge 1995. Reproduced by permission of Angus & Robertson, an imprint of HarperCollins Australia.)

A to Z of Useful Plants, Aird Books (Melbourne, Victoria, Australia), 1993.

New Plants from Old, Aird Books (Melbourne, Victoria, Australia), 1994, 2nd edition published as *New Plants from Old: Simple, Natural, No-Cost Plant Propagation,* 2007.

Book of Lavender, HarperCollins (Pymble, New South Wales, Australia), 1994.

Book of Mint, HarperCollins (Pymble, New South Wales, Australia), 1994.

Book of Rosemary, HarperCollins (Pymble, New South Wales, Australia), 1994.

Book of Thyme, HarperCollins (Pymble, New South Wales, Australia), 1994.

Book of Chili, HarperCollins (Pymble, New South Wales, Australia), 1994.

Book of Garlic, HarperCollins (Pymble, New South Wales, Australia), 1994.

Book of Parsley, HarperCollins (Pymble, New South Wales, Australia), 1994.

Book of Basil, HarperCollins (Pymble, New South Wales, Australia), 1994.

Jackie French's Guide to Companion Planting in Australia and New Zealand, Aird Books (Melbourne, Victoria, Australia), 1994.

(With Bryan Sullivan) *Switch! A Book of Home-made Power, Water, and Garbage Systems,* Aird Books (Melbourne, Victoria, Australia), 1994.

Household Self Sufficiency, Aird Books (Melbourne, Victoria, Australia), 1994.

Back Yard Self Sufficiency, Aird Books (Melbourne, Victoria, Australia), 1995.

The Organic Garden Problem Solver, HarperCollins (Pymble, New South Wales, Australia), 1995.

Plants That Never Say Die, Lothian (Port Melbourne, Australia), 1995.

Soil Food: 3,764 Ways to Feed Your Garden, Aird Books (Melbourne, Victoria, Australia), 1995.

Jackie French's Top Ten Vegetables, Aird Books (Melbourne, Victoria, Australia), 1995.

Jackie French's Cook Book, Aird Books (Melbourne, Victoria, Australia), 1995.

The Pumpkin Book, Aird Books (Melbourne, Victoria, Australia), 1996.

Yates Guide to Edible Gardening, HarperCollins (Pymble, New South Wales, Australia), 1996.

Growing Flowers Naturally, Aird Books (Melbourne, Victoria, Australia), 1996.

Making Money from Your Garden, Earth Garden Books (Trentham, Victoria, Australia), 1997.

Seasons of Content, illustrated by Gwen Harrison, Angus & Robertson (Pymble, New South Wales, Australia), 1997.

Yates Guide to Herbs, HarperCollins (Pymble, New South Wales, Australia), 1998.

Jackie French's Household Herb Book, Earth Garden Books (Trentham, Victoria, Australia), 1998.

How to Guzzle Your Garden, HarperCollins (Pymble, New South Wales, Australia), 1999.

Natural Solutions, Women's Weekly Home Library, 1999.

The Best of Jackie French: A Practical Guide to Everything from Aphids to Zuchinni Chocolate Cake, HarperCollins (Pymble, New South Wales, Australia), 2000.

The House That Jackie Built, Earthgarden (Trentham, Victoria, Australia), September, 2001.

Earthly Delights, HarperCollins (Pymble, New South Wales, Australia), 2001.

The Secret Life of Santa Claus, HarperCollins (Pymble, New South Wales, Australia), 2001.

Searching for Charlie, HarperCollins (Pymble, New South Wales, Australia), 2003.

A War for Gentlemen (historical novel), Flamingo (Pymble, New South Wales, Australia), 2004.

Rocket Your Child into Reading (nonfiction), Angus & Robertson (Pymble, New South Wales, Australia), 2004.

Regular contributor to periodicals, including *Australian Women's Weekly, Burke's Backyard,* and *Earthgarden.*

Adaptations

Hitler's Daughter was adapted as a stage play by Eva DiCesare, Sandra Eldridge, and Tim McGarry, Currency Press (Strawberry Hills, New South Wales, Australia), 2007. "Walking the Boundaries," a popular environmental children's outdoor program, was based on French's book of the same name.

Sidelights

The stories of Australian writer Jackie French are inspired by her love of the landscape Down Under, her good-natured humor, and her passionate involvement in environmental and horticultural issues. The Australian bush serves as the backdrop of books such as her highly acclaimed story collection *Rainstones,* while the continent's unique creatures stars in picture books such as *Diary of a Wombat* and *Josephine Wants to Dance.* As Kevin Steinberger noted in *Magpies,* French "explores [the native Australian flora and fauna] with a keen multi-sensory perception that indicates a genuine affinity with the land and a passion for its life." In her review for *Horn Book,* Karen Jameyson also praised the author's poignant descriptions. Readers "imbibe not just plot and character but a very distinct group of country settings as well," Jameyson wrote. "Casuarina trees sway in the breeze; mopokes call their distinctive cry; wombats grind grass in the moonlight." In addition to the Australian landscape, French has also focused on her country's history in her "Fair Dinkum History" se-

ries for middle-grade readers, and her reputation as a self-sufficiency guru has been firmly cemented with works such as *New Plants from Old, Plants That Never Say Die,* and *Household Self-Sufficiency.*

With *The Little Book of Big Questions,* French attracted critical attention from across the English-speaking world. Organized in fifteen sections, French's book presents a multitude of reflective and unanswerable questions, such as "How did the universe begin?," "What is life?," "What happens when you die?," and "Why isn't life fair?" The possible and often-contradictory answers she poses for reader consideration draw from science, philosophy, and religion. French encourages readers to come up with their own answers to these questions but also suggests that they talk with librarians, ministers, teachers, or other adults in their personal search for answers. "It takes a brave adult to encourage kids to ask questions to which they have no answers," Julian Baggini commented in a review of the book for the *Times Educational Supplement.* Although she focuses on scientific explanations for the origins of life and of the universe, the critic added that French also gives "room and respect" to other alternatives, such as creationism. *The Little Book of Big Questions* is "a

French joins frequent collaborator and artist Bruce Whatley to create the humorous picture book **Diary of a Wombat.** (Clarion Books, 2002. Illustrations copyright © Farmhouse Illustration Company Pty Limited, 2002. Reprinted by permission of Clarion Books, an imprint of Houghton Mifflin Company. All rights reserved.)

good choice for small browsers who like to mull over big issues," concluded Debbie Whitbeck in *School Library Journal.*

Although she has written several novels for adults, most of French's fiction is geared for younger readers. *Somewhere around the Corner,* a middle-grade novel, transports Barbara, an Australian foster child, from a violent labor dispute in 1990s Sydney, back to that city in 1932, in the midst of the Great Depression. Fortunately for Barbara, she meets Jim, a young boy her own age who brings her home to his family. Amid the era's hard times and misfortune, Barbara comes to know the loving warmth and support of a family for the first time. Writing for *School Library Journal,* Susan L. Rogers claimed that "thorough character development and a captivating story save the novel from preaching." *Booklist* critic Sally Estes took a similar view, writing that "French does a wonderful job of portraying the precariousness of life during the 1930s Depression as well as the courage and warmth of people who not only survived but managed, in many ways, to thrive despite adversity." "The author has an eye for setting and characterization," concluded *Voice of Youth Advocates* contributor Joyce A. Litton in a review of *Somewhere around the Corner.*

In her award-winning middle-grade novel *Hitler's Daughter,* French focuses on a boy who is pondering one of modern history's darker moments. After one of his friends tells a fictional story about the secret daughter of German Chancellor Adolph Hitler during a story-telling game, ten-year-old Mark begins to reflect on the tale's deeper implications. He puts himself in the girl's place, living during World War II, and wonders what his life would be like if a trusted adult he looked up to for guidance was actually as evil as the Nazi leader. If he was the son of Hitler, and learned that his father was killing thousands of people, what would he have done? From there, the boy turns to the deeper implications of other things happening in the world, such as the taking of aboriginal lands, resulting in what *Booklist* reviewer Hazel Rochman dubbed a "disturbing, fast-paced story" that "makes clear the roles of perpetrator and bystander."

In *Rover,* published in Australia as *They Came on Viking Ships,* French goes back in time a thousand years to tell the story of Hekja, a girl who lives in a seaside town in Sweden. Captured by a band of Viking raiders led by Freydis Eriksdottir, the daughter of Erik the Red, the twelve-year-old girl and her dog, Snarl, are taken to Greenland. Starting as a slave, Hekja becomes Freydis's friend, and eventually they help establish a settlement on Vinland, or North America. Praising *Rover* as "a captivating" novel featuring "a feisty and resourceful" young protagonist, Heather M. Campbell added in her *School Library Journal* review that French's ability to mine the Norse sagas for a wealth of "historical detail . . . lends an air of authority" to her novel.

Among French's many othe books for children that have made their way to American readers are the "Wacky Family" series. Designed to engage the imaginations of young readers, each beginning chapter book in the series features a boy or girl who is burdened with an unbelievable and totally improbable home life. In *My Dog the Dinosaur,* for example, Gunk and his family bring a strange puppy home from the local animal shelter, only to have it turn out to be a baby dinosaur. For Buster, normal means being a werewolf, and in *My Uncle the Werewolf* he balks when his uncle decides that everyone should act like humans. When Horace becomes a knight-in-training in *My Dad the Dragon,* the boy's homework assignment—to slay a dragon—is particularly problematic for his fire-breathing father.

French's picture-book collaborations with illustrator Bruce Whatley are beloved by many readers and include *Diary of a Wombat, The Secret World of Wombats, Josephine Wants to Dance,* and *Pete the Sheep-Sheep.* An entertaining introduction to an unique Australian species, *Diary of a Wombat* allows readers to keep pace with a not-so-busy wombat as her main occupation turns from sleeping away the day to begging for food once easily trainable humans arrive in her neighborhood. Whatley's amusing acrylic paintings "provide the perfect counterpoint to French's deadpan narration," according to a *Kirkus Reviews* writer. Noting French's informative text, *School Library Journal* contributor Gay Lynn Van Vleck also praised the book's "simple sentences and hilarious yet realistic" art.

In *Josephine Wants to Dance* a young kangaroo rejects the criticism of family and friends to follow her love of dancing, and proves that kangas can do more than just hop when she takes over the role of an injured prima ballerina. In a play on the role of a sheepdog, *Pete the Sheep-Sheep* focuses on Shaun, a sheep shearer living in Shaggy Gully who uses his sheep Pete to herd his flock of sheep with polite requests rather than the nips, snaps, and low grows employed by sheepdogs. When the town's other shearers object, Shaun takes up a new trade, creating sheep hairstyles that make him the talk of the town. In *School Library Journal,* Kara Schaff Dean called *Josephine Wants to Dance* "an amusing twist on the age-old story of triumphing over adversity," adding that the book will appeal to "little girls with ballerina dreams of their own." *Pete the Sheep-Sheep* was praised by a *Kirkus Reviews* writer, who described the collaboration between French and Whatley as a "sweetly fleecy tale of outsider-makes-good." Noting that *Pete the Sheep-Sheep* plays on a simple silly premise, Ilene Cooper wrote in *Booklist* that French's "text is so jaunty and the artwork so amusing" that the book will nonetheless captivate story-hour crowds.

French once told *SATA:* "I wrote my first children's book, *Rainstones,* living in a shed with a wallaby called Fred, a black snake called Gladys, and a wombat called Smudge. The editor at HarperCollins described it as the

In **Josephine Wants to Dance** *a kangaroo's dreams of life as a ballerina are brought to life by French and Whatley.* (HarperCollins Australia, 2006. Illustration © 2006 by Farmhouse Illustration Company Pty. Ltd. Reproduced by permission.)

messiest, worst spelt manuscript they'd ever received. Now, tens of thousands of readers deeply love these same short stories.

"The messiness was mostly due to Smudge, the wombat, who had a particular hatred for my typewriter (an old one I found at the dump) and so he left nightly droppings on the keyboard. But the incorrect spellings were from my dyslexia—I can't focus on single words to see if they're spelt properly or not. (I profoundly hope someone has checked this spelling before you read it.)

"I sent my first book off because I was broke, had a baby to support, and could think of no other way to do it alone in the bush. But I've always told stories. I'm a storyteller by passion and by conviction. In any age, in any place, I'd be a storyteller. But I also write because I believe that giving children fiction is one of the most valuable things you can give them.

"When you tell a child a story, you are telling them life holds other possibilities. Encouraging fantasies of mermaids, and unicorns just around the corner, may well foster creative imaginations that one day lead to social reform, or new theories of the universe or, simply, a knowing that life can be better.

"As well as my books for children, I'm one of the Australian gurus of organic growing methods, with books ranging from detailed accounts of my research into alternative methods of weed or pest control, to more popular gardening books. I'm also a regular on many radio programs around Australia. My husband, Bryan, and I also run an experimental farm.

"My other work includes adult fiction (horrible way to express it—it always sounds like I write pornography, but how else do you differentiate children's books from books for adults?), and various other books that are hard to stuff into categories I've also studied wombat ecology for many years, and will tell wombat stories at a drop of the hat—or with even less encouragement."

French lives with her family in a valley on the Southern Tablelands of New South Wales. "We live in a house we built ourselves with stone from the creek," she once told *SATA,* "with a homemade waterwheel to power the computer when it's too shady for the solar panels, a rambling garden over-endowed with fruit and roses, six wombats, a frequently drunk goanna, and a mob of lyrebirds who dig up the asparagus." Other, more recent residents include "a possum who dances on the roof every morning at 4 a.m., two wedgetail eagles who live in nests on the cliffs above us, eight geese (one of them only has one leg and none of them has many brains), a lot of chooks, and a very handsome rooster called Rodney with long black and green tail feathers (they look like he's combed them) and a loud voice, and another called Arnold Shwarzenfeather."

One of French's central passions, in addition to her family, are the many wombats that have shared her time living in the Australian bush ("I suspect the local wildlife see us as pets, not the other way around," she quipped on her home page). Although she credits the short-legged, burrowing marsupials with being a central creative inspiration, French admits that the creatures have several annoying habits. One of her wombat acquaintances, Pudge, religiously ate all the celery growing in her garden, topping that off with parts of a nearby doormat. Pudge also influenced the author's typical bedtime routine; "10:00ish—Say goodnight to wombat; go to bed. 10:30—Say a very firm goodnight to wombat. 11:30—Rescue chewed doormat and mangled garbage bin from wombat. Speak sternly to wombat. Go to sleep."

Biographical and Critical Sources

PERIODICALS

Australian Book Review, February, 1993, p. 56; June, 1993, p. 59.
Booklist, May 15, 1995, Sally Estes, review of *Somewhere around the Corner,* p. 1645; September 15, 2003, Hazel Rochman, review of *Hitler's Daughter,* p. 236; January 1, 2006, Ilene Cooper, review of *Pete the Sheep,* p. 112; January 1, 2007, Francisca Goldsmith, review of *Rover,* p. 100.
Bulletin of the Center for Children's Books, June, 1995, review of *Somewhere around the Corner,* p. 343; July, 2003, review of *Hitler's Daughter,* p. 447; November, 2003, Deborah Stevenson, review of *Diary of a Wombat,* p. 102.
Horn Book, July-August, 1992, Karen Jameyson, review of *Rainstones,* pp. 498-499; September-October, 1995, Ann A. Flowers, review of *Somewhere around the Corner,* p. 599; January-February, 2006, Kitty Flynn, review of *Pete the Sheep-Sheep,* p. 68.
Kirkus Reviews, May 15, 2003, review of *Hitler's Daughter,* p. 750; July 15, 2003, review of *Diary of a Wombat,* p. 963; October 15, 2005, review of *Pete the Sheep-Sheep,* p. 1137; February 15, 2007, review of *Rover;* September 15, 2007, review of *Josephine Wants to Dance.*
Kliatt, March, 2007, Claire Rosser, review of *Rover,* p. 12.

Magpies, March, 1992, review of *The Roo That Won the Melbourne Cup,* p. 30; July, 1993, review of *Hairy Charlie and the Frog,* p. 26; November, 1993, review of *The Boy Who Had Wings,* p. 34; March, 1995, review of *Hairy Charlie and the Pumpkin,* p. 21; March, 1996, review of *Alien Game,* p. 33; September, 1997, review of *There's an Echidna at the Bottom of My Garden,* p. 31; September, 1999, review of *Charlie's Gold,* p. 29; November, 1999, Catherine McClellan and Kay Sagar, review of *Hitler's Daughter,* p. 6; May, 2001, review of *In the Blood,* p. 38; September, 2001, review of *Dark Wind Blowing,* p. 33; July, 2002, review of *The White Ship,* p. 34; July, 2002, review of *Space Pirates on Callisto,* p. 34; November, 2002, review of *Diary of a Wombat,* p. 29; March, 2003, review of *Pigs Don't Fly!,* p. 26; November, 2003, review of *Too Many Pears!,* p. 25; November, 2004, Jo Goodman, review of *Pete the Sheep,* p. 28; November, 2006, Vikki Turton, review of *Josephine Wants to Dance,* p. 27.
Psychology Today, Paul Chance, review of *The Little Book of Big Questions,* p. 75.
Publishers Weekly, April 26, 1993, review of *Book of Lavender,* p. 73; May 15, 1995, review of *Somewhere around the Corner,* p. 73; July 21, 2003, review of *Diary of a Wombat,* p. 193.
School Library Journal, July, 1995, Susan L. Rogers, review of *Somewhere around the Corner,* p. 78; November, 2000, Debbie Whitbeck, review of *The Little Book of Big Questions,* p. 140; May, 2003, Sue Giffard, review of *Hitler's Daughter,* p. 151; August, 2003, Gay Lynn Van Vleck, review of *Diary of a Wombat,* p. 128; November, 2003, Maryann H. Owen, review of *Too Many Pears!,* November, 2005, Grace Oliff, review of *Pete the Sheep-Sheep,* p. 90; June, 2007, Heather M. Campbell, review of *Rover,* p. 144; July, 2007, Kelly Roth, reviews of *My Dad the Dragon* and *My Mom the Pirate,* pp. 75-76; November, 2007, Kara Schaff Dean, review of *Josephine Wants to Dance,* p. 91.
Times Educational Supplement, Julian Baggini, review of *The Small Book of Big Questions,* p. 23.
Voice of Youth Advocates, October, 1995, Joyce A. Litton, review of *Somewhere around the Corner,* p. 218.

ONLINE

HarperCollins Web site, http://www.harpercollins.com.au/ (January 10, 2008), "Jackie French."
Jackie French Home Page, http://www.jackiefrench.com (January 10, 2008).

*   *   *

FRENCH, Jackie Anne
See FRENCH, Jackie

G

GARÓFOLI, Viviana 1970-

Personal

Born June 30, 1970, in Buenos Aires, Argentina; married; husband's name Sergio; children: April, Emma. *Education:* Escuela National de Bellas Artes Pridiliano Pueyrredon, B.F.A., 1995. *Hobbies and other interests:* Gardening, growing orchids.

Addresses

Home—Buenos Aires, Argentina. *Agent*—Mela Bolinao, MB Artists, 10 E. 29th St., New York, NY 10016. *E-mail*—vivigarofoli@ciudad.com.ar.

Career

Illustrator and author of children's books. *Exhibitions:* Work exhibited at galleries in Buenos Aires, Argentina.

Writings

SELF-ILLUSTRATED

Princess, Marshall Cavendish (New York, NY), 2008.
Pirates, Marshall Cavendish (New York, NY), 2008.

ILLUSTRATOR

Adela Basch, *La sonrisa en la caja,* Libros del Quirquincho (Buenos Aires, Argentina), 1994.
Susana Szwarc, *Había una vez un circo,* Libros del Quirquincho (Buenos Aires, Argentina), 1996.
Graciela Repún, *Yo no picoteo como un pajarito,* Libros del Quirquincho (Buenos Aires, Argentina), 1996.
Darío Rojo and Mario Varela, *El trabajo de los animales,* Libros del Quirquincho (Buenos Aires, Argentina), 1996.
Patricia Suarez, *La historia de Gallagher,* Libros del Quirquincho (Buenos Aires, Argentina), 1997.

María Brandán Aráoz, *Magdalena en el zoológico,* Editorial Alfaguara (Buenos Aires, Argentina), 1999.
Laura Devetach, *El otro lado del mundo,* Editorial Alfaguara (Buenos Aires, Argentina), 1999.
Enrique Melantoni, *Nombres. Sobre nombres para toda ocasión,* Editorial el Ateneo (Buenos Aires, Argentina), 2000.
María Elena Walsh, *Versos tradicionales para cebollitas,* Editorial Alfaguara (Buenos Aires, Argentina), 2000.
Graciela Repún, *Mi nuevo hermanito,* Editorial Planeta Junior (Buenos Aires, Argentina), 2001.
Graciela Repún, *Famila, la mía, la tuya, la de los demás,* Editorial Planeta Junior (Buenos Aires, Argentina), 2001.
Adela Basch, *José de San Martin. Caballero del principio al fin,* Editorial Alfaguara (Buenos Aires, Argentina), 2001.
Jackie Wolf, *Night-night, Sleep Tight,* Playhouse (Akron, OH), 2004.
Kirsten Hall, *Zoom, Zoom, Zoom,* Children's Press (New York, NY), 2004.
Annie Auerbach, *My Race into Space,* Piggy Toes Press (Los Angeles, CA), 2004.
Mary Man-Kong, *The Spooky Smells of Halloween,* Golden Books (New York, NY), 2005.
Lisa Schroeder, *Baby Can't Sleep,* Sterling Publisher (New York, NY), 2005.
Dorothea DePrisco, *Mommy and Me; Daddy and Me,* Piggy Toes Press (Inglewood, CA), 2006.
Susan Middleton Elya, *Sophie's Trophy,* Putnam (New York, NY), 2006.
Jonathan London, *My Big Rig,* Marshall Cavendish (Tarrytown, NY), 2007.
Patricia Hubbell, *Firefighters!: Speeding! Spraying! Saving!,* Marshall Cavendish (Tarrytown, NY), 2007.
Patricia Hubbell, *Police!: Hurrying! Helping! Saving!,* Marshall Cavendish (Tarrytown, NY), 2008.
Barbara Park, *Ma! There's Nothing to Do Here!,* Random House (New York, NY), 2008.

Also contributor of illustrations to other books published in Argentina, including titles by A. Sapongnikof, María Granta, and Graciel Repún.

Biographical and Critical Sources

PERIODICALS

Booklist, June 1, 2006, Kay Weisman, review of *Sophie's Trophy,* p. 82; March 1, 2007, Hazel Rochman, review of *Firefighters!: Speeding! Spraying! Saving!,* p. 88; April 15, 2007, Carolyn Phelan, review of *My Big Rig,* p. 49; December 15, 2007, Julie Cummins, review of *Ma! There's Nothing to Do Here!,* p. 50.

Kirkus Reviews, May 15, 2006, review of *Sophie's Trophy,* p. 517; February 15, 2007, review of *Firefighters!* and *My Big Rig.*

Publishers Weekly, November 28, 2005, review of *Baby Can't Sleep,* p. 50; February 26, 2007, review of *My Big Rig,* p. 88; November 19, 2007, review of *Ma!,* p. 55.

School Library Journal, January, 2006, Suzanne Myers Harold, review of *Baby Can't Sleep,* p. 113; August, 2006, Amelia Jenkins, review of *Sophie's Trophy,* p. 81; May, 2007, DeAnn Okamura, review of *Firefighters!,* p. 98, and Lynn K. Vanca, review of *My Big Rig,* p. 102.

ONLINE

Imaginaria Web site, http://www.imaginaria.com/ar/ (June 5, 2002), "Viviana Garófoli."*

*   *   *

GODON, Ingrid 1958-

Personal

Born August 29, 1958, in Antwerp, Belgium; married; children: three. *Education:* Attended Sint-Marie Instituut (Antwerp) and Lierse Academie voor Schone Kunsten.

Addresses

Home—Belgium. *Office*—Leielaan 4, 2500 Liege, Belgium. *E-mail*—ingrid.godon@telenet.be.

Career

Children's book illustrator and author, beginning c. 1980.

Awards, Honors

Boekenpauw, and Vlag en Wimpel, Penseeljury, and Gouden Griffel, all 2001, all for *Wachten op Matroos* by André Sollie; Kakelbontsprijs, 2005, for *My Daddy Is a Giant* by Carl Norac.

Writings

SELF-ILLUSTRATED

Nelly et César: Sauter, danser et autres aventures, Casterman (Tornai, Belgium), 1999, translated as *Nelly and Caesar: Jumping, Dancing, and Other Adventures,* Barron's Educational (Hauppauge, NY), 2000.

Nelly et César: Large étroit et autres contraires, Casterman (Tornai, Belgium), 1999, translated as *Nelly and Caesar, Fat, Thin, and Other Opposites,* Barron's Educational (Hauppauge, NY), 2000.

Nelly et César: Dedans, dehors et autres situations, Casterman (Tornai, Belgium), 1999, translated as *Nelly and Caesar, In, Out, and Other Places,* Barron's Educational (Hauppauge, NY), 2000.

Nelly et César: Toucher, goûter et autres sensations, Casterman (Tornai, Belgium), 2000, translated as *Nelly and Caesar, Touch, Taste, and Other Senses,* Barron's Educational (Hauppauge, NY), 2001.

Theo's Rainy Day, Macmillan (London, England), 2002.

Théo construit un chariot, Bayard Jeunesse (Paris, France), 2002, translated as *Theo's Red Wagon,* Macmillan (London, England), 2002.

Théo fait un gâteau, Bayard Jeunesse (Paris, France), 2002, translated as *Theo's Cheer up Cake,* Macmillan (London, England), 2002.

Theo's Big Surprise, Macmillan (London, England), 2002.

Bonjour Monsieur Pouce!, Bayard Jeuness (Paris, France), 2003.

Théo part en bateau, Bayard Jeunesse (Paris, France), 2003.

Théo travaille au jardin, Bayard Jeunesse (Paris, France), 2003.

ILLUSTRATOR

Héloïse Antoine, *Grand catalogue des petits curieux,* translated by Vicky Holifield as *The Big Book of Words for Curious Kids,* Peachtree (Atlanta, GA), 1995.

Héloïse Antoine, *Grand catalogue des petits écoliers,* translated by Vicky Holifield as *Curious Kids Go to Preschool: Another Big Book of Words,* Peachtree (Atlanta, GA), 1996.

Héloïse Antoine, *Grand catalogue des petits vacanciers,* translated by Vicky Holifield as *Curious Kids Go on Vacation: Another Big Book of Words,* Peachtree (Atlanta, GA), 1996.

Cressida Cowell, *What Shall We Do with the Boo-Hoo Baby?,* Scholastic (New York, NY), 2000, board book edition, 2003.

André Sollie, *Wachten op matroos,* Querido (Amsterdam, Netherlands), 2000.

Marlies Bardeli, *De vogels van Heer Droogstempel,* Arifjn, 2001.

Ben Kuipers, *De wereld van Wolf en Lam,* Leopold, 2001.

Martine Oborne, *One Beautiful Baby,* Little, Brown (Boston, MA), 2002.

Ben Kuipers, *Hoe de Wereld begon,* Leopold, 2002.

Marita de Sterck, *Grote tanden,* De Eenhoorn, 2002.

André Sollie, *De bus naar Hawaii,* Querido (Amsterdam, Netherlands), 2003.

Jaak Dreesen, *Het concert,* De Eenhoorn, 2003.

Edward van de Vendel, *Anna Maria Sofia en de kleine Cor,* Querido (Amsterdam, Netherlands), 2004.

Marlies Bardeli, *Philines Zirkusreise,* Sauerlander, 2004.

Carl Norac, *Mijn papais een reus,* Leopold, 2004, translated as *My Daddy Is a Giant,* Macmillan (London, England), 2004, Clarion Books (New York, NY), 2005.

Carl Norac, *My Mummy Is Magic,* Macmillan (London, England), 2006, published as *My Mommy Is Magic,* Clarion Books (New York, NY), 2007.

Carl Norac, *My Grandpa Is a Champion,* Macmillan (London, England), 2006, published as *My Mommy Is Magic,* Macmillan (London, England), 2007.

Carl Norac, *My Grandma Is a Star,* Macmillan (London, England), 2006.

Contributor of illustrations to periodicals, including *Doopido.*

Books featuring Godon's artwork have been translated into ten languages, including English, Dutch, German, and French.

Adaptations

Godon's "Nellie and Caesar" books were adapted as an animated television series by "Averbode (Belgium)/ Planet Nemo (France), 2008.

Sidelights

An artist whose illustrations for picture-book texts by authors such as Carl Norac and Ben Kuipers are beloved by readers in her native Belgium, Ingrid Godon has also achieved international acclaim. In addition to winning awards for picture-book collaborations with writers Norac and André Sollie, Godon's popularity among young children has inspired television animators to adapt her "Nellie and Caesar" book series into an animated television series.

Godon's warm, expressive art is characterized by chalked outlines filled with pastel, water color, and gouache. Her stylized images gain a wood-cut feel through her incorporation of heavy, dark lines drawn freehand on textured paper, a technique that also adds an element of movement to her work. In a review of her illustrations for Martine Oborne's *One Beautiful Baby,* Martha Topol wrote in *School Library Journal* that Godon's "minimalist, cartoon style" pastel images "radiate warmth and genuine delight," making the counting book "perfect . . . for toddlers."

Simple and engaging, Godon's work pairs well with Norac's simple, family-centered picture books *My*

Ingrid Godon's highly textured, graphic art teams with Carl Norac's text in **My Daddy Is a Giant.** (Clarion Books, 2004. Illustrations copyright © 2004 by Ingrid Godon. Reprinted by permission of Clarion Books, an imprint of Houghton Mifflin Company. All rights reserved.)

Daddy Is a Giant, My Mother Is Magic, and *My Grandpa Is a Champion,* which depict a loving, caring parent from a toddler's perspective. In *My Daddy Is a Giant,* Godon's illustrations show the boy and father in a skewed perspective that pairs with the young narrator's assertions that his father is so high that he reaches the clouds, and can kick a ball up to the moon. Noting the value of Norac's story in building up fathers as role models for young boys, Joanna Rudge Long added in *Horn Book* that Godon's "graphic virtuosity and . . . pleasing palette" contribute to the book's success. According to *School Library Journal* contributor Amy Lilien-Harper, the illustrator's "oversize, brightly colored paint-and-pastel illustrations . . . are the real draw," and "depict the loving bond between father and son perfectly."

Biographical and Critical Sources

PERIODICALS

Booklist, January 1, 2001, GraceAnne A. DeCandido, review of *What Shall We Do with the Boo-Hoo Baby?,* p. 967; September 15, 2002, Kathy Broderick, review of *One Beautiful Baby,* p. 242; June 1, 2005, Gillian Engberg, review of *My Daddy Is a Giant,* p. 1819; February 15, 2007, Gillian Engberg, review of *My Mommy Is Magic,* p. 84.

Horn Book, May-June, 2005, Joanna Rudge Long, review of *My Daddy Is a Giant,* p. 311.

Kirkus Reviews, August 1, 2002, review of *One Beautiful Baby,* p. 1139; May 15, 2005, review of *My Daddy Is a Giant,* p. 594.

Publishers Weekly, July 24, 1995, review of *The Big Book of Words for Curious Kids,* p. 63; November 6, 2000, review of *What Shall We Do with the Boo-Hoo Baby?,* p. 89; June 6, 2005, review of *My Daddy Is a Giant,* p. 63.

School Library Journal, September, 2002, Martha Topol, review of *One Beautiful Baby,* p. 202; May, 2005, Amy Lilien-Harper, review of *My Daddy Is a Giant,* p. 94; March, 2007, Nancy Kunz, review of *My Mommy Is Magic,* p. 182.

ONLINE

Flemish Illustrators Web site, http://www.vlaamse-illustratoren.com/ (January 15, 2008), "Ingrid Godon."

Inhoud Laten Lezen Web site, http://www.leesplein.nl/ (January 10, 2008), "Ingrid Godon."*

*   *   *

GOSS, Mini 1963-

Personal

Born 1963, in Australia; children: three.

Addresses

Home and office—Australia.

Career

Author and illustrator.

Writings

SELF-ILLUSTRATED

When Mum Was Little, Black Dog Books (Fitzroy, Victoria, Australia), 2001, Kane/Miller Book Publishers (La Jolla, CA), 2004.

When Dad Was a Teenager, Black Dog Books (Fitzroy, Victoria, Australia), 2004.

Rhino Neil, New Frontier (Epping, New South Wales, Australia), 2005.

What Does Daddy Do?, Koala Books (Mascot, New South Wales, Australia), 2006.

ILLUSTRATOR

Edel Wignell, reteller, *The Cat and the Mouse: An English Folktale,* Mammoth (Port Melbourne, Victoria, Australia), 1994.

John Parker, *Fire!,* Heinemann Library (Port Melbourne, Victoria, Australia), 2000.

John Parker, *Max's Mystery Box,* Pearson Education (South Melbourne, Victoria, Australia), 2000.

Edel Wignell, adaptor, *Bendemolena: A Play Based on an American Folktale,* Pearson Education (South Melbourne, Victoria, Australia), 2001.

Andrew Whitmore, *Ark of Dreams,* Black Dog Books (Fitzroy, Victoria, Australia), 2001.

Hazel Edwards and Christine Anketell, *Sticky Bill: TV Duckstar/Cyberfarm,* Banana Books (Otford, New South Wales, Australia, 2002.

Jill McDougall, *No One Likes Me,* Era (Flinders Park, South Australia, Australia), 2002.

Nick Hughes, *Colossal Creatures,* Koala Books (Mascot, New South Wales, Australia), 2002.

Joelie Croser, *I Want to Be Me,* Era Publications (Flinders Park, South Australia, Australia), 2004.

Josephine Croser, *Pick Me,* Era (Flinders Park, South Australia, Australia), 2004.

Hazel Edwards, *Hand-Me-Down Hippo,* Penguin (Camberwell, Victoria, Australia), 2004.

Nick Hughes, *Colossal Machines,* Koala Books (Mascot, New South Wales, Australia), 2004.

Sue Whiting, *Taming Butterflies,* New Frontier (Epping, New South Wales, Australia), 2004.

Gabiann Marin, *Little Rosie Runaway,* New Frontier (Epping, New South Wales, Australia), 2005.

Tom Skinner, *Round Fish, Square Bowl,* New Frontier (Frenchs Forest, New South Wales, Australia), 2006.

Mark Carhew, *Five Little Owls,* New Frontier (Frenchs Forest, New South Wales, Australia), 2007.

Biographical and Critical Sources

PERIODICALS

Magpies, July, 2002, "Cyberfarm and Sticky Bill," p. 33; March, 2003, review of *Colossal Creatures,* p. 27; July, 2007, Annette Dale Meiklejohn, review of *Five Little Owls,* p. 26.
School Library Journal, March, 2005, Susan Weitz, review of *When Mum Was Little,* p. 172.

ONLINE

Black Dog Books Web site, http://www.bdb.com.au/ (January 6, 2007), "Mini Goss."
Kane/Miller Book Publishers Web site, http://www. kanemiller.com/ (January 6, 2007).*

*   *   *

GRAHAM, Arthur Kennon
See HARRISON, David L.

*   *   *

GRAHAM, Kennon
See HARRISON, David L.

*   *   *

GRIMLY, Gris

Personal

Male. *Education:* Graduated from art college.

Addresses

Office—Los Angeles, CA. *Agent*—Steven Malk, Writers House, 21 W. 26th St., New York, NY 10010; Peter McHugh, Gotham Group, 9255 Sunset Blvd., Los Angeles, CA 90069. *E-mail*—grisgrimly@madcreator.com.

Career

Illustrator, sculptor, painter, author, and filmmaker. Mad Creator Productions (multimedia company), Los Angeles, CA, founder and owner, 1998—. Director of *Cannibal Flesh Riot!* (independent film), 2006. Also worked as a designer and illustrator at Universal Studios, Los Angeles.

Writings

SELF-ILLUSTRATED

Gris Grimly's Wicked Nursery Rhymes, Baby Tattoo Books (Van Nuys, CA), 2003.

Gris Grimly (Photo by Steven Arouson courtesy of Marilyn Singer.)

Little Jordan Ray's Muddy Spud, Baby Tattoo Books (Van Nuys, CA), 2005.
Gris Grimly's Wicked Nursery Rhymes II, Baby Tattoo Books (Van Nuys, CA), 2006.

Creator of limited-edition miniature books, including *Helium Head Harold* and *Norbert the Seal Boy.* Creator of "Little Lou Lou's Adventures in Hell" (online comic).

ILLUSTRATOR

Marilyn Singer, *Monster Museum,* Hyperion Books for Children (New York, NY), 2001.
Carlo Collodi, *Pinocchio,* Tor (New York, NY), 2002.
Joan Aiken, *The Cockatrice Boys,* Starscape Books (New York, NY), 2002.
Marilyn Singer, *Creature Carnival,* Hyperion Books for Children (New York, NY), 2004.
Carolyn Crimi, *Boris and Bella,* Harcourt (Orlando, FL), 2004.
Edgar Allan Poe, *Edgar Allan Poe's Tales of Mystery and Madness,* Atheneum Books for Young Readers (New York, NY), 2004.

Susan Pearson, *Grimericks,* Marshall Cavendish (New York, NY), 2005.

Laura Leuck, *Santa Claws: A Scary Christmas to All,* Chronicle Books (San Francisco, CA), 2006.

Washington Irving, *The Legend of Sleepy Hollow,* Atheneum Books for Young Readers (New York, NY), 2007.

Neil Gaiman, *The Dangerous Alphabet,* HarperCollins (New York, NY), 2008.

Kelly DiPucchio, *Sipping Spiders through a Straw: Campfire Songs for Monsters,* Scholastic (New York, NY), 2008.

Contributor to *Spectrum: The Best in Contemporary Fantasy Art.* Also illustrator of book covers for Harper-Collins and Hyperion Books.

Sidelights

Gris Grimly, a painter, sculptor, and filmmaker known for his macabre yet whimsical creations, is the author and illustrator of a number of highly regarded books for young readers. Grimly, who works primarily in ink and watercolor, has been compared to Tim Burton, Edward Gorey, and Dr. Seuss, the last of whom he cites as an influence. "I would say that my stuff is a lot edgier than Dr. Seuss," Grimly told Jonathan Williams in the *Atlanta Journal-Constitution,* adding, "I have an older audience that is more pre-teen to adults, but [my work] does also appeal to children."

The founder of Mad Creator Productions, a multimedia firm, Grimly noted on his home page that he draws "inspiration from almost anything that surrounds me daily. The most obvious are music, films, fantastical images, live performances . . ., and, of course, monsters." Grimly discussed his influences further with Kevin Van Natter for the *CreatureCorner* Web site. Noting that he has "been intrigued by horror films, mainly monsters, since I was a child," Grimly recalled that his "earliest memory was seeing *The Fly* with Vincent Price. That end scene was something that I have not forgotten to this day."

Grimly worked at Universal Studios in Los Angeles, where he designed characters for themed entertainment. A gallery in nearby Beverly Hills requested that he produce the series of hand-painted miniature books that brought him to the attention of editors at Hyperion Books. In 2001 he provided the illustrations for Marilyn Singer's *Monster Museum,* a collection of poems about an unusual school field trip. Grimly's "cleverly detailed watercolors . . . steal the show with hilarious humor and offer careful readers all sorts of visual jokes," a *Kirkus Reviews* critic noted. In *Creature Carnival,* another title by Singer, a group of children tour a sideshow filled with attractions from mythology and folklore, including the Cheshire Cat, Pegasus, and Godzilla. Grimly's "illustrations create a gruesome menagerie of characters that are as buffoonish and appealing as they are grotesque," observed Gillian Engberg in *Booklist.*

Grimly's macabre view of life extends to romance in his illustrations for Carolyn Crimi's **Boris and Bella.** (Harcourt, 2004. Illustration copyright © 2004 by Gris Grimly. Reproduced by permission of Harcourt, Inc. This material may not be reproduced in any form or by any means without the prior written permission of the publisher.)

A pair of monstrous neighbors learn to overcome their differences in Carolyn Crimi's *Boris and Bella,* a "bootiful friendship tale," according to a *Kirkus Reviews* contributor. The work follows the exploits of the supremely messy Bella Lagrossi and her equally fastidious counterpart, Boris Kleanitoff. A reviewer in *Publishers Weekly* praised Grimly's "fiendish visual details," and *Booklist* contributor Gillian Engberg remarked that the illustrator's art "has a hint of Charles Addams ghoulishness." In *Santa Claws: A Scary Christmas to All,* written by Laura Leuck, Mack and Zack prepare for St. Nick's visit by hanging up their smelly socks and baking poisonberry pies. Maureen Wade, writing in *School Library Journal,* complimented Grimly's "quirky, Tim Burtonesque style art."

Grimly has also contributed illustrations to modern versions of classic tales. For a new edition of Carlo Collodi's *Pinocchio,* Grimly created "his own wacky world, which is part Gothic, part *Mad* magazine," observed *New York Times Book Review* contributor Sam Swope. In *Booklist,* Francisca Goldsmith complimented Grimly's "wonderfully ghastly" art in *Edgar Allan Poe's Tales of Mystery and Madness,* and Susan Scheps, writing in *School Library Journal,* commented that his "deliciously malevolent illustrations are the perfect complement to Poe's macabre stories." Grimly drew praise from *Horn Book* reviewer Claire E. Gross for his "Halloween-hued panel and spot illustrations" in Washington Irving's *The Legend of Sleepy Hollow*.

In his self-illustrated *Gris Grimly's Wicked Nursery Rhymes*, Grimly presents a number of ghoulish poems, including one featuring a gluttonous Bo Beep. His "efforts mock the wholesome formula" of the Mother Goose rhymes, a *Publishers Weekly* critic wrote. In another original work, *Little Jordan Ray's Muddy Spud*, the title character attempts to barter his family's only potato, encountering a mad hare, a griffin, and a grumpy troll along the way. The book "has the feel of Dr. Seuss," remarked Laurel Graeber in the *New York Times* in a nod to Grimly's artistic inspiration.

Biographical and Critical Sources

PERIODICALS

Atlanta Journal-Constitution, September 1, 2005, Jonathan Williams, "Grim Outlook at DragonCon," p. 27.

Booklist, April 1, 2004, Gillian Engberg, review of *Creature Carnival,* p. 1367; October 15, 2004, Francisca Goldsmith, review of *Edgar Allan Poe's Tales of Mystery and Madness,* p. 405; January 1, 2005, Ilene Cooper, review of *Boris and Bella,* p. 868; September 15, 2007, Jennifer Mattson, review of *The Legend of Sleepy Hollow,* p. 65.

Horn Book, November-December, 2007, Claire E. Gross, review of *The Legend of Sleepy Hollow,* p. 681.

Kirkus Reviews, September 15, 2001, review of *Monster Museum,* p. 1368; February 15, 2004, review of *Creature Carnival,* p. 185; August 15, 2004, review of *Boris and Bella,* p. 804; November 1, 2006, review of *Santa Claws: A Scary Christmas to All,* p. 1131.

New York Times, May 6, 2005, Laurel Graeber, "A Muddy Spud and How It Grew," p. E29.

New York Times Book Review, November 17, 2002, Sam Swope, "The Subject Was Noses," review of *Pinocchio,* p. 38.

Prick, January, 2006, "Gris Grimly."

Publishers Weekly, September 24, 2001, review of *Monster Museum,* p. 43; December 1, 2003, review of *Gris Grimly's Wicked Nursery Rhymes,* p. 56; August 9, 2004, review of *Boris and Bella,* p. 248; April 4, 2005, review of *Little Jordan Ray's Muddy Spud,* p. 62; September 25, 2006, review of *Santa Claws,* p. 71.

Rue Morgue, August, 2007, "Gris Grimly's *Cannibal Flesh Riot.*"

School Library Journal, November, 2001, Kay Bowes, review of *Monster Museum,* p. 152; December, 2003, Lisa Prolman, review of *Gris Grimly's Wicked Nursery Rhymes,* p. 152; April, 2004, Kathleen Whalin, review of *Creature Carnival,* p. 142; September, 2004, Donna Cardon, review of *Boris and Bella,* p. 156; October, 2004, Susan Scheps, review of *Edgar Allan Poe's Tales of Mystery and Madness,* p. 176; October, 2006, Maureen Wade, review of *Santa Claws,* p. 97.

ONLINE

Creature Corner Web site, http://www.creature-corner.com/ (July 24, 2007), Kevin Van Natter, interview with Grimly.

Gris Grimly Home Page, http://madcreator.com (December 1, 2007).

Van Eaton Galleries Web site, http://vegalleries.com/ (December 1, 2007), "Gris Grimly."

H

HAGERUP, Klaus 1946-

Personal
Born March 5, 1946, in Oslo, Norway; son of Inger Hagerup (an author); children: Hilde.

Addresses
Home and office—Gressvik, Norway.

Career
Playwright, novelist, actor, and filmmaker. National Scene (theatre), Oslo, Norway, 1968-69, then National Theater and Hålogaland Theater, actor, teacher, director, and writer. Actor in films, including *Helten På Den Grøne Øya*, 1971, *Løperjenten*, 1981, *Høvdingen*, 1984, *Noe Helt Annet*, 1985, *Plastposen*, 1986, *Måker*, 1991, and *Markus og Diana*, 1996.

Awards, Honors
Sonja Hagemanns Barnebokpris, 1990, and Certificate of Honour for Writing, International Board on Books for Young People, 1993, both for *Høyere en Himmenlen*.

Writings

NOVELS; FOR CHILDREN AND YOUNG ADULTS

Landet der Tiden Var Borte, Aschehoug (Oslo, Norway), 1989.
Høyere enn Himmelen (also see below), Aschehoug (Oslo, Norway), 1990.
I Går Var i Dag i Morgen, Aschehoug (Oslo, Norway), 1992.
(With Tande-P) *De Glødende Hjerters Liga*, 1993.
(With Jostein Gaarder) *Bibbi Bokkens Magiske Bibliotek*, Universitetsforlaget (Oslo, Norway), 1993.
Kristin og Håkon, 1993.
Drager Skal Fly, 1996.

Marie og Julesnapperen, 2000.
Kaninene Synger i Mørket, 2001.

NOVELS; "MARKUS" SERIES; FOR YOUNG ADULTS

Markus og Diana og Lyset fra Sirius (also see below), Aschehoug (Oslo, Norway), 1994, translated as *Markus and Diana*, Front Street (Asheville, NC), 2006.
Markus og Jentene, Aschehoug (Oslo, Norway), 1997.
Markus og den Store Fotballkjærligheten, Aschehoug (Oslo, Norway), 1999.
Markus og Sigmund, Aschehoug (Oslo, Norway), 2003.
Markus og Karaokekongen, Aschehoug (Oslo, Norway), 2004.

PLAYS

To Skuespill: Alice i underverdenen og Kuler i Solnedgangen (two plays), Gylendal (Oslo, Norway), 1974.
Det e Her æ høre tel og Ronnie (two plays), 1978.
To Skuespill fra Hålogaland Teater, Gylendal (Oslo, Norway), 1978.
I Denne Verden er atl Mulig (radio play/musical), Oktober (Oslo, Norway), 1979.
Roser er Røde: Skuespill, Oktober (Oslo, Norway), 1981.
Gullivers Siste Reise: Et Kjærlighetsdrama fra Verdens Begynnelse, Oktober (Oslo, Norway), 1982.
Pelle og Superstøvlene (radio play), Solum (Oslo, Norway), 1983.
Ninas Hemmelige Reise, illustrated by Bengt Olsson, Solum (Oslo, Norway), 1984.
Undrenes Tid, 1984.
Dyreklubben Møter Torden Olsen, 1986.
Heartbreak Hotel, 1987.
(With Carsten Palmær) *Såpestykket*, 1989.
Lisa og Demonen i den Gylne Byen (radio play), 1991.
Blå Fugler, 1993.
Drømmen om Sherwoodskogen og Marie og Spøkelset (two radio plays; for children), 1996.

SCREENPLAYS

Rivalen (television film), 1970.
I Denne Verden er Alt Mulig (television film), 1983.
(And director) *Nikkerne* (television film), 1984.
Høyere enn Himmelen (based on his novel), 1993.
(And assistant director) *Markus og Diana* (based on his novel *Markus og Diana og Lyset fra Sirius*), 1996.

OTHER

Slik Tenker Jeg på Dere (poetry), 1969.
(With mother, Inger Hagerup) *Alt er Så Nær Meg* (autobiography), Aschehoug (Oslo, Norway), 1988.
(With Tande-P) *God Bedring* (humor), 1991.
Seniorhumoristen (adult novel), Aschehoug (Oslo, Norway), 1994.
Maratonherren (adult novel), 1998.
Herremannen (adult novel), Aschehoug (Oslo, Norway), 2000.
(With Nils Nordberg) *Siste Akt* (crime novel), 2007.

Author of *Desperadosklubben og den Mystiske Mistenkte* (video game), 1985.

Sidelights

Norwegian author Klaus Hagerup has worked as a playwright, filmmaker, director, and actor in addition to writing fiction for teens and general readers. Sales of his first book, the poetry collection *Slik Tenker Jeg på Dere,* helped fund his education in theater. Although Hagerup initially considered himself an actor rather than writer, during the 1980s and 1990s writing became a larger part of his profession. "Today, Hagerup is considered one of the most important authors in Norway," wrote a contributor to the Internationales Literaturfestival, Berlin Web site.

Hagerup's novels are popular in and beyond Norway, and his works have been translated into several languages, including German and English. In addition, two of his novels for teens have been adapted for film. One of these, *Markus og Diana og Lyset fra Sirius,* has also been translated into English as *Markus and Diana.* In the novel, socially awkward and shy Markus is terribly afraid of girls. In order to express himself, he begins writing to celebrities by adopting various personas—a widow, a rich businessman, a track star—and asking for their autographs. When friend Sigmund persuades Markus to contact starlet Diana Mortensen, on whom Markus has a serious crush, she responds to the millionaire she thinks has written her asking for a meeting when she visits Norway. Rising to the challenge, Sigmund and Markus transform the geeky teen into a young man who could pass as the son of a millionaire.

The teens' "scheme goes awry in myriad hilarious ways," Sarah Ellis wrote in *Horn Book.* As they meet, Markus learns that hiding behind other personas may not be what he wants in life after all. "Many preteens will empathize with the boy's shyness and root for him to gain confidence," wrote Susan Riley in *School Library Journal.* Although a *Kirkus Reviews* contributor found the final meeting with Diana to be "anticlimactic," the reviewer acknowledged, "it does showcase Markus's growth and newfound willingness to take risks." The "Markus" series includes four following novels chronicling Markus's further adventures.

Along with the "Markus" series, Hagerup has written many plays and several other novels for children and young adults. His *Kaninen Synger i Mørket* is a story in the style of Lewis Carroll's *Alice in Wonderland.* Here young Else journeys into a mysterious world with rabbits who wear shorts and other bizarre creatures. He has also written an autobiography about life with his mother, Inger Hagerup, an author, playwright, and poet. Continuing the family tradition, Hagerup's daughter, Hilde Hagerup, is also an author.

Biographical and Critical Sources

PERIODICALS

Horn Book, November-December, 2006, Sarah Ellis, review of *Markus and Diana,* p. 712.

Cover of Klaus Hagerup's young-adult novel **Markus and Diana.** (Front Street, an imprint of Boyds Mills Press, Inc., 1997. Illustration © 1997 by Klaus Hagerup and H. Aschehoug & Company. Reproduced by permission.)

Kirkus Reviews, September 15, 2006, review of *Markus and Diana,* p. 954.

School Library Journal, December, 2006, Susan Riley, review of *Markus and Diana,* p. 143.

ONLINE

Boyds Mills Press Web site, http://www.boydsmillspress. com/ (December 21, 2007), "Klaus Hagerup."

Internationales Literaturfestival, Berlin Web site, http:// www.literaturfestival.com/ (December 21, 2007), "Klaus Hagerup."*

* * *

HALL, Becky 1950-

Personal

Born 1950; married; children: two. *Education:* College degree. *Hobbies and other interests:* Hiking, dogs, traveling with her family.

Addresses

Home—UT.

Career

Educator and author. Rowland Hall-St. Mark's School, Salt Lake City, UT, teacher and library media specialist.

Writings

A Is for Arches: A Utah Alphabet Book, illustrated by Katherine Larson, Sleeping Bear Press (Chelsea, MI), 2003.

Morris and Buddy: The Story of the First Seeing Eye Dog, illustrated by Doris Ettlinger, Albert Whitman (Morton Grove, IL), 2007.

Sidelights

A teacher and library media specialist, Becky Hall is also a writer whose first published book, *A Is for Arches: A Utah Alphabet Book,* introduces readers to the unique aspects of the western state where Hall lives. An interest in seeing eye dogs inspired her second book, *Morris and Buddy: The Story of the First Seeing Eye Dog,* the biography of Morris Frank. Blinded at age sixteen during a boxing match, Frank traveled from his home in New York City to Vevey, Switzerland in 1928, where he met dog trainers Dorothy Harrison Eustice and Jack Humphrey. Under the trainers' guidance, he worked with a trained German shepherd named Buddy who helped Frank learn to get around with relative independence. Although Hall ends her picture-book biography at the point where Frank completes his training and returns home to New York with Buddy, in the book's afterword she explains that Frank later became

an advocate for the blind and ultimately went on to found the Seeing Eye School to train guide dogs for other blind people. Praising Hall for her "clearly written story," Carolyn Phelan wrote in *Booklist* that *Morris and Buddy* serves as "a fresh and engaging nonfiction choice" for elementary-grade readers. In *School Library Journal,* Kathleen Kelly MacMillan was equally enthusiastic, writing that the nonfiction work "reads like a story" and "ends on a high note."

In an interview for the *Utah Children's Writers and Illustrators* Web site, Hays advised beginning writers to read a wide range of children's literature and spend time around their intended audience. "You need to know the crazy way kids think and react to the world," she added. "Picking a mentor text is a good idea too. I don't mean copying someone else's style, but if you have a writer who is a mentor for you, you begin to notice what makes their writing work. That includes typing out their text and really studying it. Then a writer has to find his own style and have lots of faith, grit and determination. Never give up."

Biographical and Critical Sources

PERIODICALS

Booklist, March 1, 2007, Carolyn Phelan, review of *Morris and Buddy: The Story of the First Seeing Eye Dog,* p. 82.

Cover of Becky Hall's Morris and Buddy, *a true story about the first seeing eye dog that features illustrations by Doris Ettlinger.* (Albert Whitman, 2007. Illustration © 2007 by Doris Ettlinger. Reproduced by permission.)

School Library Journal, May, 2007, Kathleen Kelly Mac-Millan, review of *Morris and Buddy,* p. 116.

ONLINE

Utah Children's Writers and Illustrators Web site, http://www.ucwi.org/ (November 5, 2003), interview with Hall.*

*   *   *

HARRISON, David L. 1937-
(Arthur Kennon Graham, Kennon Graham)

Personal

Born March 13, 1937, in Springfield, MO; son of John Alexander (a businessman) and Laura Neva (a homemaker) Harrison; married Sandra Sue Kennon (a high school counselor), May 23, 1959; children: Robin Lynn Harrison Williams, Jeffrey Scott. *Education:* Drury College, A.B. (biology), 1959; Emory University, M.S. (parasitology), 1960; Evansville University, graduate studies, 1960-63.

Addresses

Office—928 S. Glenstone, Springfield, MO 65802. *E-mail*—dharrison@mchsl.com.

Career

Writer. Mead Johnson Co., Evansville, IN, pharmacologist, 1960-63; Hallmark Cards, Kansas City, MO, editorial manager, 1963-73; Glenstone Block Co. (manufacturer and supply house of building materials), Springfield, MO, president and owner, 1973—. President and member of Springfield Board of Education, 1983-88; member of board, Springfield Public Schools Foundation, 1988-96; member of board of trustees, Ozarks Technical Community College, 1992-94; member of advisory board, *Springfield Parent* magazine, 1994-97. Has been a professional musician, music teacher, and principal trombonist in the Springfield Symphony. Active in various activities supporting literacy, 1982—; presenter and speaker at workshops and conferences.

Member

Society of Children's Book Writers and Illustrators, Missouri Writers Guild.

Awards, Honors

Christopher Award, Christopher Foundation, 1973, for *The Book of Giant Stories;* award for Outstanding Contributions to Children's Literature, Central State University, 1978; Distinguished Alumni Award, Drury College,

1981; Kentucky Blue Grass Award nominee, Kentucky State Reading Association, 1993, for *Somebody Catch My Homework;* Celebrate Literacy Award, Springfield Council of the International Reading Association (IRA), 1994 and 2002; Celebrate Literacy Award, Missouri State Reading Association, 1994; Friend of Education Award, Missouri State Teachers Association, 1994 and 2002; Children's Choice Award, IRA/Children's Book Council, 1994, for *Somebody Catch My Homework,* 1995, for *When Cows Come Home,* and 1997, for *A Thousand Cousins;* inclusion on Recommended Reading List, Kansas State Reading Association, 1995, and Master List of Virginia Young Readers Program, Virginia State Reading Association, 1996-97, both for *When Cows Come Home;* IRA Local Council Community Service Award, 2001, for "Sky High on Reading" literacy project; Missouri Governor's Humanities Award, 2001.

Writings

The Boy with a Drum, Golden Press (Racine, WI), 1969.
Little Turtle's Big Adventure, Random House (New York, NY), 1969.
The Little Boy in the Forest, Albert Whitman (Racine, WI), 1969.
About Me, Childcraft Education Corp., 1969.
The World of American Caves, Reilly & Lee, 1970.
The Case of Og the Missing Frog, Rand McNally (Chicago, IL), 1972.
(With Mary Loberg) *The Backyard Zoo,* Hallmark Books (Shelby, OH), 1972.
(With Mary Loberg) *The Kingdom of the Sea,* Hallmark Books (Shelby, OH), 1972.
(With Mary Loberg) *The World of Horses,* Hallmark Books (Shelby, OH), 1972.
(With Mary Loberg) *The Terrible Lizards,* Hallmark Books (Shelby, OH), 1972.
The Book of Giant Stories, illustrated by Philippe Fix, McGraw, 1972.
The Little Boy and the Giant, Golden Press (Racine, WI), 1973.
Let's Go Trucks!, Golden Press (Racine, WI), 1973.
Children Everywhere, Rand McNally (Chicago, IL), 1973.
Piggy Wiglet and the Great Adventure, Golden Press (Racine, WI), 1973.
The Huffin Puff Express, Albert Whitman (Racine, WI), 1974.
The Love Bug: Herbie's Special Friend, Golden Press (Racine, WI), 1974.
The Busy Body Book, Albert Whitman (Racine, WI), 1975.
Monster! Monster!, Golden Press (Racine, WI), 1975.
The Pink Panther in Z-Land, Albert Whitman (Racine, WI), 1976.
The Circus Is in Town, Golden Press (Racine, WI), 1978.
Detective Bob and the Great Ape Escape, illustrated by Ned Delaney, Parents Magazine Press (New York, NY), 1980.
My Funny Bunny Phone Book, illustrated by Lyn McClure Butrick, Golden Press (Racine, WI), 1980.

What Do You Know!: Mind-boggling Questions, Astonishing Answers, illustrated by Rod Ruth, Rand McNally (Chicago, IL), 1981.

The Snoring Monster, illustrated by Richard Walz, Golden Press (Racine, WI), 1985.

Busy Machines, illustrated by Richard Walz, Golden Press (Racine, WI), 1985.

Wake up, Sun!, illustrated by Hans Wilhelm, Random House (New York, NY), 1986, reprinted, 2003.

Little Boy Soup, Ladybird Books (England), 1989.

Somebody Catch My Homework: Poems, illustrated by Betsy Lewin, Boyds Mills Press (Honesdale, PA), 1993.

When Cows Come Home, illustrated by Chris L. Demarest, Boyds Mills Press (Honesdale, PA), 1994.

The Boy Who Counted Stars: Poems, illustrated by Betsy Lewin, Boyds Mills Press (Honesdale, PA), 1994.

A Thousand Cousins: Poems of Family Life, illustrated by Betsy Lewin, Boyds Mills Press (Honesdale, PA), 1996.

The Animals' Song, Boyds Mills Press (Honesdale, PA), 1997.

The Purchase of Small Secrets: Poems, Wordsong (Honesdale, PA), 1998.

Wild Country: Outdoor Poems for Young People, Wordsong (Honesdale, PA), 1999.

(With Bernice E. Cullinan) *Easy Poetry Lessons That Dazzle and Delight,* Scholastic Professional Books (New York, NY), 1999.

Farmer's Garden: Rhymes for Two Voices, illustrated by Arden Johnson-Petrov, Wordsong (Honesdale, PA), 2000.

(Adaptor) *The Big Sleepover* (based on "Clifford the Big Red Dog" series), Scholastic (New York, NY), 2001.

(Adaptor) *The Big Surprise* (based on "Clifford the Big Red Dog" series), Scholastic (New York, NY), 2001.

(Adaptor) *Dogs and Cats* (based on "Clifford the Big Red Dog" series), Scholastic (New York, NY), 2001.

Johnny Appleseed: My Story, Random House (New York, NY), 2001.

(Adaptor) *The Doggy Detectives* (based on "Clifford the Big Red Dog" series), Scholastic (New York, NY), 2001.

Dylan, the Eagle-hearted Chicken, Boyds Mills Press (Honesdale, PA), 2002.

The Alligator in the Closet, and Other Poems around the House, illustrated by Jane Kendall, Boyds Mills Press (Honesdale, PA), 2003.

The Mouse Was out at Recess, illustrated by Eugenie Fernandes, Boyds Mills Press (Honesdale, PA), 2003.

Wake up, Sun!, illustrated by Hans Wilhelm, Random House (New York, NY), 2003.

Connecting Dots: Poems of My Journey (memoir), illustrated by Kelley Cunningham Cousineau, Wordsong (Honesdale, PA), 2004.

Miss Grubb, Super Sub!: A Write-in Reader, illustrated by Page Eastburn O'Rourke, Random House (New York, NY), 2005.

Farmer's Dog Goes to the Forest: Rhymes for Two Voices, illustrated by Arden Johnson-Petrov, Wordsong (Honesdale, PA), 2005.

Sounds of Rain: Poems of the Amazon, photographs by Doug Duncan, Wordsong (Honesdale, PA), 2006.

Piggy Wiglet, Boyds Mills Press (Honesdale, PA), 2007.

Cave Detectives: Unraveling the Mystery of an Ice Age Cave, illustrated by Ashley Mims, photographs by Edward Biamonte, Chronicle Books (San Francisco, CA), 2007.

Bugs: Poems about Creeping Things, illustrated by Rob Shepperson, Wordsong (Honesdale, PA), 2007.

Pirates, illustrated by Dan Burr, Wordsong (Honesdale, PA), 2008.

"EARTHWORKS" SERIES; NONFICTION

Caves: Mysteries beneath Our Feet, illustrated by Cheryl Nathan, Boyds Mills Press (Honesdale, PA), 2001.

Rivers: Nature's Wondrous Waterways, illustrated by Cheryl Nathan, Boyds Mills Press (Honesdale, PA), 2002.

Volcanoes: Nature's Incredible Fireworks, illustrated by Cheryl Nathan, Boyds Mills Press (Honesdale, PA), 2002.

Oceans: The Vast, Mysterious Deep, illustrated by Cheryl Nathan, Boyds Mills Press (Honesdale, PA), 2003.

Earthquakes: Earth's Mightiest Moments, illustrated by Cheryl Nathan, Boyds Mills Press (Honesdale, PA), 2004.

Mountains: The Tops of the World, illustrated by Cheryl Nathan, Boyds Mills Press (Honesdale, PA), 2005.

Glaciers: Nature's Icy Caps, illustrated by Cheryl Nathan, Boyds Mills Press (Honesdale, PA), 2006.

UNDER PSEUDONYM KENNON GRAHAM

Smokey Bear Saves the Forest, Albert Whitman (Racine, WI), 1971.

Lassie and the Big Clean-up Day, Golden Press (Racine, WI), 1971.

Eloise and the Old Blue Truck, Albert Whitman (Racine, WI), 1971.

Lassie and the Secret Friend, Golden Press (Racine, WI), 1972.

My Little Book of Cars and Trucks, Albert Whitman (Racine, WI), 1973.

Woodsy Owl and the Trail Bikers, Golden Press (Racine, WI), 1974.

Land of the Lost: Surprise Guests, Golden Press (Racine, WI), 1975.

The Pink Panther in the Haunted House, Golden Press (Racine, WI), 1975.

The Pink Panther Rides Again, Albert Whitman (Racine, WI), 1976.

My Little Book about Flying, Albert Whitman (Racine, WI), 1978.

Bugs Bunny in Escape from Noddington Castle, illustrated by Darrell Baker, Golden Press (Racine, WI), 1979.

EDITOR

Peter Pan, Hallmark Books (Shelby, OH), 1964.

Cinderella, Hallmark Books (Shelby, OH), 1964.

Pinocchio, Hallmark Books (Shelby, OH), 1964.

The Adventures of Doctor Dolittle, Hallmark Books (Shelby, OH), 1965.

A Christmas Carol, Hallmark Books (Shelby, OH), 1965.

The Three Pigs, Hallmark Books (Shelby, OH), 1966.

Goldilocks and the Three Bears, Hallmark Books (Shelby, OH), 1966.

(With Sandy Asher) *Dude!: Stories and Stuff for Boys,* Dutton (New York, NY), 2006.

OTHER

Writing Stories: Fantastic Fiction from Start to Finish, Scholastic Reference (New York, NY), 2004.

Contributor of stories and poems to anthologies. Contributor of short stories, under pseudonyms Arthur Kennon Graham and Kennon Graham, to *The Witch Book,* edited by Dorothy F. Haas, Rand McNally (Chicago, IL), 1976. Contributor to periodicals, including *Highlights for Children, Family Circle, Journal of Reading, Creative Classroom, Hello Reader!, Senior Living,* and *Springfield News-Leader.* Articles and interviews have appeared in *Reading Today* and state IRS reading journals.

Author's work has been translated into more than twelve languages.

Adaptations

Harrison's works have been adapted for audiocassette and for production on television and radio throughout the world. *Somebody Catch My Homework* was adapted for CD-ROM, Discis, 1994. Sandy Asher used Harrison's poetry as inspiration for the play *Somebody Catch My Homework,* 2002.

Sidelights

Educated as a scientist, David L. Harrison worked as both a pharmacologist and an editor before going on to establish a business in his native Missouri. At the same time, he also established a successful second career as a children's book author. In the dozens of books he has written for young people, Harrison draws on his interest in science as well as on the many other interests that have enriched his life, producing award-winning stories, poetry, and retellings of classic tales in addition to nonfiction works. "By the time I was twenty-one," the author once explained, "I had worked in a pet shop, done yard work, taught music, dug ditches, unloaded boxcars, played in dance bands, poured concrete, worked in the entomology department at a university, mined uranium, and explored caves. I had also begun to write seriously, but it took nearly six more years before my first story was accepted for publication." In addition to writing, Harrison has also teamed with Sandy Asher to edit *Dude!: Stories and Stuff for Boys,* an anthology of eighteen stories, poems, and plays that, taken together, "offer an array of characters and experiences" designed to inspire curiosity in middle-grade boys, according to *Booklist* reviewer Shelle Rosenfeld.

David L. Harrison's poetry strays to the whimsical in **The Alligator in the Closet,** *a verse collection brought to life by Jane Kendall's art.* (Wordsong, an imprint of Boyds Mills Press. Illustration © 2003 by Jane Kendall. Reproduced by permission.)

In one of Harrison's best-known books, the award-winning *The Book of Giant Stories,* the author blends limericks and stories together to create a world where giants live among men. In one fantasy tale, a young boy escapes from the hands of giants by telling them a secret; in another a clever lad calms a temperamental giant by teaching him to whistle; a third story finds a boy helping an unfortunate giant who has been cursed by a wicked witch. A reviewer in *Publishers Weekly* described Harrison's book as "farfetched and funny," while Evelyn Stewart noted in *Library Journal* that the "believable fantasy is perfect for reading aloud" to younger readers.

Featuring an easy-to-read text, *Wake up, Sun!* chronicles the humorous attempts of barnyard animals to awaken the sun when they arise one morning before daybreak. *Piggy Wiglet* and *When Cows Come Home* also feature a barnyard setting. The first is the story of a curious pig who decides to catch the sun despite the effort of others to stop him, while in *When Cows Come Home* Harrison reveals what really happens on the farm when the farmer's back is turned. As soon as the farmer tends to other business, all of his cows explode in silly and whimsical stunts, such as square dancing, riding bicycles, and playing tag. Harrison's "rhyming text" combines with watercolor illustrations by Karen Stormer Brooks to "contribute to the cheerful tone of this pleasant story," wrote Linda L. Walkins in a *School Library Journal* ap-

A lost pig is the hero of Harrison's picture book **Piggy Wiglet,** *featuring artwork by Karen Stormer Brooks.* (Boyds Mills Press, Inc., 2007. Illustration © 2007 by Karen Stormer Brooks. Reproduced by permission.)

praisal of *Piggy Wigglet.* Reviewing *When the Cows Come Home,* a *Kirkus Reviews* critic complimented Harrison's "skillful versifying," while in *School Library Journal* Mary Lou Budd admired the book's "rhythmic and evocative text." A *Publishers Weekly* reviewer described *When Cows Come Home* as "a bright, appealing volume with a mischievous nature."

Harrison's picture book *Dylan, the Eagle-hearted Chicken* takes the nature-versus-nurture theory down to a child's level. After Ethel the chicken decides to take a break from sitting on her egg, it is snatched away by an old crow. The thief deposits the egg in an eagle nest, and when hatching time comes the mother eagle is surprised when a small yellow chick suddenly appears. The story continues as Dylan searches for his real mother while his eagle "siblings" contemplate eating him for lunch. A *Kirkus Reviews* writer thought that

Harrison's story has a "droll wit that bespeaks the silliness of the situation."

Many of Harrison's books feature rhyming texts geared for young readers. In *Somebody Catch My Homework* he gathers a variety of poems addressing the trials and tribulations children often have about school. Missing-homework excuses, asking timely permission for restroom privileges, and complaints about playground bullies are set to verse and salted with a sense of humor that makes them accessible to children. According to *School Library Journal* contributor Lee Bock, *Somebody Catch My Homework* is "reminiscent of the styles of [Jack] Prelutsky and [Shel] Silverstein." Writing in *Booklist,* Hazel Rochman applauded Harrison for his "immediacy and slapstick," while a *Kirkus* reviewer described *Somebody Catch My Homework* as a "genuinely funny" book "to read aloud, pass around, and chortle over again."

In *A Thousand Cousins: Poems of Family Life* Harrison provides a light-hearted look at family situations which often confuse and confound children. The poet explores the relationships between siblings and extended family members and makes light of situations common to many children, such as fathers snoring loudly and mothers incessantly reminding their kids to keep clean. A critic in *Kirkus Reviews* observed that most of the poems "have punchy endings; each revolves around some gimmick." *School Library Journal* contributor Marjorie Lewis asserted that these poems will "elicit giggles from young readers and listeners." A similar topical familiarity informs *The Alligator in the Closet: And Other Poems around the House.* The verses in this collection focus on such commonplace household moments as the disruption posed by a new baby, a barking dog, a pesky spider, or the lack of toilet paper in the bathroom. *Booklist* correspondent Carolyn Phelan felt that the "familiar, homely topics and straightforward approach" make *The Alligator in the Closet* a good choice for reading out loud.

In *The Purchase of Small Secrets* Harrison compiles thirty-eight free-verse poems about a boy growing up in the country, while *Wild Country: Outdoor Poems for Young People* collects several short poems about Harrison's observations in the wild. *Wild Country* is separated into four sections: "Mountains," "High Country," "Forest," and "Sea." Also drawing from anture, *The Animals' Song* is a book-length nonsense rhyme that includes children playing instruments and animals making their respective noises.

Turning to more exotic locales, *Sounds of Rain: Poems of the Amazon* brings to life the many animals and plants that populate the rainforests surrounding the Amazon River in South America. Inspired by a trip to the Amazon region, the book is formatted like a scrapbook and features photographs by fellow traveler Doug Duncan. Harrison's trip to the Amazon is part of a much larger tapestry, as he shows in *Connecting Dots: Poems of My Journey,* a memoir composed of fifty-four poems. Moving from childhood to his teenage years to adulthood, Harrison's short poems express the wisdom he has gained throughout life, resulting in "an interesting endeavor," in the opinion of *School Library Journal* contributor Laura Reed.

In his "Earthwork" nonfiction series Harrison focuses on Earth science. He introduces young readers to cave formation in *Caves: Mysteries beneath Our Feet* offers scientific information in the form of a story. When Farmer Howe's cow leaves the pasture to stand in front of the entrance to a cave, the curious farmer discovers that breezes from the underground caves are keeping the cow cool. The book also describes how caves evolve and what is inside them. In *Booklist* Kelly Milner Halls called *Caves* "science with grace."

The "Earthworks" series continues with *Rivers: Nature's Wondrous Waterways, Volcanoes: Nature's Incredible Fireworks, Oceans: The Vast, Mysterious Deep, Earthquakes: Earth's Mightiest Movements, Glacier: Nature's Icy Caps,* and *Mountains: The Tops of the World.* In *Rivers* Harrison discusses the water cycle, ecology, geology, and environmental awareness while focusing mainly on rivers in his rhyming text. *Volcanoes* explains how volcanoes form, where they can be found, and what happens when they erupt while *Oceans* introduces readers to Earth's water cycle and phenomena such as tsunamis, el niño, and hurricanes. *Glaciers* and *Mountains* both focus on the slow but relentless changes occurring on Earth's surface. *School Library Journal* contributor Lynn Dye noted in her review of *Rivers* that Harrison's explanation of how a river forms is written in "clear, poetic prose." Although a critic for *Kirkus Reviews* maintained that the book leaves many questions unanswered, Carolyn Phelan praised *Volcanoes* in *Booklist* for its "surprisingly graceful text." *Oceans* "could inspire a deeper exploration of the subject," concluded *School Library Journal* reviewer Dona Ratterree, and Phelan praised *Mountains* for presenting a "simple, clear discussion" of the sometimes complex and still unfolding science of plate tectonics.

Other nonfiction works include *Cave Detectives: Unraveling the Mystery of an Ice Age.* Readers can follow the discovery and exploration of Riverbluff Cave, a Missouri cave that, in 2001, was found to contain the oldest fossil remains yet discovered in North America. Revealed by a road crew engaged in blasting a roadbed into the side of a hill, the cave rewarded scientists with a look back tens of thousands of years into the past, to the ice age. Citing the book's "inviting design," Marcia Kochel praised *Cave Detectives* in her *School Library Journal* review, noting that Harrison's "narrative is smooth and easy to follow" and is likely to inspire readers to learn more about the work of modern paleontologists.

Reflecting on his decades-long career as a writer, Harrison once commented on the way "folks react if you tell them you write for young people. They used to say something like, 'Oh?' beneath arched eyebrows, signifying that it was a darned pity you couldn't make it as a real writer. Thanks to our nation's well-founded concerns about educating and developing our newest generations, writing for young people is now recognized as a worthy goal. Writers have always known that they must grow with their work. What could be a better strategy for success than to choose an audience that also must keep growing?" In an effort to contribute to the success of others in the same field, Harrison has also produced *Writing Stories: Fantastic Fiction from Start to Finish,* which provides suggestions and examples geared for budding middle-grade writers. Praising the work for its "enthusiastic tone," Linda Wadleigh added in *School Library Journal* that *Writing Stories* will inspire "students . . . to start their own writing careers."

Harrison casts his poet's eye on nature in **Rivers,** *an informational picture book featuring captivating artwork by Cheryl Nathan.* (Boyds Mills Press, Inc., 2002. Illustration © 2002 by Cheryl Nathan. Reproduced by permission.)

Biographical and Critical Sources

PERIODICALS

Booklist, May 1, 1994, Janice Del Negro, review of *When Cows Come Home,* p. 1608; April 1, 1997, Hazel Rochman, review of *The Animals' Song,* p. 1337; November 15, 1999, Carolyn Phelan, review of *Wild Country: Outdoor Poems for Young People,* p. 620; September 1, 2000, Ellen Mandel, review of *A Farmer's Garden: Rhymes for Two Voices,* p. 122; September 15, 2001, Kelly Milner Halls, review of *Caves: Mysteries beneath Our Feet,* p. 228; February 1, 2002, Carolyn Phelan, review of *Johnny Appleseed: My Story,* p. 949; April 1, 2002, Shelley Townsend-Hudson, review of *Rivers: Nature's Wondrous Waterways,* p. 1330; July, 2002, Carolyn Phelan, review of *Volcanoes: Nature's Incredible Fireworks,* p. 1851; April 1, 2003, Carolyn Phelan, review of *The Alligator in the Closet, and Other Poems around the House,* p. 1408; January 1, 2004, Stephanie Zvirin, review of *Oceans: The Vast, Mysterious Deep,* p. 864; November 1, 2004, GraceAnne A. DeCandido, review of *Writing Stories,* p. 478; September 1, 2005, Hazel Rochman, review of *Farmer's Dog Goes to the Forest: Rhymes for Two Voices,* p. 144; November 1, 2005, Carolyn Phelan, review of *Mountains: The Tops of the World,* p. 49; April 1, 2006, Carolyn Phelan, review of *Glaciers: Nature's Icy Caps,* p. 45; July 1,

2006, Shelle Rosenfeld, review of *Dude!: Stories and Stuff for Boys,* p. 86; March 1, 2007, Hazel Rochman, review of *Bugs: Poems about Creeping Things,* p. 86; May 1, 2007, Carolyn Phelan, review of *Cave Detectives: Unraveling the Mystery of an Ice Age Cave,* p. 90.

Kirkus Reviews, March 15, 2002, review of *Rivers,* p. 412; August 1, 2002, review of *Volcanoes,* p. 1131; August 15, 2002, review of *Dylan, the Eagle-hearted Chicken,* p. 1225; August 15, 2003, review of *The Mouse Was out at Recess: Poems,* p. 1074; August 15, 2004, review of *Earthquakes,* p. 806; November 15, 2004, review of *Connecting Dots: Poems of My Journey,* p. 1089; August 15, 2005, review of *Mountains,* p. 1027; June 1, 2006, review of *Dude!,* p. 568; November 1, 2006, review of *Sounds of Rain: Poems of the Amazon,* p. 1122; February 15, 2007, review of *Bugs;* May 15, 2007, review of *Cave Detectives.*

Library Journal, January 15, 1973, Evelyn Stewart, review of *The Book of Giant Stories,* p. 253.

Publishers Weekly, November 29, 1993, p. 64; December 17, 2001, review of *The Book of Giant Stories,* p. 94.

School Library Journal, March, 1997, Patricia Pearl Doyle, review of *The Animals' Song,* p. 160; November 1, 1998, Angela J. Reynolds, review of *The Purchase of Small Secrets,* p. 136; December, 1999, Carolyn Angus, review of *Wild Country,* p. 151; November, 2000, Susan Scheps, review of *Farmer's Garden,* p. 122; October, 2001, Catherine Threadgill, review of *Mysteries beneath Our Feet,* p. 140; May, 2002, Lynn

Dye, review of *Rivers*, p. 138; August, 2002, Gay Lynn Van Vleck, review of *Dylan, the Eagle-hearted Chicken*, p. 156; March, 2003, Nancy Palmer, review of *The Alligator in the Closet*, p. 218; September, 2003, John Peters, review of *The Mouse Was out at Recess*, p. 199; January, 2004, Dona Ratterree, review of *Oceans*, p. 117; November, 2004, Sandra Welzenbach, review of *Earthquakes*, p. 124; December, 2004, Laura Reed, review of *Connecting Dots*, p. 162; January, 2005, Linda Wadleigh, review of *Writing Stories: Fantastic Fiction from Start to Finish*, p. 148; September, 2005, Marilyn Taniguchi, review of *Farmer's Dog Goes to the Forest*, p. 192; October, 2005, Eva Elisabeth Von Ancken, review of *Mountains*, p. 138; August, 2006, Coop Renner, review of *Dude!*, p. 113; August, 2006, Michael Santangelo, review of *Glaciers*, p. 105; December, 2006, Kathleen Whalin, review of *Sounds of Rain*, p. 163; May, 2007, Linda L. Walkins, review of *Piggy Wiglet*, p. 98; June, 2007, Julie Roach, review of *Bugs*, p. 133; August, 2007, Marcia Kochel, review of *Cave Detectives*, p. 134.

ONLINE

Drury University Web site, http://www.drury.edu/ (January 10, 2008), "Alumni Profile: David L. Harrison, '59."*

*   *   *

HAYASHI, Nancy 1939-

Personal

Born November 11, 1939, in Bucyrus, OH; daughter of Howard (a building contractor) and Janette (a homemaker) Schieber; married Tom Hayashi (a computer field engineer), April 12, 1969; children: Brian, David. *Education:* Denison University, B.A., 1962; attended Cleveland Art Institute, 1962-65. *Hobbies and other interests:* Reading, hiking, camping, travel.

Addresses

Home and office—Los Angeles, CA.

Career

Author and illustrator. Layout artist at Higbee's Department Store, 1964-66; art director at Bowes Advertising, 1966-75, and Baxter, Gurian & Mazzei Advertising, 1975-77; freelance writer and illustrator.

Member

Society of Children's Book Writers and Illustrators, Southern California Council on Literature for Children and Young People.

Writings

SELF-ILLUSTRATED

Cosmic Cousin (middle-grade novel), Dutton (New York, NY), 1988.

The Fantastic Stay-Home-from-School Day (middle-grade novel), Dutton (New York, NY), 1992.
Superbird to the Rescue, Dutton (New York, NY), 1995.

ILLUSTRATOR

Paula Kursbad Feder, *Did You Lose That Car Again?*, Dutton (New York, NY), 1990.
Cynthia Rylant, *Bunny Bungalow*, Harcourt (New York, NY), 1999.
Effin Older, *My Two Grandmothers*, Harcourt (New York, NY), 2000.
Kerry Arquette, *What Did You Do Today?*, Harcourt (San Diego, CA), 2002.
Eileen Spinelli, *Wanda's Monster*, Albert Whitman (Morton Grove, IL), 2002.
Eileen Spinelli, *I Know It's Autumn*, HarperCollins (New York, NY), 2004.
Barbara Bottner, *Raymond and Nelda*, Peachtree (Atlanta, GA), 2007.

Biographical and Critical Sources

PERIODICALS

Booklist, October 15, 2000, Carolyn Phelan, review of *My Two Grandmothers*, p. 446; August, 2004, Carolyn Phelan, review of *I Know It's Autumn*, p. 1944.
Bulletin of the Center for Children's Books, January, 1989, review of *Cosmic Cousin*, p. 123; May, 1995, review of *Superbird to the Rescue*, p. 309.
Horn Book, January-February, 2003, Betty Carter, review of *Wanda's Monster*, p. 63.
Publishers Weekly, January 27, 1992, review of *The Fantastic Stay-Home-from-School Day*, p. 98.
School Library Journal, February, 1989, review of *Cosmic Cousin*, p. 81; August, 1992, Rita Soltan, review of *The Fantastic Stay-Home-from-School Day*, p. 136; May, 1995, Blair Christolon, review of *Superbird to the Rescue*, p. 106; October, 2002, Be Astengo, review of *Wanda's Monster*, p. 132; August, 2004, Kathleen Kelly MacMillan, review of *I Know It's Autumn*, p. 94.*

*   *   *

HICKMAN, Pamela 1958-

Personal

Born December 4, 1958, in Cooksville, Ontario, Canada; daughter of Melville (an Air Canada Express manager) and Marguerite (a homemaker) Hunter; married P. Douglas Hickman (an environmental consultant), June 27, 1981; children: Angela Lindsey, Connie Marie, Jennifer Lee. *Education:* University of Waterloo, B.S. (with honors; environmental studies/biology), 1980. *Hobbies and other interests:* Gardening, camping, collecting antiques, reading, travel.

Addresses

Office—Box 296, Canning, Nova Scotia B0P 1H0, Canada.

Career

Writer and naturalist. Alberta Environment, mosquito control technician, Edmonton, Alberta, Canada, 1979, plant-sciences technician in Vegreville, Alberta, 1980-81; Federation of Ontario Naturalists, Toronto, Ontario, Canada, education coordinator, 1982-90; freelance writer, beginning 1989. Apple Tree Landing Children's Centre, Canning, Nova Scotia, Canada, chairperson of board of directors, beginning 1994. Glooscap Home and School Association, member of executive committee, beginning 1992.

Member

World Wildlife Fund, Canadian Children's Book Centre, Writers Federation of Nova Scotia, Federation of Ontario Naturalists.

Awards, Honors

Ann Connor Brimer Award shortlist, 1993, for *Wetlands,* and 1998, for *Animal Senses;* Lilla Sterling Memorial Award, Canadian Authors Association, 1995, for *Habitats;* Red Cedar Book Award shortlist, 1998, for *Jumbo Book of Nature Science* and *Night Book;* Hackmatack Children's Choice Award finalist, 2000, for *At the Seashore.*

Writings

Getting to Know Nature's Children: A Parent's Guide, Grolier (Danbury, CT), 1985.

Birdwise: Forty Fun Feats for Finding out about Our Feathered Friends, illustrated by Judie Shore, Kids Can Press (Toronto, Ontario, Canada), 1988.

Bugwise: Thirty Incredible Insect Investigations and Arachnid Activities, illustrated by Judie Shore, Kids Can Press (Toronto, Ontario, Canada), 1990.

Plantwise, illustrated by Judie Shore, Kids Can Press (Toronto, Ontario, Canada), 1991.

Habitats: Making Homes for Animals and Plants, illustrated by Sarah Jane English, Kids Can Press (Toronto, Ontario, Canada), 1993.

Wetlands, illustrated by Judie Shore, Kids Can Press (Toronto, Ontario, Canada), 1993.

The Night Book: Exploring Nature after Dark with Activities, Experiments, and Information, illustrated by Suzanne Mogensen, Kids Can Press (Toronto, Ontario, Canada), 1996.

At the Seashore, Formac (Halifax, Nova Scotia, Canada), 1996.

The Jumbo Book of Nature Science, illustrated by Judie Shore, Kids Can Press (Toronto, Ontario, Canada), 1996.

The Kid's Canadian Plant Book, illustrated by Heather Collins, Kids Can Press (Toronto, Ontario, Canada), 1996.

The Kid's Canadian Bird Book, illustrated by Heather Collins, Kids Can Press (Toronto, Ontario, Canada), 1996.

The Kid's Canadian Bug Book, illustrated by Heather Collins, Kids Can Press (Toronto, Ontario, Canada), 1996.

The Kid's Canadian Tree Book, illustrated by Heather Collins, Kids Can Press (Toronto, Ontario, Canada), 1996.

A Seed Grows: My First Look at a Plant's Life Cycle, Kids Can Press (Toronto, Ontario, Canada), 1997.

Hungry Animals: My First Look at a Food Chain, illustrated by Heather Collins, Kids Can Press (Toronto, Ontario, Canada), 1997.

A New Butterfly: My First Look at Metamorphosis, Kids Can Press (Toronto, Ontario, Canada), 1997.

Animal Senses: How Animals See, Hear, Taste, Smell, and Feel, illustrated by Pat Stephens, Kids Can Press (Toronto, Ontario, Canada), 1998, revised by David MacDonald as *How Animals Use Their Senses,* 2007.

In the Woods, illustrated by Twila Robar-DeCoste, Formac (Halifax, Nova Scotia, Canada), 1998.

A New Frog: My First Look at the Life Cycle of an Amphibian, illustrated by Heather Collins, Kids Can Press (Toronto, Ontario, Canada), 1999.

A New Duck: My First Look at the Life Cycle of a Bird, illustrated by Heather Collins, Kids Can Press (Toronto, Ontario, Canada), 1999.

Animals in Motion: How Animals Swim, Jump, Slither, and Slide, illustrated by Pat Stevens, Kids Can Press (Toronto, Ontario, Canada), 2000, revised by David MacDonald as *How Animals Move,* 2007.

Animals Eating: How Animals Chomp, Chew, Slurp, and Swallow, illustrated by Pat Stevens, Kids Can Press (Toronto, Ontario, Canada), 2001, revised by David MacDonald as *How Animals Eat,* 2007.

Animals and Their Young: How Animals Produce and Care for Their Babies, illustrated by Pat Stevens, Kids Can Press (Toronto, Ontario, Canada), 2003.

Animals and Their Mates: How Animals Attract, Fight for, and Protect Each Other, illustrated by Pat Stephens, Kids Can Press (Toronto, Ontario, Canada), 2004.

Animals Hibernating: How Animals Survive Extreme Conditions, illustrated by Pat Stevens, Kids Can Press (Toronto, Ontario, Canada), 2005.

Turtle Rescue ("Changing the Future for Endangered Wildlife" series), Firefly Books (Buffalo, NY), 2005.

Birds of Prey Rescue ("Changing the Future for Endangered Wildlife" series), Firefly Books (Buffalo, NY), 2006.

It's Moving Day, illustrated by Geraldo Valério, Kids Can Press (Toronto, Ontario, Canada), 2008.

Writer for "Kids Canadian Nature Series," Kids Can Press (Toronto, Ontario, Canada), 1995-96.

Sidelights

Active in environmental issues that draw on her life-long interest in the biological sciences, Pamela Hickman specializes in introducing young readers to the world of plants and animals. Born and raised in Ontario, Canada, and now a resident of Nova Scotia, she began writing for children while working as education coordinator for the Federation of Ontario Naturalists. Beginning her new career as a children's book author in the late 1980s, Hickman shares her love of nature with beginning readers in books such as *Birds of Prey Rescue, Animals and Their Young: How Animals Produce and Care for Their Babies,* and *It's Moving Day,* the last a picture book pairing Hickman's simple text with colorful art by Geraldo Valério. Praising *Birds of Prey Rescue* in *Resource Links,* Angela Thompson cited Hickman's contribution to the nonfiction nature books available to young readers, noting that her writing "reflects a wealth of research and personal knowledge."

Many of Hickman's books focus specifically on the ecosystems native to Canada. In *The Kid's Canadian Tree Book,* which features illustrations by Heather Collins, Hickman combines hands-on activities, interesting facts, and useful observations to help readers learn to distinguish tree species near their homes. Other volumes, such as *Animal Senses: How Animals See, Hear, Taste, Smell, and Feel, Hungry Animals: My First Look at a Food Chain,* and *A New Duck: My First Look at the Life Cycle of a Bird,* focus on the habitat, life cycle, and other characteristics of the many creatures that inhabit North America. Reviewing *Animal Senses* in *Booklist,* Carolyn Phelan wrote that the book matches "pick-me-up visual appeal with solid facts about animal senses." Discussing a companion volume, *Animals and Their Young,* Karen McKinnon praised the "lovely illustrations" by Pat Stephens in her *Resource Links* review and described the work as "a great little book for students" in search of "not too well-known information about some common and some not so common animals."

Hickman gets much of the inspiration for her nature books from living in Nova Scotia. "Our property . . . includes a wooded ravine, marsh and meadow," she commented on the *Kids Can Press* Web site. "I can watch birds, hear cicadas and smell the wildflowers as I work. Nature offers unlimited scope for new discoveries, and I know it will continue to challenge and intrigue me throughout my life." As she once told *SATA,* the most rewarding part of her career as a nonfiction author "is that I learn so much as I do my research. I also love the fact that I can go out bird-watching or down to the seashore, walk in the woods, or stroll through a meadow and still be working! Everything I see, smell, touch, taste, and hear can become part of a book. I find it much easier to write about something I have experienced firsthand. My main motivation for writing is to share my love and enthusiasm for nature with my readers, and I hope to kindle a similar lifelong joy in them."

Biographical and Critical Sources

PERIODICALS

Booklist, May 15, 1998, Carolyn Phelan, review of *Animal Senses: How Animals See, Hear, Taste, Smell, and Feel,* p. 1623; May 1, 2000, Carolyn Phelan, review of *Animals in Motion: How Animals Swim, Jump, Slither, and Glide,* p. 1664; March 1, 2003, Diane Foote, review of *Animals and Their Young: How Animals Produce and Care for Their Babies,* p. 1194; October 15, 2004, Carolyn Phelan, review of *Animals and Their Mates: How Animals Attract, Fight for, and Protect Each Other,* p. 401; November 1, 2005, John Peters, review of *Animals Hibernating: How Animals Survive Extreme Conditions,* p. 43.

Kirkus Reviews, February 1, 2003, review of *Animals and Their Young,* p. 231; September 1, 2004, review of *Animals and Their Mates,* p. 866; August 15, 2005, review of *Animals Hibernating,* p. 915; February 15, 2007, review of *How Animals Eat.*

Resource Links, June, 2000, review of *Animals in Motion,* pp. 11-12; June, 2006, Angela Thompson, review of *Birds of Prey Rescue,* p. 34; February, 2007, Karen McKinnon, review of *How Animals Use Their Senses,* p. 4.

School Library Journal, May, 2001, Cynthia M. Sturgis, review of *Animals Eating: How Animals Chomp, Chew, Slurp, and Swallow,* p. 142; June, 2003, Nancy Call, review of *Animals and Their Young,* p. 128; October, 2005, Sandra Welzenbach, review of *Animals Hibernating,* p. 140; June, 2006, Gail E. Wellman, review of *Turtle Rescue,* p. 178.

ONLINE

Kids Can Press Web site, http://www.kidscanpress.com/ (January 10, 2008), "Pamela Hickman."

Writers' Federation of Nova Scotia Web site, http://www. writers.ns.ca/ (January 10, 2008), "Pamela Hickman."*

*   *   *

HILL, Stuart 1958-

Personal

Born 1958, in Leicester, England. *Education:* University graduate.

Addresses

Home and office—Leicester, England.

Career

Bookseller and children's writer. Worked previously as a car trimmer, an archaeologist, and a teacher.

Awards, Honors

Ottakars Prize for best new children's novel, for *The Cry of the Icemark.*

Writings

The Cry of the Icemark, Scholastic (New York, NY), 2005.
Blade of Fire, Scholastic (New York, NY), 2007.

Adaptations

The Cry of the Icemark was optioned by film. Hill's novels have also been adapted as audiobooks.

Sidelights

Bookseller and children's writer Stuart Hill learned to read later than most of his peers. "I couldn't read or write until I was seven and I can still remember that almost magical feeling when those strange angular symbols actually began to have a meaning," he told an interviewer at the *DoubleCluck* Web site. "After that I couldn't stop playing with words and their sounds and meaning." Though his grades were only average, Hill "was fortunate to have a teacher who inspired in him a lifelong love of reading," wrote a contributor to the *Scholastic Web site.* While further honing his interest in reading, Hill worked as a car trimmer, then later as a teacher and an archaeologist.

Hill's first published novel, *The Cry of the Icemark,* was written during the coffee breaks he had in his job working in a bookstore. The novel spins a fantasy about a young queen name Thirrin, who must unite with ancient enemies to defeat the foe who comes marching

Cover of Stuart Hill's fantasy novel **The Cry of the Icemark,** *featuring cover art by Gary Blythe.* (Scholastic, 2005. Parisi, Elizabeth B., book designer. Front cover art copyright © 2005 by Gary Blythe and Carol Lawson. Reprinted by permission of Scholastic Inc.)

onto her land. With the aid of her friend, advisor, and romantic interest Oskan the Warlock, Thirrin travels to gain the aid of the vampire king and queen, the werewolves who live on her borders, and the giant snow leopards that claim the woodlands as their own. Although her story is firmly set in the realms of fantasy, Thirrin is based on someone from Hill's life: his sister, Kathleen, who died of leukemia when he was a teen.

Jennifer Mattson, writing in *Booklist,* called *The Cry of the Icemark* an "extravagant first novel" and added that "Hill's affection for his characters . . . will prove infectious." Noting that the novel incorporates several elements more traditionally associated with horror or urban fantasy, Michele Winship noted in *Kliatt* that Hill "skillfully reinvents them to fit into his world." A *Publishers Weekly* contributor observed that the author "braids these elements smoothly, and his winning heroine will lead readers through." Jane P. Fenn, reviewing *The Cry of the Icemark* for *School Library Journal,* concluded that "fantasy fans and those with some familiarity with ancient history will enjoy this inventive tale."

Told from the point of view of her children, Thirrin's saga continues in *Blade of Fire.* Thirrin's youngest son, Charlemagne or "Sharly," suffered from polio and is lame. Unable to defend his nation when the enemy approaches the border again, Thirrin sends her son with the refugees being transported to safer southern lands so he can serve as the regent for their community. In the lands of these desert people, Sharly discovers that he may be the center of a prophecy regarding the preservation of his homeland. "Readers will be drawn to the likeable Sharly, cheering him on as he finds his place in the world," wrote Winship in *Kliatt.* Mattson described the book as "epic in scope" and noted that "the high-fantasy action moves right along." Tina Everitt, reviewing *Blade of Fire* for *Bookseller,* concluded: "I cannot wait for the next installment."

When asked by an interviewer at the *DoubleCluck* Web site about his ideal time and place for writing, Hill replied: "My ideal time and place would be an oak-paneled study with hours of uninterrupted leisure in which to enjoy the process of writing. The reality is a little different, i.e., a scruffy bedroom with a tired old laptop on which I desperately bang out a few paragraphs whenever I get the chance in a frantic day. Oh yes, and Mr. B. (my cat) likes to stuff his tail up my nose just when I'm coming to a difficult bit."

Biographical and Critical Sources

PERIODICALS

Booklist, February 15, 2005, Jennifer Mattson, review of *The Cry of the Icemark,* p. 1072; March 15, 2007, Jennifer Mattson, review of *Blade of Fire,* p. 47.

seemingly abandoned, while her dad's
becomes a spell and an overly strict teacher
he role of Wicked Witch.

adance as an "endearing" protagonist "whose
n and ability with language" make her stand
he novel's other teen characters, Claire Rosser
liatt that "Holmes' novel-in-letters balances
nny" commentary with more sober reflections
ily in crisis." The author captures "the con-
l tone characteristic of middle graders," noted
rs Weekly reviewer, the critic adding that the
"poignant" letters to her unknown recipient
o thoughtful readers involved" in the girl's
life. In *Kirkus Reviews* a writer noted that,
Iolmes' efforts to balance humor with more
atters may confuse readers, her story's "con-
s can be intriguing" and "may . . . cast a
some readers." *Letters from Rapunzel* cap-
universal angst of adolescence," observed D.
Rocco in her *School Library Journal* review,
concluding of Cadance that Holmes' preteen
st "leaves readers with the wisdom that one
ie oneself before rescuing others."

her fictional heroine, Holmes commented to
loved fairy tales as a kid; they were full of
and danger and love and courage and most
gic, which I totally believed in. Everything
red was there. For Cadence, not only are fairy
ething she shares with her dad, but they're
vay of making sense of what's happening. I
right to look for other explanations, to search
n words, to make her own magic and find her
y ending. Don't we all want that?"

hical and Critical Sources

LS

f *the Center for Children's Books,* May, 2007,
  Coats, review of *Letters from Rapunzel,* p. 371.
iews, February 15, 2007, review of *Letters from
  zel.*
rch, 2007, Claire Rosser, review of *Letters from
  zel,* p. 14.
Weekly, March 19, 2007, review of *Letters from
  zel,* p. 64.
ibrary Journal, February, 2007, D. Maria
  co, review of *Letters from Rapunzel,* p. 118.

e *Forest* Web site, http://www.theedgeoftheforest.
  (January 15, 2008), interview with Holmes.
is *Holmes Blog* site, http://saralewisholmes.
  ot.com/ (January 15, 2008).
is *Holmes Home Page,* http://www.saralewis
  s.com (January 15, 2008).

HUBBELL, Patricia 1928-

Personal
Born July 10, 1928, in Bridgeport, CT; daughter of Franklin H. (a watershed manager) and Helen (a homemaker) Hubbell; married Harold Hornstein (a newspaper editor), March 10, 1954; children: Jeffrey, Deborah. *Education:* University of Connecticut, B.A., 1950. *Politics:* "Independent." *Hobbies and other interests:* Painting, crafts, gardening, reading, horses.

Addresses
Home—Easton, CT. *E-mail*—PatHubbell@kidspoet.com.

Career
Author. *Newtown Bee,* Newtown, CT, member of staff, 1950-51; *Westport Town Crier,* Westport, CT, reporter, 1951-54; *Bridgeport Sunday Post,* Bridgeport, CT, horse and dog columnist, 1958-68; author of children's poetry and picture books, beginning 1963; freelance writer specializing in gardening and nature, 1968-88.

Member
Authors Guild, Authors League, Society of Children's Book Writers and Illustrators.

Awards, Honors
Nick, Jr. magazine Best Books of the Year list, Oppenheim Toy Group Gold Medal, and Bank Street College Best Books of the Year list, all for *Bouncing Time; Parents* Best Books of the Year list, and American Booksellers Association Kids' Pick of the Lists designation, both for *Wrapping Paper Romp;* Bank Street College Best Books of the Year, and *Parenting* magazine Reading Magic Award, both 1999, both for *Sidewalk Trip;* Sequoyah Oklahoma Children's Book Award finalist, for *A Grass Green Gallop;* Children's Book Award finalist, Connecticut Center for the Book, 2004, Children's Gallery Award masterlist, National Christian School Association 2005-06, and Crown Gallery Award nomination, all for *Black All Around!*

Writings

POETRY

The Apple Vendor's Fair, illustrated by Julie Maas, Atheneum (New York, NY), 1963.
8 A.M. Shadows, illustrated by Julie Maas, Atheneum (New York, NY), 1965.
Catch Me a Wind, illustrated by Susan Trommler, Atheneum (New York, NY), 1968.
The Tigers Brought Pink Lemonade (poems), illustrated by Ju-Hong Chen, Atheneum (New York, NY), 1988.

Hill's fantasy saga continues in **Blade of Fire,** *featuring cover art by* ***Gary Blythe.*** (Scholastic, 2007. Parisi, Elizabeth B. and Jensen, Leyah, jacket designers. Jacket art copyright © 2007 by Gary Blythe and Carol Lawson. Reprinted by permission of Scholastic Inc.)

Bookseller, October 20, 2006, Tina Everitt, review of *Blade of Fire,* p. 15.

Bulletin of the Center for Children's Books, April, 2005, Timnah Card, review of *The Cry of the Icemark,* p. 339.

Kirkus Reviews, April 1, 2005, review of *The Cry of the Icemark,* p. 418.

Kliatt, May, 2005, Michele Winship, review of *The Cry of the Icemark,* p. 13; January, 2007, Michele Winship, review of *Blade of Fire,* p. 12.

Publishers Weekly, review of *The Cry of the Icemark,* 61.

School Library Journal, May, 2005, Sue Giffard, review of *The Cry of the Icemark,* p. 128; November, 2006, Jane P. Fenn, review of *The Cry of the Icemark,* p. 63; June, 2007, Marie C. Hansen, review of *Blade of Fire,* p. 146.

Voice of Youth Advocates, June, 2005, Sarah Flowers, review of *The Cry of the Icemark,* p. 148; April, 2007, Sarah Flowers, review of *Blade of Fire,* p. 65.

ONLINE

BookBrowse Web site, http://www.bookbrowse.com/ (December 21, 2007), "Stuart Hill."

DoubleCluck Web site, http://w
cember 21, 2007), interviev
Scholastic Web site, http://wwv
ber 21, 2007), "Stuart Hill.'

*   *

HOLMES, Sara Lewis

Personal

Married; children: two. *Educa.*
of North Carolina at Chapel
and Mary, B.A. (government).
ests: Fitness, golf, theatre, rea
tales, poetry.

Addresses

Home—Lorton, VA. *E-mail*—
com.

Career

Author of novels and short fict

Member

Society of Children's Book Wr
thors Guild.

Awards, Honors

Ursula Nordstrom Fiction Cont
ters from Rapunzel.

Writings

Letters from Rapunzel, HarperC
2007.

Contributor of short stories to
Spider and *Cricket,* and to anth
tains of the Moon.

Sidelights

Sara Lewis Holmes won the
Fiction Contest for the manus
Letters from Rapunzel. Holmes
tive premise: As a way to deal v
ther's hospitalization for clini
year-old Cadance Brogan
correspondence with the unkno
Box 5667. The box-holder is
corresponded with prior to his
Cadance the letters allow her to
phor for her situation. Within t
sided correspondence, she bec

lated a
depress
assumes

Praising
imagina
out from
noted i
"wildly
on "a f.
versatio
a *Publis*
narrator
"will ke
emotior
althoug
serious
tradicti
spell ov
tures "t
Maria I
the criti
protago
must re

Regardi
SATA:
real blo
of all,
that ma
tales so
also her
think sh
for her
own ha

Biogra

PERIOD

Bulletin
Kar
Kirkus
Raj
Kliatt,
Raj
Publishe
Raj
School
LaF

ONLINE

Edge of
con
Sara L
blog
Sara L
holu

A Grass Green Gallop, illustrated by Ronald Himler, Atheneum (New York, NY), 1990.

Boo!: Halloween Poems and Limericks, illustrated by Jeff Spackman, Marshall Cavendish (New York, NY), 1998.

Earthmates, illustrated by Jean Cassels, Marshall Cavendish (New York, NY), 1999.

City Kids, illustrated by Teresa Flavin, Marshall Cavendish (New York, NY), 2001.

Black Earth, Gold Sun, illustrated by Mary Newell De-Palma, Marshall Cavendish (New York, NY), 2001.

Rabbit Moon: A Book of Holidays and Celebrations, illustrated by Wendy Watson, Marshall Cavendish (New York, NY), 2002.

PICTURE BOOKS

(With Bethany Roberts) *Camel Caravan,* illustrated by Cheryl Munro Taylor, Tambourine (New York, NY), 1996.

(With Bethany Roberts) *Eleven Elephants Going Up!,* illustrated by Minh Uong, Whispering Coyote Press (Boston, MA), 1996.

Pots and Pans, illustrated by Diane de Groat, HarperFestival (New York, NY), 1998.

Wrapping Paper Romp, illustrated by Jennifer Plecas, HarperFestival (New York, NY), 1998.

Sidewalk Trip, illustrated by Mari Takabayashi, HarperFestival (New York, NY), 1999.

Bouncing Time, illustrated by Melissa Sweet, HarperCollins (New York, NY), 2000.

Sea, Sand, Me!, illustrated by Lisa Campbell Ernst, HarperCollins (New York, NY), 2001.

Black All Around!, illustrated by Don Tate, Lee & Low (New York, NY), 2003.

I Like Cats, illustrated by Pamela Paparone, North-South Books (New York, NY), 2003.

Trucks: Whizz! Zoom! Rumble!, illustrated by Megan Halsey, Marshall Cavendish (New York, NY), 2003.

Hurray for Spring!, illustrated by Taia Morley, NorthWord Books (Minnetonka, MN), 2005.

Trains: Steaming! Pulling! Huffing!, illustrated by Megan Halsey and Sean Addy, Marshall Cavendish (New York, NY), 2005.

Cars: Rushing! Honking! Zooming!, illustrated by Megan Halsey and Sean Addy, Marshall Cavendish (New York, NY), 2006.

Firefighters: Speeding! Spraying! Saving!, illustrated by Viviana Garófoli, Marshall Cavendish (New York, NY), 2007.

Papa Fish's Lullaby, illustrated by Susan Eaddy, NorthWord Books (Minnetonka, MN), 2007.

Airplanes: Soaring! Diving! Turning!, illustrated by Megan Halsey and Sean Addy, Marshall Cavendish (New York, NY), 2007.

Police: Hurrying! Helping! Saving!, illustrated by Viviana Garofoli, Marshall Cavendish (New York, NY), 2008.

My First Airplane Ride, illustrated by Nancy Speir, Marshall Cavendish (New York, NY), 2008.

OTHER

Pig Picnic (chapter book), illustrated by Nadine Bernard Westcott, Golden Books (New York, NY), 1999.

Pig Parade (chapter book), illustrated by Nadine Bernard Westcott, Golden Books (New York, NY), 2002.

Contributor of poems to anthologies, textbooks, and magazines.

Sidelights

Patricia Hubbell is the author of a number of highly regarded picture books, including *Sidewalk Trip* and *Black All Around!,* as well as of poetry collections for children such as *Earthmates* and *City Kids.* "I think the reason I began to love poetry so much is because my mother and grandmother read a great deal of poetry to me when I was very young," Hubbell once told *SATA.* "The wonderful word-pictures and rhythms got into my head at an early age—and never left. I began writing poems myself when I was in the third grade. Sometimes, I would write them out on the cardboard pieces that came with shirts returned from the laundry and draw pictures around the edges.

"One of the first poems I remember doing was about a fox that I saw in the meadow across from our house. He was leaping in the sun and his coat was shining

Patricia Hubbell's rhythmic, rhyming text in **City Kids** *is reflected in Teresa Flavin's stylized, urban-inspired art.* (Marshall Cavendish, 2001. Illustrations copyright © 2001 by Teresa Flavin. Reproduced by permission of the publisher.)

Hubbell presents a picture-book paean to a dramatic hue in **Black All Around!,** *featuring artwork by Don Tate.* (Lee & Low Books, Inc., 2003. Illustration copyright © 2003 by Don Tate. Reproduced by permission of Lee & Low Books, Inc.)

gold and red. He looked like a dancer! Many years later, that same fox put in an appearance in a poem that was published in my first book, *The Apple Vendor's Fair.* He was still dancing, but now I knew that what he was really doing was going after a mouse; the poem was titled 'Prey Ballet.'"

Hubbell, who has worked as a journalist and reporter, first began writing books when she was at home with her children, often using the kitchen table as her office while they played on the floor. "There really aren't any rules or steps for writing a poem," she noted on her home page. "For me, sometimes a poem starts with a sound I hear, or a bit of conversation, or a rhythm, or with something I see. Sometimes a few words that sound like the start of a poem come into my head and I work from there." Hubbell writes mostly rhyming verse, short poems that are often accompanied by illustrations. For example, *The Tigers Brought Pink Lemonade* is a set of twenty-one poems, accompanied by graphic illustrations that combine with the collection to create a "picture book," noted Betsy Hearne in the *Bulletin for the Center of Children's Books.*

Pots and Pans, a story about a toddler emptying out kitchen cupboards to accompanying rhymes and sounds, is another one of Hubbell's rhyming picture books. In

the book, the author "skillfully epitomiz[es] . . . the boundless inquisitiveness of toddlers" in a "lively impromptu performance," noted a *Kirkus Reviews* critic. Hubbell's rhymes pair with de Groat's accompanying illustrations to make *Pots and Pans* a "fine candidate for a lap-sit story," in the opinion of John Peters in *School Library Journal.* Another toddler is the focus of *Wrapping Paper Romp,* in which Hubbell's rhyming couplets describe the child's antics as he tears apart a brightly wrapped present. Carolyn Phelan, writing in *Booklist,* described this book as one "that young children will enjoy opening again and again."

Critics have noted the realistic quality of Hubbell's writing, especially when she is recreating the world of young children. Although the characters in her stories have no names and she mentions no specific places, critics have consistently remarked on the concrete nature of her plots and her ability to present a child's viewpoint. In *Sidewalk Trip,* which recounts a little girl and her mother's trip to the ice-cream truck, Hubbell's text and the accompanying illustrations are "almost jet-propelled by enthusiasm," said a critic in *Kirkus Reviews.* In *Earthmates,* the author focuses on animals, writing thirty-five poems about various creatures, including minnows, deer, elephants, and even barnacles. Barbara Chatton, writing in *School Library Journal,* was especially appreciative of the realistic illustrations as well as vivid images invoked by Hubbell's writing, characterizing the work as a "lovely collection." Hazel Rochman, writing in *Booklist,* noted that "the rhythm and sound of the very short lines reinforce the sense of the wild, astonishing creatures" introduced in the entertaining story. In *Bouncing Time,* Hubbell describes a baby's trip to the zoo with her mother. The "vibrant" illustrations and "playfulness of the text" make this book a "romp to read any time of day," noted Marta Segal in a *Booklist* review. Again, Hubbell was praised for the powerfully realistic portrayal of the events in her book, with a *Publishers Weekly* critic writing that the "mom and child almost seem to dance—and readers will want to join in" this "slice of pure pleasure."

The tone of Hubbell's *City Kids* is slightly different from her earlier works as she focuses this time on children playing in the city. Although the poems focus on the fun the children are having, the book is tinged with sadness via the mention of the mugging of one child's grandmother. Although, characteristically, there is no specific city or even neighborhood mentioned, Hubbell writes a "concrete poem" from the "child's viewpoint," concluded Rochman.

In *Black Earth, Gold Sun* Hubbell "describes, discovers, and celebrates" the garden in a series of poems that are written in a "contemplative mood," according to Nina Lindsay in *School Library Journal.* The metaphors are rich and the poems are written in the voices of "children, adults, and even plants" wrote *Booklist* critic Gillian Engberg. As the critic noted, the "sophisti-

Hubbell's picture book **Black Earth, Gold Sun** ***features warm-toned art by Mary Newell DePalma.*** (Marshall Cavendish, 2001. Illustrations copyright 2001 © Mary Newell DePalma. Reproduced by permission of the publisher.)

cated language" and comparisons evoked by Hubbell are "powerful and exciting."

A small girl and her mother spend a day at the beach in *Sea, Sand, Me!* During the visit, the youngster romps in the surf, builds a sand castle, and meets a new friend. Genevieve Ceraldi, writing in *School Library Journal,* praised Hubbell's "bouncy rhyming text," and Phelan noted that the "energy and simplicity of the words" are matched by Lisa Campbell Ernst's ink-and-pastel illustrations. In *Black All Around!,* an African-American girl marvels at the many wonderful things in her world that are black in color, including the night sky, a limousine, and her father's arms. "The author's rhymes try hard to make black an intriguing, special shade," remarked a *Kirkus Reviews* contributor, and *Booklist* critic Ilene Cooper stated that Hubbell's narrative "brings a bundle of new objects and ideas about the depth and beauty of darkness."

Hubbell celebrates felines—both real and imaginary—in *I Like Cats.* Whether describing a cat snoozing in a sink or showing off behind the wheel of a convertible, the author's "jaunty text expresses her admiration for these cuddly critters," *School Library Journal* reviewer Be Astengo noted. Engberg applauded the pairing of Hubbell's verse with Pamela Paparone's artwork, stating that "the charming paintings and rhythmic words offer plenty of fun." In *Hurray for Spring!* a young boy passes the day splashing in puddles, planting seeds, and watching red-winged blackbirds. Here "Hubbell uses specific sensory images and lighthearted wordplay to re-create the boy's world," Phelan commented. "Large print, short sentences, and rhyming text make this title accessible to new readers," observed Maryann H. Owen in *School Library Journal.*

In works like *Trucks: Whizz! Zoom! Rumble!* and *Trains: Steaming! Pulling! Huffing!* Hubbell introduces youngsters to the wonders of transportation. *Trucks* humorously showcases a host of vehicles, cargos, and drivers, including an elephant operating a flatbed that is loaded with peanuts. Kay Weisman, writing in *Booklist,* complimented the author's "succinct, cleverly written rhymed text." In *Trains* "Hubbell takes a wild ride with locomotives both past and present," according to a critic in *Kirkus Reviews.* The work explores not only the many types of trains but the noises they make and the places they travel. "The text will have readers building up steam and momentum until the very last page," remarked Genevieve Gallagher in *School Library Journal.* The automotive industry is the subject of *Cars: Rushing! Honking! Zooming!,* "a snappy, stylish presentation of a subject with perennial appeal," as Phelan remarked. Hubbell's "rollicking text features witty rhymes," wrote *School Library Journal* critic Karen Ostergard, and a *Kirkus Reviews* critic lauded the author's "clipped, energetic verses."

Hubbell once told *SATA* that her work reflects the delight she feels when "playing with words, thoughts and dreams" as well as the pleasure she derives from her "surroundings." She added, "I think writing poems is a lot like gardening. When you garden you choose a plant, set it in place, move it if it's not doing well, weed out unwanted plants, tend it carefully and try for something beautiful. When you write poetry you do the same thing—only with words!"

Biographical and Critical Sources

BOOKS

Speaking of Poets 2: More Interviews with Poets Who Write for Children and Young Adults, National Council of Teachers of English (Urbana, IL), 1994.

PERIODICALS

Booklist, December 1, 1998, Carolyn Phelan, review of *Wrapping Paper Romp,* p. 670; September 15, 1999, Kathy Broderick, review of *Sidewalk Trip,* p. 268; March 15, 2000, Hazel Rochman, review of *Earthmates: Poems,* p. 383; April 1, 2000, Marta Segal, review of *Bouncing Time,* p. 469; March 1, 2001, Hazel Rochman, review of *City Kids,* p. 1283; May 1, 2001, Carolyn Phelan, review of *Sea, Sand, Me!,* p. 1694; September 15, 2001, Gillian Engberg, review of *Black Earth, Gold Sun,* p. 220; October 15, 2003, Gillian Engberg, review of *I Like Cats,* p. 419; February 15, 2003, Ilene Cooper, review of *Black All Around!,* p. 1089; April 15, 2003, Kay Weisman, review of *Trucks: Whizz! Zoom! Rumble!,* p. 1478; May 15, 2005, Carolyn Phelan, review of *Hurray for Spring!,* p. 1665; October 1, 2005, Diane Foote, review of *Trains: Steaming! Pulling! Huffing!,* p. 63; November 1, 2006, Carolyn Phelan, review of *Cars: Rushing! Honking! Zooming!,* p. 60; March 1, 2007, Hazel Rochman, review of *Firefighters: Speeding! Spraying! Saving!,* p. 88.

Bulletin of the Center for Children's Books, January, 1989, Betsy Hearne, review of *The Tigers Brought Pink Lemonade,* p. 124.

Children's Book Review Service, October, 1998, review of *Boo! Halloween Poems and Limericks,* p. 15.

Kirkus Reviews, June 1, 1998, review of *Pots and Pans,* p. 812; June 1, 1999, review of *Sidewalk Trip,* p. 883; February 15, 2003, review of *Trucks,* p. 308; March 15, 2003, review of *Black All Around!,* p. 468; August 1, 2005, review of *Trains,* p. 850; August 1, 2006, review of *Cars,* p. 788; February 15, 2007, review of *Firefighters.*

Publishers Weekly, May 8, 2000, review of *Bouncing Time,* p. 220; June 11, 2001, review of *Sea, Sand, Me!,* p. 84; March 10, 2003, review of *Black All Around!,* p. 70.

School Library Journal, fall, 1989, Nancy A. Gifford, review of *The Tigers Brought Pink Lemonade,* p. 78; June, 1998, John Peters, review of *Pots and Pans,* p. 109; September, 1998, Judith Constantinides, review of *Boo!,* p. 192; February, 1999, Blair Christolon, review of *Wrapping Paper Romp,* p. 84; March, 2000, Barbara Chatton, review of *Earthmates,* p. 226; July, 2000, Janet M. Bair, review of *Bouncing Time,* p. 80; July, 2001, Alicia Eames, review of *City Kids,* p. 94; August, 2001, Genevieve Ceraldi, review of *Sea, Sand, Me!,* p. 154; November, 2001, Nina Lindsay, review of *Black Earth, Gold Sun,* p. 146; June, 2002, Piper L. Nyman, review of *Rabbit Moon: A Book of Holidays and Celebrations,* p. 97; May, 2003, Ajoke'

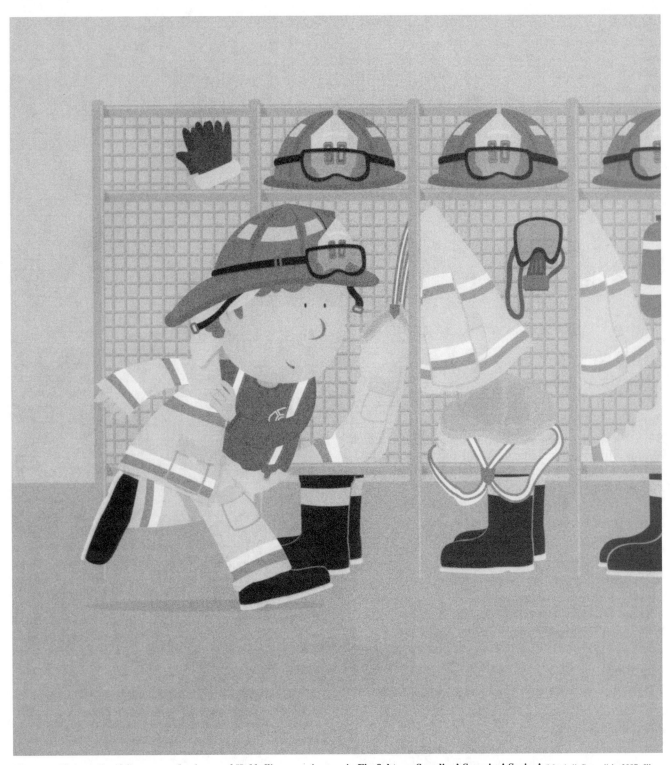

Illustrator Viviana Garófoli captures the drama of Hubbell's energetic story in **Firefighters: Speeding! Spraying! Saving!** (Marshall Cavendish, 2007. Illustrations copyright © 2007 by Marshall Cavendish Corporation. Reproduced by permission.)

T.I. Kokodoko, review of *Black All Around!,* p. 120; January, 2004, Be Astengo, review of *I Like Cats,* p. 98; April, 2005, Maryann H. Owen, review of *Hurray for Spring!,* p. 99; September, 2005, Genevieve Gallagher, review of *Trains,* p. 174; November, 2006, Karen Ostergard, review of *Cars,* p. 96; May, 2007, DeAnn Okamura, review of *Firefighters,* p. 98.

ONLINE

Lee & Low Web site, http://www.leeandlow.com/ (December 1, 2007), "Booktalk with Patricia Hubbell."

Patricia Hubbell Home Page, http://www.kidspoet.com (December 1, 2007).

J

JOHANSEN, Krista V.
See JOHANSEN, K.V.

*　　*　　*

JOHANSEN, K.V. 1968-
(Krista V. Johansen)

Personal
Born 1968, in Kingston, Ontario, Canada. *Education:* Mount Allison University, B.A. (history and English; with honors), 1990; University of Toronto, M.A. (medieval studies), 1991; McMaster University, M.A. (English), 1994. *Hobbies and other interests:* Gardening, "growing exotic trees indoors."

Addresses
Home—Eastern Canada.

Career
Writer. Presenter at children's writing workshops.

Member
Writers' Union of Canada.

Awards, Honors
New Brunswick Lieutenant Governor's Award for Early Childhood Literacy, 2000, for *Pippin and the Bones;* Eileen Wallace research fellowship in children's literature, University of New Brunswick, 2001; Frances E. Russell Award, International Board on Books for Young People, 2004; Silver Birch Award nomination, Diamond Willow Award nomination, and Lilla Stirling Award, Canadian Authors' Association, all 2006, all for *Torrie and the Pirate Queen;* Ontario Library Association Top-

K.V. Johansen (Reproduced by permission.)

Ten Children's Books designation, and Canadian Children's Book Centre (CCBC) Choice selection, both 2006, both for *Torrie and the Firebird;* CCBC Choice designation, Canadian Association of Children's Librarians Book of the Year for Children Award shortlist, both 2007, both for *The Cassandra Virus;* Silver Birch Award nomination, 2008, for *Torrie and the Snake-Prince.*

Writings

FOR CHILDREN

The Serpent Bride: Stories from Medieval Danish Ballads, Thistledown Press (Saskatoon, Saskatchewan, Canada), 1998.

The Cassandra Virus, Orca Book Publishers (Victoria, British Columbia, Canada), 2006.

The Drone War (sequel to *The Cassandra Virus*), Sybertooth (Sackville, New Brunswick, Canada), 2007.

"TORRIE QUESTS" SERIES; FOR CHILDREN

Torrie and the Dragon, illustrated by Dean Bloomfield, Roussan Publishing (Montreal, Quebec, Canada), 1997.

Torrie and the Pirate-Queen, illustrated by Christine Delezenne, Annick Press (Toronto, Ontario, Canada), 2005.

Torrie and the Firebird, illustrated by Christine Delezenne, Annick Press (Toronto, Ontario, Canada), 2006.

Torrie and the Snake-Prince, illustrated by Christine Delezenne, Annick Press (Toronto, Ontario, Canada), 2007.

"PIPPIN AND MABEL"SERIES; FOR CHILDREN

Pippin Takes a Bath, illustrated by Bernice Lum, Kids Can Press (Toronto, Ontario, Canada), 1999.

Pippin and the Bones, illustrated by Bernice Lum, Kids Can Press (Toronto, Ontario, Canada), 2000.

Pippin and Pudding, illustrated by Bernice Lum, Kids Can Press (Toronto, Ontario, Canada), 2001.

Author's books have been translated into French.

"WARLOCKS OF TALVERDIN" FANTASY SERIES

Nightwalker, Orca Book Publishers (Custer, WA), 2007.

Treason in Eswy, Orca Book Publishers (Custer, WA), 2008.

OTHER

Quests and Kingdoms: A Grown-up's Guide to Children's Fantasy Literature, Sybertooth (Sackville, New Brunswick, Canada), 2005.

Beyond Window Dressing?: Canadian Children's Fantasy at the Millenium, Sybertooth (Sackville, New Brunswick, Canada), 2007.

Contributor of articles and short fiction to magazines, including *Phantastes, On Spec, Rural Delivery, Atlantic Horse and Pony, Farm Woman, Resource Links,* and *Atlantic Forestry Review.*

Author's works have been translated into several languages, including Danish, French, and Macedonian.

Sidelights

Canadian fantasy writer K.V. Johansen earned advanced degrees in both English and medieval studies before embarking on her career as a novelist for young readers. "I've always told stories," she once told *SATA*. "When I was eight or nine I started writing them down, and I find it hard to imagine myself doing anything else." Among Johansen's award-winning books for young readers are her "Torrie Quests" and "Warlocks of Talverdin" fantasy novels, as well as a science-fiction adventure that takes place in the near future and plays out in *The Cassandra Virus* and *The Drone War.*

Johansen began her career with *Torrie and the Dragon,* the first novel in her "Torrie Quests" series. The series is narrated by a resourceful creature name Torrie, who lives in a medieval-esque fantasy world called Erythroth, and recounts the adventures of his youth to the other Old Things that gather in the forest to swap stories. In *Torrie and the Dragon* Torrie joins enchantress Cossypha to rescue a prince from the dungeons of Cossypha's evil father, Sporryl, and find the magic sword that will help Prince Rufik rid his kingdom of a predatory dragon. In *Torrie and the Pirate-Queen* Erythroth is ruled by Cossypha's granddaughter. Torrie's adventures take him to sea aboard the *Shrike,* where he helps young Captain Anna save her father from an evil pirate-queen and encounters everything from treasure and a cursed kingdom to a prince who they rescue from a deserted island.

The adventures of Torrie and Anna continue in *Torrie and the Firebird,* as they help a young boy prove his innocence of a terrible crime by tracking down one of the most destructive powers in their world. In *Torrie and the Snake-Prince* the oldest of the Old Things meets Wren, a poor, lame girl who is unaware of what the fates have in store for her. Helped by Torrie, Wren joins in the effort to rescue Prince Liasis from an evil sorcerer and his goblin henchmen. Comparing the "Torrie's Quest" series to books by C.S. Lewis and J.R.R. Tolkien, *Resource Links* critic David Ward noted that Johansen incorporates the medieval elements of her fantasy world "with a rhythm and vocabulary that bring the reader close to this Dark Ages fantastical environment," resulting in a setting that is "remarkably resilient, fresh, and consistent."

Describing her "Pippin and Mabel" books—*Pippin Takes a Bath, Pippin and the Bones,* and *Pippin and Pudding*—as "an aberration" because there's "not a dragon, demon, or troll in sight," Johansen explained the genesis of the three-book series. "Pippin is based on my own dog, Pippin, who is a Husky/German Shepherd/Labrador mix. But in [the real] Pippin's case, life usu-

Cover of Johansen's middle-grade adventure novel Torrie and the Snake-Prince, *featuring artwork by Christine Delezenne.* (Annick Press, 2007. Illustrations copyright © 2007 Christine Delezenne. Reproduced by permission.)

ally imitates art, rather than the other way around. He was never sprayed by a skunk until after I wrote *Pippin Takes a Bath,* and a few months after *Pippin and Pudding* (in which Pippin finds a kitten) was published, a stray cat showed up and adopted us. Pippin still hasn't found any ancient bones, so far as I know." In *Resource Links,* Judy Cottrell praised *Pippin and Pudding* as "a good read-aloud for . . . animal lovers" and an effective resource in "lessons on friendship, bonding and emotions."

Nightwalker is the first volume in Johansen's "Warlocks of Talverdin" fantasy series. Taking place on an island called Eswiland, the novel introduces readers to wizards called Nightwalkers because they can see the unseen in the dark. Orphaned as an infant, Maurey has always stood out from his fellow villagers because of his dark eyes and strange appearance. When it is discovered that he is a nightwalker, Maurey is tossed into the dungeon on orders of the king. Rescued from certain death by Annot, a young baroness, Maurey now learns to harness his special skills and realizes that he alone holds the key to saving the secret kingdom that serves as the Night-eyes' only refuge. Hailing the novel as a "prom-

ising start" to a new series, *Booklist* contributor Diana Tixier Herald wrote that Johansen's "fast-paced" and "fully realized fantasy" features "compelling characters and conflicts that make sense" within the bounds of the story's fantastic premise.

In both *The Cassandra Virus* and *The Drone War,* Johansen turns to science fiction. In the first book readers meet thirteen-year-old Helen, who is working to save one of the few frog species still living on a near-future Earth. When Helen's bored, super-smart friend Jordan creates a virtual computer that inhabits and grows on the World Wide Web, the two friends soon find themselves in the middle of a government operation, hoping to keep Cassandra away from those who would use it for evil purposes. Because of her work in artificial intelligence, Jordan's older sister Cassie finds herself the target of spies in *The Drone War.* Soon Jordan has marshaled Helen and Cassandra to help keep his sibling safe, although the group must grapple with questions as to how far they can stray from what is right to fight evil. Noting the humor Johansen weaves within her suspenseful plot, Vicki Reutter concluded in *School Library Journal* that computer-savvy teens "will enjoy the technology aspects as well as the characters" in *The Cassandra Virus.* Calling the novel "well researched and topical," Eva Wilson also praised *The Cassandra Virus* in her *Resource Links* review and referred to Johansen's prose style as "engaging and light." Praising the novel for being refreshingly "Canadian in content," Lesley Little noted in the same periodical that *The Drone War* features an "up-to-the-minute" storyline that, despite its technological focus, is "easy to read but not facile or condescending."

Biographical and Critical Sources

PERIODICALS

Booklist, November 15, 1999, Shelley Townsend-Hudson, review of *Pippin Takes a Bath,* p. 636; August, 2000, Susan Dove Lempke, review of *Pippin and the Bones,* p. 2147; April 1, 2007, Diana Tixier Herald, review of *Nightwalker,* p. 45.
Bulletin of the Center for Children's Books, May, 2007, review of *Nightwalker,* p. 372.
Kids' Home Library, September 8, 1999, review of *Pippin Takes a Bath.*
Publishers Weekly, August 23, 1999, review of *Pippin Takes a Bath,* p. 57.
Resource Links, April, 1999, Connie Hall, review of *The Serpent Bride: Stories from Medieval Danish Ballads,* p. 25; February, 2000, review of *Pippin Takes a Bath,* pp. 4-5; April, 2001, Jody Cottrell, review of *Pippin and Pudding,* p. 4; June, 2000, review of *Pippin and the Bones,* p. 3; June, 2005, David Ward, review of *Torrie and the Pirate-Queen,* p. 14; June, 2006, Leslie L. Kennedy, review of *Torrie and the Firebird,* p. 6; April, 2007, Eva Wilson, review of *The Cassandra Vi-*

rus, p. 14; October, 2007, David Ward, review of *Torrie and the Snake-Prince,* p. 15, and Lesley Little, review of *The Drone War,* p. 30.

School Library Journal, November, 1999, Anne Chapman, review of *Pippin Takes a Bath,* p. 120; August, 2000, Elaine Lesh Morgan, review of *Pippin and the Bones,* p. 158; November, 2006, Vickie Reutter, review of *The Cassandra Virus,* p. 136; September, 2007, Emily R. Brown, review of *Nightwalker,* p. 200.

ONLINE

Canadian Review of Materials Online, http://www.uman itoba.ca/cm/ (February 12, 1999), Joanne Peters, review of *The Serpent Bride;* (January 19, 2001) Catherine Hoyt, review of *Pippin Takes a Bath;* (May 11, 2001) Catherine Hoyt, review of *Pippin and Pudding.*

K.V. Johansen Home Page, http://www.pippin.ca (January 20, 2007), "K.V. Johansen."

*   *   *

JOHNSON, Kathleen Jeffrie 1950-

Personal

Born 1950, in Washington, DC; daughter of Jacie (a painter) and Roy (an engineer); married; husband's name Stephen. *Education:* Earned A.A.

Addresses

Home—Germantown, MD. *E-mail*—yak@kathleenjeff riejohnson.com.

Career

Writer of teen novels. Previously worked as a library technician.

Writings

The Parallel Universe of Liars, Roaring Brook Press (Brookfield, CT), 2002.
Target, Roaring Brook Press (Brookfield, CT), 2003.
A Fast and Brutal Wing, Roaring Brook Press (Brookfield, CT), 2004.
Dumb Love, Roaring Brook Press (New Milford, CT), 2005.
Gone, Roaring Brook Press (New Milford, CT), 2007.

Contributor of essay to *The World of the Golden Compass: The Otherworldly Ride Continues,* edited by Scott Westerfeld, Benbella Books, 2007; and of short fiction to *Owning It: Stories about Teen with Disabilities,* edited by Donald R. Gallo, Candlewick Press (New York, NY), 2008.

Sidelights

Kathleen Jeffrie Johnson is the author of teen novels that do not shy away from controversial issues. Although often dealing with serious topics such as rape, incest, and mental illness in her stories, Johnson attempts to offset those themes with humor. "My books have been called dark, edgy, full of risk," the author noted on her home page. "But there's humor, too. To go into the darkness without carrying a light of some kind is just too difficult for me." It took Johnson some time to figure out the kind of book she wanted to write. She tried writing for adults and writing for children, but nothing seemed to work until she focused on adolescents. As she wrote on her home page, "I spent my whole life trying to become a writer. . . . I finally found my fiction voice writing novels for teenagers."

Johnson's first novel, *The Parallel Universe of Liars,* is a story about the sexual awakening of Robin Davis, a normal teen dealing with an abnormal family situation. Her parents are divorced and her body-conscious mother is preparing for a second marriage, encouraging Robin to lose weight before the wedding. Robin's father is already remarried to beautiful, young China, who is having an affair with next-door neighbor Frankie, the subject of Robin's own crush. When Robin meets Tri, she is given the chance to form a healthy romantic relationship, if only she can convince herself that love is not always about lying and cheating. Given the number of plot elements, including race issues resulting from Tri's biracial identity, *Booklist* critic Ilene Cooper felt that "first-time novelist Johnson does a remarkable job of juggling." A *Kirkus Reviews* contributor, while describing the cast of the book as "unappealing," added that "Johnson knows how to turn a phrase and her heroine's voice is incisive and sadly authentic." A *Publishers Weekly* critic, on the other hand, found Robin to be "a refreshingly ordinary narrator living among realistically flawed family and friends," and Miriam Lang Budin concluded in *School Library Journal* that *The Parallel Universe of Liars* "is the work of a promising writer."

In *Target,* sixteen-year-old Grady West has a normal life. Then, while walking home from a failed date one night, Grady is assaulted by two men and brutally raped. Everything reminds Grady of that night, and he transfers to a new school in the hopes that he can just blend in and disappear. At his new school, outgoing and likeable Jess Williams tries to get the now-silent and anorexic Grady to come out of his shell. "*Target* meticulously portrays [Grady's] long-term healing, and how he finds a spark of light here and there, through trust and caring friends," wrote J.A. Ksazuba Locke in her review for *Bookloons* online. "The story moves at a glacier's pace, but necessarily so: for Grady, every movement, every word is excruciating, each minute of the day a challenge," wrote a contributor to *Publishers Weekly.* Alison Follos, reviewing the novel for *School Library Journal,* concluded of *Target* that "there are no easy solutions or quick fixes here—but there are sound friendships from credible characters." A *Kirkus Reviews* contributor called the novel "painful and riveting."

A Fast and Brutal Wing is the story of Niki and Emmet, two siblings who have been abandoned by their father. Other characters include their sympathetic class-mate Doug, who struggles through grief about his mother's death. Told through letters and e-mails, snippets of articles from a newspaper, and short-story excerpts, readers learn that Doug reported Emmet and Niki for attacking a reclusive local author, accusing them of possibly even changing into animals—something he recants. Emmet is put into an institution, even though he claims the idea that he can shapeshift is a fancy of his sister's. Niki is monitored from home, writing a short story that further reveal her own belief about her supernatural abilities. There are additional hints that Emmet and Niki have an incestuous relationship, which Doug fervently denies. "Mature readers will be drawn into—and chilled by—this suspenseful novel," predicted a *Publishers Weekly* contributor. A *Kirkus Reviews* critic called *A Fast and Brutal Wing* "a memorable read that allows fantasy, mystery, and realistic fiction fans alike to examine the power of love." In *Booklist* Frances Bradburn concluded of Johnson's novel that it is one "readers will remember long after turning the final page."

In *Dumb Love* Johnson moves away from the serious themes of her earlier books and introduces teenage advice columnist Carlotta. Carlotta is determined to get the attention of her crush, Pete, and her quest for love is the focus of the romantic tale. As she told Cynthia Leitich Smith in *Cynsations* online: "Ever since I'd had a library job, years ago, where I processed paperback romance novels . . . I knew I had a romance novel in me; I just needed the right moment to give it birth." Reviewing *Dumb Love* for *Booklist,* Gillian Engberg cited the story's "unforgettable characters and Johnson's southern-tinged prose." A *Publishers Weekly* critic also predicted that readers "will take a shine to these characters," and concluded that *Dumb Love* is "big on funny moments, details and big-hearted characters."

Johnson returns to more serious themes in *Gone,* the tale of an illicit relationship between recently graduated Connor and his former history teacher. Connor has had difficult relationships with his parents, both of whom are alcoholics. When readers meet the teen, his mother has abandoned the family and his dad is in a nursing home due to an alcohol-related accident, leaving Connor with his aunt. Unsure of what to do with his life after high school, Connor decides to pursue a relationship with Ms. Corinna Timms, a teacher who has a host of her own issues as well as a mysterious past. When Corinna decides to move to New Mexico, Connor plans to accompany her, hoping to find a place he can call home. "Readers will find it easy to sympathize with Connor," wrote a *Publishers Weekly* contributor. Jennifer Mattson, reviewing *Gone* for *Booklist,* maintained that in Johnson's prose "crushing emotions are beautifully drawn."

"While I am currently working on another 'realistic, edgy' teen novel, in the books that come next I hope to pick up the fantastic thread I started in *A Fast and*

Brutal Wing," Johnson told *SATA.* "Not the *same* thread, but one of the many that shimmer in that blurred spot between what is real and what isn't. Why stick with only what we call 'the truth'? The mind is capable of so many interesting, if sometimes weird, interpretations of reality." In an interview for the *Random House Web site,* Johnson offered advice to young authors. "My tip for aspiring writers, besides 'Read, read, read,' is—'write!' Nothing else will substitute. You either need to do it or you don't. But give yourself and your words time to grow."

Biographical and Critical Sources

PERIODICALS

Booklist, September 15, 2002, Ilene Cooper, review of *The Parallel Universe of Liars,* p. 227; December 15, 2004, Frances Bradburn, review of *A Fast and Brutal Wing,* p. 736; September 15, 2005, Gillian Engberg, review of *A Fast and Brutal Wing,* p. 76; March 15, 2007, Jennifer Mattson, review of *Gone,* p. 42.

Bulletin of the Center for Children's Books, November, 2003, Deborah Stevenson, review of *Target,* p. 109; December, 2004, Krista Hutley, review of *A Fast and Brutal Wing,* p. 173; March, 2007, Deborah Stevenson, review of *Gone,* p. 296.

Kirkus Reviews, October 1, 2002, review of *The Parallel Universe of Liars,* p. 1471; August 1, 2003, review of *Target,* p. 1018; October 1, 2004, review of *A Fast and Brutal Wing,* p. 962.

Publishers Weekly, October 7, 2002, review of *The Parallel Universe of Liars,* p. 74; November 3, 2003, review of *Target,* p. 76; November 22, 2004, review of *A Fast and Brutal Wing,* p. 61; October 17, 2005, review of *Dumb Love,* p. 69; February 26, 2007, review of *Gone,* p. 92.

School Library Journal, December, 2002, Miriam Lang Budin, review of *The Parallel Universe of Liars,* p. 142; December, 2003, Alison Follos, review of *Target,* p. 153; November, 2005, Emily Garrett, review of *Dumb Love,* p. 138; July, 2006, review of *A Fast and Brutal Wing,* p. 37; May, 2007, Sheila Fiscus, review of *Gone,* p. 134.

Voice of Youth Advocates, December, 2002, review of *The Parallel Universe of Liars,* p. 384; April, 2005, review of *A Fast and Brutal Wing,* p. 12; April, 2007, Mary Ann Harlan, review of *Gone,* p. 50.

ONLINE

Adams Literary Agency Web site, http://www.adamsliterary.com/ (December 21, 2007), "Kathleen Jeffrie Johnson."

Cynsations, http://cynthialeitichsmith.blogspot.com/ (October 19, 2005), Cynthia Leitich Smith, interview with Johnson.

Bookloons, http://www.bookloons.com/ (December 21, 2007), J.A. Kaszuba Locke, review of *Target.*

Kathleen Jeffrie Johnson Blog site, http://thefustyblob. blogspot.com/ (December 21, 2007).

Kathleen Jeffrie Johnson Home Page, http://www. kathleenjeffriejohnson.com (December 21, 2007).

Random House Web site, http://www.randomhouse.com/ (December 21, 2007), interview with Johnson.

*   *   *

JOLIN, Paula

Personal

Married; children: one son, one daughter. *Education:* Brown University, degree; attended Institute for Teaching Arabic to Foreigners; McGill University, M.A. (Islamic studies).

Addresses

Home and office—NC. *E-mail*—paula@paulajolin.com.

Career

Author.

Writings

In the Name of God, Roaring Brook Press (New Milford, CT), 2007.

Sidelights

Although Paula Jolin always wanted to be a writer, as she admitted in a *BookPage.com* interview, as a young adult she "didn't have anything to say." Finding a subject to capture her interest was actually "one of the reasons I started traveling," she admitted. Jolin traveled to many unusual locations while studying for her undergraduate and graduate degrees, including Syria where her first novel takes place. *In the Name of God* centers on the region's Muslim culture and beliefs; in fact, one of Jolin's hopes in writing the novel was to educate young American readers about a different culture. In her *BookPage* online interview, Jolin commented that she also wanted to "show someone who's in a place we couldn't imagine being."

Critics have acknowledged *In the Name of God* for its suspenseful plot and its ability to clearly detail a culture that is foreign to American teens. The novel's main character, Nadia, is a typical seventeen-year-old Muslim who is devout to her religion and to her parents. However, things change for Nadia when her cousin is arrested and mistreated for publicly criticizing the government. Angry, Nadia becomes an extremist and is eventually convinced to become a suicide bomber. In *School Library Journal,* Kathleen Isaacs regarded Jolin's novel as a "believable depiction of the growth of

religious zealotry." Margaret Hall in her review for *Washington Report on Middle East Affairs,* commented on Jolin's use of journal entries as a way to portray her lead character, and concluded that the first-time novelist creates a "compelling portrayal of the viewpoint of would-be suicide bombers." In *Kirkus Reviews* a critic acknowledged Jolin for her ability to breathe "life into each of her well-drawn characters and their complicated world."

Biographical and Critical Sources

PERIODICALS

Booklist, April 15, 2007, Gillian Engberg, review of *In the Name of God,* p. 38.

Kirkus Reviews, April 1, 2007, review of *In the Name of God.*

Library Media Connection, August, 2007, Sheila Acosta, review of *In the Name of God,* p. 70.

Publishers Weekly, March 26, 2007, review of *In the Name of God,* p. 95.

School Library Journal, April, 2007, Kathleen Issacs, review of *In the Name of God,* p. 140.

Voice of Youth Advocates, April, 2007, Cindy Faughnan, review of *In the Name of God,* p. 50.

Washington Report on Middle East Affairs, September-October, 2007, Margaret Hall, review of *In the Name of God,* p. 64.

ONLINE

BookPage.com, http://www.bookpage.com/ (December 15, 2007), "Opening a Window on an Unfamiliar Culture."

Class of 2k7 Web site, http://classof2k7.com/ (December 15, 2007), "Paula Jolin."*

*   *   *

JONES, Traci L.

Personal

Born in Monmouth, IL; daughter of Regis F. (a politician) and Ada L. Groff; married; husband's name Tony; children: Desiree, Andrew, Isaiah, Brooke. *Education:* Bachelor's degree (psychology); attended University of Denver.

Addresses

Home—Denver, CO.

Career

Author.

Awards, Honors

Coretta Scott King/John Steptoe New Talent Author Award, for *Standing against the Wind.*

Writings

Standing against the Wind (young adult novel), Farrar, Straus & Giroux (New York, NY), 2006.

Sidelights

Traci L. Jones won the 2006 Coretta Scott King/John Steptoe New Talent Author Award for her debut work of young-adult fiction, *Standing against the Wind.* The novel concerns Patrice Williams, an inner-city teen struggling to adjust to her own often-difficult circumstances. "I think there are some emotions that most preteens and teens go through, regardless of their economic status or their geographic location," Jones told an interviewer on the *Embracing the Child* Web site. "I just tapped into some of the feelings I remembered going through and wrote about them as honestly as I could."

Born in Monmouth, Illinois, Jones was raised in Denver, Colorado, in the same home where she now lives with her husband and four children. The daughter of former Colorado State Senator Regis F. Groff and Ada L. Groff, Jones developed an interest in reading and writing at an early age. "I read everywhere—in the car, at basketball games, at football games, at parties, even during church," she remarked on her home page. "Where ever I went I had a book with me." Jones began writing one Christmas after she received a manual typewriter as a present from her mother. She later served on the school paper at her high school but found that she preferred penning fiction to nonfiction. Her dreams of becoming an author were almost dashed in college, however, when her counselor, a professor who also taught English, harshly criticized her work. Disheartened, Jones changed her major to psychology, stopped reading books for pleasure, and did not register for another English course until her senior year. After the birth of her first child, though, Jones decided to take a writing course at the University of Denver. As she stated on her home page, "My love for writing returned with a vengeance and I haven't quit writing yet."

Standing against the Wind, which Jones began while attending the University of Denver, centers on Patrice, a studious eighth grader who has been transplanted from her grandmother's home in Georgia to live with her aunt in a Chicago housing project. Patrice must endure the harsh Midwestern winter and daily harassment from gang members, yet she continues to excel academically—so much so that the principal at her school encourages her to apply for a scholarship to a prestigious African-American boarding school. Patrice gets support and assistance from an unlikely source: Monty, a troubled neighbor who takes Patrice under his wing. According to Rainbow Lightfoot-Mayer, writing in the *Journal of Adolescent & Adult Literacy,* "Patrice must find her voice and stand up for herself and her beliefs. As she finds her own strength (and it takes a while), she refuses to abandon her values and blend in to the crowd." "I love the fact that Patrice knows her strengths and is steadfast in the face of peer pressure," Jones remarked in her *Embracing the Child* interview, adding, "Patrice would rather be smart than socially accepted, which is a hard choice for teens to make."

Standing against the Wind received praise from a number of critics. In the words of a *Kirkus Reviews* contributor, the author "vividly and painfully portrays the deadening effects of poverty, hopelessness and dysfunctional and ever-changing family relationships." In *School Library Journal,* Faith Brautigan commented that readers "will appreciate the strength that underlies Patrice's quiet and unassuming exterior," and Hazel Rochman, writing in *Booklist,* described *Standing against the Wind* as a "gripping story of a contemporary kid who works to make her dreams come true."

Biographical and Critical Sources

PERIODICALS

Booklist, July 1, 2006, Hazel Rochman, review of *Standing against the Wind,* p. 60.
Bulletin of the Center for Children's Books, December, 2006, Karen Coats, review of *Standing against the Wind,* p. 175.
Horn Book, March-April, 2007, "Coretta Scott King/John Steptoe New Talent Author Award," p. 220.
Journal of Adolescent & Adult Literacy, November, 2006, Rainbow Lightfoot-Mayer, review of *Standing against the Wind,* p. 243.
Kirkus Reviews, September 15, 2006, review of *Standing against the Wind,* p. 956.
School Library Journal, November, 2006, Faith Brautigan, review of *Standing against the Wind,* p. 138.
Voice of Youth Advocates, February 2007, Sherrie Williams, review of *Standing against the Wind,* p. 527.

ONLINE

Embracing the Child Web site, http://www.embracing thechild.org/ (December 20, 2007), interview with Jones.
Farrar, Straus & Giroux Web site, http://www.fsgkids books.com/ (December 20, 2007), "Traci L. Jones."
Traci L. Jones Home Page, http://tracijones.com (December 20, 2007).*

K-L

KEHLENBECK, Angela 1959-

Personal
Born May, 1959; married; children: Kater, Pony (daughters). *Education:* Earned diploma in art.

Addresses
Home—Bremen, Germany.

Career
Illustrator. Worked for an advertising agency; freelance illustrator. Head of seminar for advanced training for art instructors.

Awards, Honors
Art included in Bologna Illustrator's Exhibition, 1986.

Illustrator
Nina Schindler, *Wenn ich eine Hexe wär . . .*, Neugebauer Verlag (Zurich, Switzerland), 1998.
Nina Schindler, *Mein Schatz,* Arena, 1999.
Bruno Háchler, *Das geheimnis der bären,* Neugebauer Verlag (Zurich, Switzerland), 2000, adapted and translated by J. Alison James as *The Bears' Christmas Surprise,* North-South Books (New York, NY), 2000.
Sjoerd Kuyper, *Das buch von Josie,* Saurländer (Oberentfelden, Switzerland), 2002.
Dodo Kresse, *Der Petzonaut,* Buchverlag, 2003.
Karla Schneider, *Kapitän Neo taught auf,* Buchverlag, 2005.
Géraldine Elschner, *Pashmina, das Weihnachtszicklein,* Minedition (Salzburg, Austria), 2006, translation published as *Pashmina: The Little Christmas Goat,* Minedition (New York, NY), 2006.

Biographical and Critical Sources

PERIODICALS

Booklist, December 1, 2006, Carolyn Phelan, review of *Pashmina: The Little Christmas Goat,* p. 51.
Kirkus Reviews, November 1, 2006, review of *Pashmina,* p. 1128.
Publishers Weekly, September 25, 2006, review of *Pashmina,* p. 71.
School Library Journal, October, 2006, Eva Mitnick, review of *Pashmina,* p. 96.

ONLINE

Minedition Web site, http://www.minedition.com/ (January 15, 2007), "Angela Kehlenbeck."*

* * *

KOSTICK, Conor 1964-

Personal
Born 1964, in Ireland; son of a math teacher and a special-needs teacher; partner's name Aoife. *Education:* Trinity College, Dublin, Ph.D. (medieval history).

Addresses
Home—Dublin, Ireland.

Career
Writer and historian. Trinity College, Dublin, Dublin, Ireland, professor of medieval history. Editor of *Socialist Worker.* Previously worked for Treasure Trap (game company), as an engineering clerk for Case International, at a nature conservancy on the Island of Rhum, Scotland, as an archaeologist, and as a political activist.

Member
Irish Writers' Union (former chairman).

Awards, Honors
International Board on Books for Young People Honour List, 2006, and Best Books selection, *School Library Journal,* and Top Ten Fantasy Books for Youth designation, *Booklist Online,* both 2007, all for *Epic.*

Writings

Epic, O'Brien (Dublin, Ireland), 2004, Viking (New York, NY), 2007.
Saga, O'Brien (Dublin, Ireland), 2006, Viking (New York, NY), 2008.
The Book of Curses, O'Brien (Dublin, Ireland), 2007.
Move, O'Brien (Dublin, Ireland), 2008.

ADULT NONFICTION

Revolution in Ireland: Popular Militancy, 1917 to 1923, Pluto Press (Chicago, IL), 1996.
(With Lorcan Collins) *The Easter Rising: A Guide to Dublin in 1916,* O'Brien (Dublin, Ireland), 2000.
(Editor, with Katherine Moore) *Irish Writers against War,* O'Brien (Dublin, Ireland), 2003.
The Social Structure of the First Crusade, Brill (Leiden, Netherlands), 2008.

Contributor of reviews to *Journal of Music in Ireland.*

Sidelights

Conor Kostick was twelve years old when, inspired by writers such as Michael Moorcock, J.R.R. Tolkien, and Andre Norton, he tried his hand at writing. Unhappy with the result, he turned to a different creative endeavor: working as a designer for Treasure Trap, a game company that developed the first live-action role-playing-game (RPG). After this experience, Kostick had trouble taking jobs seriously, and he worked in a number of fields before turning to academia and completing his doctorate in medieval history at Trinity College, Dublin.

While following his academic path, Kostick published several nonfiction books for adults and continued his interest in RPGs. Contemplating the online-game phenomenon, he wondered what the world would be like if one's success in an online fantasy game could also impact one's actual life. This idea is explored in his first novel for young adults, *Epic.* In New Earth, violence is illegal, and disputes are settled through the massive computer game called Epic. Real-world power is determined by one's ability to accumulate wealth and power in the game, and an elite group of players, manipulates the outcome for many others. Relying on the game to solve real-world problems ultimately undermines New Earth's economy and cripples those people, like Erik's father, who refuse to play. Erik is frustrated with the game, and as a player, instead of following the standard patterns, he begins experimenting with different ways to play, including having a female persona. When he defeats a red dragon and becomes one of the wealthiest people in the game, he becomes a threat to the elite who run New Earth.

Although Kostick's storyline in *Epic* "is nonstop, it's easy to keep track of who's who, and the story flows seamlessly as characters move between worlds, main-

taining their individuality in both," according to Sally Estes in her *Booklist* review of the novel. "Well written and engaging, *Epic* will easily draw in avid readers and video-game players," predicted Dylan Thomarie in *School Library Journal,* while a *Publishers Weekly* critic noted that the novel's "elegant conclusion will linger with readers." In *Kliatt* Paula Rohrlick noted that "readers will be eager to continue the adventure in the sequel."

In an interview on the O'Brien Web site, Kostick discussed the themes of *Epic* and noted that experimenting with ideas against the crowd can be a good thing. "Just because very many people accept certain ideas and ways of doing something does not necessarily mean that their approach is the best way," he noted. "I like the character of Erik for several reasons, but this is probably the main one, that he is not afraid of trying something new, in fact he only enjoys Epic when experimenting with it."

Kostick considered his future as a writer with an interviewer at the Ask about Writing Web site. "I am going to stay in children's writing for the foreseeable future," he explained. "There is quite a thriving children's lit-

Cover of Conor Kostick's novel Epic, *featuring artwork by Tony Sahara.* (Viking, 2004. Jacket art copyright © Tony Sahara, 2007. Reproduced by permission.)

erature industry in Ireland that has an international impact." In addition to writing, he is a professor of medieval history at Trinity College, Dublin.

Biographical and Critical Sources

PERIODICALS

Booklist, March 1, 2007, Sally Estes, review of *Epic,* p. 84.

Bulletin of the Center for Children's Books, April, 2007, Cindy Welch, review of *Epic,* p. 333.

Kliatt, March, 2007, Paula Rohrlick, review of *Epic,* p. 16.

Publishers Weekly, May 21, 2007, review of *Epic,* p. 57.

School Library Journal, May, 2007, Dylan Thomarie, review of *Epic,* p. 136.

Voice of Youth Advocates, June, 2007, Heidi Dolomore, review of *Epic,* p. 164.

ONLINE

Ask about Writing Web site, http://www.askaboutwriting. net/ (December 20, 2007), interview with Kostick.

Conor Kostick's Web log, http://conorkostick.blogspot.com (July 18, 2007).

Irish Writers Online, http://www.irishwriters-online.com/ (December 20, 2007), profile of Kostick.

O'Brien Web site, http://www.obrien.ie/ (December 20, 2007), interview with Kostick.*

* * *

L'ENGLE, Madeleine 1918-2007
(Madeleine L'Engle Camp, Madeleine Franklin, Madeleine L'Engle Franklin, Madeleine L'Engle Camp Franklin, Madeleine Camp Franklin L'Engle)

OBITUARY NOTICE—

See index for *SATA* sketch: Born November 29, 1918, in New York, NY; died September 6, 2007, in Litchfield, CT. Novelist, children's author, poet, playwright, memoirist, educator, and librarian. L'Engle is remembered as the award-winning author of children's books featuring the Murry family, even though, ironically, she claimed that she never intended to write for children. In fact, most of the sixty-plus books she published in her fifty-year career were for adults. Yet her immortality may well rest on her "Time Fantasy" series about young Meg Murry and her quest to save her father from dark forces on a distant planet that could only be reached by traveling through time. *A Wrinkle in Time* (1962) became a best-seller and earned L'Engle a Newbery award from the American Library Association, but it also became one of the most banned children's books in

history. Initially, the book almost never went to press, as an adult novel featuring a juvenile protagonist was hard to market. As a children's novel, the story depended on time travel in a universe governed by principles reminiscent of quantum physics and was deemed too complicated for young readers. Finally published, L'Engle's combination of myth and mysticism with science and fiction disturbed many conservative Christians. Despite this, *A Wrinkle in Time* became an unqualified popular success, and four more "Time Fantasy" novels followed. L'Engle described herself as an Episcopalian and worked for many years as a librarian at the Cathedral of St. John the Divine in New York City. Her adult writings included novels, poetry, plays, prayer collections, and spiritual meditations, none of which provoked religious controversy. She also adapted several Bible stories for children and also wrote the "Austin Family" series for children, both ventures which proved non-controversial. Much of L'Engle's fiction reflected her background as an only child raised by middle-aged parents in the United States and abroad, and educated at boarding schools. She worked as an actress and married Hugh Franklin, a successful television actor. She worked briefly as a schoolteacher and raised her family. Through all of it she remained first and foremost a writer, but when it came to fantasy, L'Engle herself claimed that her stories sometimes seemed to write themselves. She accepted comments describing *A Wrinkle in Time* as an allegory with spiritual overtones, but her own interpretation of its message varied over the years. L'Engle's later books reflect the wide range of her writings; they include *An Acceptable Time* (1996), the final "Time Fantasy" novel; *Mothers and Sons* (1999); *The Other Dog* (2001), a children's picture book; and the autobiographical novel *The Joys of Love,* which was written in the 1940s but not published until after her death.

OBITUARIES AND OTHER SOURCES:

BOOKS

Contemporary Popular Writers, St. James Press (Detroit, MI), 1997.

L'Engle, Madeleine, *A Circle of Quiet,* Farrar, Straus & Giroux (New York, NY), 1972.

L'Engle, Madeleine, *The Summer of the Great-Grandmother,* Farrar, Straus & Giroux (New York, NY), 1974.

L'Engle, Madeleine, *The Irrational Season,* Seabury Press (New York, NY), 1977.

L'Engle, Madeleine, *Two-Part Invention,* Farrar, Straus & Giroux (New York, NY), 1988.

L'Engle, Madeleine, *My Own Small Place: Developing the Writing Life,* Harold Shaw (Wheaton, IL), 1998.

L'Engle, Madeleine, *Madeleine L'Engle Herself: Reflections on a Writing Life,* collected by Carol Chase, WaterBrook Press (Colorado Springs, CO), 2001.

St. James Guide to Children's Writers, 5th edition, St. James Press (Detroit, MI), 1999.

PERIODICALS

Los Angeles Times, September 8, 2007, p. B10.
New York Times, September 8, 2007, p. A13.
Times (London, England), September 25, 2007, p. 60.

*   *   *

L'ENGLE, Madeleine Camp Franklin
See L'ENGLE, Madeleine

*   *   *

LALICKI, Tom 1949-
(Tom L. Matthews)

Personal

Born 1949, in Scranton, PA; married; wife's name Barbara. *Education:* Brooklyn College, graduated. *Hobbies and other interests:* Indian cooking, photography and digital manipulation of images, travel, gardening.

Addresses

Home—Westchester County, NY. *E-mail*—Tom. Lalicki@gmail.com.

Career

Author. Author and director of corporate videos for twenty years.

Member

Authors Guild, Authors League.

Awards, Honors

Best Books for Young Adults selection, American Library Association, for *Spellbinder;* Notable Social Studies Trade Book designation, National Council for the Social Studies/Children's Book Council, and 100 Titles for Reading and Sharing selection, New York Public Library, both for *Always Inventing;* Best Children's Book selection, Bank Street College of Education, 2007, for *Danger in the Dark.*

Writings

"HOUDINI AND NATE" SERIES; FICTION

Danger in the Dark, illustrated by Carlyn Cerniglia, Farrar, Straus & Giroux (New York, NY), 2006.
Shots at Sea, illustrated by Carlyn Cerniglia, Farrar, Straus & Giroux (New York, NY), 2007.

NONFICTION

Spellbinder: The Life of Harry Houdini, Holiday House (New York, NY), 2000.

Grierson's Raid: A Daring Cavalry Strike through the Heart of the Confederacy, illustrated with maps by David Cain, Farrar, Straus & Giroux (New York, NY), 2004.

NONFICTION; UNDER NAME TOM L. MATTHEWS

Light Shining through the Mist: A Photobiography of Dian Fossey, National Geographic (Washington, DC), 1998.
Always Inventing: A Photobiography of Alexander Graham Bell, National Geographic (Washington, DC), 1999.

Sidelights

Tom Lalicki is the author of a number of critically acclaimed works of fiction and nonfiction. His interest in famed magician and escape artist Harry Houdini led him to write *Spellbinder: The Life of Harry Houdini,* as well as the young-adult novels *Danger in the Dark* and *Shots at Sea,* two books in his "Houdini and Nate Mystery" series. Lalicki has also published *Grierson's Raid: A Daring Cavalry Strike through the Heart of the Confederacy,* an account of a Union raid during the U.S. Civil War. Writing as Tom L. Matthews, Lalicki has also produced biographies of scientists Dian Fossey and Alexander Graham Bell.

Lalicki's passion for literature began at the age of eleven, when he was bedridden for several months after breaking bones in his foot, ankle, and leg. "Month after month, I had nothing to do but read all the books a thoughtful teacher delivered every week," Lalicki recalled on his home page. "Thus began a lifelong love of history, biography and historical fiction—interrupted by a business career." Lalicki worked as a writer and director of corporate videos for twenty years before attempting his first book, *Light Shining through the Mist: A Photobiography of Dian Fossey.* As the author admitted, "I've certainly never regretted making the switch."

In *Light Shining through the Mist,* Lalicki explores the controversial career of primatologist Fossey, who founded the Karisoke Research Center in Rwanda and dedicated her life to the preservation of mountain gorillas. Roger Sutton, writing in *Horn Book,* stated that the narrative "does a fine job of tracing the life of a troubled woman." A reviewer in *Publishers Weekly* applauded Lalicki's "flowing text and stunning photos," adding that his "fascinating biography will surely snare the attention of young animal lovers and aspiring anthropologists." The inventor of the telephone is the subject of *Always Inventing: A Photobiography of Alexander Graham Bell.* According to a contributor in *Horn Book,* "Bell's inexhaustible curiosity emerges as his wide range of experiments are outlined" in Lalicki's text.

In *Grierson's Raid* Lalicki recounts an 1863 expedition, led by Colonel Benjamin H. Grierson, into Mississippi and Alabama. For sixteen days Union soldiers damaged rail lines, destroyed bridges, and disrupted communications; the campaign successfully diverted the attention of Confederate commanders before the siege of Vicksburg. *Booklist* reviewer Ed Sullivan described the work as "accessibly written and scrupulously researched," and in *School Library Journal* Elizabeth M. Reardon remarked that *Grierson's Raid* "is told in an accessible style that reads more like an adventure story than a history text."

While researching *Spellbinder,* Lalicki noted on the Farrar, Straus & Giroux Web site, "it became clear that Houdini was an A-plus celebrity before the A-list was invented. . . . [and] has a hold on the popular psyche unsurpassed by any of his contemporaries. Even so, while everyone knows the name Houdini, very few people know anything real about him." In his biography, Lalicki examines not only Houdini's feats of daring, including the Chinese Water-Torture Cell escape, but also his personal life, from his childhood in Wisconsin to his death in 1926. "Lalicki successfully presents Houdini as a man remarkable for his confidence, determination, and hard work," Phelan commented, and a *Publishers Weekly* critic stated that "readers will be inspired by both Houdini's magic and enduring mysteries and by this subject's timeless message about the power of hard work and dedication."

Lalicki's debut work of fiction, *Danger in the Dark,* centers on the relationship between Houdini and Nate Fuller, a young clerk working in Manhattan. After Nate meets David Douglas Trane, an unsavory gentleman who holds late-night seances in his family's parlor, he suspects foul play and enlists the help of the celebrated daredevil to expose the charlatan. "The action is nonstop," commented Francisca Goldsmith in *Booklist,* and Connie Tyrell Burns, reviewing *Danger in the Dark* for *School Library Journal,* stated that Lalicki "brings the period to life with many historical references." In a sequel, *Shots at Sea,* Houdini and Nate board the ocean liner *Lusitania* to order to prevent the assassination of former U.S. President Theodore Roosevelt. "Readers interested in fiction with historical characters will drink this one up," noted a *Kirkus Reviews* critic.

Biographical and Critical Sources

PERIODICALS

Booklist, September 15, 1998, Carolyn Phelan, review of *Light Shining through the Mist: A Photobiography of Dian Fossey,* p. 223; June 1, 1999, Carolyn Phelan, review of *Always Inventing: A Photobiography of Alexander Graham Bell,* p. 1822; September 1, 2000, Carolyn Phelan, review of *Spellbinder: The Life of Harry Houdini,* p. 110; August, 2004, Ed Sullivan, review of *Grierson's Raid: A Daring Cavalry Strike through the Heart of the Confederacy,* p. 1917; November 15, 2006, Francisca Goldsmith, review of *Danger in the Dark,* p. 48.

Horn Book, September-October, 1998, Roger Sutton, review of *Light Shining through the Mist,* p. 622; July, 1999, review of *Always Inventing,* p. 481; July-August, 2004, Betty Carter, review of *Grierson's Raid,* p. 468.

Kirkus Reviews, March 1, 2004, review of *Grierson's Raid,* p. 225; September 15, 2006, review of *Danger in the Dark,* p. 959; September 1, 2007, review of *Shots at Sea.*

Publishers Weekly, June 22, 1998, review of *Light Shining through the Mist,* p. 93; July 17, 2000, review of *Spellbinder,* p. 197.

School Library Journal, September, 2000, Carol Fazioli, review of *Spellbinder,* p. 250; December, 2001, Kathleen Baxter, "We Could Be Heroes," review of *Spellbinder,* p. 39; June, 2004, Elizabeth M. Reardon, review of *Grierson's Raid,* p. 168; September, 2005, Kathleen Baxter, review of *Grierson's Raid,* p. 35; October, 2006, Connie Tyrell Burns, review of *Danger in the Dark,* p. 160.

ONLINE

Farrar, Straus & Giroux Web site, http://www.fsgkidsbooks.com/ (January 1, 2008), "Q&A with Tom Lalicki."

Kidsreads.com, http://www.kidsreads.com/ (December 1, 2007), Robert Oksner, review of *Danger in the Dark.*

Tom Lalicki Home Page, http://www.houdiniandnate.com (December 1, 2007).*

*   *   *

LANGSTON, Laura 1958-

Personal

Born August 25, 1958, in Victoria, British Columbia, Canada; married Barry Nazarko; children: Tlell (daughter), Zachary. *Education:* British Columbia Institute of Technology, degree.

Addresses

Home—Victoria, British Columbia, Canada. *E-mail*—info@lauralangston.com.

Career

Author. Has also worked as a bank teller, journalist with Canadian Broadcasting Corporation, and radio broadcaster in Langley, British Columbia, and Richmond, British Columbia, Canada.

Member

Canadian Society of Children's Authors, Illustrators, and Performers, Writers Union of Canada, Society of Children's Book Writers and Illustrators.

Awards, Honors

Red Cedar Award nomination, and Silver Birch Award shortlist, both for *Pay Dirt!;* New York Public Library Books for the Teen Age selection, 2003, for *A Taste of*

Perfection; Blue Spruce Award nomination, Shining Willow Award nomination, CILIP Kate Greenaway Medal nomination, and Notable Social Studies Trade Book for Young People designation, National Council for the Social Studies/Children's Book Council, all for *Mile-High Apple Pie;* Snow Willow Award nomination, Rocky Mountain Book Award shortlist, Manitoba Young Readers' Choice Award shortlist, and Kobzar Literary Award, all 2006, all for *Lesia's Dream.*

Writings

JUVENILE

No Such Thing as Far Away, illustrated by Robert Amos, Orca Book Publishers (Victoria, British Columbia, Canada), 1994.

Pay Dirt!: The Search for Gold in British Columbia, illustrated by Stuart Duncan, Orca Book Publishers (Victoria, British Columbia, Canada), 1994.

The Magic Ear, illustrated by Victor Bosson, Orca Book Publishers (Victoria, British Columbia, Canada), 1995.

The Fox's Kettle, illustrated by Victor Bosson, Orca Book Publishers (Victoria, British Columbia, Canada), 1998.

A Taste of Perfection, Stoddart Kids (Toronto, Ontario, Canada), 2002.

Lesia's Dream, HarperTrophy Canada (Toronto, Ontario, Canada), 2003.

Mile-High Apple Pie, illustrated by Lindsey Gardiner, Bodley Head (London, England), 2004, published as *Remember, Grandma?,* Viking (New York, NY), 2004.

Chan Hon Goh: Prima Ballerina, Pearson Education Canada (Don Mills, Ontario, Canada), 2005.

Rosemary Brown: Political Pioneer, Pearson Education Canada (Don Mills, Ontario, Canada), 2005.

Exit Point, Orca Book Publishers (Victoria, British Columbia, Canada), 2006.

Finding Cassidy, HarperTrophy Canada (Toronto, Ontario, Canada), 2006.

Perfectly Blue, Fitzhenry & Whiteside (Toronto, Ontario, Canada), 2008.

The Trouble with Cupid, Fitzhenry & Whiteside (Toronto, Ontario, Canada), 2008.

My Bully, illustrated by Cynthia Nugent, Fitzhenry & Whiteside (Toronto, Ontario, Canada), 2008.

OTHER

Your Guide to Herb Gardening: Cooking, Crafts and Medicinal Herbs, Garden and Container Cultivation, Recipes and Instructions, Coles (Toronto, Ontario, Canada), 1999.

Contributor to periodicals, including *Canadian Gardening.*

Sidelights

Laura Langston is an award-winning Canadian author of picture books for children, novels for young adults, and general nonfiction. Growing up in Victoria, British Columbia, Langston surrounded herself with books and decided to pursue an author's life while she was just a youngster. "I wanted to be a writer by the time I was in grade four," she recalled on her home page. "It's my mother's fault. She kept our house loaded with books and trips to the library were considered Very Special."

After graduating from high school, Langston took a job as a bank teller and later studied journalism while working for the Canadian Broadcasting Corporation (CBC). "I didn't know any writers and I had no idea how to get paid to write, other than becoming a reporter and writing about current events," she later recalled. She eventually landed in the newsroom at the CBC's Winnipeg office, where she mixed reporting with documentary work. "Even in radio when I was paid to write the facts, I dreamed of writing fiction," she remarked in a *Canadian Review of Materials* interview. After her daughter was born, Langston began a career as a freelance writer, publishing a number of stories and articles.

In 1994 Langston produced her debut title, *No Such Thing as Far Away.* Based on the author's childhood memories of Victoria's Chinatown, *No Such Thing as Far Away* focuses on a young boy who grows concerned when his family prepares to move to a new neighborhood. Marion Scott, writing in *Canadian Review of Materials,* called the work "a satisfying, reassuring treatment of the theme of leaving loved places and loved ones."

On her next two picture books, *The Magic Ear* and *The Fox's Kettle,* Langston collaborated with illustrator Victor Bosson. "Vic's not Japanese, but he does Japanese art, and he's incredibly talented," Langston commented in her *Canadian Review of Materials* interview. "After I saw his art, I was blown away by it, and I really wanted to do something with him." *The Magic Ear,* adapted from a Japanese folk tale, follows a peasant who saves the life of a tiny fish and is rewarded with a powerful gift. According to Ian McClaren in *Canadian Review of Materials,* "the rich descriptiveness of Langston's writing is undeniable."

Langston spent a year researching Japanese mythology in preparation for writing *The Fox's Kettle,* which centers on a storyteller's complex and unusual relationship with a trio of magical foxes. "Langston is clearly comfortable with her material; her story has the directness and logic of folktale," observed *Quill & Quire* reviewer Annette Goldsmith of the picture book.

In *Mile-High Apple Pie* (also published as *Remember, Grandma?*), Langston explores the special bond between a young girl and her beloved grandmother, a woman who suffers from Alzheimer's disease. The author "has captured the voice of her young narrator beautifully," Valerie Nielsen commented in *Canadian Review of Materials.* "Langston's approach to the topic is both sensitive and gentle," noted *Resource Links* critic

Laura Langston shares a warm multigenerational tale in **Remember, Grandma?**, *a picture book featuring art by Lindsay Gardiner.* (Viking, 2004. Illustration © 2004 by Lindsey Gardiner. Reproduced by permission.)

Brenda Power, the critic adding that *Mile-High Apple Pie* "is touching, while at the same time it is not over-emotional or sentimental."

Langston has also found success with her novels for teenage readers. In *A Taste of Perfection,* twelve-year-old Erin Morris spends a summer training Lavender Blue, her grandmother's show dog, and reinventing her own physical appearance. When Blue loses a leg in an accident caused by Erin, the youngster must overcome her guilt to nurture the "imperfect" creature. "Langston's text reads smoothly," observed *Resource Links* contributor Lisa Strong, and Barbara Auerbach remarked in *School Library Journal* that "the resolution is realistic and satisfying."

Lesia's Dream, a work of historical fiction, concerns a little-known episode in Canadian history: the internment of some 5,000 Ukrainian immigrants, who were deemed "enemy agents," from 1914 to 1920. The novel centers on Lesia, a fifteen year old who helps restore the family farm after her father and older brother are placed in an internment camp. In *Canadian Review of Materials,* Joan Marshall called *Lesia's Dream* "a compelling story of the horrors faced by a particular immigrant family who quickly become endeared to the reader." In Langston's supernatural work, *Exit Point,* a sixteen-year-old accident victim must tend to unfinished business on earth before he reaches the afterlife. "With a fast-paced plot and the constant pull of tension," *Kli-*

att reviewer Amanda MacGregor noted that "Langston manages to pack a lot of action into a brief story."

"Writing is the best job in the world, Langston concluded to *SATA.* "I can wear slippers to work and I get to meet all sorts of interesting people: my characters. If I spend enough time with them, I end up with a story. With any luck, it's a story that makes people laugh or cry, or maybe even a little of both!"

Biographical and Critical Sources

PERIODICALS

Canadian Review of Materials, September, 1994, Marion Scott, review of *No Such Thing as Far Away,* p. 132; September 15, 1995, Ian McClaren, review of *The Magic Ear;* November 27, 1998, Joan Payzant, review of *The Fox's Kettle;* September 5, 2003, Joan Marshall, review of *Lesia's Dream;* April 15, 2005, Valerie Nielsen, review of *Mile-High Apple Pie;* October 13, 2006, Jane Bridle, review of *Exit Point.*
Kliatt, January, 2007, Amanda McGregor, review of *Exit Point,* p. 24.
Quill & Quire, June, 1998, Annette Goldsmith, review of *The Fox's Kettle,* p. 59.
Resource Links, June, 2003, Lisa Strong, review of *A Taste of Perfection,* p. 27; December, 2005, Brenda Power, review of *Mile-High Apple Pie,* p. 5; October, 2006, Maria Forte, review of *Exit Point,* p. 36.
School Library Journal, March, 1999, Nancy A. Gifford, review of *The Fox's Kettle,* p. 178; May, 2003, Barbara Auerbach, review of *A Taste of Perfection,* p. 156; August, 2006, Carol Schene, review of *Exit Point,* p. 123.
Voice of Youth Advocates, February, 2007, Laura Woodruff, review of *Exit Point,* p. 528.

ONLINE

Canadian Review of Materials Web site, http://www.umanitoba.ca/cm/profiles/ (October 8, 2003), interview with Langston.
Canadian Society of Children's Authors, Illustrators, and Performers Web site, http://www.canscaip.org/ (December 20, 2007), "Laura Langston."
Laura Langston Home Page, http://www.lauralangston.com (December 20, 2007).

*   *   *

LEW-VRIETHOFF, Joanne

Personal

Married; children: one daughter. *Education:* Art Center College of Design, degree, 1995.

Addresses

Home and office—Amsterdam, Netherlands. *E-mail*—jo@josgreatesthits.com.

Career

Illustrator, graphic designer, and artist. DiVision Studio, New York, NY, graphic designer and art director, 1997; Gazworks.com, Kuala Lumpur, Malaysia, art director; freelance graphic designer and illustrator. Designer of handbags. *Exhibitions:* Works exhibited in galleries in Germany, New York, NY, and Los Angeles, CA.

Member

Society of Children's Book Writers and Illustrators.

Illustrator

Milton Schafer, *I'm Big!,* Dial Books for Young Readers (New York, NY), 2006.

Eileen Spinelli, *Summerhouse Time,* Alfred A. Knopf (New York, NY), 2007.

Biographical and Critical Sources

PERIODICALS

Booklist, February 15, 2007, Ilene Cooper, review of *Summerhouse Time,* p. 80.

School Library Journal, September, 2006, Suzanne Myers Harold, review of *I'm Big!,* p. 183; May, 2007, Nancy Brown, review of *Summerhouse Time,* p. 144.

ONLINE

Joanne Lew-Vriethoff Home Page, http://www.josgreatesthits.com/ (January 6, 2008).

Thumbtack Press Web site, http://www.thumbtackpress.com/ (January 10, 2008), "Jo Lew-Vriethoff."*

*   *   *

LOUIS, Catherine 1963-

Personal

Born 1963, in Neuveville, Switzerland. *Education:* Attended École d'Arts Visuels de Bienne. *Hobbies and other interests:* Designing puppets.

Addresses

Home—Switzerland.

Career

Illustrator and author. École d'Art de la Chaux-de-Fonds, Chaux-de-Fonds, Switzerland, instructor in illustration. Has also worked as a set designer. Card designer for UNICEF and Nouvelles Images, Paris, France. *Exhibitions:* Work included in Biennale de Bratislava, 1989, 1990, 1997; and in other exhibitions.

Awards, Honors

International Board on Books for Young People (IBBY) Honor List for Swiss illustration, 1990; Paolo Vergerio à Padoue European prize, 1993, for *La Force du Berger* by Azouz Begag; IBBY Honor List for Swiss illustration, 1997, for "Léon et Ciboulette" series; U.S. Board on Books for Young People Outstanding listee, 2008, for *Legend of the Chinese Dragon* by Marie Sellier.

Writings

SELF-ILLUSTRATED

L'Escargot et le papillon, Librairie de l'Etat de Berne (Berne, Switzerland), 1982.

Cinquante histoires courtes et amusantes, Editions Lito (Champigny sur Marne, France), 1989.

Les quatre saisons du renard, Editions Flick Flack (Paris, France), 1989.

Trois histoires de robots, Editions Lito (Champigny sur Marne, France), 1989.

Mon journal à l'hôpital, Editions La Joie de Lire (Geneva, Switzerland), 1990.

Mon journal en avion, Editions La Joie de Lire (Geneva, Switzerland), 1992.

Julien dans l'île aux cerfs-volants, collect., Editions Bordas (Paris, France), 1992.

Mon journal à la poste, Editions La Joie de Lire (Geneva, Switzerland), 1994.

L'oiseau Charpentier, Mimi Barthé lé my, tiré à compte d'auteur à 300 exemplaires en sérigraphie, disponible *Chez C. Louis* (exhibition catalogue), Edition à Compte d'Auteur 1998.

Fernand Fainéant, Editions Nord-Sud (Paris, France), 2000.

Amour, Picquier Jeunesse (Arles, France), 2001.

Le don de Lucas, Lehrmittelverlag, 2001.

Liu et l'oiseau, calligraphy by Feng Xiao Min, Picquier Jeunesse (Arles, France), 2003, translated by Sibylle Kazeroid as *Liu and the Bird: A Journey in Chinese Calligraphy,* North-South Books (New York, NY), 2006.

Mon imagier chinois, calligraphy by Shi Bo, Picquier Jeunesse (Arles, France), 2004, translated as *My Little Book of Chinese Words,* North-South Books (New York, NY), 2008.

SELF-ILLUSTRATED; "LÉON ET CIBOULETTE" SERIES

Le bateau, Editions La Joie de Lire (Geneva, Switzerland), 1996.

Le bouton, Editions La Joie de Lire (Geneva, Switzerland), 1996.

Le fil, Editions La Joie de Lire (Geneva, Switzerland), 1996.

La peinture, Editions La Joie de Lire (Geneva, Switzerland), 1996.

L'ombre, Editions La Joie de Lire (Geneva, Switzerland), 1996.

Le livre, Editions La Joie de Lire (Geneva, Switzerland), 1996.

ILLUSTRATOR

Jean-Pierre Fily, *Les petites lettres ont pris la fuite,* Editions Lito (Champigny sur Marne, France), 1987.

Barbara Haupt, *Die Möwe Fridolin,* Editions Atlantis Chez Pro Juventute (Zurich, Switzerland), 1988.

Hans Peter Scheier, *Le voyage de Maximilien au bout du monde,* Editions Atlantis chez Pro Juventute (Zurich, Switzerland), 1989.

Véronique Borg, *Le balcon d'en dessous,* Editions Casterman (Brussels, Belgium), 1989, translated as *The Next Balcony Down,* Child's World (Mankato, MN), 1992.

Chantal Crovi, *Les sept Mamm-goz et la pâte à crêpes,* Editions Milan (Milan, Italy), 1990.

Miette Marsol, *Fifine et le fantôme,* Editions Milan (Milan, Italy), 1990.

Eleonor Nilson, *Le 89e chaton,* Editions Milan (Milan, Italy), 1990.

Azouz Begag, *Les voleurs d'écritures,* Editions du Seuil (Paris, France), 1990.

Sarah Cohen-Scali, *Danger d'amour,* Editions Casterman (Brussels, Belgium), 1991.

Azouz Begag, *La force du berger,* Editions La Joie de Lire (Geneva, Switzerland), 1991.

Barbara Haupt, *Gré gor le microbe,* Editions Atlantis chez Pro Juventute (Zurich, Switzerland), 1992.

Véronique Borg, *Mozart et moi,* Editions du Seuil (Paris, France), 1992.

Anne-Lise Grobéty, *Une bouffée de bonheur,* [Zurich, Switzerland], 1992.

Uwe Timm, *Rudi la truffe,* Editions Milan (Milan, Italy), 1993.

Azouz Begag, *Une semaine à Cap Maudit,* Editions du Seuil (Paris, France), 1994.

Azouz Begag, *Le temps des villages,* Editions La Joie de Lire (Geneva, Switzerland), 1994.

Bernard Friot, *C'est Noêl,* Editions Hachette (Paris, France), 1994.

Azouz Begag, *Ma maman est devenue une é toile,* Editions La Joie de Lire (Geneva, Switzerland), 1995.

Frauke Nahrgang, *Katja und die Buchstaben,* Beltz & Gelberg (Weinheim, Germany), 1995.

Catherine Challandes, *Symphonie pour piano et patins à roulettes,* Editions La Joie de Lire (Geneva, Switzerland), 1995.

Azouz Begag, *Mona et le bateau-livre,* Editions du Chardon Bleu (Plantagenet, Ontario, Canada), 1996.

Catherine Nesi, *Escalier pour la terre,* Département de l'Instruction Publique (Neuchâtel, Switzerland), 1997.

Bernard Friot, *Encore des histoires pressées,* Editions Milan (Milan, Italy), 1997.

Gardi Hutter, *Mamma mia, ma mère est une sorcière,* Editions Nord-Sud (Paris, France), 1997.

Gardi Hutter, *Mamma mia, qu'est-ce qu'on a pleuré,* Editions Nord-Sud (Paris, France), 1999.

Andreas Venzke, *Carlos kann doch Tore schiessen,* Nagel & Kimche (Zurich, Switzerland), 1999.

Nathalie Beau, *Jojo et son pot; Jojo n'a pas sommeil; Jojo à l'école; Jojo et Ouistiti,* Editions Milan (Milan, Italy), 2000.

Daniel Badraun, *Weinachten mit Solanima,* Lehrmittelverlag des Kantons (Zurich, Switzerland), 2000.

Sprachfenster, Manuel d'enseignement de l'allemand, Lehrmittelverlag des Kantons (Zurich, Switzerland), 2000.

Véronique Borg, *Le don de Lucas,* Lehrmittelverlag des Kantons (Zurich, Switzerland), 2001.

Gardi Hutter, *Mamma Mia, ne t'en va pas,* Editions Nord-Sud (Paris, France), 2001.

Azouz Begag, *Un train pour chez nous,* Editions Thierry Magnier (Paris, France), 2001.

Jonier Marin, *L'arbre é lé phant,* Editions Vents d'Ailleurs (La Roque d'Anthéron, France), 2001.

Marie-José Auderset, *Amidou,* Editions Callicéphale (Strasbourg, France), 2002.

Bernard Friot, *Pour vivre,* Martinière Jeunesse, 2005.

Marie Sellier, *Naissance du dragon,* Picquier Jeunesse (Arles, France), 2006 translated by Sibylle Kazeroid as *Legend of the Chinese Dragon,* North-South Books (New York, NY), 2008.

Bernard Friot, *Tu veux être ma maman,* Petit Clown (Milan, Italy), 2007.

Marie Sellier, *La naissance de Ganesh,* Picquier Jeunesse (Arles, France), 2007.

Marie Sellier, *Le rat m'a dit,* Picquier Jeunesse (Arles, France), 2008.

Books featuring Louis's art have been translated into Dutch, Korean, Chinese, English, and Czech.

Sidelights

Catherine Louis is an award-winning illustrator and graphic artist whose work is familiar to children throughout Europe. A native of Switzerland, she has created artwork to pair with numerous French-language authors, such as Azouz Begag, Marie Sellier, Catherine Nesi, and frequent collaborator Bernard Friot. Praising her work for Sellier's *Legend of the Chinese Dragon,* *Booklist* contributor Linda Perkins dubbed it "stately" while in *School Library Journal* Margaret A. Chang commented on Louis's "rough-hewn woodcuts executed in black and bright primary colors."

In addition to creating artwork for books by others, Louis has also channeled her interest in Chinese art into several original picture books. Among those reaching English-language readers in translation are *Liu and the Bird: A Journey in Chinese Calligraphy* and *My Little Book of Chinese Words. Liu and the Bird* focuses on a Chinese girl who dreams of traveling over the mountains to the home of her grandfather, guided by a small bird. This imaginary trip, illustrated in three-part woodcut images printed on textured, torn-paper collage and highlighted by calligraphy by Feng Xiao Min, allows Louis to introduce readers to thirty Chinese pictographs. In *Booklist,* Carolyn Phelan noted Louis's skill in pairing "striking artwork and an unusual concept," and Chang described *Liu and the Bird* as "both evocative and educational" in her *School Library Journal* appraisal. Despite remarking that the sophisticated concept may not be apparent to younger children, a *Kirkus Reviews* writer described Louis's book as a "dreamy narrative" that is paired with "handsome linocut and painted-paper collage scenes."

Biographical and Critical Sources

PERIODICALS

Booklist, April 15, 2006, Carolyn Phelan, review of *Liu and the Bird: A Journey in Chinese Calligraphy,* p. 52; December 15, 2007, Linda Perkins, review of *Legend of the Chinese Dragon,* p. 47.

Kirkus Reviews, March 1, 2006, review of *Liu and the Bird,* p. 234.

School Library Journal, April, 2006, Margaret A. Chang, review of *Liu and the Bird,* p. 112; December, 2007, Margaret A. Chang, review of *Legend of the Chinese Dragon,* p. 100.

ONLINE

Exposition Catherine Louis Web site, http://www.ordp. vsnet.ch/fr/ressources/mediatheque/expo/ (November 3, 2003).*

*   *   *

LUCAS, Margeaux

Personal

Female. *Hobbies and other interests:* Travel.

Addresses

Home—New York, NY. *Agent*—Mela Bolino, MB Artists, 10 E. 29th St., Ste. 40G, New York, NY 10016.

Career

Illustrator.

Illustrator

Burton Albert, *The Pirates of Bat Cave Island: A Treasure-hunting Flap Book,* Little Simon (New York, NY), 1997.

Cathy Dubowski, *Santa's Biggest Little Helper,* Golden Books (New York, NY), 1997.

Eileen Spinelli, *Sadie Plays House: A Really Messy Sticker Book!,* Little Simon (New York, NY), 1998.

Sally Lucas, *Dancing Dinos Go to School,* Golden Books (New York, NY), 1998.

Michael Christie, *Olive, the Orphan Reindeer,* New Canaan Publishing (New Canaan, CT), 2000.

Betsy Franco, *My Pinkie Finger,* Children's Press (New York, NY), 2001.

Danielle Blood, *Fifteen Greek Mini-Books,* Instructor Books, 2001.

Ken Nesbitt, *The Aliens Have Landed!: Poems,* Meadowbrook Press (Minnetonka, MN), 2001.

Debbie Dadey, *Swamp Monster in Third Grade,* Scholastic (New York, NY), 2002.

Ellen Weiss, *The Nose Knows,* Kane Press (New York, NY), 2002.

Tanya Lee Stone, *P Is for Passover: A Holiday Alphabet Book,* Price, Stern Sloan (New York, NY), 2003.

Charles Haddad, *Calliope Day Falls . . . in Love?,* Delacorte Press (New York, NY), 2003.

AnnMarie Harris, *Countdown to Halloween,* Price Stern Sloan (New York, NY), 2003.

Susan Goldman Rubin, *Art against the Odds: From Slave Quilts to Prison Paintings,* Crown (New York, NY), 2004.

Debbie Dadey, *Lizards in the Lunch Line,* Scholastic (New York, NY), 2004.

Jo S. Kittinger, *When I Grow Up,* Children's Press (New York, NY), 2004.

Sally Lucas, *Dancing Dinos Go to School,* Random House (New York, NY), 2005.

Debbie Dadey, *Great Green Gator Graduation,* Scholastic (New York, NY), 2006.

Carlene Morton, *Alpha Betti,* Upstart Books (Fort Atkinson, WI), 2007.

David Parker, *My Sister Has a New Computer,* Scholastic (New York, NY), 2008.

David Parker, *A New Person in My Class,* Scholastic (New York, NY), 2008.

Contributor to periodicals, including *Highlights for Children.*

Biographical and Critical Sources

PERIODICALS

Booklist, May 1, 2003, Lauren Peterson, review of *Calliope Day Falls . . . in Love?,* p. 1591; February 15, 2004, Gillian Engberg, review of *Art against the Odds: From Slave Quilts to Prison Paintings,* p. 1058; August 1, 2006, Hazel Rochman, review of *Dancing Dinos Go to School,* p. 95.

Kirkus Reviews, June 15, 2006, review of *Dancing Dinos Go to School,* p. 635.

School Library Journal, October, 2000, review of *Olive, the Orphan Reindeer,* p. 58; January, 2003, Nancy A. Gifford, review of *The Nose Knows,* p. 114; August, 2003, Catherine Ensley, review of *Calliope Day Falls . . . in Love?,* p. 128; October, 2006, Tracy Bell, review of *Dancing Dinos Go to School,* p. 116.

ONLINE

MB Artists Web site, http://www.hkportfolio.com/ (January 15, 2008), "Margeaux Lucas."*

M

MATTHEWS, Tom L.
See LALICKI, Tom

* * *

McDONNELL, Kathleen 1947-

Personal
Born 1947, in Chicago, IL; immigrated to Canada; partner's name Alec; children: two daughters. *Education:* University of Toronto, B.A.

Addresses
Home—Toronto Island, Ontario, Canada. *E-mail*—kathleen@kathleenmcdonnell.com.

Career
Playwright, author of fiction and nonfiction, and editor. Contributor to CBC Radio. Speaker and workshop leader at conferences. Young People's Theater, Toronto, Ontario, Canada, playwright-in-residence, 1999-2000.

Member
Writers Union of Canada, Playwrights Union of Canada.

Awards, Honors
National Women's Playwriting Award (Canada), 1980, for *Risk Factors;* Chalmers Canadian Children's Play Award, 1994, for *Loon Boy;* Dora Award for best performance, 2003, for *The Seven Ravens.*

Writings

FOR CHILDREN AND YOUNG ADULTS

Ezzie's Emerald (also see below), illustrated by Sally J.K. Davies, Second Story Press (Toronto, Ontario, Canada), 1990.

The Nordlings ("Notherland Journeys" saga), Second Story Press (Toronto, Ontario, Canada), 1999.
The Shining World ("Notherland Journeys" saga), Second Story Press (Toronto, Ontario, Canada), 2003.
1212: Year of the Journey, Second Story Press (Toronto, Ontario, Canada), 2006.
The Songweavers ("Notherland Journeys" saga), Second Story Press (Toronto, Ontario, Canada), 2008.

PLAYS

(With Francine Volker) *Six-East,* produced 1979.
Risk Factors, produced 1980.
Different, produced 1987.
The Cookie War, produced at Blyth Festival, 1988.
Precipitous, produced 1992.
Loon Boy (also see below), produced 1994.
Ezzie's Emerald (adapted from the novel of the same title; also see below), music by Phyllis Cohen, produced 1995.
Unpacking, produced 1995.
Foundlings (also see below), produced in Toronto, Ontario, Canada, 1999.
(With Anne Barber and Brad Harley) *Right of Passage,* produced in Toronto Island, Ontario, Canada, 2000.
The Seven Ravens (also see below), produced in Montreal, Quebec, Canada, 2001.
Putting on a Show: Theater for Young People (includes *Foundlings, Ezzie's Emerald, Loon Boy,* and *The Seven Ravens*), Second Story Press (Toronto, Ontario, Canada), 2004.
The New Mother, produced in Montreal, Quebec, Canada, 2005.

OTHER

Not an Easy Choice: A Feminist Re-examines Abortion, South End (Boston, MA), 1984, revised edition, Second Story Press (Toronto, Ontario, Canada), 2002.
(Editor with Mariana Valverde) *The Healthsharing Book: Resources for Canadian Women,* Women's Press (Toronto, Ontario, Canada), 1985.

(Editor) *Adverse Effects: Women and the Pharmaceutical Industry,* Women's Press (Toronto, Ontario, Canada), 1986.

Kid Culture: Children and Adults and Popular Culture, Pluto Press Australia (Annadale, New South Wales, Australia), 2000.

Honey, We Lost the Kids: Re-thinking Childhood in the Multimedia Age, Second Story Press (Toronto, Ontario, Canada), 2001.

Contributor to periodicals, including Toronto *Globe and Mail, Toronto Star, Chatelaine, Maclean's,* and *Utne Reader.*

Sidelights

Kathleen McDonnell is an award-winning children's playwright and the author of books for both children and adults. Born in Chicago, Illinois, McDonnell moved to Canada to attend the University of Toronto, and she began her writing career shortly thereafter. In 1979, her first play, co-written with Francine Volker, was produced, and her next play, *Risk Factors,* received the National Women's Playwriting Award in 1980. From 1999 to 2000, she served as playwright-in-residence at the Young People's Theater in Toronto.

The year 1999 was a memorable year for McDonnell for other reasons: the first volume of her "Notherland Journeys" children's fantasy saga was released. Titled *The Nordlings,* the book introduces headstrong Peggy who is transported to a world she thought she had made up as a child. Peggy is, in fact, the world's creator, and now that the world is in trouble from an outside evil, she must decide whether to attempt to save it or abandon it and return to her normal life. McDonnell had developed the idea for the saga years before, while she was working on a nonfiction work titled *Kid Culture: Children and Adults and Popular Culture.* Recalling her idea of "paracosms"—imaginary worlds made up by children—she wrote on her home page: "I knew right away that I wanted to write a story around this idea, and that it would involve a grown-up who returns to an imaginary childhood world to save it from extinction."

Peggy's journey continues in *The Shining World* as she and her companions search for the lost sky-spirit Mi. Their quest takes them through a number of dream worlds as Mi tries to make it to the Shining World, where his wounds will be healed. When the Evil Angel bars the way, Peggy must call upon her own special magic, found in her musical ability, to clear Mi's path. Noting the themes of real-world danger to children that hover around the edges of the narrative, Teresa Hughes wrote in *Resource Links* that "*The Shining World* is a very good read." *The Songweavers,* the final book in the "Notherland Journeys" series, was released in 2008.

Departing from the "Notherland Journeys," McDonnell's next novel, *1212: Year of the Journey,* is a recounting of the Children's Crusade. Etienne, Abel, and Blanche all hope that their peaceful crusade will spread

Christianity without violence, but sadly, many of the children who journey with them are sold into slavery or die due to the journey's hardships. "While *1212* is a very demanding read at times, it is also an extremely valuable read as the religious persecutions and tensions throughout the novel mirror many contemporary issues," wrote Emily Springer in a review of the book for *Resource Links.* Though Krista Hutley noted in *Booklist* that the novel's notes do not include sources for students wishing to research the late Middle Ages, she concluded that "McDonnell brings the period alive." Claire Rosser, writing in *Kliatt,* also made note of the historical detail, writing that "readers interested in religious history and European history will appreciate McDonnell's fine work."

McDonnell has continued to write plays in addition to her fiction. In 2004, several of her works for the stage were collected in a guide for theater teachers titled *Putting on a Show: Theater for Young People.* The book includes an introduction that "eloquently describes" suspending disbelief, according to Lynda Pogue in *Childhood Education,* as well as short essays about history, and cross-cultural performance themes. Adriane Pettit, reviewing the work for *Resource Links,* recommended the book as "an excellent handbook for any elementary drama teacher."

As McDonnell explained on her home page, she writes for and about kids, "*for* because . . . I find that children's stories are usually the best medium to express what I want to say; and *about* because I have a burning interest in kids and their culture, how they think and feel about the world they're growing up in."

Biographical and Critical Sources

PERIODICALS

Booklist, April 15, 2007, Krista Hutley, review of *1212: Year of the Journey,* p. 50.

Canadian Book Review Annual, 2004, David E. Kemp, review of *Putting on a Show: Theater for Young People,* p. 571.

Childhood Education (annual), 2005, Lynda Pogue, review of *Putting on a Show,* p. 301.

Kliatt, January, 2007, Claire Rosser, review of *1212,* p. 24.

Quill & Quire, October, 1999, review of *The Nordlings,* p. 46.

Resource Links, February, 2004, Teresa Hughes, review of *The Shining World,* p. 36; April, 2005, Adriane Pettit, review of *Putting on a Show,* p. 48; February, 2007, Emily Springer, review of *1212,* p. 38.

School Library Journal, March, 2007, Renee Steinberg, review of *1212,* p. 214.

Voice of Youth Advocates, February, 2007, Megan Lynn Isaac, review of *1212,* p. 529.

ONLINE

Kathleen McDonnell Home Page, http://www.kathleen mcdonnell.com (December 20, 2007).
Second Story Press Web site, http://www.secondstorypress. ca/ (December 20, 2007), "Kathleen McDonnell."

* * *

McKINTY, Adrian

Personal

Born in Carrickfergus, Northern Ireland; immigrated to United States, c. 1992. *Education:* Attended Oxford University.

Addresses

Home—CO.

Career

Novelist, attorney, and educator. Worked variously as a security guard, construction worker, postman, bartender, door-to-door salesman, rugby coach, bookstore clerk, and school teacher; former attorney.

Writings

NOVELS

Orange Rhymes with Everything, William Morrow (New York, NY), 1997.
Dead I Well May Be, Scribner (New York, NY), 2003.
Hidden River, Scribner (New York, NY), 2005.
The Dead Yard, Scribner (New York, NY), 2006.
The Lighthouse Land (part of "Lighthouse" trilogy), Amulet (New York, NY), 2006.
The Bloomsday Dead, Scribner (New York, NY), 2007.
The Lighthouse War (part of "Lighthouse" trilogy), Amulet (New York, NY), 2007.

Adaptations

Dead I Well May Be was adapted for film by John Lee Hancock, for Universal Pictures.

Sidelights

Novelist and educator Adrian McKinty was born in Carrickfergus, Northern Ireland, and grew up in the late 1960s and 1970s, during the height of the Troubles—a nearly thirty-year period of violent conflict and civil strife. Trained as an attorney, he came to the United States in the early 1990s, after his legal career stalled. A variety of jobs followed, including working as a school teacher.

Orange Rhymes with Everything, McKinty's first novel, was written for adults and tells about the Troubles from the point of view of an Irish Protestant. The mundane life of an unnamed, physically disabled schoolgirl in Belfast is juxtaposed with the violent activities of her father, a Protestant terrorist and fugitive who is attempting to elude authorities in New York City. Although the man's hatred is deep and his brutality seems second nature, his fondest desire is to return to Northern Ireland to see his daughter.

In *Hidden River,* another novel for adult readers, Alexander Lawson was a Royal Ulster Constabulary officer. Now a disgraced heroin addict, Lawson immigrates to the United States to escape the wrath of corrupt former colleagues. He also intends to investigate the death of his high-school love Victoria Patawasti, who has been murdered in Denver. Lawson convinces Victoria's family to let him solve her murder and bring the perpetrator to justice. "McKinty still knows how to write elegantly horrifying death scenes . . . and spot-on endings that make the journey worthwhile," commented *Booklist* reviewer Frank Sennett.

In *Dead I Well May Be* McKinty introduces Michael Forsythe, a man on the run from the law in his native Belfast who illegally enters the United States and effortlessly slides into a job as an enforcer for Irish mobster Darkey White. Although Forsythe tries to keep local violence to a minimum, the constant conflict between the Irish mob, Dominican gangs, and other rivals fighting for control of the streets eventually causes him to rack up numerous kills. Trouble brews when Forsythe meets White's girlfriend Bridget Callaghan and finds her irresistible. An bogus drug deal in Mexico sets Forsythe and three friends up for a fall, and they land in a brutal prison, from which only Forsythe emerges. After his ordeal, revenge on White is Forsyth's prime goal. Sennett deemed *Dead I Well May Be* a "profoundly satisfying book from a major new talent." In *Kirkus Reviews* a contributor called McKinty "a storyteller with the kind of style and panache that blur the line between genre and mainstream," and concluded that *Dead I Well May Be* is "top-drawer."

The mercenary Forsythe returns in *The Dead Yard,* and this time the F.B.I. has coerced him into infiltrating an Irish terrorist cell. McKinty rounds out Forsythe's adventures in *The Bloomsday Dead,* which finds the hired gun directly in the sights of Bridget. Tracked down by his former flame while in hiding in South America, Forsythe returns to Dublin to discover the whereabouts of Bridget's daughter, who is being held by kidnappers. "McKinty hooks readers early with vivid action sequences and brutal bits of foreshadowing," wrote Sennett in a review of *The Dead Yard* for *Booklist.* Calling the novel "literate" and "expertly crafted," a *Publishers Weekly* critic hailed McKinty as "one of his generation's leading talents." Reviewing *The Bloomsday Dead* in *Booklist,* Sennett commended McKinty's novel for rewarding readers with the author's "trademark dark lyricism, one great red herring, and a masterful plot twist" leading to a surprise ending. Calling the concluding volume of the trilogy the author's "most visceral, satisfying effort yet," a *Publishers Weekly* contributor enjoyed the literary allusions to noted Irish novelist James Joyce.

McKinty turns to younger readers in his "Lighthouse Trilogy" of science-fiction novels. The trilogy begins with *The Lighthouse Land,* in which thirteen-year-old New Yorker Jamie O'Neill joins his mom in a move to a new home on an island off the coast of Ireland. Stricken with bone cancer, Jamie has lost an arm but has otherwise recovered physically. The emotional problems remain, however, as Jamie has not spoken a word since his arm was amputated. Although emotionally withdrawn, he is befriended by a local boy named Ramsay, and in their exploration of a nearby lighthouse the two young teens discover a golden artifact that transports them to another planet. On Altair Jamie's arm is restored, as is his voice, and he quickly joins in the fight of the resident Aldanese to battle an army of invaders. Calling Jamie "a sympathetic and thoughtful character" who sticks to his values, *Kliatt* reviewer Donna Scanlon added that *The Lighthouse Land* features a story that "is fresh and unique." In *School Library Journal* Sharon Rawlins wrote that McKinty draws readers into "an interesting setting," while a *Kirkus Reviews* writer dubbed *The Lighthouse Land* "an entertaining adventure." McKinty "brings an attuned ear for dialogue and a taut pacing to his first YA outing," wrote a *Publishers Weekly* critic, the critic observing that the author's inclusion of "pop-culture references," the creation of "an intelligent, open-ended mythology," and engaging dialogue combine to make *The Lighthouse Land* "an enjoyable trip" for young-adult readers.

Biographical and Critical Sources

PERIODICALS

Booklist, September 1, 2003, Frank Sennett, review of *Dead I Well May Be,* p. 71; November 1, 2004, Frank Sennett, review of *Hidden River,* p. 468; December 15, 2005, Frank Sennett, review of *The Dead Yard,* p. 28; November 15, 2006, Cindy Dobrez, review of *The Lighthouse Land,* p. 49; December 1, 2006, Frank Sennett, review of *The Bloomsday Dead,* p. 28.

Kirkus Reviews, August 1, 2003, review of *Dead I Well May Be,* p. 982; September 1, 2004, review of *Hidden River,* p. 828; September 15, 2006, review of *The Lighthouse Land,* p. 962.

Kliatt, November, 2006, Donna Scanlon, review of *The Lighthouse Land,* p. 14; November, 2007, Donna Scanlon, review of *The Lighthouse Land,* p. 14.

Library Journal, October 15, 004, Lisa Hanson, review of *Hidden River,* p. 54.

Publishers Weekly, November 4, 1996, review of *Orange Rhymes with Everything,* p. 63; September 1, 2003, review of *Dead I Well May Be,* p. 62; December 6,
2004, Patrick Millikin, interview with McKinty, p. 44; December 6, 2004, review of *Hidden River,* p. 44; January 9, 2006, review of *The Dead Yard,* p. 32; October 16, 2006, review of *The Lighthouse Land,* p. 3; January 1, 2007, review of *The Bloomsday Dead,* p. 32.

ONLINE

Washington Post Online, http://www.washingtonpost.com/ (December 20, 2004), Patrick Anderson, review of *Hidden River.**

*   *   *

MELLING, David

Personal

Born in Oxford, England; married; children: two. *Education:* Studied art in college.

Addresses

Home—Oxfordshire, England.

Career

Author and illustrator of children's books. Has also worked as a painter and designer in an animation studio.

Awards, Honors

Smarties Book Award shortlist, 1994, for *Brilliant the Dinosaur;* Kate Greenaway Medal longlist, for *What's That Noise?,* and shortlist for *The Kiss That Missed;* Pulcinella Award shortlist for Best TV Movie, 2005, for *The Tale of Jack Frost.*

Writings

SELF-ILLUSTRATED

Cartwheels in the Kitchen, Hodder Children's Books (London, England), 2001.
Just like My Dad, Hodder Children's Books (London, England), 2002.
The Kiss That Missed, Barron's (New York, NY), 2002.
The Tale of Jack Frost, Barron's (New York, NY), 2003.
The Ghost Library, Barron's (New York, NY), 2004.
Good Knight Sleep Tight, Barron's (New York, NY), 2005.
The Scallywags, Barron's, (New York, NY), 2006.
Two by Two and a Half, Hodder Children's Books (London, England), 2007.

ILLUSTRATOR

Richard Stilgoe, *Brilliant the Dinosaur,* Pavilion (London, England), 1994.

(With Colin Reeder) Nicola Baxter, *The Little Red Car,* Ladybird (Loughborough, England), 1995.

Sandi Toksvig, *If I Didn't Have Elbows,* De Agostini Children's Books (New York, NY), 1996.

Diane Bentley, *Monty at the Seaside,* Heinemann Educational (Oxford, England), 1996.

Diana Bentley, *Monty and the Ghost Train,* Heinemann Educational (Oxford, England), 1996.

Diana Bentley, *Monty at McBurgers,* Heinemann Educational (Oxford, England), 1996.

Diana Bentley, *Monty at the Party,* Heinemann Educational (Oxford, England), 1996.

Francesca Simon, *What's That Noise?,* Barron's (Hauppage, NY), 1996.

Jim Eldridge, *Tractor and Digger Save the Day,* Bloomsbury (London, England), 1997.

Nigel Boswall, *Jerry's Trousers,* Macmillan Children's Books (London, England), 1998.

Vivian French, *Iggy Pig's Party,* Hodder Children's Books (London, England), 1998.

Vivian French, *Iggy Pig's Skippy Day,* Hodder Children's Books (London, England), 1998.

Hilary McKay, *Cold Enough for Snow,* Hodder Children's Books (London, England), 1998.

Hilary McKay, *A Birthday Wish,* Hodder Children's Books (London, England), 1998.

Francesca Simon, *Where Are You?,* Peachtree (Atlanta, GA), 1998.

Vivian French, *Iggy Pig's Big Bad Wolf Trouble,* Scholastic (New York, NY), 1998.

Vivian French, *Iggy Pig's Dark Night,* Hodder Children's Books (London, England), 1999.

Vivian French, *Iggy Pig's at the Seaside,* Hodder Children's Books (London, England), 1999.

Vivian French, *Iggy Pig's Shopping Day,* Hodder Children's Books (London, England), 1999.

Vivian French, *Iggy Pig's Snowy Day,* Hodder Children's Books (London, England), 1999.

Hilary McKay, *A Strong Smell of Magic,* Hodder Children's Books (London, England), 1999.

Ian Whybrow, *Jump In!,* Barron's (Hauppage, NY), 1999.

Neil Morris, *My First Words to See and Learn,* Passport Books (Chicago, IL), 1999, published as *My First Oxford Book Of Words,* Oxford University Press (Oxford, England), 1999.

Joan Powers, editor, *Over the Moon!: A Collection of Best-loved Nursery Rhymes,* Templar Publishing (London, England), 1999, Dutton (New York, NY), 2000.

Neil Morris, *My First Spanish Words to See and Learn,* Passport Books (Chicago, IL), 1999, published as *My First Oxford Spanish Words,* Oxford University Press (Oxford, England), 2000, bilingual edition published as *Oxford First Spanish Words,* 2002.

Neil Morris, *My First French Words to See and Learn,* Passport Books (Chicago, IL), 1999, published as *My First Oxford French Words,* Oxford University Press (Oxford, England), 1999, bilingual edition published as *Oxford First French Words,* 2002.

Haiwyn Oram, *Gerda the Goose,* Barron's (Hauppage, NY), 2000.

Peter Patilla, *My First Oxford Book of Numbers,* Oxford University Press (Oxford, England), 2000.

Margaret Ryan, *Rainbow to the Rescue,* Hodder Children's Books (London, England), 2000.

Margaret Ryan, *Smiler Gets Toothache,* Hodder Children's Books (London, England), 2000, Scholastic, (New York, NY), 2003.

Neil Morris, *My First Oxford German Words,* Oxford University Press (Oxford, England), 2000, bilingual edition, 2002.

James and Deborah Howe, *Bunnicula: A Rabbit-Tale of Mystery,* Hodder Children's Books (London, England), 2000.

James Howe, *Bunnicula Strikes Again!,* Hodder Children's Books (London, England), 2000.

James Howe, *Howliday Inn: The Nightmare Hotel,* Hodder Children's Books (London, England), 2000.

James Howe, *Return to Howliday Inn,* Hodder Children's Books (London, England), 2000.

James Howe, *The Celery Stalks at Midnight,* Hodder Children's Books (London, England), 2000.

James Howe, *Nighty-Nightmare,* Hodder Children's Books (London, England) 2000.

Mike Haines, *Count Down to Bedtime,* Hyperion Books (New York, NY), 2001.

Margaret Ryan, *Bumpy's Rumbling Tummy,* Hodder Children's Books (London, England), 2001.

Ian Whybrow, *All Change!,* Barron's (New York, NY), 2001.

Margaret Ryan, *Fuzzbuzz Takes a Tumble,* Hodder Children's Books (London, England), 2001, Scholastic (New York, NY), 2003.

Francesca Simon, *The Adventures of Harry,* Hodder Children's Books (London, England), 2004.

Lucy Daniels, *Hattie's New House,* Hodder Children's Books (London, England), 2004.

Mike Haines, *First Adventures of Fidget and Quilly,* Hodder Children's Books (London, England), 2004.

Lucy Daniels, *Oscar's Best Friends,* Hodder Children's Books (London, England), 2004.

Lucy Daniels, *Party Time, Poppy!,* Hodder Children's Books (London, England), 2004.

Lucy Daniels, *Fergal's Flippers,* Hodder Children's Books (London, England), 2005.

Lucy Daniels, *Sammy's Secret,* Hodder Children's Books (London, England), 2005.

Adaptations

The Tale of Jack Frost was adapted as an animated television show, produced by British Broadcasting Corporation, 2004.

Sidelights

David Melling is a popular and prolific illustrator of books for young readers. Born in Oxford, England, Melling has provided the artwork for titles by such respected authors as Vivian French, Francesca Simon, and James Howe. "Becoming a children's book illustrator came about through a natural progression of events rather than an early inspiration," he told a *Children's Bookcase* online interviewer. One of Melling's early influences was his father, a sculptor, and he chose to study art in college. After pursuing a career in photography, Melling took a job at an animation studio, where he drew backgrounds, painted cells, and assisted with design work. "By now I had become very interested in drawing characters and telling stories with pictures and, eventually I met someone who suggested I look at illustrating children's books," he remarked. "This was such a revelation for me as I realised immediately that this was what I wanted to do."

Melling made his literary debut in 1994 when he illustrated Richard Stilgoe's *Brilliant the Dinosaur,* an environmental tale. He has since worked on dozens of other books, including *Where Are You?* by Francesca Simon. In this story, a small dog named Harry becomes distracted by the smell of cupcakes while shopping with his grandfather. When the doggie duo realizes they have become separated, each frantically winds his way through the aisles in search of the other. "Melling's pictures are both comic and dramatic," noted *School Library Journal* contributor Stephanie Zvirin in her review of the book.

Over the Moon!: A Collection of Best-loved Nursery Rhymes, edited by Joan Powers, features such favorite verses as "Humpty Dumpty," "Little Miss Muffet," and "Hickory Dickory Dock." "Melling's cartoonish spreads add fun details," observed a reviewer in *Publishers Weekly.* In Melling's artwork for *Count Down to Bedtime,* a lift-the-flap book by Mike Haines, Bandit the raccoon and Spike the porcupine find plenty of things to keep them busy—including brushing their teeth and checking under the bed for monsters—in the ten minutes before they turn in. "Brightened with colorful washes, the cartoonlike drawings are clearly delineated and easy to follow," wrote Carolyn Phelan in *Booklist.*

Melling has also published a number of highly regarded self-illustrated works. In *The Kiss That Missed,* a king blows an enchanted kiss toward his young son, but it sails past its intended target and enters a forest that is guarded by a dragon. "The tale is refreshingly original and relevant, showing a busy family full of love," remarked *School Library Journal* contributor Be Astengo. Another story dealing with royalty, *Good Knight Sleep Tight,* concerns a loyal knight's quest for the perfect stuffing to repair the baby princess' damaged pillow. "Melling's watercolor-and-ink pictures bubble with a pleasing slapstick tone . . . and a mock-serio theatricality," noted a *Publishers Weekly* critic, and Piper L. Nyman, writing in *School Library Journal,* commented that "dramatic shifts in perspective and the inclusion of comic-style mini-illustrations add to the absurdity and sense of adventure" in Melling's art.

A mysterious boy with unusual powers helps the enchanted creatures of the forest fend off a gaggle of nasty goblins in *The Tale of Jack Frost.* "Readers who like their fairy tales served with physical comedy will revel in the detailed illustrations" in this book, a reviewer in *Publishers Weekly* stated. The members of a disgusting family of wolves attempt to change their ways, with surprising results, in *The Scallywags,* "a thoroughly delightful romp" by Melling, according to Judith Constantinides in *School Library Journal.* "Melling turns cartoon-style art, which in lesser hands would seem ordinary, into an art form," concluded *Booklist* contributor Ilene Cooper of *The Scallywags,* and in the London *Guardian* Julia Eccleshare praised the author-illustrator's "thought-provoking and refreshing storyline."

Biographical and Critical Sources

PERIODICALS

Booklist, December 1, 1998, Stephanie Zvirin, review of *Where Are You?,* p. 672; December 1, 2000, Ilene Cooper, review of *Over the Moon!: A Collection of Best-loved Nursery Rhymes,* p. 728; June 1, 2001, Carolyn Phelan, review of *Countdown to Bedtime,* p. 1890; February 1, 2006, Connie Fletcher, review of *Good Knight, Sleep Tight,* p. 56; February 1, 2007, Ilene Cooper, review of *The Scallywags,* p. 46.

Guardian (London, England), August 10, 1999, review of *What's That Noise?,* p. 5; February 6, 2001, Lindsey Fraser, review of *If I Didn't Have Elbows,* p. 57; January 20, 2007, Julia Eccleshare, review of *The Scallywags,* p. 20.

Kirkus Reviews, December 15, 2006, review of *The Scallywags,* p. 1271.

Publishers Weekly, July 20, 1998, review of *Where Are You?,* p. 217; October 30, 2000, review of *Rhyme and Reason,* p. 78; October 27, 2003, review of *The Tale of Jack Frost,* p. 68; January 2, 2006, review of *Good Knight, Sleep Tight,* p. 60; February 5, 2007, review of *The Scallywags,* p. 57.

School Library Journal, May, 1999, Christie J. Flynn, review of *Where Are You?,* p. 97; July, 2001, Kathleen Simonetta, review of *Countdown to Bedtime,* p. 82; December, 2002, Be Astengo, review of *The Kiss That Missed,* p. 102; March, 2004, Lee Bock, review of *The Tale of Jack Frost,* p. 178; March, 2006, Piper L. Nyman, review of *Good Knight, Sleep Tight,* p. 199; March, 2007, Judith Constantinides, review of *The Scallywags,* p. 182.

Scotsman, November 17, 2000, Jane Ellis, review of *Countdown to Bedtime,* p. 13.

ONLINE

Children's Bookcase Web site, http://www.thechildrens bookcase.com/ (December 20, 2007), interview with Melling.*

*　　*　　*

MILLER, Ruth White
See WHITE, Ruth C.

**MISKELL, Clifford
See BAYOC, Cbabi**

*   *   *

MOORE, Cyd 1957-

Personal

Born July 4, 1957, in GA; daughter of Henry and Joy (an art teacher) Shealy; children: Branden, Lindsay. *Education:* University of Georgia, B.F.A. *Hobbies and other interests:* Painting, yoga, running, cooking, gardening, mosaics.

Addresses

Home—Sylvan Lake, MI. *E-mail*—mail@cydmoore.com.

Career

WMAZ-TV/Radio, Macon, GA, art director, 1978-80; *Macon Telegraph & News,* Macon, staff artist, 1980-83; freelance illustrator/designer, 1983—. *Exhibitions:* Works have been exhibited at solo shows in galleries in Birmingham and Montgomery, AL, and Birmingham, MI; work exhibited at group-show of children's book art in New York, NY.

Writings

ILLUSTRATOR

Jane Yolen, *Jane Yolen's Songs of Summer,* Boyds Mills Press (Honesdale, PA), 1993.

Fay Robinson, compiler, *A Frog inside My Hat,* Troll (Mahwah, NJ), 1993.

Judy Barron, *I Want to Learn to Fly* (with audio cassette), Scholastic (New York, NY), 1994.

Shulamith Levey Oppenheim, *I Love You Bunny Rabbit,* Boyds Mills Press (Honesdale, PA), 1994.

Charles Ghigna, *Tickle Day: Poems from Father Goose,* Hyperion (New York, NY), 1994.

Rozanne L. Williams, *Scaredy Cat,* Creative Teaching Press (Huntington Beach, CA), 1995.

Marlene Beierel, *What Comes in Threes?,* Creative Teaching Press (Huntington Beach, CA), 1995.

Rozanne L. Williams, *The Time Song,* Creative Teaching Press (Huntington Beach, CA), 1995.

Rozanne L. Williams, *Scaredy Cat Runs Away,* Creative Teaching Press (Huntington Beach, CA), 1995.

Eileen Spinelli, *Where's the Night Train Going?,* Boyds Mills Press (Honesdale, PA), 1996.

Shulamith Levey Oppenheim, *What Is the Full Moon Full Of?,* Boyds Mills Press (Honesdale, PA), 1997.

Cyd Moore (Photo courtesy of Cyd Moore.)

Steven J. Simmons, *Alice and Greta: A Tale of Two Witches,* Charlesbridge Publishers (Watertown, MA), 1997.

Lisa McCourt, *I Love You, Stinky Face,* Troll (Mahwah, NJ), 1997.

Lisa McCourt, *It's Time for School, Stinky Face,* Troll-Bridgewater Books (Mahwah, NJ), 1997.

Rozanne L. Williams, *Can You Read a Map?,* Creative Teaching Press (Huntington Beach, CA), 1997.

Big Book: Goldilocks and the Three Bears, William Sadlier (New York, NY), 1997.

Lisa McCourt, *I Miss You, Stinky Face,* Bridgewater Books (Mahwah, NJ), 1999.

Steven J. Simmons, *Greta's Revenge: More Alice and Greta,* Crown Publishers (New York, NY), 1999.

Lisa McCourt, *Good Night, Princess Pruney-Toes,* Troll-Bridgewater (Mahwah, NJ), 2001.

Steven J. Simmons, *Alice and Greta's Color Magic,* Knopf (New York, NY), 2001.

Roni Schotter, *Missing Rabbit,* Clarion Books (New York, NY), 2001.

Amy Gary, *Picturebook 2001,* WaterMark, 2001.

Lisa McCourt, *Merry Christmas, Stinky Face,* Bridgewater (Mahwah, NJ), 2002.

Roni Schotter, *Room for Rabbit,* Clarion Books (New York, NY), 2003.

Lisa McCourt, *The Most Thankful Thing,* Bridgewater (Mahwah, NJ), 2003.

Lesléa Newman, *A Fire Engine for Ruthie,* Clarion Books (New York, NY), 2004.

Raffi, adaptor, *If You're Happy and You Know It,* Knopf (New York, NY), 2005.

Tony Johnston, *Sticky People,* HarperCollins (New York, NY), 2006.

Jeanie Franz Ransom, *What Do Parents Do (When You're Not Home)?,* Peachtree (Atlanta, GA), 2007.

Lisa McCourt, *Happy Halloween, Stinky Face,* Scholastic (New York, NY), 2007.

Marjorie Blain Parker, *Your Kind of Mommy,* Dutton (New York, NY), 2007.

Lisa McCourt, *Granny's Dragon,* Dutton (New York, NY), 2008.

Denise Brennan Nelson and Rosemarie Brennan, *Willow,* Sleeping Bear Press (Chelsea, MI), 2008.

EDITOR

(With Amy Gary) *Picturebook '98: The Directory of Children's Illustration,* Menasha Ridge Press, 1999.

(With Amy Gary) *Picturebook '99: The Directory of Children's Illustration,* WaterMark, 1999.

(With Amy Gary) *Picturebook 2K: The Directory of Children's Illustration,* WaterMark, 2000.

Also coeditor, with Amy Gary, of *Picturebook 2001: The Directory of Children's Illustration.*

Sidelights

As a children's book illustrator, artist Cyd Moore chooses from among a variety of styles and palettes in order to accentuate the unique qualities of each story she brings to life. Her work has been paired with tales by Lisa McCourt, Fay Robinson, Steven J. Simmons, and Eileen Spinelli, among others, always with upbeat results. Reviewing Moore's work for Lesléa Newman's *A Fire Engine for Ruthie,* which finds a little girl more interested in playing with toy trains and trucks than dolls, a *Publishers Weekly* contributor concluded that the book's "vibrant watercolors pack in plenty of detail and the cheery hues of the busy spreads echo Ruthie's sunny optimism." Turning to another example from the illustrator's long list of successes, a *Kirkus Reviews* writer noted that Moore's detailed illustrations "will prove engrossing for young readers" of Marjorie Blain Parker's *Your Kind of Mommy.*

Growing up in Georgia, Moore was encouraged in her creative endeavors by her mother, also an artist. In school, her artistic talent earned her the job of designing posters as well as a position on the yearbook

Moore brings to life the animated characters in Lisa McCourt's popular picture book It's Time for School, Stinky Face. (Scholastic, 2000. Illustration copyright © 2000 by Cyd Moore. Reprinted by permission of Scholastic, Inc.)

Moore's endearing art reflects the close bond that is the focus of McCourt's picture book **The Most Thankful Thing.** (Scholastic, 2004. Illustration copyright © 2004 by Cyd Moore. Reprinted by permission of Scholastic, Inc.)

committee. After high school, Moore attended the University of Georgia, where she earned her B.F.A. and then started on a career as a graphic illustrator, creating art for newspapers, television, and product advertisements. In the mid-1980s she decided to make the shift to book illustration, where children's picture books were the perfect fit for her humorous, whimsical approach.

In her art for McCourt's picture-book series that includes *I Love You, Stinky Face, I Miss You, Stinky Face,* and *Happy Halloween, Stinky Face,* Moore contributes neon-colored monsters and brightly colored scenes to emphasize the unlikely nature of the child's fears and the consequent humor of imagining they could really happen. Reviewing *I Love You, Stinky Face,* in which a little boy being put to bed tests his mother's love with frightful scenarios, Hazel Rochman wrote in *Booklist* that "Moore's paintings, in neon colors with lots of

purple and green, contrast the gentle bedtime caresses with the wild scenarios." A similar scene is enacted in *I Miss You, Stinky Face,* in which Mom, phoning her son while away on business, is questioned closely about her ability to overcome a series of unlikely obstacles that might delay her return, while *Merry Christmas, Stinky Face* continues the amusing interchange between mother and son. Reviewing *It's Time for School, Stinky Face,* Tim Wadham wrote in *School Library Journal* that Moore's "lively cartoon style is perfect for the over-the-top scenarios" presented in McCourt's text, while Rochman praised the illustrator's ability to "express the rambunctious party fun as well as the tender family bond" in *Merry Christmas, Stinky Face.*

Other collaborations with McCourt also center on the love between a parent and child. In *Good Night, Princess Pruney Toes* the two tell the story of a father bathing and putting his daughter to bed, creating "a delightful romp," according to Susan Marie Pitard in *School Library Journal.* Moore's "exuberant watercolors include warm domestic details" readers will easily identify with, according to a contributor to *Publishers Weekly. The Most Thankful Thing,* another team effort, pairs McCourt's "breezy" text about a mother and daughter's perusal of a family photo album with McCourt's "effective" pastel-hued cartoon art, according to *Booklist* critic Carolyn Phelan. In *School Library Journal* Deborah Rothaug dubbed *The Most Thankful Thing* "a wonderful, reassuring read-aloud for storytime and for individual sharing," and in *Publishers Weekly* a critic concluded that the illustrator's "heartfelt, cartoonish illustrations manage to keeps things lively."

Moore contributes cheerful watercolors to Robinson's poetry collection *A Frog inside My Hat* as well as to Charles Ghigna's *Tickle Day: Poems from Father Goose.* Her watercolor-and-pencil compositions for the latter reflect the poet's optimism through "vaguely Chagall-like touches" and the use of "rich and vibrant" colors, according to a contributor to *Publishers Weekly.* For Spinelli's collection of poems titled *Where Is the Night Train Going?,* Moore creates a crew of shaggy cartoon characters in a style that recalls the reassuring art of illustrator Mercer Mayer.

A range of emotions are reflected in Moore's paintings in Shulamith Levey Oppenheim's *I Love You, Bunny Rabbit,* in which a little boy's favorite rabbit becomes so dirty that he (briefly) contemplates giving it up in favor of a new toy. A *Publishers Weekly* contributor dubbed *I Love You, Bunny Rabbit* "a winsome tale of love remaining love in spite of dirt and grime." Another rabbit stars in *Missing Rabbit* and *Room for Rabbit,* two "reassuring" picture books by Roni Schotter that feature "Moore's warm, cartoonlike watercolors," according to *School Library Journal* contributor Kathleen Kelly MacMillan. "Gentle humor is also reflected in Moore's illustrations for Oppenheim's *What Is the Full Moon Full Of?* Here, a little boy asks the title question of a cow, a firefly, a squirrel, and his grandmother, and finally comes up with his own idea. "Moore's pictures are lighthearted and goofy," remarked Stephanie Zvirin in her *Booklist* review.

Moore fittingly gives way to flights of illustrative fancy in *I Want to Learn to Fly!,* lyrics written by Judy Barron and sung by Maureen McGovern that focuses on a child's wish for adventure. "Fanciful, full-page illustrations . . . playfully depict the girl's exotic destinations," remarked a *Publishers Weekly* reviewer of the work. Other lyrics brought to life through Moore's art include popular singer/storyteller Raffi's version of *If You're Happy and You Know It.*

Two toddlers spend a day involved in one sticky object after another in Tony Johnston's *Sticky People,* a picture book that is injected with even more humor via Moore's watercolor art. The story's illustrations depict the two toddlers as they move from breakfast with jam to playing in the mud, and pasting together craft projects, until they wind up in the bathtub after a playful dinner with their parents. Moore's art sets the story within a loving family in which the "feeling of familiarity" show "characters . . . having so much fun readers will want to join right in," according to a *Kirkus Reviews* writer. In a turn of the tables, adults cause the mess in the pages of Jenanie Franz Ransom's *What Do Parents Do (When You're Not Home?).* In watercolor-and-pencil illustrations, Moore contributes what *School Library Journal* critic Linda L. Walkins described as "humorous details" to Ransom's revelations regarding parents who get into all sorts of trouble while their children are spending the night at Grandma's.

Moore has teamed up with author Steven J. Simmons in a number of picture-book projects. Among these are the "Alice and Greta" stories about two little witches, one always good and the other always bad. In her art, Moore plays with the meanings associated with color: In *Alice and Greta: A Tale of Two Witches* she dresses sweet Alice in pink while poisonous Greta wears a nasty shade of green. The tables are turned in *Greta's Revenge: More Alice and Greta,* as nasty Greta casts a spell on Alice to make her mean, and formerly pink Alice turns green. In *Alice and Greta's Color Magic* Greta succeeds in casting a spell that drains the entire world of color, even the vile shade of green that she adores. Sharon McNeil, writing in *School Library Journal,* praised Moore's humorous, pastel-colored cartoons in *Alice and Greta's Color Magic,* noting that "the facial expressions of all of the characters are very telling."

Moore once told *SATA:* "Illustration does not have to be just a picture of the words written on a page. It can be and, in my opinion, *must* be more than that. Illustration, approached with a larger purpose, is art of the highest form . . . just as important and inspiring as an oil painting in the finest museum. My single purpose in illustrating each book is to make that book more than the words . . . to go beyond the words . . . to lift readers young and old to places within themselves that make their lives more than they were a moment before. One beautifully painted picture, filled with imagination and love, does that to those who are able to see.

"Great art must flow from higher spaces through the artist's hands and onto a smooth white page. It is always spontaneous and never contrived. It is like a living thing that must have a vehicle by which to travel in order to arrive where it needs to be. Great art can arrive anywhere: in a gallery, in a subway, in a children's book. It only depends upon the spirit of the artist and whether he can or *will* allow that art to come. The goal is to be that open every time for every page in every book that is illustrated. The goal is hard and frustrating at times. Deadlines and time schedules must be factored in to all of this wonderful *flow.* But when the goal is grasped even once, the feeling of getting it right forces you to try again and again for that perfection.

Raffi's picture-book version of a favorite song in **If You're Happy and You Know It** *is enriched by Moore's upbeat characters.* (Alfred Knopf, 2005. Illustrations copyright © 2005 by Cyd Moore. Used by permission of Alfred A. Knopf, an imprint of Random House Children's Books, a division of Random House, Inc.)

"These may seem like lofty statements for the illustration of children's books. But I remember some of the pictures in some of my books from childhood to this day. I remember how they made me feel. Children and their parents don't go to museums much. Museums can be boring and hard to understand. Video games are a lot more fun, and so is golf on Saturday. But most kids get to open a book and look at the pictures, and sometimes the parents share those moments. And if those pictures happen to have some substance behind them . . . some magic . . . then the artist's show has been viewed, hopefully a spark has been lit, and the artist's job has been well done."

Biographical and Critical Sources

PERIODICALS

Booklist, June 1, 1993, Deborah Abbott, review of *Jane Yolen's Songs of Summer,* p. 1846; January 1, 1995, April Judge, review of *I Love You, Bunny Rabbit,* p. 826; January 1, 1996, Hazel Rochman, review of *Where's the Night Train Going?,* p. 841; October 15, 1997, Hazel Rochman, review of *I Love You, Stinky Face,* p. 403; December 1, 1997, Stephanie Zvirin, review of *What Is the Full Moon Full Of?,* p. 643; May 1, 2002, Gillian Engberg, review of *Missing Rabbit,* p.

1536; September 15, 2002, Hazel Rochman, review of *Merry Christmas, Stinky Face,* p. 246; March 1, 2003, Gillian Engberg, review of *Room for Rabbit,* p. 1204; November 1, 2003, Carolyn Phelan, review of *The Most Thankful Thing,* p. 502; August, 2004, Ilene Cooper, review of *A Fire Engine for Ruthie,* p. 1944; April 1, 2007, Abby Nolan, review of *What Do Parents Do (When You're Not Home)?,* p. 60; September 1, 2007, Ilene Cooper, review of *Happy Halloween, Stinky Face,* p. 126.

Bulletin of the Center for Children's Books, February, 1995, review of *I Love You, Bunny Rabbit,* p. 211; September, 2004, Hope Morrison, review of *A Fire Engine for Ruthie,* p. 33; April, 2007, Deborah Stevenson, review of *What Do Parents Do (When You're Not Home)?,* p. 342.

Kirkus Reviews, February 15, 2002, review of *Missing Rabbit,* p. 265; November 1, 2002, review of *Merry Christmas, Stinky Face,* p. 1622; July 1, 2004, review of *A Fire Engine for Ruthie,* p. 625; May 1, 2006, review of *Sticky People,* p. 461; February 1, 2007, review of *Your Kind of Mommy,* p. 128.

Oakland Press (Oakland, MI), October 12, 2004, Garry Graff, "Moore, Moore, Moore," pp. D1-D2.

Publishers Weekly, July 26, 1993, review of *A Frog inside My Hat,* p. 70; September 12, 1994, review of *Tickle Day: Poems from Father Goose,* p. 91; December 12, 1994, review of *I Love You, Bunny Rabbit,* p. 61; March 20, 1995, review of *I Want to Learn to Fly!,* p. 31; February 5, 1996, review of *Where's the Night*

Train Going?, p. 90; August 18, 1997, review of *Alice and Greta: A Tale of Two Witches,* p. 91; August 25, 1997, review of *I Love You, Stinky Face,* p. 70; July 19, 1999, review of *Alice and Greta,* p. 197; September 6, 1999, review of *Greta's Revenge: More Alice and Greta,* p. 103; February 5, 2001, review of *Good Night, Princess Pruney Toes,* p. 88; January 21, 2002, review of *Missing Rabbit,* p. 88; August 25, 2003, review of *Alice and Greta's Color Magic,* p. 67; November 3, 2003, review of *The Most Thankful Thing,* p. 73; September 6, 2004, review of *A Fire Engine for Ruthie,* p. 61; December 6, 2004, review of *The Most Thankful Thing,* p. 58.

School Library Journal, August, 1993, Jane Marino, review of *Jane Yolen's Songs of Summer,* p. 162; October, 1993, Barbara Chatton, review of *A Frog inside My Hat,* p. 121; September, 1994, Kathleen Whalin, review of *Tickle Day,* p. 208; February, 1995, Lynn Cockett, review of *I Love You, Bunny Rabbit,* p. 78; April, 1996, Liza Bliss, review of *Where's the Night Train Going?,* p. 130; October, 1997, Elizabeth Trotter, review of *I Love You, Stinky Face,* p. 104; December, 1997, Peggy Morgan, review of *What Is the Full Moon Full Of?,* p. 99; January, 1998, Tana Elias, review of *Alice and Greta,* p. 93; May, 1999, Linda Ludke, review of *I Miss You, Stinky Face,* p. 92; December, 1999, Maryann H. Owen, review of *Greta's Revenge,* p. 112; October, 2000, Tim Wadham, review of *It's Time for School, Stinky Face,* p. 130; May, 2001, Susan Marie Pitard, review of *Good Night, Princess Pruney Toes,* p. 129; October, 2001, Sharon McNeil, review of *Alice and Greta's Color Magic,* p. 132; April, 2002, Susan Weitz, review of *Missing Rabbit,* p. 122; April, 2003, Kathleen Kelly MacMillan, review of *Room for Rabbit,* p. 138; August, 2003, Deborah Rothaug, review of *The Most Thankful Thing,* p. 138; September, 2004, Roxanne Burg, review of *A Fire Engine for Ruthie,* p. 176; July, 2006, Julie Roach, review of *Sticky People,* p. 79; March, 2007, Martha Topol, review of *Your Kind of Mommy,* p. 184; June, 2007, Linda L. Walkins, review of *What Do Parents Do (When You're Not Home)?,* p. 120.

ONLINE

Cyd Moore Home Page, http://www.cydmoore.com (January 15, 2007).

Embracing the Child Web site, http://www.embracingthe child.org/ (January 10, 2007), "Cyd Moore."

*   *   *

MORA, Pat 1942-

Personal

Born January 19, 1942, in El Paso, TX; daughter of Raul Antonio (an optician and business owner) and Estela (a homemaker) Mora; married William H. Burnside, Jr., July 27, 1963 (divorced 1981); married Vernon Lee Scarborough (an archaeologist and professor), May

Pat Mora (Cynthia Farah-Haines, photographer. Reproduced by permission.)

25, 1984; children: (first marriage) William Roy, Elizabeth Anne, Cecilia Anne. *Education:* Texas Western College (now University of Texas—El Paso), B.A., 1963; University of Texas—El Paso, M.A., 1967. *Politics:* Democrat. *Religion:* "Ecumenical." *Hobbies and other interests:* Reading, walking, cooking, gardening, museums, traveling, visiting with family and friends.

Addresses

Home—Santa Fe, NM. *Agent*—Elizabeth Harding, Curtis Brown Ltd., Ten Astor Place, New York, NY 10003.

Career

Writer, educator, administrator, lecturer, and activist. El Paso Independent School District, El Paso, TX, teacher, 1963-66; El Paso Community College, part-time instructor in English and communications, 1971-78; University of Texas—El Paso, part-time lecturer in English, 1979-81, assistant to vice president of academic affairs, 1981-88, director of university museum and assistant to president, 1988-89; full-time writer, 1989—. Distinguished Visiting Professor, Garrey Carruthers chair in honors, University of New Mexico, 1999; Civitella Ranieri fellow to Umbria, Italy, 2003. Member of Ohio

Arts Council panel, 1990. W.K. Kellogg Foundation, consultant, 1990-91, and member of advisory committee for Kellogg National Fellowship Program, 1991-94. Helped institute El día de los niños/El día de los libros, during National Poetry Month, to celebrate childhood and bilingual literacy, beginning April 30, 1997; helped establish Estela and Raúl Mora Award, National Association to Promote Library Service to the Spanish-Speaking and Latinos, 2000. Host of radio program *Voices: The Mexican-American in Perspective,* KTEP, 1983-84; gives poetry readings and presentations throughout the world.

Member

Academy of American Poets, International Reading Association, National Association of Bilingual Educators, Society of Children's Book Writers and Illustrators, Texas Institute of Letters, Friends of the Santa Fe Library, Museum of New Mexico Foundation, Spanish Colonial Arts Society, National Council of La Raza.

Awards, Honors

Award for Creative Writing, National Association for Chicano Studies, 1983; Poetry Award, *New America,* 1984; Harvey L. Johnson Book Award, Southwest Council of Latin American Studies, 1984; Southwest Book Award, Border Regional Library, 1985, for *Chants;* Kellogg national leadership fellowship, 1986-89; Leader in Education Award, El Paso Women's Employment and Education, 1987; Chicano/Hispanic Faculty and Professional Staff Association Award, University of Texas—El Paso, 1987, for outstanding contribution to the advancement of Hispanics; Southwest Book Award, 1987, for *Borders,* 1994, for *A Birthday Basket for Tía;* named to Writers Hall of Fame, *El Paso Herald-Post,* 1988; Poetry Award, Conference of Cincinnati Women, 1990; National Endowment for the Arts fellowship in creative writing, 1994; Americas Award commendation, Consortium of Latin Americas Studies Program, Choice designation, Cooperative Children's Book Center, "Children's Books Mean Business" listee, Children's Book Council, and Notable Books for a Global Society designation, International Reading Association, all 1996, all for *Confetti;* Premio Aztlan Literature Award, and Women of Southwest Book Award, both 1997, both for *House of Houses;* Washington Children's Choice Picture Book Award nomination, 1997, for *Pablo's Tree* illustrated by Cecily Lang; Tomás Rivera Mexican-American Children's Book Award, Southwest Texas State University, 1997, *Skipping Stones* Book Award, 1998, and Apollo Children's Book Award nomination, Apollo Reading Center (FL), 2002, all for *Tomás and the Library Lady;* Book Publishers of Texas Award, Texas Institute of Letters, 1998, and PEN Center USA West Literary Award finalist, 1999, both for *The Big Sky;* Pellicer-Frost Bi-national Poetry Award, 1999, for collection of odes; Alice Louis Wood Memorial Ohioana Award for Children's Literature, 2001; Teddy Award, Writers' League of Texas, and Books for

the Teen Age selection, New York Public Library, both 2001, both for *My Own True Name;* named Literary Light for Children, Associates of the Boston Library, 2002; Distinguished Alumna honor, 2004, from University of Texas—El Paso; Golden Kite Award, 2005, and Pura Belpre Illustrator Medal, Pura Belpre Honor Book, and ALA Notable Book designation, all 2006, all for *Doña Flor;* National Hispanic Cultural Center Literary Award, 2006; honorary D.L., State University of New York, Buffalo, 2006; Roberta Long Medal for Distinguished Contributions to Celebrating the Cultural Diversity of Children, University of Alabama at Birmingham, 2007; International Latino Book Award for Best Poetry in English, Spur Poetry Award finalist, Western Writers of America, and Bronze Medal in Poetry, Independent Publisher Book Awards, all 2007, all for *Adobe Odes.*

Writings

PICTURE BOOKS; FOR CHILDREN

A Birthday Basket for Tía, illustrated by Cecily Lang, Macmillan (New York, NY), 1992.

Listen to the Desert/Oye al desierto, illustrated by Francesco X. Mora, Clarion Books (New York, NY), 1994.

Agua, Agua, Agua (concept book), illustrated by José Ortega, GoodYear Books (Reading, MA), 1994.

Pablo's Tree, illustrated by Cecily Lang, Macmillan (New York, NY), 1994.

(With Charles Ramirez Berg) *The Gift of the Poinsettia,* Piñata Books (Houston, TX), 1995, adapted as the play *Los posadas and the Poinsettia.*

(Reteller) *The Race of Toad and Deer,* illustrated by Maya Itzna Brooks, Orchard Books (New York, NY), 1995, revised edition, illustrated by Domi, Groundwood/Douglas & McIntyre (Toronto, Ontario, Canada), 2001.

Tomás and the Library Lady (biography), illustrated by Raul Colón, Knopf (New York, NY), 1997, published as *Thomas and the Library Lady,* Dragonfly Books (New York, NY), 1997.

Delicious Hullabaloo/Pachanga deliciosa, illustrated by Francesco X. Mora, Spanish translation by Alba Nora Martinez and Pat Mora, Piñata Books (Houston, TX), 1998.

The Rainbow Tulip, illustrated by Elizabeth Sayles, Viking (New York, NY), 1999.

(Reteller) *The Night the Moon Fell,* illustrated by Domi, Groundwood/Douglas & McIntyre (Toronto, Ontario, Canada), 2000.

The Bakery Lady/La señora de la panadería, illustrated by Pablo Torrecilla, translated with Gabriela Baeza Ventura, Piñata Books (Houston, TX), 2001.

A Library for Juana: The World of Sor Juana Inés (biography), illustrated by Beatriz Vidal, Knopf (New York, NY), 2002.

Maria Paints the Hills, illustrated by Maria Hesch, Museum of New Mexico Press (Santa Fe, NM), 2002.

Doña Flor: A Tall Tale about a Giant Woman with a Great Big Heart, illustrated by Raúl Colón, Knopf (New York, NY), 2005.

The Song of Francis and the Animals, illustrated by David Frampton, Eerdmans (Grand Rapids, MI), 2005.

Let's Eat! = A comer!, illustrated by Maribel Surez, Rayo (New York, NY), 2007.

Join Hands!, illustrated by George Ancona, Charlesbridge (Watertown, MA), 2008.

POETRY; FOR CHILDREN

The Desert Is My Mother/El desierto es mi madre, art by Daniel Lechon, Piñata Books (Houston, TX), 1994.

Confetti: Poems for Children, illustrated by Enrique O. Sanchez, Lee & Low Books (New York, NY), 1995.

Uno, dos, tres/One, Two, Three, illustrated by Barbara Lavallee, Clarion Books (New York, NY), 1996.

The Big Sky, illustrated by Steve Jenkins, Scholastic (New York, NY), 1998.

My Own True Name: New and Selected Poems for Young Adults, 1984-1999, illustrated by Anthony Accardo, Piñata Books (Houston, TX), 2001.

Love to Mama: A Tribute to Mothers (anthology), illustrated by Paula S. Barragán, Lee & Low Books (New York, NY), 2001.

Marimba!: Animales from A to Z, illustrated by Doug Cushman, Clarion (New York, NY), 2006.

Yum! Mmmm! Que Rico!: Americas' Sproutings (haiku), illustrated by Rafael López, Lee & Low (New York, NY), 2007.

POETRY; FOR ADULTS

Chants, Arte Público Press (Houston, TX), 1984.

Borders, Arte Público Press (Houston, TX), 1986.

Communion, Arte Público Press (Houston, TX), 1991.

Agua Santa/Holy Water, Beacon Press (Boston, MA), 1995.

Aunt Carmen's Book of Practical Saints, Beacon Press (Boston, MA), 1997.

Adobe Odes, University of Arizona Press (Tucson, AZ), 2006.

FICTION AND NONFICTION; FOR ADULTS

Nepantla: Essays from the Land in the Middle, University of New Mexico Press (Albuquerque, NM), 1993.

House of Houses (memoir), Beacon Press (Boston, MA), 1997.

Work represented in anthologies, including *New Worlds of Literature,* Norton (New York, NY); *Revista Chicano-Ripueña: Kikirikí/Children's Literature Anthology,* Arte Público (Houston, TX), 1981; *Tun-Ta-Ca-Tún,* Arte Público, 1986; *The Desert Is No Lady: Southwestern Landscapes in Women's Writing and Art* (also see below), edited by Vera Norwood and Janice Monk, University of Arizona Press (Tucson, AZ), 1997; *Many Voices: A Multicultural Reader,* edited by Linda Watkins-Goffman and others, Prentice-Hall (Englewood

Cliffs, NJ), 2001; and *Wachale! Poetry and Prose about Growing Up Latino in America,* edited by Ilan Stevens, Cricket Books, 2001. Contributor of poetry and essays to periodicals, including *Best American Poetry 1996, Calyx, Daughters of the Fifth Sun, Horn Book, Kalliope, Latina, Ms., New Advocate,* and *Prairie Schooner.*

Mora's books have been translated into several languages, including Bengali and Italian.

Sidelights

One of the most distinguished Hispanic writers working in the United States, Pat Mora is also an advocate working to advance cultural appreciation and literacy as well as conservation. An educator and speaker, Mora dedicates her writing to advance the recognition and preservation of Mexican-American culture. Her books for children, in particular, work to instill in young Latinos pride in their heritage. Characteristically, Mora's books are set in the southwestern United States, often in her birthplace of El Paso, Texas, and the surrounding desert. Celebrating the Mexican-American experience while also encouraging unity among all cultures, her written work for children includes picture books, biographies, concept books, and retellings of Mayan folktales. In titles such as *A Birthday Basket for Tía, The Gift of the Poinsettia,* and *The Desert Is My Mother,* she shares Hispanic history, customs, and traditions with children of all cultures. As a poet, Mora has also compiled verse anthologies for both children and young adults and has edited or contributed to poetry collections for more general readers.

In her children's books, Mora addresses several of the subjects and themes that constitute her books for adults, such as Mexican-American culture, nature (especially the desert), and the importance of family. Her spare but evocative prose is filled with descriptions and imagery; she also includes basic Spanish phrases in her works, most of which are published in both English and Spanish. A *Dictionary of Hispanic Biography* essayist noted that "Mora has been essential to the movement to understand and uphold Mexican-American culture. . . . She provides an excellent model for young Hispanics who are just beginning to understand the past and are about to experience promising futures. . . . As a successful Hispanic writer, and a writer who writes about and for Hispanics, Mora is an exemplary role model for the young people of an increasingly multicultural America."

Born in El Paso, Texas, of parents of Mexican descent, Mora and her siblings were taught both English and Spanish while growing up. She has often acknowledged the influence of her maternal grandmother and aunt, who lived with the family. She attended a Roman Catholic grade school and devoured, equally, comic books, novels, and biographies of famous Americans such as Clara Barton, Davy Crockett, Amelia Earhart, Betsy Ross, William Penn, Dolly Madison, and Jim Bowie. In high school she began writing poetry, mostly religious in focus. As Mora related in a *Scholastic Authors On-line Library* interview, "I always liked reading, and I always liked writing, but I don't think I thought of being a writer."

Although she enjoyed her family's Mexican traditions, Mora downplayed her ethnicity at school, and did not reveal to her friends that she was bilingual. "There were times when I wished that my Mexican heritage were a part of my school day," she recalled in her *Scholastic Authors Online Library* interview. "I wished that we had had books that had Spanish in them. And I wished that I had seen things about Mexican culture on the bulletin boards and in the library. One of the reasons that I write children's books is because I want Mexican culture and Mexican-American culture to be a part of our schools and libraries."

After graduating from high school, Mora thought about becoming a doctor, then decided to be a teacher. She attended Texas Western College (now the University of Texas—El Paso) and received her bachelor's degree in 1963. Shortly after graduation, she married William H. Burnside, Jr., with whom she would have three children: William, Elizabeth, and Cecilia. Mora began to teach English and Spanish at grade and high schools in El Paso. She earned her master's degree in 1967, then became a part-time instructor in English and communications at El Paso Community College. In 1981, she moved into administration. Several years later, after going through a divorce, she turned to her past: in addition to writing, she also began to educate herself about her heritage. Awarded for her early efforts, she published her first adult poetry collection, *Chants,* in 1984, the same year she married Vernon Lee Scarborough, an archeologist and professor whom she had met at college. Five years later she left her administrative job to become a full-time writer and speaker.

In 1992, Mora produced her first book for children, *A Birthday Basket for Tía.* A picture book inspired by an incident from the life of her aunt, the story describes how young narrator Cecilia finds the perfect present for her ninety-year-old great-aunt, Tía, by collecting objects that recall the many happy times they have shared. Written in a repetitive text, *A Birthday Basket for Tía* is both a story and a counting book that helps readers count to ninety. A *Publishers Weekly* reviewer called the work "poignant" and added that Mora's text "flows smoothly from one event to the next, and clearly presents the careful planning behind Cecilia's gift-gathering mission." Writing in *School Library Journal,* Julie Corsaro called *A Birthday Basket for Tía* a "warm and joyful story," while *Horn Book* critic Maeve Visser Knoth called Cecilia "an irrepressible child."

Featuring a multigenerational focus, *Pablo's Tree* takes place during the fifth birthday of its protagonist, a boy who has been adopted and who lives with his single mother. Pablo is excited because he is going to be with

Barbara Lavallee's colorful artwork brings to life Mora's Mexican-inspired bilingual concept book Uno, Dos Tres: One, Two, Three. (Clarion Books, 1996. Text copyright © 1996 by Pat Mora. Illustrations copyright © 1996 by Barbara Lavallee. Reprinted by permission of Clarion Books, an imprint of Houghton Mifflin Company. All rights reserved.)

his abuelito, or grandfather, for whom he is named. Lito has established a tradition for his grandson: every year, he decorates a special tree in the boy's honor, leaving the decorations as a surprise. In past years, the tree has been festooned with balloons, colored streamers, paper lanterns, and bird cages; this year, Lito has chosen bells and wind chimes as his theme. Pablo and Lito celebrate the day by eating apples and listening to the music coming from the tree; Lito also tells Pablo the story of the tree, which was planted when Pablo's mother adopted him. Writing in the *Bulletin of the Center for Children's Books,* Deborah Stevenson commented that *Pablo's Tree* "has a celebratory aspect that makes it appealing not just to adoptees but to kids generally.'" In *Booklist,* Annie Ayres called the picture book "lovely and resonant," with a story that "rings with happiness and family love."

Based on a family story from Mora's mother, *The Rainbow Tulip* is set in El Paso during the 1920s and features Estelita, a first grader caught between two cultures. Estelita realizes that her heritage sets her apart: she sees her mother, who speaks no English and dresses in dark clothes, as old-fashioned. The girls in Estelita's class are dressing as tulips for the upcoming May Day parade, and she wants her costume to be different from the others. When the big day arrives, she comes dressed in all the colors of the rainbow, then successfully executes a maypole dance and wins her teacher's approval. The girl's mother then explains that being different can be both sweet and sour, much like the lime sherbet that is their favorite dessert, and Estelita recognizes her mother's quiet love for her. According to *Library Journal* critic Ann Welton, in *The Rainbow Tulip* "Mora succeeds in creating a quiet story to which children will respond. . . . This tale of family love and support

A true story about a young writer's early inspiration is the focus of Mora's picture book Tomás and the Library Lady, *featuring artwork by Raul Colón.* (Alfred A. Knopf, 1997. Illustrations copyright © 1997 by Raul Colón. Used by permission of Alfred A. Knopf, Inc, an imprint of Random House Children's Books, a division of Random House, Inc.)

crosses cultural boundaries and may remind youngsters of times when their families made all the difference."

Another picture book, *Tomás and the Library Lady,* combines two of Mora's characteristic themes: the joy of reading and the special quality of intergenerational relationships. Based on an incident in the life of Hispanic author and educator Tomás Rivera, Mora's fictionalized biography describes how young Tomás, the son of migrant workers, is introduced to the world of books by a sympathetic librarian. Tomás's grandfather has told him wonderful stories, but has run out of them; he tells Tomás to go to the library for more. At the library, Tomás meets a kindly librarian, who gives him books in English—signed out on her own card. In return, Tomás teaches Spanish to the librarian. In *Publishers Weekly* a critic predicted that "young readers and future librarians will find this an inspiring tale." Interestingly, *Tomás and the Library Lady* actually was the first of Mora's books to be accepted for publication. However, due to the difficulty in finding an appropriate illustrator, the manuscript was delayed for almost a decade before it was published, together with Raul Colón's evocative art.

Mora transports readers back to seventeenth-century Mexico in *A Library for Juana: The World of Sor Juana Inés.* The story focuses on the childhood of Sor Juana

Inéz de la Cruz, a nun and noted intellectual who became known for her poetry, songs, and stories and who is acknowledged as one of Mexico's most noted women writers. Reviewing *A Library for Juana* in *Kirkus Reviews,* a critic praised the book as a "magnificent offering" that is enhanced by "exquisite gouache-and-watercolor" paintings that are "filled with authentic details" by illustrator Beatriz Vidal. "Mora laces her narrative with lively anecdotes," noted a *Publishers Weekly* writer, and in *Booklist* Gillian Engberg praised the author's "inspiring . . . account of a Latin American woman who loved learning during a time when few women were educated." "Mora's beautifully crafted text does credit to its subject," concluded Ann Welton in *School Library Journal,* calling *A Library for Juana* "an exceptional introduction to an exceptional woman."

As a girl, Sor Juana loved to read, and in *Doña Flor: A Tall Tale about a Giant Woman with a Great Big Heart* Mora introduces another enthusiastic reader. Set in the American Southwest, *Doña Flor* focuses on a giantess who is beloved by the normal-sized children living nearby. When a loud, mysterious sound is heard, terrifying the locals, the giant woman tracks down what proves to be its very surprising source. Mora graces her "economical, poetic text with vivid, fanciful touches," in the opinion of Engberg, and Colón's "signature" art injects "texture and movement," according to *School Library Journal* contributor Linda M. Kenton.

Folk tales and other traditional stories take center stage in books such as *The Gift of the Poinsettia* and *The Song of Francis and the Animals.* Praised by a *Publishers Weekly* contributor as a "celebratory" work, *The Song of Francis and the Animals* introduces readers to the Catholic saint who was able to communicate with animals, while *The Gift of the Poinsettia* tells the story of the young Mexican girl whose search for a gift for the baby Jesus is transformed into the brilliant red plant that comes into bloom during the Christmas season. In *School Library Journal,* Jane Barrer described Mora's text for *The Song of Francis and the Animals* as "more poetry than story," and Engberg concluded that Mora's text "brings close the spiritual connection between Francis and the animals." As Barrer added, David Frampton's woodcut illustrations accentuate this focus, depicting the saint's faith in the gentleness of all creatures.

Mora's first verse collection for young readers, *Confetti: Poems for Children,* features free-verse narrative poems that describe the American Southwest as seen through the eyes of a young Mexican-American girl. The child, who lives in the desert, describes the region and its inhabitants throughout the space of a day, from early morning to nightfall. The sun, clouds, leaves, and wind are the focus of some poems, while others feature a wood sculptor, a grandmother, and a baker. In *Kirkus Reviews* a critic noted that the "best of these poems that mix English and Spanish . . . warmly evokes familiar touchstones of Mexican-American life." Writing in

School Library Journal, Sally R. Dow called *Confetti* a "welcome addition" and stated that the poems "capture the rhythms and uniqueness of the Southwest and its culture."

Marimba!: Animales from A to Z follows an after-hours party at a city zoo in Mora's rhyming bilingual text, as animals of all sorts turn to song as the zookeepers take a nap. In *Yum! Mmmm! Que Rico!* Her poetry takes a twist as she includes a baker's dozen of haiku introducing thirteen foods unique to the Americas. In *Kirkus Reviews,* a critic dubbed *Marimba!* as "an inviting introduction to both Spanish and the animal kingdom," and also praised the energetic, high-contrast cartoon art by Doug Cushman. Described by *Booklist* contributor Julie Cummins as an "inventive stew," *Yum! Mmmm!* features "stylized Mexican" art by Rafael Lopez.

Another verse collection, *The Big Sky,* celebrates the land, people, and creatures of the Southwest in fourteen poems, and also includes poems set in Mora's then home state of Ohio. Subjects include the sky, a grandmother, a huge mountain, an old snake, a horned lizard, and coyotes. A *Publishers Weekly* reviewer predicted that the poems in *The Big Sky* "will delight readers of all ages with their playfully evocative imagery," and in *School Library Journal* Lisa Falk dubbed it a "gem [that] is both a lovely poetry book and an evocative look at a magical place." Calling Mora's words "wonderful," Marilyn Courtot commented in *Children's Literature* that the collection's "spare and dramatic poems transport readers to the American Southwest."

My Own True Name: New and Selected Poems for Young Adults, 1984-1999 contains sixty poems primarily selected by Mora from among those published in her adult books. The metaphor of a cactus, which represents human existence, joins the poems thematically: blooms represent love and joy, thorns represent sorrow and hardship, and roots represent family, home, strength, and wisdom. Autobiographical, the poems address Mora's life as a Latina in the Southwest, her search for identity, and her experience as a mother. She also weaves Mexican phrases, historical figures, and cultural symbols into her poems. Writing in *School Library Journal,* Nina Lindsay stated that Mora's verses "are accessible to, yet challenging for, teens. . . . and . . . should find many readers." Calling the poems "powerful," Gillian Engberg noted in *Booklist* that "the rich, symbolic imagery, raw emotion, and honesty will appeal to mature teens." Delia Culberson concluded in *Voice of Youth Advocates* that in *My Own True Name* Mora "reaches out to her young adult readers with affection and encouragement."

In 1997, Mora lobbied successfully to establish a national day to celebrate childhood and bilingual literacy. Called El día de los niños/El día de los libros, the day is part of National Poetry Month. In 2000, Mora and her siblings established the Estela and Raúl Mora Award, a prize named in honor of their parents. This

In Marimba! *Doug Cushman's high-energy animal characters keep pace with Mora's rhythmic storyline as they dance through the alphabet.* (Clarion Books, 2006. Illustrations copyright © 2006 by Doug Cushman. Reprinted by permission of Houghton Mifflin Company. All rights reserved.)

award, which is coordinated by REFORMA, the National Association to Promote Library Service to Latinos, is designed to promote El día de los niños/El día de los libros. In an essay for *Horn Book,* Mora explained what has motivated her to write: "I write because I am a reader. I want to give to others what writers have given me, a chance to hear the voices of people I will never meet . . . I enjoy the privateness of writing and reading. I write because I am curious. I am curious about me. Writing is a way of finding out how I feel about anything and everything. . . . Writing is my way of saving my feelings. . . . I write because I believe that Hispanics need to take their rightful place in American literature. I will continue to write and to struggle to say what no other writer can say in quite the same way."

Biographical and Critical Sources

BOOKS

Children's Literature Review, Volume 58, Gale (Detroit, MI), 2000.
Dictionary of Hispanic Biography, Gale (Detroit, MI), 1996.

One of the most important of family relationships is Mora's focus in Love to Mama: A Tribute to Mothers, *featuring ethnic-inspired paintings by Paula S. Barragan.* (Lee & Low Books Inc., 2001. Reproduced by permission of Lee & Low Books, Inc.)

Dictionary of Literary Biography, Volume 209: *Chicano Writers,* 3rd series, Gale (Detroit, MI), 1996.

Ikas, Karen Rosa, *Chicana Ways: Conversations with Ten Chicana Writers,* University of Nevada Press (Reno, NV), 2001.

Mora, Pat, *House of Houses,* Beacon Press (Boston, MA), 1997.

Mora, Pat, *Nepantla: Essays from the Land in the Middle,* University of New Mexico Press (Albuquerque, NM), 1993.

This Is about Vision: Interviews with Southwestern Writers, edited by William Balassi and others, University of New Mexico Press (Albuquerque, NM), 1990.

PERIODICALS

Booklist, November 1, 1994, Annie Ayres, review of *Pablo's Tree,* p. 507; November 15, 1998, Isabel Schon, review of *Tomás and the Library Lady,* p. 599; March 15, 2000, Gillian Engberg, review of *My Own True Name: New and Selected Poems for Young Adults, 1984-1999,* p. 1377; November 15, 2002, Gillian Engberg, review of *A Library for Juana: The World of Sor Juana Inéz,* p. 605; December 15, 2002, Hazel Rochman, review of *Maria Paints the Hills,* p. 760; October 15, 2005, Gillian Engberg, review of *The Song of Francis and the Animals,* p. 58; December 1, 2005, Gillian Engberg, review of *Doña Flor: A Tall Tale about a Giant Woman with a Great Big Heart,* p. 55; December 1, 2007, Julie Cummins, review of *Yum! Mmmm! Que rico!,* p. 45.

Bulletin of the Center for Children's Books, September, 1994, Deborah Stevenson, review of *Pablo's Tree,* p. 20; February, 2006, Hope Morrison, review of *Doña Flor,* p. 276.

Horn Book, July-August, 1990, Pat Mora, "Why I Am a Writer," pp. 436-437; January-February, 1993, Maeve Visser Knoth, review of *A Birthday Basket for Tía,* pp. 76-77; November-December, 1994, Maeve Visser Knoth, review of *Pablo's Tree,* pp. 723-724; July, 2001, Nell D. Beram, review of *Love to Mama: A Tribute to Mothers,* p. 468; September-October, 2005, Deirdre F. Baker, review of *The Song of Francis and the Animals,* p. 565.

Kirkus Reviews, October 1, 1996, review of *Confetti: Poems for Children,* p. 1476; November 15, 2002, review of *A Library for Juana,* p. 1699; August 1, 2005, review of *The Song of Francis and the Animals,* p. 854; September 15, 2005, review of *Doña Flor,* p. 1031; October 15, 2006, review of *Marimba!: Animales from A to Z,* p. 1075; September 15, 2007, review of *Yum!*

New Advocate, fall, 1998, Pat Mora, "Confessions of a Latina Author," pp. 279-289.

Publishers Weekly, August 31, 1992, review of *A Birthday Basket for Tía,* p. 77; July 21, 1997, review of *Tomas and the Library Lady,* p. 201; March 23, 1998, review of *The Big Sky,* p. 99; October 28, 2002, review of *A Library for Juana,* p. 71; June 27, 2005, review of *The Song of Francis and the Animals,* p. 67.

School Library Journal, September 15, 1992, Julie Corsaro, review of *A Birthday Basket for Tía,* p. 156; November, 1996, Sally R. Dow, review of *Confetti,* p. 100; July, 1998, Lisa Falk, review of *The Big Sky,* p. 90; November, 1999, Ann Welton, review of *The Rainbow Tulip,* p. 126; July, 2000, Nina Lindsay, review of *My Own True Name,* p. 119; April, 2001, Ann Welton, review of *Love to Mama,* p. 165; November, 2002, Ann Welton, review of *A Library for Juana,* p. 146; October, 2005, Jane Barrer, review of *The Song of Francis and the Animals,* p. 123; October, 2005, Linda M. Kenton, review of *Doña Flor,* p. 122; September, 2007, Marilyn Taniguchi, review of *Yum!,* p. 185.

Voice of Youth Advocates, April, 2001, Delia Culberson, review of *My Own True Name,* p. 20.

ONLINE

Children's Literature, http://www.childrenslit.com/ (January 9, 2008), "Pat Mora."

Pat Mora Web Site, http://www.patmora.com (January 15, 2008).

Scholastic Authors Online Library, http://www.teacher/ scholastic.com/ (May 19, 2002), interview with Mora.

Voices from the Gaps: Women Writers of Color Web site, http://voices.cla.umn.edu/ (May 19, 2002), Delia Abreu and others, "Pat Mora."

OTHER

The Desert Is No Lady (film), Women Who Make Movies, 1995.*

N-O

NAU, Thomas

Personal
Married Janet Pederson (an illustrator); children: Graham.

Addresses
Home and office—Brooklyn, NY.

Career
Author and photographer.

Writings

Walker Evans: Photographer of America, Roaring Brook Press (New Milford, CT), 2007.

Biographical and Critical Sources

PERIODICALS

Booklist, March 1, 2007, Jennifer Mattson, review of *Walker Evans: Photographer of America,* p. 72.
Horn Book, May-June, 2007, Betty Carter, review of *Walker Evans,* p. 303.
School Library Journal, March, 2007, Carol Schene, review of *Walker Evans,* p. 233.*

* * *

NEVIUS, Carol 1955-

Personal
Born 1955, in upstate NY; married Hugh Jones; children: three children. *Education:* Brandeis University, B.A. (psychology), 1976; attended University of Manchester (Manchester, England), 1974-75. *Hobbies and other interests:* Sailing, travel, swimming, music, growing orchids.

Addresses
Home—Coral Springs, FL.

Career
Children's author and educator. Worked variously as a sailing charter cook, snorkeling and fishing guide, and U.S. Coast Guard-licensed boat captain. Westglades Middle School, Coral Gables, FL, language arts teacher. Visiting teacher and writing instructor in public schools.

Writings

Karate Hour, illustrated by Bill Thomson, Marshall Cavendish (New York, NY), 2004.
Building with Dad, illustrated by Bill Thomson, Marshall Cavendish (New York, NY), 2006.
Baseball Hour, illustrated by Bill Thomson, Marshall Cavendish (New York, NY), 2008.

Also author of *911 to Ten,* illustrated by Kimberly Kulaff, RBC Publishing.

Sidelights
Teaming up with artist Bill Thomson, Carol Nevius has created several picture-book stories that are designed to appeal to active youngsters. In *Karate Hour,* which she was inspired to write when her youngest child began taking karate lessons, she introduces young children to karate. As class begins, students—both boys and girls—practice stances, blocks, and kicks under the guidance of their sensei, their efforts documented in Nevius's simple, rhythmic text. Similar in focus, *Baseball Hour* focuses on a young team in the making. Beginning their practice with calisthenics, teammates hone their fielding

and base-running skills before dividing up into teams to play a game. Praising the text of *Karate Hour* for effectively "capturing both the precepts and the movements in relatively few words," *Booklist* contributor Ilene Cooper also praised Thomson's "amazing artwork," with its dramatic use of contrast and detail. Young readers "will definitely feel like participants in this visit to a children's karate class," concluded a *Kirkus Reviews* contributor in another favorable appraisal of *Karate Hour.*

Featuring dramatic acrylic-and-colored pencil artwork by Thomson that reflects a young child's view of the adult world, *Building with Dad* finds a boy accompanying his father to work: a local construction site where a new school building is underway. Fans of heavy machinery will enjoy the detailed images of dump trucks, graders, steamrollers, and other earth-moving machines that work to prepare the ground, while fans of building blocks can follow the steps required to create floors, walls, and ceilings in the new building. *Building with Dad* was described as an "energetic picture book with visual punch" by *Booklist* critic Gillian Engberg, and "Nevius's simple, incisive rhymes capture what's salient from a kid's point of view," according to a *Publishers Weekly* critic. "Thomson's dramatically foreshortened framing" pairs with his use of dramatic perspective to "make for an experience that's both larger than life and deliciously dizzying," the critic added.

Cover of Carol Nevius's picture book Building with Dad, *featuring Bill Thomson's dramatic detailed art.* (Marshall Cavendish, 2006. Illustrations copyright © 2006 by Bill Thomson. Reproduced by permission.)

Biographical and Critical Sources

PERIODICALS

Booklist, September 1, 2004, Ilene Cooper, review of *Karate Hour,* p. 114; September 1, 2006, Gillian Engberg, review of *Building with Dad,* p. 138.
Kirkus Reviews, August 15, 2004, review of *Karate Hour,* p. 810; August 1, 2006, review of *Building with Dad,* p. 793.
Publishers Weekly, October 9, 2006, review of *Building with Dad,* p. 55.
School Library Journal, December, 2004, Grace Oliff, review of *Karate Hour,* p. 114; October, 2006, Judith Constantinides, review of *Building with Dad,* p. 120.

ONLINE

Balkin Buddies Web site, http://www.balkinbuddies.com/ (February 1, 2008), "Carol Nevius."*

*   *   *

O'CONNOR, Jane 1947-

Personal

Born December 30, 1947, in New York, NY; daughter of Norman and Dovie Abramson; married Jim O'Connor, December 9, 1973; children: Robert, Teddy. *Education:* Smith College, B.A., 1969.

Addresses

Home—New York, NY. *Office*—Penguin USA, 345 Hudson St., New York, NY 10014.

Career

Hastings House Publishers, New York, NY, editorial staff member, beginning 1971; Scholastic, Inc., New York, NY, editor, 1977-83; Random House, New York, NY, 1983-89, became editor-in-chief of children's books; Penguin Putnam, Books for Young Readers, New York, NY, president of mass market division, 1989-99; Penguin USA Books for Young Readers, editor-at-large, 1999—.

Writings

JUVENILE NOVELS

Yours till Niagara Falls, Abby, illustrated by Margot Apple, Hastings House (New York, NY), 1979.
Just Good Friends, Harper & Row (New York, NY), 1983.
(With Joyce Milton) *The Dandee Diamond Mystery,* Scholastic (New York, NY), 1983.

(With Joyce Milton) *The Amazing Bubble Gum Caper,* Scholastic (New York, NY), 1984.

(With husband, Jim O'Connor) *The Magic Top Mystery,* Scholastic (New York, NY), 1984.

BEGINNING READERS

Lulu and the Witch Baby, illustrated by Emily Arnold McCully, Harper & Row (New York, NY), 1986.

(Reteller) *The Teeny Tiny Woman,* illustrated by R.W. Alley, Random House (New York, NY), 1986, reprinted, 2003.

Lulu Goes to Witch School, illustrated by Emily Arnold McCully, Harper & Row (New York, NY), 1987.

Sir Small and the Dragonfly, illustrated by John O'Brien, Random House (New York, NY), 1988, reprinted, 2003.

(With Jim O'Connor) *The Ghost in Tent Nineteen,* illustrated by Charles Robinson, Random House (New York, NY), 1988.

Molly the Brave and Me, illustrated by Sheila Hamanaka, Random House (New York, NY), 1990, reprinted, 2003.

(With Jim O'Connor) *Slime Time,* illustrated by Pat Porter, Random House (New York, NY), 1990.

(With son, Robert O'Connor) *Super Cluck,* illustrated by Megan Lloyd, HarperCollins (New York, NY), 1991.

Eek! Stories to Make You Shriek, illustrated by G. Brian Karas, Grosset & Dunlap (New York, NY), 1992.

Nina, Nina Ballerina, illustrated by DyAnne DiSalvo-Ryan, Grosset & Dunlap (New York, NY), 1993.

Splat!, illustrated by Marilyn Mets, Grosset & Dunlap (New York, NY), 1994.

Kate Skates, illustrated by DyAnne DiSalvo-Ryan, Grosset & Dunlap (New York, NY), 1995.

The Bad-Luck Penny, illustrated by Horatio Elena, Grosset & Dunlap (New York, NY), 1996.

Dragon Breath, illustrated by Jeff Spackman, Grosset & Dunlap (New York, NY), 1997.

Benny's Big Bubble, illustrated by Tomie De Paola, Putnam (New York, NY), 1997.

Nina, Nina, Star Ballerina, illustrated by DyAnne DiSalvo-Ryan, Grosset & Dunlap (New York, NY), 1997.

Nina, Nina and the Copycat Ballerina, illustrated by DyAnne DiSalvo-Ryan, Grosset & Dunlap (New York, NY), 2000.

Snail City, illustrated by Rick Brown, Grosset & Dunlap (New York, NY), 2001.

Dear Tooth Fairy, illustrated by Joy Allen, Grosset & Dunlap (New York, NY), 2002.

(With Jessie Hartland) *The Perfect Puppy for Me!,* illustrated by Jessie Hartland, Viking (New York, NY), 2003.

Sir Small and the Sea Monster, illustrated by John O'Brien, Random House (New York, NY), 2005.

The Snow Globe Family, illustrated by S.D. Schindler, Putnam (New York, NY), 2006.

Ready, Set, Skip!, illustrated by Ann James, Viking (New York, NY), 2007.

"HERE COME THE BROWNIES" SERIES

Corrie's Secret Pal, illustrated by Laurie Struck Long, Grosset & Dunlap (New York, NY), 1993.

Sarah's Incredible Idea, illustrated by Laurie Struck Long, Grosset & Dunlap (New York, NY), 1993.

Make up Your Mind, Marsha!, illustrated by Laurie Struck Long, Grosset & Dunlap (New York, NY), 1993.

Amy's (Not So) Great Camp-out, illustrated by Laurie Struck Long, Grosset & Dunlap (New York, NY), 1993.

Think, Corrie, Think!, illustrated by Laurie Struck Long, Grosset & Dunlap (New York, NY), 1994.

Lauren and the New Baby, illustrated by Laurie Struck Long, Grosset & Dunlap (New York, NY), 1994.

"FANCY NANCY" SERIES

Fancy Nancy, illustrated by Robin Preiss Glasser, HarperCollins (New York, NY), 2006.

Fancy Nancy and the Posh Puppy, illustrated by Robin Preiss Glasser, HarperCollins (New York, NY), 2007.

Fancy Nancy at the Museum, illustrated by Robin Preiss Glasser, HarperCollins (New York, NY), 2008.

Fancy Nancy: Bonjour, Butterfly, illustrated by Robin Preiss Glasser, HarperCollins (New York, NY), 2008.

Fancy Nancy's Collection of Fancy Words: From Accessories to Zany, illustrated by Robin Preiss Glasser, HarperCollins (New York, NY), 2008.

Fancy Nancy and the Boy from Paris, illustrated by Robin Preiss Glasser, HarperCollins (New York, NY), 2008.

NONFICTION

(With Katy Hall) *Magic in the Movies: The Story of Special Effects,* Doubleday (New York, NY), 1980.

The Care Bears' Party Cookbook, illustrated by Pat Sustendal, Random House (New York, NY), 1985.

The Emperor's Silent Army: Terracotta Warriors of Ancient China, Viking (New York, NY), 2002.

Henri Matisse: Drawing with Scissors, illustrated by Jessie Hartland, Grosset & Dunlap (New York, NY), 2002.

Mary Cassatt: Family Pictures, illustrated by Jennifer Kalis, Grosset & Dunlap (New York, NY), 2003.

If the Walls Could Talk: Family Life at the White House, illustrated by Gary Hoving, Simon & Schuster (New York, NY), 2004.

FOR ADULTS

Dangerous Admissions: Secrets of a Closet Sleuth (novel), Avon Books (New York, NY), 2007.

Sidelights

In addition to her work as editor at New York City publisher Penguin Books for Young Readers, Jane O'Connor has written a number of works of fiction for children. Specializing in beginning readers with imaginative plots—reflected in such titles as *Lulu and the Witch*

A young girl attempts to master a new sport, with some help, in Jane O'Connor's Kate Skates, *a book featuring illustrations by DyAnne DiSalvo-Ryan.* (Grosset & Dunlap, 1995. Illustrations copyright © 1995 by DyAnne DiSalvo-Ryan. Reproduced by permission of Grosset & Dunlap, a division of Penguin Putnam Inc.)

Baby, The Ghost in Tent Nineteen, and *Snail City*—O'Connor encourages students in the early primary grades to build their reading confidence and find reading fun. In addition to her novels, which include several installments in the "Here Come the Brownies" series about a fictitious Girl Scout troop, O'Connor has penned several titles in her bestselling "Fancy Nancy" series of picture books, has contributed works about artists Henri Matisse and Mary Cassatt to the "Smart about Art" series, and has written an award-winning book about the first emperor of China titled *The Emperor's Silent Army: Terracotta Warriors of Ancient China.*

Born in New York City in 1947, O'Connor attended Smith College, graduating in 1969. Two years later she got her first job in publishing, working in the editorial department of Hastings House Publishers. From 1977 to 1983, O'Connor was an editor at Scholastic, Inc.; then she moved to Random House, where she became editor-in-chief of children's books. In 1989 she moved to Grosset & Dunlap (now a division of Penguin USA). O'Connor wrote her debut novel, *Yours till Niagara Falls, Abby,* in 1979. The book's success with readers was an encouragement, and O'Connor has since turned writing children's books into a second occupation, one

she sometimes engages in with the help of family members. Her younger son, Teddy, wrote his own book, *A New Brain for Igor,* published by Random House in 2001.

Yours till Niagara Falls, Abby is one of a group of middle-grade novels O'Connor authored early in her writing career. Taking place during a torturous two months at Pinecrest overnight summer camp, the novel introduces Merle and Abby, who have been longtime best friends. When Merle's parents opt to send their teen daughter to camp rather than on a far-more-exciting family vacation, Abby works out a way whereby her parents can send her too. Unfortunately, Merle breaks her leg during a dancing class just before the start of camp and winds up confined at home, leaving Abby to suffer camp on her own. Fortunately, the trials of camp life—difficulties with cabin mates and less-than-sympathetic camp counselors, participating in sports at which one is hopelessly bad, catching poison ivy, and the like—become easy to endure with the help of new best friend Roberta. Abby solves the dilemma of reconciling Merle and Roberta as co-best friends by the end of the novel. A *Publishers Weekly* critic praised O'Connor's "fluent, sunny [prose] style," while *School Library Journal* contributor Liza Graybill Bliss added that the author's tone "is funny" and "relaxed." "Readers feel the pain of each setback and the pride of each accomplishment," added Bliss, as the heroine moves "toward self-confidence."

In addition to consistent praise from reviewers, *Yours till Niagara Falls, Abby* won the Nebraska Golden Sower award in 1982, encouraging O'Connor to continue her writing. Her *Just Good Friends,* published in 1983, finds thirteen-year-old Joss frustrated over her blossoming figure, which is proving to be more than either she or her platonic friend Fletcher can handle. Besides dealing with Fletcher's unwanted, immature sexual advances, Joss must also come to terms with her suspicion that her college lecturer father is having an extramarital affair with an attractive college coed. Meanwhile, her mother, who has returned to school to complete her degree after raising her children, seems increasingly preoccupied and withdrawn. There is a bright spot for Joss, however, when the boy she has a crush on shows signs that he returns her feelings. Reviewing the novel, *Bulletin of the Center for Children's Books* reviewer Zena Sutherland commented that *Just Good Friends* "has good flow and pace" and characters who are "vividly real." The lesson that "we cannot always predict people's qualities and roles is imparted by the author with a subtle capability," in the opinion of *School Library Journal* contributor Catherine VanSonnenberg. In her appraisal of *Just Good Friends* for *Growing Point,* Margery Fisher wrote that "there are moments of disarming humour and of warm sympathy in this account of a family whose members are all trying to reconcile their own needs with their responsibilities for one another."

Lulu, a spunky young witch, is one of many characters O'Connor has invented to populate her beginning readers. In *Lulu and the Witch Baby,* as well as the follow-up *Lulu Goes to Witch School,* the fed-up young witch gets tired of her baby sister, who she hates "more than eating lizard liver" because the tiny witchling gets far more attention and never seems to get scolded for all the trouble she causes. To solve her problem, Lulu mixes up bat's blood, fly legs, swamp water, and cat hair into a spell designed to make her sister disappear. When it works she is glad for a while, but then compassion sets in. Worried that the little witch will feel alone and scared being invisible, Lulu undoes her spell, and her small sister returns to view. Unknown to Lulu—but known to the reader—it was actually the girl's mother who caused the infant to disappear, by taking baby sister away for a bath. "Kids will identify immediately with the authenticity of Lulu's feelings," noted a reviewer for *School Library Journal.* In *Lulu Goes to Witch School,* Lulu's spell-making abilities come under the scrutiny of the warty-nosed Miss Slime. Calling O'Connor's story "an absurd and fun idea," a *Publishers Weekly* critic praised it for being "funny and full of the 'gross' details kids love," while in *Booklist,* Ilene Cooper commented that *Lulu Goes to Witch School* "packs plenty of child appeal with its everyday situations, witchy ambience," and easy-to-grasp vocabulary.

O'Connor has contributed to several beginning reader series for a variety of publishers. Her contributions to the "All Aboard Reading" series include *Nina, Nina Ballerina* and *Kate Skates,* both of which feature young, likeable protagonists. In *Nina, Nina Ballerina,* which *School Library Journal* contributor Sharron McElmeel called a "gentle, appealing title for emerging readers," a hard-working young dance student worries that her mother will not be able to spot her in the crowd of similarly costumed dancing butterflies at an upcoming dance recital, until she is reassured by both her mother and her instructor. When Kate's younger sister Jen inherits Kate's old double-bladed ice skates after she receives new ones as a birthday gift in *Kate Skates,* Jen seems to be a natural. She quickly learns to get around on the ice without falling, and falling becomes Kate's job, as she clumsily tries to get used to her new, larger single-blade skates. Eventually, with practice, Kate learns to maneuver in her new skates. When bullies knock her sister down the following week, she is able to help in a story that "gives a little nod to what it means to be a good big sister," according to Stephanie Zvirin in her *Booklist* review.

Other books written by O'Connor with beginning readers in mind include several volumes in the "Eek! Sto-

O'Connor's imaginative tale of a small-scale world is brought to life in S.D. Schindler's illustrations for **The Snow Globe Family.** (G.P. Putnam's Sons, 2006. Illustrations copyright © 2006 by S.D. Schindler. Reproduced by permission..)

ries to Make You Shriek" series, including *The Bad-Luck Penny* and *Dragon Breath.* Her two installments in the "Step into Reading" series were also well received by critics. *The Teeny Tiny Woman,* an adaptation of a folktale O'Connor first published in 1986, contains a repetitive text that is "perfect for a beginning reader," according to *School Library Review* contributor Nancy Palmer. In *Sir Small and the Dragonfly,* published in 1988, O'Connor creates a tale of brave miniature knights who ride ants, loyal peasants no taller than toothpicks, and a beautiful but diminutive maiden abducted by a dragonfly from her home in the town of Pee Wee. Gale W. Sherman noted in *School Library Journal* that O'Connor's tale is "simple but clearly crafted," and praised the author for a "delightful story" of the rescue of a damsel in distress. Phillis Wilson agreed in her *Booklist* appraisal, dubbing *Sir Small and the Dragonfly* "a hit" containing "an engagingly humorous story line" with a vocabulary that practicing readers will not find too daunting. O'Connor also penned a sequel titled *Sir Small and the Sea Monster.*

Several of O'Connor's books have been collaborations with family members such as husband Jim O'Connor. In addition, O'Connor's older son, Robert, has also worked with his mother. While a sixth grader, Robert O'Connor collaborated on *Super Cluck,* the story of a chicken from outer space. Adopted by kind-hearted Mrs. Cluck, given the name Chuck, and raised as one of her own, the alien chicken is soon attracting attention due to his size, strength, and his ability to fly long distances. While such differences set him apart and cause the other chicks to poke fun at him, Chuck eventually saves the day and gains everyone's admiration after he rescues the barnyard from an egg-hungry rat and saves a number of young chicks. Noting that *Super Cluck* could serve as a "role model" for would-be writers, a *School Library Journal* contributor felt that the story would have special appeal to children in the early elementary grades who are "attracted to 'Super Hero' characters."

Young readers can learn more about famous artists through O'Connor's contributions to the "Smart about Art" series: *Henri Matisse: Drawing with Scissors* and *Mary Cassatt: Family Pictures.* Both books take an innovative approach to the artists in question, by presenting the books as projects being produced by students. In *Mary Cassatt,* Claire becomes interested in the American painter after seeing Cassatt's work on a postcard, then the Internet, and then during a family trip to the Metropolitan Museum of Art in New York City. Woven into Claire's discovery are tidbits of information on Cassatt's life and painting techniques. *School Library Journal* reviewer Toniann Scime praised the "exuberant introduction to Cassatt's life and art." *Henri Matisse* begins with an "assignment" from a schoolteacher and continues as Keesia Johnson fulfills that assignment by learning about the latter stages of Matisse's artistic career. In *School Library Journal,* Augusta R. Malvagno called *Henri Matisse* "a creative way to instill an appreciation of art in children."

Another early reader, *Snail City,* subtly introduces the concept of individuality by exploring the adventures of Gail, a snail who gets teased for being speedy. Only after Gail's quick actions save a baby snail do her more sedate playmates understand her special talents. In the picture book *The Perfect Puppy for Me!,* a young narrator does his homework in anticipation of getting his very first puppy. He meets many different breeds of dogs and learns the differences in their appearance and personality. In the end his choice is a hybrid, a "Labradoodle," a mix between a Labrador and a poodle. "This book wins Best in Show," enthused a *Publishers Weekly* reviewer, who added that *A Perfect Puppy for Me!* is "a wonderful starting point for kids who want a dog."

The Snow Globe Family, called an "enticing, snappily written tale-within-a-tale" by a *Publishers Weekly* reviewer, centers on the parallel lives of two Victorian families. While the members of one family live in a sprawling house atop a large hill, a miniature family resides behind the curved walls of their glass home, which sits idly upon a mantle in the large mansion. When a snowstorm sends the big family out to play, one youngster stays behind and manages to topple the snow globe, creating a long-awaited blizzard for its inhabitants. According to *Booklist* critic Gillian Engberg, "kids will like the notion of a tiny, unseen world within our own," and a contributor in *Kirkus Reviews* described *The Snow Globe Family* as "a small and gentle foray into imagination."

In *Ready, Set, Skip!,* a work told in verse, a small girl hopes to learn to skip as well as she can whistle, skate, and somersault. With the help of her understanding mother, the youngster soon masters a new skill. "O'Connor's deft turns of phrase masterfully capture the initial glumness and ensuing buoyancy," remarked a critic in *Kirkus Reviews,* and Carolyn Phelan, writing in *Booklist,* noted that the author "keeps the text moving lightly along and the focus centered on the child's concern."

In 2006 O'Connor introduced her popular heroine Nancy, the perky, precocious, and fashion-conscious protagonist of *Fancy Nancy,* "a book sure to appeal to girls' inner princesses—and inspire new ensembles and décor," wrote Shelle Rosenfeld in *Booklist.* Illustrated by Robin Preiss Glasser, the work follows Nancy as she attempts to enrich the lives of her less-than-flamboyant family members. "The message here is welcome—fanciness (unlike physical beauty) is available to anyone with a can-do spirit—and the writing is adorable," remarked *New York Times Book Review* critic Emily Jenkins. "Nancy's joy is infectious, and her over-the-top elegant vocabulary pays off in a warm twist."

O'Connor continues the exploits of the imaginative youngster in such titles as *Fancy Nancy and the Posh Puppy* and *Fancy Nancy at the Museum.* "I think as an adult I am quite understated—which is a fancy word for plain," O'Connor told *Publishers Weekly* contributor

Cover of O'Connor's picture-book The Perfect Puppy for Me!, *featuring artwork by Jessie Harland.* (Puffin Books, 2003. Jacket illustration copyright © Jessie Hartland, 2003. Reproduced by permission.)

Sally Lodge. "But as a child, whenever my grandma and other relatives would arrive for a Sunday visit, I was all ready for them in my tutu and cape, galumphing around the house. And I think *that* is in every little girl. Sometimes as a kid it's hard to get noticed, and for little girls it's fun to dress up in things that glitter. There is definitely a part of me in Nancy."

Turning to older elementary-grade readers, O'Connor has written *The Emperor's Silent Army.* This nonfiction account introduces readers to the discovery and excavation of the 1,000-year-old army of life-sized terracotta figures, commissioned by an emperor of China to accompany his tomb. "This book provides an intriguing glimpse at one of China's greatest treasures and at one of its most famous emperors," wrote Barbara Scotto in *School Library Journal.* In *Booklist,* Cooper called the title "an enticing example of nonfiction; it leads children into unfamiliar, exciting places."

In *If the Walls Could Talk: Family Life at the White House* O'Connor presents a variety of facts about the forty-three men who have served as president of the United States. She notes, among other things, that Martin Van Buren sold off unattractive furniture, Warren Harding lost a set of china during a poker game, and John F. Kennedy had a tired-looking White House lawn dyed green for visitors. The author "compiles much entertaining and amusing information, sure to send aspiring historians off to seek more," remarked a *Publishers Weekly* contributor. *If the Walls Could Talk* "should appeal both to schoolchildren and to their parents," observed Cokie Roberts in the *New York Times Book Review.*

Biographical and Critical Sources

PERIODICALS

Booklist, October 1, 1987, Ilene Cooper, review of *Lulu Goes to Witch School,* p. 326; March 1, 1989, Phillis Wilson, review of *Sir Small and the Dragonfly,* p.

1199; January 1-15, 1996, Stephanie Zvirin, review of *Kate Skates*, p. 850; April 15, 2002, Ilene Cooper, review of *The Emperor's Silent Army: Terracotta Warriors of Ancient China*, p. 1398; May 15, 2003, Julie Cummins, review of *The Perfect Puppy for Me!*, p. 1672; August, 2004, Ilene Cooper, review of *If the Walls Could Talk: Family Life at the White House*, p. 1939; January 1, 2006, Shelle Rosenfeld, review of *Fancy Nancy*, p. 118; October 1, 2006, Gillian Engberg, review of *The Snow Globe Family*, p. 60; April 15, 2007, Gillian Engberg, "An Inconvenient Truth," p. 44; July 1, 2007, Carolyn Phelan, review of *Ready, Set, Skip!*, p. 66.

Bulletin of the Center for Children's Books, March, 1983, Zean Sutherland, review of *Just Good Friends*, p. 133.

Growing Point, December, 1984, Margery Fisher, review of *Just Good Friends*, p. 4313.

Horn Book, November-December, 2006, Martha V. Parravano, review of *The Snow Globe Family*, p. 702; May-June, 2007, Jennifer M. Brabander, review of *Ready, Set, Skip!*, p. 271.

Kirkus Reviews, August 1, 2004, review of *If the Walls Could Talk*, p. 747; September 1, 2006, review of *The Snow Globe Family*, p. 910; April 15, 2007, review of *Ready, Set, Skip!*

Miami Herald, January 11, 2006, Sue Corbett, "'Fancy Nancy's' Creator Comes with Frills Attached."

New York Times Book Review, October 17, 2004, Cokie Roberts, review of *If the Walls Could Talk*, p. 20; March 12, 2006, Emily Jenkins, review of *Fancy Nancy*, p. 24; December 17, 2006, Julie Just, review of *The Snow Globe Family*, p. 19; August 19, 2007, Chelsea Cain, review of *Dangerous Admissions: Secrets of a Closet Sleuth*, p. 11.

Publishers Weekly, February 22, 1980, review of *Yours till Niagara Falls, Abby*, p. 109; September 25, 1987, review of *Lulu Goes to Witch School*, p. 107; April 21, 2003, review of *The Perfect Puppy for Me!*, p. 61; September 13, 2004, review of *If the Walls Could Talk*, p. 78; January 9, 2006, review of *Fancy Nancy*, p. 53; October 23, 2006, review of *The Snow Globe Family*, p. 50; March 19, 2007, review of *Fancy Nancy and the Posh Puppy*, p. 63; May 7, 2007, review of *Ready, Set, Skip!*, p. 59; June 4, 2007, review of *Dangerous Admissions*, p. 29.

School Library Journal, December, 1979, Liza Graybill Bliss, review of *Yours till Niagara Falls, Abby*, p. 103; January, 1984, Catherine VanSonnenberg, review of *Just Good Friends*, p. 88; December, 1986, review of *Lulu and the Witch Baby*, p. 124; December, 1988, Nancy Palmer, review of *The Teeny Tiny Woman*, pp. 122-123; February, 1989, Gale W. Sherman, review of *Sir Small and the Dragonfly*, pp. 74-75; April, 1991, review of *Super Cluck*, pp. 100-101; August, 1993, Sharron McElmeel, review of *Nina, Nina Ballerina*, pp. 148-149; August, 2001, Maura Bresnahan, review of *Snail City*, p. 156; April, 2002, Barbara Scotto, review of *The Emperor's Silent Army*, p. 179; July, 2002, Augusta R. Malvagno, review of *Henri Matisse: Drawing with Scissors*, p. 110; July, 2003, Toniann Scime, review of *Mary Cassatt: Family Pictures*, p.

115; September, 2004, Donna Cardon, review of *If the Walls Could Talk*, p. 191; February, 2006, Kathleen Whalin, review of *Fancy Nancy*, p. 108; December, 2006, Amy Lilien-Harper, review of *The Snow Globe Family*, p. 112; July, 2007, Judith Constantinides, review of *Ready, Set, Skip!*, p. 82.

ONLINE

Fancy Nancy Web site, http://www.fancynancybooks.com (December 20, 2007).

Publishers Weekly Online, http://www.publishersweekly.com/ (February 1, 2007), Sally Lodge, "From Sparkles to Sales, Nancy Is Fancy Indeed."*

*   *   *

ODRIOZOLA, Elena

Personal

Born in Spain.

Addresses

Home—Spain. *Agent*—Pencil ilustradores, Menendez Pelayo No. 2 Oficina 10, 47001 Valladolid, Spain.

Career

Illustrator. Worked in an advertising agency for eight years, including as art director; illustrator, beginning 1997. *Exhibitions:* Work exhibited at Garabat galería, Bilbao, Spain, 2006.

Awards, Honors

Premio Anaya de Literatura Infantil y Juvenil, 2004, for *El arca y yo* by Vicente Muñoz Puelles; second prize, Department of Culture, 2005, for *La princesa que bostezaba a todas horas* by Carmen Gil.

Illustrator

Maite Gonzalez Esnal, *Maiderren taupada bilduma*, Alberdania, 2002.

Marjaleena Lembcke, *Los despistes de Matias*, translation by Pilar Galindez, Edelvives, 2003.

Hans Christian Andersen, *La princesa y el guisante/The Princess and the Pea*, Grupo Anaya Comercial, 2004.

Vicente Muñoz Puelles, *El arca y yo*, Grupo Anaya Comercial, 2004.

Susan Chandler, *Vegetable Glue*, Meadowside Children's Books (London, England), 2004.

Patxi Zubizarreta, *Magali por fin lo sabe*, Grupo Anaya Comercial, 2005.

Juan Kruz Igerabide, *Botoi bat bezala/Como un boton* (stories), Grupo Anaya Comercial, 2005.

Juan Kruz Igerabide, *Hosto gorri, hosto berde = Hoja roja, hoja verde = Feuille rouge, feuille verte*, 2nd edition, Centro de Linguistica Aplicada Atenea (Madrid, Spain), 2005.

Stephanie Rosenheim, *Supersonic Tonic,* Meadowside Children's Books (London, England), 2005.

Carmen Gil, *La princesa que bostezaba a todas horas,* Ogo, 2005.

Manuel L. Alonso, *Rumbo Sur/ Going South,* Luis Vives Editorial, 2005.

Maria Baranda, *Marte y las princesas voladores,* Fondo de Cultura Economica, 2006.

Kenneth Grahame, *El viento en los sauces/The Wind in the Willows,* Grupo Anaya Comercial, 2006.

Tom MaCrae, *The Opposite,* Peachtree (Atlanta, GA), 2006.

Txabi Arnal, *Tres hermanas ladronas,* OQO (Pontevedra, Spain), 2007.

Stephanie Rosenheim, *The Story of Noah,* Meadowside Children's Books (London, England), 2007.

Ferida Wolff and Harriet May Savitz, *The Story Blanket,* Andersen Press (London, England), 2008.

Antonio Ventura, *Cuando sale la luna,* Thul Ediciones, 2008.

Also illustrator of *El brujo del viento/The Wind Wizard: 176 (el barco de vapor/The Steamboat),* by Paloma Sanchez.

Biographical and Critical Sources

PERIODICALS

Kirkus Reviews, August 15, 2006, review of *The Opposite,* p. 848.
Publishers Weekly, September 11, 2006, review of *The Opposite,* p. 54.
School Librarian, autumn, 2006, Rosemary Woodman, review of *The Opposite,* p. 128.
School Library Journal, October, 2006, Genevieve Gallagher, review of *The Opposite,* p. 118.

ONLINE

Pencil, Agencia de ilustradores Web site, http://www.pencil-ilustratores.com/ (February 1, 2008), "Elena Odriozola."*

P

PALLOTTA, Gerard Larry
See PALLOTTA, Jerry

*   *   *

PALLOTTA, Jerry 1953-
(Gerard Larry Pallotta)

Personal

Born Gerard Larry Pallotta, March 26, 1953, in Boston, MA; son of Joe and Mary Pallotta; married, wife's name Linda; children: Sheila, Neil, Eric, Jill. *Education:* Graduated from Georgetown University.

Addresses

Home and office—P.O. Box 920760, Needham, MA 02492. *E-mail*—linda@jerrypallotta.com.

Career

Author, 1985—, and public speaker. Worked as an insurance agent, until 1991.

Writings

The Ocean Alphabet Book, illustrated by Frank Mazzola, Jr., Peggotty Beach Books 1986, republished, Charlesbridge Publishing (Watertown, MA), 1989.
The Icky Bug Alphabet Book, illustrated by Ralph Masiello, Quinlan Press (Boston, MA), 1986.
The Bird Alphabet Book, illustrated by Edgar Stewart, Quinlan Press (Boston, MA), 1987.
The Flower Alphabet Book, illustrated by Leslie Evans, Quinlan Press (Boston, MA), 1988.
The Yucky Reptile Alphabet Book, illustrated by Ralph Masiello, Charlesbridge Publishing (Watertown, MA), 1989.

The Frog Alphabet Book, illustrated by Ralph Masiello, Charlesbridge Publishing (Watertown, MA), 1990.
Going Lobstering, illustrated by Rob Bolster, Charlesbridge Publishing (Watertown, MA), 1990.
The Dinosaur Alphabet Book, illustrated by Ralph Masiello, Charlesbridge Publishing (Watertown, MA), 1991.
The Furry Animal Alphabet Book, illustrated by Edgar Stewart, Charlesbridge Publishing (Watertown, MA), 1991.
The Underwater Alphabet Book, illustrated by Edgar Stewart, Charlesbridge Publishing (Watertown, MA), 1991.
The Icky Bug Counting Book, illustrated by Ralph Masiello, Charlesbridge Publishing (Watertown, MA), 1992.
(With Bob Thomson) *The Victory Garden Alphabet Book,* illustrated by Edgar Stewart, Charlesbridge Publishing (Watertown, MA), 1992.
The Extinct Alphabet Book, illustrated by Ralph Masiello, Charlesbridge Publishing (Watertown, MA), 1993.
The Desert Alphabet Book, illustrated by Mark Astrella, Charlesbridge Publishing (Watertown, MA), 1994.
The Spice Alphabet Book: Herbs, Spices, and Other Natural Flavors, illustrated by Leslie Evans, Charlesbridge Publishing (Watertown, MA), 1994.
(With Brian Cassie) *The Butterfly Alphabet Book,* illustrated by Mark Astrella, Charlesbridge Publishing (Watertown, MA), 1995.
The Freshwater Alphabet Book, illustrated by David Biedrzycki, Charlesbridge Publishing (Watertown, MA), 1996.
The Icky Bug Alphabet Pop-up Book, illustrated by Ralph Masiello, Charlesbridge Publishing (Watertown, MA), 1996.
(With Pam Muñoz Ryan) *The Crayon Counting Book,* illustrated by Frank Mazzola, Jr., Charlesbridge Publishing (Watertown, MA), 1996.
(With Fred Stillwell) *The Airplane Alphabet Book,* illustrated by Rob Bolster, Charlesbridge Publishing (Watertown, MA), 1997.
(With Pam Muñoz Ryan) *The Crayon Counting Board Book,* illustrated by Frank Mazzola, Jr., Charlesbridge Publishing (Watertown, MA), 1997.

The Boat Alphabet Book, illustrated by David Biedrzycki, Charlesbridge Publishing (Watertown, MA), 1998.

The Hershey's Milk Chocolate Bar Fractions Book, illustrated by Rob Bolster, Cartwheel Books (New York, NY), 1999.

The Jet Alphabet Book, illustrated by Rob Bolster, Charlesbridge Publishing (Watertown, MA), 1999.

Dory Story, illustrated by David Biedrzycki, Talewinds (Watertown, MA), 2000.

The Icky Bug Alphabet Board Book, illustrated by Ralph Masiello, Charlesbridge Publishing (Watertown, MA), 2000.

Reese's Pieces Count by Fives, illustrated by Rob Bolster, Scholastic (New York, NY), 2000.

The Hershey's Kisses Addition Book, illustrated by Rob Bolster, Scholastic (New York, NY), 2001.

Twizzlers Percentages Book, illustrated by Rob Bolster, Scholastic (New York, NY), 2001.

Underwater Counting: Even Numbers, illustrated by David Biedrzycki, Charlesbridge Publishing (Watertown, MA), 2001.

Apple Fractions, illustrated by Rob Bolster, Scholastic (New York, NY), 2002.

The Hershey's Kisses Subtraction Book, illustrated by Rob Bolster, Scholastic (New York, NY), 2002.

Icky Bug Colors, illustrated by David Biedrzycki, Scholastic (New York, NY), 2002.

The Hershey's Milk Chocolate Multiplication Book, illustrated by Rob Bolster, Scholastic (New York, NY), 2002.

Hershey's Milk Chocolate Weights and Measures, illustrated by Rob Bolster, Scholastic (New York, NY), 2002.

The Skull Alphabet Book, illustrated by Ralph Masiello, Charlesbridge Publishing (Watertown, MA), 2002.

Twizzlers Shapes and Patterns, illustrated by Rob Bolster, Scholastic (New York, NY), 2002.

Count to a Million: 1,000,000, illustrated by Rob Bolster, Scholastic (New York, NY), 2003.

Hershey's Kisses Multiplication and Division, illustrated by Rob Bolster, Scholastic (New York, NY), 2003.

How to Draw Icky Bugs, illustrated by Bonnie Gee, Scholastic (New York, NY), 2003.

Icky Bug Numbers 12345, illustrated by David Biedrzycki and Rob Bolster, Scholastic (New York, NY), 2003.

Jerry Pallotta creates an alphabet book to match every interest, as in **The Jet Alphabet Book,** *featuring art by Rob Bolster.* (Charlesbridge, 1999. Text copyright © by Jerry Pallotta. Illustrations copyright © 1999 by Rob Bolster. Used with permission by Charlesbridge Publishing, Inc. All rights reserved.)

The Ocean Alphabet Board Book, illustrated by Frank Mazzola, Jr., Charlesbridge Publishing (Watertown, MA), 2003.

(With Sammie Garnett) *U.S. Navy Alphabet Book,* illustrated by Rob Bolster, Charlesbridge Publishing (Watertown, MA), 2004.

The Beetle Alphabet Book, illustrated by David Biedrzycki, Charlesbridge Publishing (Watertown, MA), 2004.

The Icky Bug Counting Board Book, illustrated by Ralph Masiello, Charlesbridge Publishing (Watertown, MA), 2004.

Read a Zillion Books, Richard C. Owen Publishers (Katonah, NY), 2004.

Ocean Counting: Odd Numbers, illustrated by Shennen Bersani, Charlesbridge Publishing (Watertown, MA), 2005.

Who Will Guide My Sleigh Tonight?, illustrated by David Biedrzycki, Scholastic (New York, NY), 2005.

The Yummy Alphabet Book: Herbs, Spices, and Other Natural Flavors, illustrated by Leslie Evans, Charlesbridge Publishing (Watertown, MA), 2005.

The Addition Book, illustrated by Rob Bolster, Scholastic (New York, NY), 2006.

The Construction Alphabet Book, illustrated by Rob Bolster, Charlesbridge Publishing (Watertown, MA), 2006.

Who Will Help Santa This Year?, illustrated by David Biedrzycki, Scholastic (New York, NY), 2006.

Going Lobstering, illustrated by Rob Bolster, Charlesbridge Publishing (Watertown, MA), 2007.

The Subtraction Book, illustrated by Rob Bolster, Scholastic (New York, NY), 2007.

Adaptations

Sidelights

Prolific children's author Jerry Pallotta, known in literary circles as the "Alphabet Man," has published such highly regarded works as *The Icky Bug Alphabet Book,* *The Skull Alphabet Book,* and *The Airplane Alphabet Book.* In addition, Pallotta explores basic math concepts

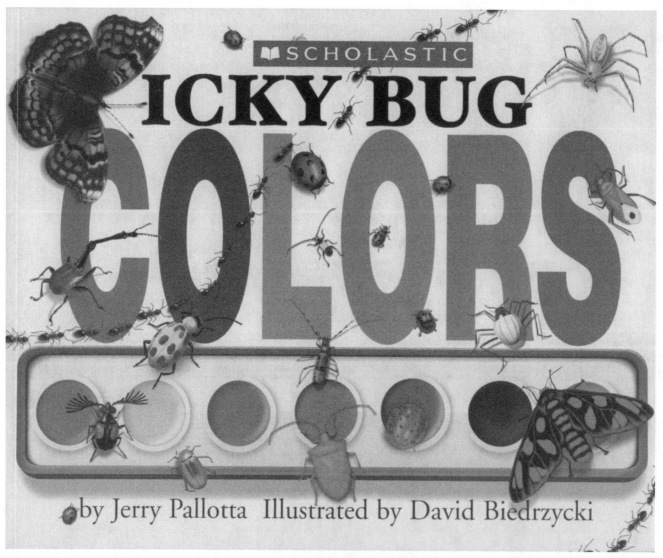

Cover of Pallotta's **Icky Bug Colors,** *an unusual concept book featuring artwork by David Biedrzycki.* (Scholastic, 2002. Illustrations copyright © 2002 by David Biedrzycki. Reprinted by permission of Scholastic Inc.)

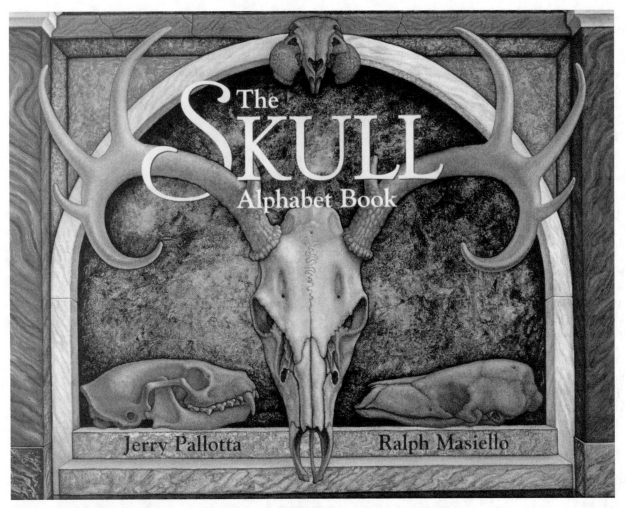

Cover of Pallotta's The Skull Alphabet Book, *featuring detailed illustrations by Ralph Masiello.* (Charlesbridge, 2002. Text copyright © 2002 by Jerry Pallotta. Illustrations copyright © 2002 by Ralph Masiello. Used with permission by Charlesbridge Publishing, Inc. All rights reserved.)

in such works as *The Hershey's Kisses Addition Book* and *Twizzlers Shapes and Patterns.* A contributor to *Publishers Weekly* praised the "fastidiously researched information" in Pallotta's works, adding that his "meatier books appeal to a broader range of readers, including elementary-school students who use his texts as research tools for school projects." "My goal has always been to write interesting, fact-filled, fun to read, beautifully illustrated color children's books," the author noted on his home page.

A former insurance salesman, Pallotta began his writing career in 1985 after becoming frustrated by the lack of interesting, informative alphabet books available for his children. "All the books were the same, A for apple and Z for zebra, but without any other text," Pallotta told *Boston Herald* interviewer Thomas Grillo. "So I thought I'd write my own." For the work, Pallotta drew on his own memories of growing up in Scituate, Massachusetts. "As a teenager I kept lobster traps, harvested seaweed and rode on fishing draggers," he remarked to an interviewer in *Publishers Weekly.* "I thought it would be a great idea to write a book that introduced my own kids to all the little creatures I knew as a child at the beach."

Using his cousin, Frank Mazzola, as the book's illustrator, Pallotta self-published 10,000 copies of *The Ocean Alphabet Book* in 1986. "I was scared," he admitted to Grillo. "Scared that I'd sell one book to my mother and have 9,999 copies in my cellar, and my wife would give me a lifetime of grief." Instead, he convinced Boston's New England Aquarium to carry the work, and it quickly became a bestseller. Realizing he needed help with distribution, Pallotta signed with Charlesbridge Publishing, which has since published more than two dozen of his titles. "I'd rather be with a smaller publisher and let my books be a major focus of the company," he remarked in *Publishers Weekly.*

Pallotta's early works focused on the natural world, as in *The Extinct Alphabet Book,* which features the Hallucigenia, a spiny, wormlike creature, and the Xerces Blue, a butterfly that once lived in San Francisco. According to a reviewer in *Publishers Weekly,* "the alphabet device serves to marshal the roster of extinct species without rebuffing adventurous preschoolers." In *The Skull Alphabet Book,* Pallotta presents the skulls of twenty-six mammals, including a baboon, an elephant, and a ram, and invites young readers to guess the animals' identities. "Touches of offbeat humor are found throughout," observed a *Kirkus Reviews* critic, "showing that for those who use their heads, science can be both educational and fun." Aerial lifts, jackhammers, and zippers are the focus of *The Construction Alphabet Book,* a departure from the author's usual subjects. "Pallotta provides more information than most picture books about the topic for this age group," *Booklist* contributor Carolyn Phelan wrote.

Pallotta is also the author of several popular counting books. In *Underwater Counting: Even Numbers,* the author introduces a variety of exotic creatures, such as manta rays and leopard sharks. According to *Booklist* reviewer Lauren Peterson, young readers will "enjoy searching the illustrations for the featured number, which is cleverly hidden in each scene." In a companion volume, *Ocean Counting: Odd Numbers,* Pallotta examines green crabs to limpets and sand dollars. Patricia Manning, writing in *School Library Journal,* called the work "a colorful, engaging, and intriguing slant" on counting techniques.

Pallotta frequently lectures at conferences and workshops and speaks to students at more than 150 schools a year. "I love writing books and I love visiting schools all over the United States," he remarked on his home page. "I think I have the best job in the world!"

Biographical and Critical Sources

PERIODICALS

Booklist, February 1, 1997, Hazel Rochman, review of *The Airplane Alphabet Book,* p. 943; February 1, 2000, Tim Arnold, review of *Dory Story,* p. 1019; March 1, 2001, Lauren Peterson, review of *Underwater Counting: Even Numbers,* p. 1284; September 1, 2002, Susan Dove Lempke, review of *The Skull Alphabet Book,* p. 118; February 1, 2005, Karin Snelson, review of *Ocean Counting: Odd Numbers,* p. 963; July 1, 2006, Carolyn Phelan, review of *The Construction Alphabet Book,* p. 62.

Boston Herald, August 9, 1998, Thomas Grillo, "ABCs of Writing Spell Success," p. 3.

Kirkus Reviews, July 15, 2002, review of *The Skull Alphabet Book,* p. 1040; February 1, 2005, review of *Ocean Counting: Odd Numbers,* p. 180.

Publishers Weekly, August 2, 1993, review of *The Extinct Alphabet Book,* p. 78; August 26, 1996, review of *The Crayon Counting Book,* p. 96; March 3, 1997, "The ABCs of Success," p. 26.

School Library Journal, January, 1994, Eva Elisabeth Von Ancken, review of *The Extinct Alphabet Book,* p. 96; March, 2000, Sue Sherif, review of *Dory Story,* p. 210; April, 2001, Joy Fleishhacker, review of *Underwater Counting: Even Numbers,* p. 133; July, 2002, Steven Engelfried, review of *The Skull Alphabet Book,* p. 110; May, 2004, Corrina Austin, review of *The Beetle Alphabet Book,* p. 134; March, 2005, Patricia Manning, review of *Ocean Counting: Odd Numbers,* p. 200; August, 2006, Lynn K. Vanca, review of *The Construction Alphabet Book,* p. 108; October, 2006, Linda Israelson, review of *Who Will Guide My Sleigh Tonight?,* p. 99.

ONLINE

Alphabet Man Web site, http://www.alphabetman.com/ (December 20, 2007).

Jerry Pallotta Home Page, http://www.jerrypallotta.com (December 20, 2007).*

*   *   *

PARSONS, Ellen
See DRAGONWAGON, Crescent

*   *   *

PETRONE, Valeria

Personal

Female. *Education:* Attended St. Martin School of Art (London, England).

Addresses

Home and office—Italy. *E-mail*—valeria@valeriapetrone.com.

Career

Illustrator.

Member

Italian Association of Illustrators (vice president), Society of Illustrators of NY.

Illustrator

Carol Watson, *If You Were a Puppy,* Dinosaur (London, England), 1989.

Wes Magee, *Morning Break, and Other Poems,* Cambridge University (New York, NY), 1990.

Dennis Bond, *The Granny Who Wasn't like Other Grannies,,* 1993, new edition, Coach House (London, England), 2003.

Incy Wincy Spider, and Other Nursery Rhymes, Ladybird (London, England), 1994.

Linda Jennings, *This Little Piggy,* Levinson Books (London, England), 1997.

Kate Burns, *Round and Round the Garden,* Levinson Books (London, England), 1997.

Denis Bond, *The Shark Who Bit Things He Shouldn't,* Little Hippo (London, England), 1998.

Lori Haskins, *Ducks in Muck,* Random House (New York, NY), 2000.

Nancy Smiler Levinson, *Say Cheese!,* Golden Books (New York, NY), 2000.

Mary Serfozo, *Plumply, Dumply Pumpkin,* Margaret K. McElderry Books (New York, NY), 2001.

Marion Dane Bauer, *Uh-oh!: A Lift-the-Flap Story,* Little Simon (New York, NY), 2002.

Leslie Parrott, *God Made You Nose to Toes,* Zonderkidz (Grand Rapids, MI), 2002.

Teresa Imperato, *Colors All Around,* Piggy Toes Press (Los Angeles, CA), 2003.

Joan N. Keener *God Thought of It First,* Standard Publishing, 2003.

Anna Jane Hays, *The Pup Speaks Up: A Phonics Reader,* Random House (New York, NY), 2003.

Teresa Imperato, *How Many Ducks in a Row?,* Piggy Toes Press (Los Angeles, CA), 2003.

Stuart J. Murphy, *Double the Ducks,* HarperCollins (New York, NY), 2003.

Jan Peck, *Way Down Deep in the Deep Blue Sea,* Simon & Schuster Books for Young Readers (New York, NY), 2004.

Valeria Petrone's naive-styled artwork adds an air of whimsy to Jan Peck's rhyming story in **Way Down Deep in the Deep Blue Sea.** (Simon & Schuster Books for Young Readers, 2004. Illustrations copyright © 2004 Valeria Petrone. Reprinted with the permission of Simon & Schuster Books for Young Readers, an imprint of Simon & Schuster Children's Publishing Division.)

Helen Bannerman, *The Boy and the Tigers,* Golden Books (New York, NY), 2004.

Cari Meister, *Luther's Halloween,* Viking (New York, NY), 2004.

Jan Peck, *Way up High in a Tall Green Tree,* Simon & Schuster Books for Young Readers (New York, NY), 2005.

Patricia Ryan, *My Blankie: A Book to Touch and Feel,* Little Simon (New York, NY), 2005.

Michelle Knudsen, *Fish and Frog,* Candlewick Press (Cambridge, MA), 2005.

Jan Peck, *Way Far away on a Wild Safari,* Simon & Schuster Books for Young Readers (New York, NY), 2006.

Shari Becker, *Horris Grows Down,* G.P. Putnam's Sons (New York, NY), 2007.

Kersten Hamilton, *Red Truck,* Viking Children's Books (New York, NY), 2008.

Sidelights

Artist Valeria Petrone is internationally known as a children's book illustrator. Although her images appear primarily in stories by English-language authors, books featuring Petrone's art have also reached young readers in Japan, France, and her native Italy through translation. Petrone's work is inspired by English book illustration—she trained at London's St. Martin School of Art—and it has been paired with texts by such well-known children's authors as Jan Peck, Stuart J. Murphy, Cari Meister, and Marion Dane Bauer. In her *School Library Journal* appraisal of Peck's picture book *Way up High in a Tall Green Tree,* Suzanne Meyers-Harold cited Petrone for contributing "bold, colorful, digitally rendered" images that are distinguished by a "creative use of perspective," and a *Kirkus Reviews* writer cited the illustrator's "bold touch."

Petrone uses her signature bold colors and digital images in her illustrations for Shari Becker's *Horris Grows Down.* In the 2007 picture book, Horris is an overgrown four year old who towers over his parents. Told by his parents to find a job, the oversized preschooler is hampered by the fact that he can neither read nor count. In creating art for Becker's quirky tale, Petrone uses vivd colors, creating "smooth digital illustrations, which mimic acrylic painting in retro oranges and turquoise," as noted by a *Publishers Weekly* reviewer. Julie Cummins, in her review of *Horris Grows Down* for *Booklist,* compared Petrone's unique images to those of other eccentric artists and wrote that her "wacky illustrations . . . call up the work of J. Otto Seibold and Dan Yaccarino."

Biographical and Critical Sources

PERIODICALS

Booklist, April 15, 2000, Hazel Rochman, review of *Ducks in Muck,* p. 1555; September 1, 2001, Shelle Rosenfeld, review of *Plumply, Dumply Pumpkin,* p. 122; March 15, 2003, Hazel Rochman, review of *Double the Ducks,* p. 1328; July, 2003, Ilene Cooper, review of *The Pup Speaks Up: A Phonics Reader,* p. 1899; February 15, 2007, Julie Cummins, review of *Horris Grows Down,* p. 82.

Books, February 11, 2007, Mary Harris Russell, review of *Horris Grows Down,* p. 7.

Bulletin of the Center for Children's Books, September, 2004, Gay Lynn Van Vleck, review of *Luther's Halloween,* p. 174; September, 2005, Hope Morrison, review of *Way up High in a Tall Green Tree,* p. 34; February, 2007, Deborah Stevenson, review of *Horris Grows Down,* p. 244.

Kirkus Reviews, July 1, 2001, review of *Plumply, Dumply Pumpkin,* p. 947; December 1, 2002, review of *Double the Ducks,* p. 1770; April 1, 2004, review of *Way Down Deep in the Deep Blue Sea,* p. 335; July 1, 2004, review of *Luther's Halloween,* p. 633; June 15, 2005, review of *Way up High in a Tall Green Tree,* p. 688; May 1, 2006, review of *Way Far Away on a Wild Safari,* p. 465; December 15, 2006, review of *Horris Grows Down,* p. 1264.

Publishers Weekly, January 4, 1999, review of *Round and Round the Garden,* p. 92; May 29, 2000, review of *Round and Round the Garden,* p. 84; September 24, 2001, review of *Plumply, Dumply Pumpkin,* p. 42; May 10, 2004, review of *Way Down Deep in the Deep Blue Sea,* p. 57; August 9, 2004, review of *Luther's Halloween,* p. 31; January 22, 2007, review of *Horris Grows Down,* p. 184.

School Librarian, November, 1989, review of *If You Were a Puppy,* p. 146; August, 1993, review of *The Granny Who Wasn't like Other Grannies,* p. 101.

School Library Journal, August, 2000, Susan Hepler, review of *Give a Little Love: Stories of Love and Friendship,* p. 164; February, 2001, Barb Lawler, review of *Ducks in Muck,* p. 100; September, 2001, Piper L. Myman, review of *Plumply, Dumply Pumpkin,* p. 206; July, 2004, Julie Roach, review of *Way Down Deep in the Deep Blue Sea,* p. 84; August, 2005, Melinda Piehler, review of *Fish and Frog,* p. 98; September, 2005, Suzanne Myers Harold, review of *Way up High in a Tall Green Tree,* p. 184; June, 2006, Marge Loch-Wouters, review of *Way Far Away on a Wild Safari,* p. 124; February, 2007, Maryann H. Owen, review of *Horris Grows Down,* p. 84.

ONLINE

Valeria Petrone Home Page, http://www.valeriapetrone.com (December 15, 2007).*

*　　*　　*

PROTOPOPESCU, Orel (Orel Odinov Protopopescu)

Personal

Born in Hempstead, NY; daughter of a lawyer and an elementary school teacher; married; children: two daughters.

Addresses

Home and office—P.O. Box 709, Miller Place, NY 11764.

Career

Author, educator, and poet. Has also worked as a storyteller and a writer and producer of educational films.

Awards, Honors

New York Public Library Books for the Teen Age selection, 2003, for *A Thousand Peaks;* poetry prize, *Oberon* magazine, 2006.

Writings

(Under name Orel Odinov Protopopescu) *Since Lulu Learned the Cancan,* illustrated by Sandra Forrest, Green Tiger Press (New York, NY), 1991.

(Under name Orel Odinov Protopopescu) *The Perilous Pit,* illustrated by Jacqueline Chwast, Green Tiger Press (New York, NY), 1993.

(With Siyu Liu) *A Thousand Peaks: Poems from China,* illustrated by Liu, Pacific View Press (Berkeley, CA), 2001.

Metaphors and Similes You Can Eat and Twelve More Great Poetry Writing Lessons, Scholastic Teaching Resources (New York, NY), 2003.

Two Sticks, illustrated by Anne Wilsdorf, Farrar, Straus & Giroux (New York, NY), 2007.

Contributor of poems to periodicals, including *Spoon River Poetry Review.*

Sidelights

Orel Protopopescu, a poet and educator, is the author of a number of humorous books for young readers, including *The Perilous Pit* and *Two Sticks.* Protopopescu, who was named after a city in her father's homeland, Russia, credits her parents with nurturing her interest in literature. As she noted on the Farrar, Straus & Giroux Web site, "My mother was a dedicated third-grade teacher in an inner-city school. I devoured all the books she brought me. My father, a lawyer who preferred bridge and backgammon to the law, taught me chess and told stories that made me laugh." Protopopescu now shares her love of the written word with students of all ages by training at writing teachers and conducting prose and poetry workshops.

A former storyteller and film producer, Protopopescu began writing for children after the birth of her daughters and her debut work, *Since Lulu Learned the Cancan,* was published in 1991. The tale concerns a lively young ostrich who dances wherever and whenever she pleases, much to the consternation—and sometimes the delight—of her family. In the author's next work, *The*

Perilous Pit, a youngster carelessly discards a peach pit, starting a chain of events involving a frightened cat, an out-of-control automobile, a gushing fire hydrant, a daredevil skateboarder who is swept out to sea, and rescue teams from the Navy, the Coast Guard, and the Air Force. Michele Landsberg, writing in *Entertainment Weekly,* praised the author's "witty, energetic prose," and a contributor in *Publishers Weekly* stated that "Protopopescu's story, a run-on sentence separated into unrhymed stanzas, leaves readers breathless."

In *A Thousand Peaks: Poems from China,* Protopopescu and coauthor Siyu Liu—who also illustrated the work—offer thirty-five poems spanning 2,000 years of Chinese history. Each poem is presented in Chinese characters as well as in a pinyin transliteration, a literal English translation, and a "poetic" English interpretation. "This unique collection invites readers to get into the act by comparing the Chinese original with this [poetic] version, and perhaps exercising their own poetic skills," observed Margaret A. Chang in *School Library Journal.* A *Washington Post* contributor similarly noted that "the real beauty of this book is that it gives readers the chance to peek behind" the original works of Chinese literature. Reviewing *A Thousand Peaks* in *Booklist,* Gillian Engberg described Protopopescu and Liu's work as "an unusual, informative resource for cross-curricular use."

An energetic youngster's love of percussion is the subject of *Two Sticks,* a work told in verse. When Little Maybelle's parents can no longer tolerate their daughter's nonstop drumming, they ask Maybelle to play outdoors in the surrounding bayou. Maybelle taps so forcefully, however, that she shatters a log bridge and falls into a swamp full of alligators. Instead of devouring the young girl, the gators are charmed by Maybelle's talents and follow the pied piper of the bayou back to her home. "Protopopescu weaves whimsical sense and nonsense into the bouncing rhymes," Engberg commented, and Nicholas A. Basbanes, writing in the *Pittsburgh Tribune-Review,* stated that the author "writes with a fresh, tongue-twisting vitality."

Biographical and Critical Sources

PERIODICALS

Booklist, June 1, 1993, Julie Corsaro, review of *The Perilous Pit,* p. 1860; March 15, 2002, Gillian Engberg, review of *A Thousand Peaks: Poems from China,* p. 1250; February 15, 2007, Gillian Engberg, review of *Two Sticks,* p. 86.

Entertainment Weekly, July 23, 1993, Michele Landsberg, review of *The Perilous Pit,* p. 72.

New York Times Book Review, June 20, 1993, review of *The Perilous Pit,* p. 23.

Pittsburgh Tribune-Review, March 18, 2007, Nicholas A. Basbanes, review of *Two Sticks.*

Publishers Weekly, May 24, 1993, review of *The Perilous Pit,* p. 84.

School Library Journal, September, 1993, Anna DeWind, review of *The Perilous Pit,* p. 218; February, 2002, Margaret A. Chang, review of *A Thousand Peaks,* p. 147; March, 2007, Nancy Kunz, review of *Two Sticks,* p. 184.

Washington Post Book World, February 24, 2002, review of *A Thousand Peaks.*

ONLINE

Farrar, Straus & Giroux Web site, http://www.fsgkids books.com/ (December 20, 2007), "Orel Protopopescu."*

*   *   *

PROTOPOPESCU, Orel Odinov
See PROTOPOPESCU, Orel

R-S

REEVE, Rosie

Personal
Born in England; married; children.

Addresses
Home and office—London, England.

Career
Illustrator.

Illustrator
Margrit Cruickshank, *We're Going to Feed the Ducks,* Frances Lincoln (London, England), 2003.

Tony Payne, *Oh No, Annie!,* Dolphin (London, England), 2004.

Tony Payne, *Not Again, Annie!,* Dolphin (London, England), 2004.

Ian Whybrow, *Hey, I Love You!,* Macmillan Children's Books (London, England), 2004.

Tony Payne, *It's Only Annie,* Dolphin (London, England), 2005.

Ian Whybrow, *Bella Gets Her Skates On,* Harry Abrams Books for Young Readers (New York, NY), 2007.

Jeanne Willis, *Delilah D. at the Library,* Clarion Books (New York, NY), 2007.

Jeanne Willis, *Delilah Darling Is in the Classroom,* Puffin (London, England), 2007.

Biographical and Critical Sources

PERIODICALS

Booklist, February 1, 2007, Ilene Cooper, review of *Delilah D. at the Library,* p. 49.

ONLINE

Houghton Mifflin Books Web site, http://www.houghton mifflinbooks.com/ (January 8, 2008), "Rosie Reeve."*

REX, Adam

Personal
Married; wife an astrophysicist. *Education:* University of Arizona, B.F.A. (illustration).

Addresses
Home—Philadelphia, PA. *Agent*—Steve Malk, Writers House, 21 W. 26th St., New York, NY 10010. *E-mail*—adamrex@earthlink.net.

Career
Author and illustrator. Creator of card art.

Awards, Honors
Golden Kite Award, Society of Children's Book Writers and Illustrators, Parents' Choice Gold Medal, and International Reading Association (IRA) Notable Book selection, all 2004, all for *The Dirty Cowboy;* Jack Gaughan Award for Best Emerging Artist, 2005; IRA Notable Book selection, 2006, for *Ste-e-e-eamboat A-comin'!*

Writings

ILLUSTRATOR

Amy Timberlake, *The Dirty Cowboy,* Farrar, Straus & Giroux (New York, NY), 2003.

Katy Kelly, *Lucy Rose: Here's the Thing about Me,* Delacorte (New York, NY), 2004.

Jill Esbaum, *Ste-e-e-eamboat A-comin!,* Farrar, Straus & Giroux (New York, NY), 2005.

Katy Kelly, *Lucy Rose: Big on Plans,* Delacorte (New York, NY), 2005.

Katy Kelly, *Lucy Rose: Busy like You Can't Believe,* Delacorte (New York, NY), 2006.

Adam Rex (Courtesy of Adam Rex.)

Elvira Woodruff, *Small Beauties: The Journey of Darcy Heart O'Hara,* Knopf (New York, NY), 2006.

SELF-ILLUSTRATED

Frankenstein Makes a Sandwich; and Other Stories You're Sure to Like, Because They're All about Monsters, And Some of Them Are Also about Food. You Like Food, Don't You? Well, All Right, Harcourt (Orlando, FL), 2006.
Tree-ring Circus, Harcourt (Orlando, FL), 2006.
Pssst!, Harcourt (Orlando, FL), 2007.
The True Meaning of Smekday (novel), Hyperion (New York, NY), 2007.
Frankenstein Takes the Cake, Harcourt (Orlando, FL), 2008.

OTHER

Author of *Editpus Rex* Blog, located at http://www.adamrex.blogspot.com. Contributor of illustrations to periodicals, including *Amazing Stories, Cricket,* and *Spider.* Illustrator of books used in role-playing games *Dungeons & Dragons, Forgotten Realms,* and *Magic: The Gathering.*

Sidelights

Adam Rex is an award-winning illustrator of such children's books as *The Dirty Cowboy* and *Small Beauties: The Journey of Darcy Heart O'Hara.* In addition, Rex has published a number of humorous self-illustrated works, including *Pssst!,* which features a youngster's

visit to an unusual zoo, and *The True Meaning of Smekday,* a middle-grade novel about the alien conquest of Earth. "I think I write first and foremost for myself," Rex stated in an interview on the *Seven Impossible Things before Breakfast* Web site. He added, "I just kind of trust that if I write something that I find compelling or funny, and it's appropriate for kids in tone and language, that some kids will find it compelling or funny, too."

Rex developed an interest in children's literature as a teenager, while working at a bookstore. "I was hearing about Lane Smith, William Joyce, Steve Johnson and Lou Fancher, and so forth," he told Kelly R. Fineman on the *Writing and Ruminating* Web site. "The market seemed so utterly different from the books I remembered from my childhood. These were very vibrant, painterly, irreverent . . . . So at sixteen or seventeen I decided picture books might be a way to reconcile my love of making pictures and inventing stories."

Rex made his literary debut in 2003, providing the illustrations for Amy Timberlake's *The Dirty Cowboy.* In the work, a filthy cowpoke heads to the river for his annual bath, leaving his faithful dog to guard his clothes. When the canine doesn't recognize his sweet-swelling owner, however, a raucous battle for the duds ensues. "Rex's rich paintings add sparkle to the story's dramatic telling," noted *Booklist* contributor Todd Morning, and a *Publishers Weekly* reviewer applauded the artist's "farcical golden-and copper-toned illustrations, which call to mind the tall-tale humor of Andrew Glass."

The picture books of Rex, such as **Pssst!,** *reflect the high-energy perspective of their creator.* (Harcourt Inc., 2007. Copyright © 2007 by Adam Rex. Reproduced by permission of Harcourt, Inc. This material may not be reproduced in any form or by any means without the prior written permission of the publisher.)

Based on a passage from Mark Twain's memoir *Life on the Mississippi, Ste-e-e-eamboat A-comin!,* written by Jill Esbaum, describes the excitement surrounding the arrival of a steamship in a small river town. "Rex depicts the hubbub with Norman Rockwell-esque realism," observed a *Kirkus Reviews* critic. Elvira Woodruff's *Small Beauties* concerns Darcy Heart O'Hara, an Irish lass who immigrates to North America with her family after their potato crop fails. Rex's illustrations "are strongly designed, with good use of the golden light of mist, memory and longing," noted a contributor in *Kirkus Reviews.* "Rich in detail of the Irish landscape," commented Lee Bock in *School Library Journal,* "the art gives a deeper understanding of this powerful story."

In 2006 Rex published his first self-illustrated work, *Frankenstein Makes a Sandwich,* a collection of poems that spoofs famous Hollywood monsters such as the Creature from the Black Lagoon and Count Dracula. "Rex demonstrates a dizzying yet fitting variety of artistic styles, layouts and lettering," a *Publishers Weekly* critic stated. "Some of the styles were chosen because they just seemed natural for the poem in question," the illustrator remarked on the *Harcourt Books* Web site. "'Dr. Jekyll and Mr. Henderson,' for example, takes place largely at a society ball, so I tried my best to imitate the look of turn-of-the-[twentieth-]century century fashion and society artists like Charles Dana Gibson." According to Bock, *Frankenstein Makes a Sandwich* "is fresh, creative, and funny, with just enough gory detail to cause a few gasps."

In the cumulative rhyming tale *Tree-ring Circus,* a fast-growing tree provides shelter for a bevy of forest creatures and escaped circus animals. Debbie Stewart Hoskins, writing in *School Library Journal,* described Rex's self-illustrated story as "carefully designed, humorously detailed, and appropriately silly." A young girl receives a host of strange requests from the residents of her local zoo in *Pssst!,* a "gleefully postmodern romp," according to a *Kirkus Reviews* contributor. A reviewer in *Publishers Weekly* stated that Rex "conveys [the animals'] personalities with an astringent attitude and a refreshing brake on the cuteness" and deemed the work "a very funny excursion."

In Rex's illustrated middle-grade novel *The True Meaning of Smekday,* eleven-year-old Gratuity Tucci joins forces with renegade alien J. Lo to rescue the youngster's mother from the Boov, a race of extraterrestrials hoping to force all humans to live on reservations in Florida. *School Library Journal* critic Jane Henriksen Baird praised Rex's "imaginative, wacky, hilarious sci-fi story," and Lisa Von Drasek, writing in the *New York Times Book Review,* predicted that the tale "will captivate fans of the wordplay and characters in Terry Pratchett's 'Discworld' [series] and of the outrageously entertaining satire of Douglas Adams's *Hitchhiker's Guide to the Galaxy.*"

Cover of Rex's highly animated, self-illustrated picture book **Tree-Ring Circus.** (Harcourt, 2006. Copyright © 2006 by Adam Rex. Reproduced by permission of Harcourt, Inc. This material may not be reproduced in any form or by any means without the prior written permission of the publisher.)

Biographical and Critical Sources

PERIODICALS

Booklist, September 1, 2003, Todd Morning, review of *The Dirty Cowboy,* p. 131; November 1, 2004, Ilene Cooper, review of *Lucy Rose: Here's the Thing about Me,* p. 485; October 15, 2006, Kay Weisman, review of *Lucy Rose: Busy like You Can't Believe,* p. 44; October 1, 2007, Jennifer Hubert, review of *The True Meaning of Smekday,* p. 59.

Horn Book, November-December, 2007, Tanya D. Auger, review of *The True Meaning of Smekday,* p. 685.

Kirkus Reviews, June 15, 2003, review of *The Dirty Cowboy,* p. 865; March 15, 2005, review of *Ste-e-e-eamboat A-comin!,* p. 350; June 1, 2005, review of *Lucy Rose: Big on Plans,* p. 638; June 1, 2006, review of *Tree-ring Circus,* p. 579; August 1, 2006, review of *Frankenstein Makes a Sandwich,* p. 795; August 15, 2006, review of *Small Beauties: The Journey of Darcy Heart O'Hara,* p. 854; August 1, 2007, review of *Pssst!*

New York Times Book Review, November 11, 2007, Lisa Von Drasek, "Me and My Alien," review of *The True Meaning of Smekday.*

Publishers Weekly, July 14, 2003, review of *The Dirty Cowboy,* p. 75; July 10, 2006, review of *Tree-ring*

Circus, p. 80; August 28, 2006, review of *Franken-stein Makes a Sandwich,* p. 53; September 10, 2007, review of *Pssst!,* p. 59; October 1, 2007, review of *The True Meaning of Smekday,* p. 57.

School Library Journal, March, 2005, Nancy Menaldi-Scanlan, review of *Ste-e-e-eamboat A-comin'!,* p. 170; September, 2006, Lee Bock, review of *Small Beauties,* p. 188, and review of *Frankenstein Makes a Sandwich,* p. 196; October, 2006, Shawn Brommer, review of *Lucy Rose: Busy like You Can't Believe,* p. 114, and Debbie Stewart Hoskins, review of *Tree-ring Circus,* p. 124; November, 2007, Rick Margolis, "Adam Rex: Space Cadet," p. 37, and Jane Henriksen Baird, review of *The True Meaning of Smekday,* p. 135.

ONLINE

Adam Rex Home Page, http://www.adamrex.com (December 20, 2007).

Editpus Rex Blog site, http://www.adamrex.blogspot.com/ (December 20, 2007).

Harcourt Book Web site, http://www.harcourtbooks.com/ (December 20, 2007), interview with Rex.

Ironic Sans Web site, http://www.ironicsans.com/ (September 5, 2006), David Friedman, interview with Rex.

Nerds with Kids Web site, http://www.nerdswithkids.com/ (August 29, 2007), Doug Slack, interview with Rex.

Seven Impossible Things before Breakfast Web site, http://blaine.org/sevenimpossiblethings/ (September 6, 2007), Eisha and Julie Danielson, interview with Rex.

Tiny Treasury Web site, http://www.tinytreasury.com/ (April 26, 2007), "Friday Fifteen: Adam Rex."

Writing and Ruminating Web site, http://kellyrfineman. blogspot.com/ (March 1, 2007), Kelly R. Fineman, interview with Rex.

* * *

SALDAÑA, René, Jr.

Personal

Born in McAllen, TX; married; wife's name Tina; children: Lukas, Mikah. *Education:* Bob Jones University, B.A.; Clemson University, M.A.; Georgia State University, Ph.D. (English and creative writing).

Addresses

Home—Lubbock, TX. *Office*—Texas Tech University, College of Education, Box 41071, Lubbock, TX 79409. *E-mail*—rene.saldana@sbcglobal.net; rene.saldana@ttu. edu.

Career

Author and educator. University of Texas-Pan American, Edinburgh, assistant professor of English; Texas Tech University, Lubbock, assistant professor of language and literacy, 2006—. Also taught middle school and high school in Texas for six years.

Awards, Honors

Humanities Texas grant.

Writings

The Jumping Tree (novel), Delacorte Press (New York, NY), 2001.

Finding Our Way (stories), Wendy Lamb Books (New York, NY), 2003.

The Whole Sky Full of Stars (novel), Wendy Lamb Books (New York, NY), 2007.

Contributor of stories to anthologies, including *Face Relations: Stories from beneath the Skin,* Simon & Schuster (New York, NY), 2004, *Every Man for Himself: Stories about Being a Guy,* Dial Books for Young Readers (New York, NY), 2005; *Make Me Over: Eleven Stories about Transformation,* Dutton (New York, NY), 2005; *Guys Write for GUYS READ,* Viking (New York, NY), 2005; and *Owning It: Stories about Teens with Disabilities,* Candlewick Press (Cambridge, MA), 2008. Contributor of stories, poems, and reviews to periodicals, including *Boy's Life, Southwestern American Literature, Multicultural Review,* and *American Book Review.*

Sidelights

René Saldaña, Jr., is the author of critically acclaimed fiction for young adults, including the novels *The Jumping Tree* and *The Whole Sky Full of Stars.* Saldaña's short stories and novels are loosely based on the author's experiences growing up in southern Texas near the U.S.-Mexico border. A native of McAllen, Texas, Saldaña was raised in nearby Nuevo Peñitas, a town that often serves as the setting for his tales. His writings also reflect his Hispanic heritage: Saldaña's mother and father were both born in Mexico.

Saldaña's debut novel, *The Jumping Tree,* was inspired by his years as a middle-school and high school teacher in Texas. While helping his students prepare for the essay portion of the state exam, Saldaña decided to eschew the prescribed topics and instead have them write personal narratives. To provide his students with examples, he began telling stories from his own life, which he later recorded and published.

A series of interrelated vignettes, *The Jumping Tree* centers on Rey Castenada, a Mexican-American boy living in a Texas border town. The work follows Rey from sixth through eighth grade, during which the youth experiences bigotry, learns to question authority, and struggles with what it means to be a man. "Saldaña has immersed the reader in the texture and detail of hardscrabble family life," observed *New York Times Book Review* contributor Patrick Markee. Gillian Engberg, writing in *Booklist,* noted that the author's "lively, poignant work . . . asks universal questions while remain-

ing culturally specific, filled with Chicano language and customs." In *The Jumping Tree,* according to *School Library Journal* critic Gail Richmond, "Saldaña draws extended family together and binds one boy's growth into manhood with real emotion and believable events."

Saldaña's next work, the short-story collection *Finding Our Way,* focuses on a group of adolescents in Georgia and Texas. Comparing *Finding Our Way* with his earlier novel, the author told Kim Underwood in the *Winston-Salem Journal* that the story collection "is rawer and not as pretty. . . . It's not a pretty life that these young people lead these days." In the story "Alternative," for example, Arturo is expelled from school for using illegal drugs and sent to an alternative center; "Manny Calls" concerns a young man who compulsively dials the phone number of his deceased grandfather; and "The Dive" centers on a girl who attempts to prove her maturity through a dangerous rite of passage. "With a deft touch, the author creates a clear, concise picture of time and place," Richmond stated, and a *Publishers Weekly* contributor noted that Saldaña "adroitly extracts meaning from quiet moments of reflection, illustrating the emotional states of his protagonists as they approach crossroads."

In *The Whole Sky Full of Stars* Saldaña "delivers another moving coming-of-age novel about the perils of friendship and the burdens of parental expectations," according to *Booklist* reviewer Bill Ott. When Barry Esquivel learns that his best friend, Alby Alonzo, has incurred large gambling debts, he reluctantly agrees to enter a local boxing competition, hoping to split the prize money with Alby and his own widowed mother. Writing in *Kliatt,* Janis Flint-Ferguson described *The Whole Sky Full of Stars* "as a morality tale of sorts, illuminating the importance of honesty and family and best friends."

Biographical and Critical Sources

PERIODICALS

Atlanta Journal-Constitution, May 9, 2001, Rick Badie, "Life's Lessons in a First Book," p. J1.

Booklist, May 15, 2001, Gillian Engberg, review of *The Jumping Tree,* p. 1747; November 15, 2001, Hazel Rochman, review of *The Jumping Tree,* p. 567; February 15, 2003, Ed Sullivan, review of *Finding Our Way,* p. 1065; March 15, 2007, review of Bill Ott, review of *The Whole Sky Full of Stars,* p. 48.

Book Report, November-December, 2001, Barbara Siegel, review of *The Jumping Tree,* p. 66.

Horn Book, March-April, 2003, Susan P. Bloom, review of *Finding Our Way,* p. 216.

Kirkus Reviews, January 1, 2003, review of *Finding Our Way,* p. 66; January 15, 2007, review of *The Whole Sky Full of Stars,* p. 81.

Kliatt, March, 2007, Janis Flint-Ferguson, review of *The Whole Sky Full of Stars,* p. 18.

New York Times Book Review, September 16, 2001, Patrick Markee, review of *The Jumping Tree,* p. 27.

Publishers Weekly, February 3, 2003, review of *Finding Our Way,* p. 76.

School Library Journal, June, 2001, Gail Richmond, review of *The Jumping Tree,* p. 155; March, 2003, Gail Richmond, review of *Finding Our Way,* p. 237; July, 2005, Coop Renner, review of *The Jumping Tree,* p. 45; May, 2007, Marie Orlando, review of *The Whole Sky Full of Stars,* p. 142.

Winston-Salem Journal, August 22, 2004, Kim Underwood, "Deep Roots, Strong Hold," p. F1.

ONLINE

Papertigers.org, http://www.papertigers.org/ (September, 2007), Jeannine Stronach, review of *The Whole Sky Full of Stars.*

René Saldaña Web log, http://www.renesaldanajr.blogspot.com (January 1, 2008).

Teenreads, http://www.teenreads.com/ (December 20, 2007), Ashley Hartlaub, review of *Finding Our Way,* and Jana Siciliano, review of *The Whole Sky Full of Stars.*

Texas Tech University Web site, http://www.ttu.edu/ (December 20, 2007), "René Saldaña."

*   *   *

SCHNEIDER, Nina 1913-2007
(Nina Zimet Schneider)

OBITUARY NOTICE—

See index for *SATA* sketch: Born January 29, 1913, in Antwerp, Belgium; died of a stroke, September 8, 2007, in Martha's Vineyard, MA. Children's science writer and adult novelist. For many years Schneider was content to write science books for children, working with her husband, Herman Schneider. In the early years, she also wrote a few children's books on her own, including a book of classic myths for the youngest readers. After nearly eighty books, when she was nearly seventy years old, Schneider published a novel that stunned the literary world. *The Woman Who Lived in a Prologue* (1980) is the story of an aging Jewish grandmother who looks back on a life filled with one traumatic event after another. It is a tale of misplaced love, abortion, suicide, mental illness, adultery, and more. Only at the end does the narrator begin to see herself as a distinct individual—apart from the others who had such an overpowering influence on the direction of her life. The impact of the story is heightened by its intimate tone, framed as it is in the form of a memoir. Critics predicted that if *The Woman Who Lived in a Prologue* turned out to be Schneider's only adult novel, which it was, her unexpectedly talented voice would still resonate for a very long time.

OBITUARIES AND OTHER SOURCES:

PERIODICALS

New York Times, September 27, 2007, p. A28.

*   *   *

SCHNEIDER, Nina Zimet
See SCHNEIDER, Nina

*   *   *

SHAPIRO, Karen Jo 1964-

Personal

Born 1964; married; husband's name Steven; children: Elina, David. *Education:* Colby College, B.A. (English); Massachusetts School of Professional Psychology, Psy.D.

Addresses

Home and office—Greensboro, NC. *E-mail*—kj@ Kjshapiro.com.

Career

Author and psychologist. Center for Creative Leadership, member of adjunct faculty.

Member

National Register of Psychologists, Society of Children's Book Writers and Illustrators, Association of Booksellers for Children.

Writings

Because I Could Not Stop My Bike, and Other Poems, illustrated by Matt Faulkner, Whispering Coyote (Watertown, MA), 2003.
I Must Go down to the Beach Again, and Other Poems, illustrated by Judy Love, Charlesbridge (Watertown, MA), 2007.

Sidelights

A practicing psychologist, Karen Jo Shapiro developed an early love of poetry that she indulged throughout high school and into college, where she majored in English and Spanish. As Shapiro noted on her home page, along her way to her current career were "lots of different kind of jobs trying to help people have better lives." As a writer, she has inspired readers to share her love of verse, producing the books *Because I Could Not Stop My Bike, and Other Poems* and *I Must Go down to the Beach Again, and Other Poems.*

In her verse collections, Shapiro parodies classical poems and re-fashions each traditina verse favorite into a kid-friendly version highlighted with humor. For instance, the title poem of *Because I Could Not Stop My Bike, and Other Poems* imitates the rhyme and rhythm of Emily Dickinson's famous "Because I Could Not Stop for Death." Critics have praised Shapiro's fun and unique spin on such classical poems, *Childhood Education* critic Bruce Herzig noting that the book "works well as an introduction to poetry" and is even more appealing when it is read out loud. Likewise, Hazel Rochman noted in her *Booklist* review that Shapiro's "singing rhythms and rhymes show the fun of poetry" and will be even more appreciated by young children when read aloud.

Biographical and Critical Sources

PERIODICALS

Booklist, February 15, 2007, Hazel Rochman, review of *I Must Go down to the Beach Again, and Other Poems,* p. 81.

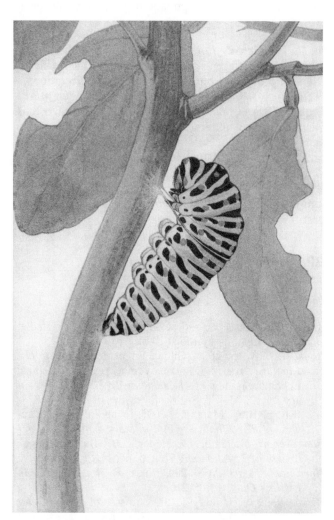

Karen Jo Shapiro introduces children to the transforming power of nature in **Butterflies,** *featuring illustrations by Jean Cassels.* (Scholastic, 2001. Illustrations copyright © 2001 by Jean Cassels. Reprinted by permission of Scholastic Inc.)

Children Education, summer, 2004, Bruce Herzig, review of *Because I Could Not Stop My Bike, and Other Poems,* p. 213.

Kirkus Reviews, December 15, 2006, review of *I Must Go down to the Beach Again, and Other Poems,* p. 1272.

Library Media Connection, February, 2004, review of *Because I Could Not Stop My Bike, and Other Poems,* p. 75.

Publishers Weekly, June 9, 2003, review of *Because I Could Not Stop My Bike, and Other Poems,* p. 51.

School Library Journal, August, 2003, Lauralyn Persson, review of *Because I Could Not Stop My Bike, and Other Poems,* p. 185; February, 2007, Kathleen Whalin, review of *I Must Go down to the Beach Again, and Other Poems,* p. 145.

ONLINE

Charlesbridge Publishing Web site, http://www.charlesbridge.com/ (December 15, 2007), "Karen Jo Shapiro" (includes teacher's guide).

Karen Jo Shapiro Home Page, http://www.kjshapiro.com (December 15, 2007).

*   *   *

SHETH, Kashmira

Personal

Born in Bhavangar, Gujarat, India; immigrated to United States at age seventeen; married; husband's name Rajan (a civil engineer); children: Rupa, Neha (daughters). *Education:* Iowa State University, B.S. (microbiology). *Hobbies and other interests:* Traveling, cooking, reading, gardening, yoga, walking.

Addresses

Home—Madison, WI.

Career

Author and scientist. Wisconsin Department of Agriculture, Trade, and Consumer Protection, Madison, microbiologist. Also teaches Indian dance to children.

Awards, Honors

Oppenheim Toy Portfolio Platinum Award, 2005, and Paul Zindel First Novel Award, both for *Blue Jasmine.*

Writings

JUVENILE FICTION

Blue Jasmine (novel), Hyperion Books (New York, NY), 2004.

Koyal Dark, Mango Sweet (novel), Hyperion Books (New York, NY), 2006.

My Dadima Wears a Sari, illustrated by Yoshiko Jaeggi, Peachtree (Atlanta, GA), 2007.

Keeping Corner (novel), Hyperion Books (New York, NY), 2007.

Sidelights

Kashmira Sheth is the author of such highly regarded young-adult novels as *Blue Jasmine* and *Koyal Dark, Mango Sweet,* as well as the picture book *My Dadima Wears a Sari.* Born in Bhavangar, India, Sheth often incorporates her memories of her homeland into her works. "My own journey from India to America and the need to tell that story in order to come full circle with the immigrant experience was a catalyst for my writing," the author stated in an interview on the Debbie Michiko Florence Web site. "I believe it is emotionally exhausting to leave one country and make a home in another. Writing about it has made me a stronger person."

Sheth came to the United States at age seventeen to attend Iowa State University, where her uncle taught. After graduating with a degree in microbiology, she landed a job with the Wisconsin Department of Agriculture, Trade, and Consumer Protection. Following the birth of

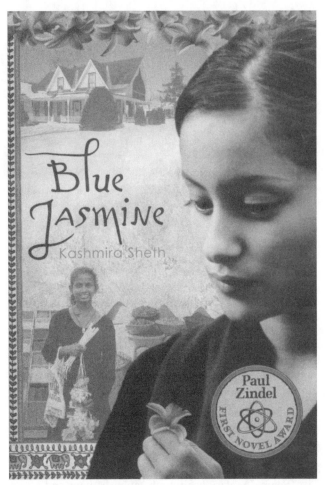

Cover of Kashmira Sheth's middle-grade novel Blue Jasmine, *featuring artwork by Kim McGillivray.* (Hyperion Books for Children, 2004. Text copyright © 2004 by Kashmira Sheth. Cover art copyright 2004 by Kim McGillivray. Reprinted by permission of Hyperion Books for Children. All rights reserved.)

Children can explore a new culture in the pages of Sheth's **My Dadima Wears a Sari,** *a picture book featuring Yoshiko Jaeggi's detailed art.* (Peachtree Publishers, 2007. Illustrations copyright © 2007 by Hoshiko Jaeggi. Reproduced by permission.)

her daughters, Sheth developed an interest in children's literature and began recording her life experiences. The author recalled that she was influenced by stories from the Indian epics *Ramayana* and *Mahabharata,* as well as by a letter she received from a relative describing his childhood in India. "It made me think that writing can make a difference," Sheth told Marla C. Maeder in the *Capital Times.* "He described everything in detail—of the spring coming, how kids would eat the tender leaves of the mango trees and make their tongues turn purple. It was very inspiring."

Sheth published her debut work of fiction, *Blue Jasmine,* in 1994. *Blue Jasmine,* which garnered the Paul Zindel First Novel Award, concerns twelve-year-old Seema Trivedi, who must adjust to U.S. culture and customs after her family moves from India to Iowa City. Seema's relationship with Mukta, a poor and often misunderstood playmate in India, helps the youngster overcome her difficulties with a bully at her new school. "Sheth deftly traces the stages of her heroine's emo-

tional development and her expanding perspective of the world," a critic in *Publishers Weekly* observed, and a contributor in *Kirkus Reviews* described the work as "a realistic emigration story told with empathy and sincerity."

Set in Mumbai, India, *Koyal Dark, Mango Sweet* centers on sixteen-year-old Jeeta, a free-thinking high schooler who considers the traditions practiced by her mother, including arranged marriages, to be restrictive and sexist. When Jeeta falls for Neel, the cousin of her new friend, they enter a clandestine romance to avoid the disapproval of Jeeta's parents. "This first-person narrative is a lush and loving exploration of coming of age," noted *School Library Journal* critic Kathleen Isaacs, and Mary Beth Cecchini, writing in *Papertigers. org,* remarked, "Sheth has created an earnest work that captures the familiar struggle to bridge modern culture with conservative tradition."

A woman explains the many and varied uses of her favorite garment to her granddaughters in Sheth's picture book *My Dadima Wears a Sari*, "a sweet story about tradition and the power of imagination," wrote *Papertigers.org* contributor Kristen Daniel. "Stories portraying Indian or Indian American families are rare for this age group," noted *Booklist* contributor Gillian Engberg, the critic praising the "continuous, loving exchange" between the family members in Sheth's story.

Keeping Corner, a work of historical fiction, is set in 1918 India. The novel is based on Sheth's great-aunt, who became a child widow during this epoch in history. The novel concerns twelve-year-old Leela, whose husband dies unexpectedly, requiring her to stay indoors, or "keep corner," for one year. Inspired by her older brother and her female tutor, both disciples of Mohandas Gandhi, Leela becomes an advocate for social change. "This powerful and enchanting novel juxtaposes Leela's journey to self-determination with the parallel struggle" of the Indian people to achieve independence from Great Britain, observed a critic in *Kirkus Reviews*.

Biographical and Critical Sources

PERIODICALS

Booklist, August, 2004, Linda Perkins, review of *Blue Jasmine*, p. 1937; April 1, 2006, Jennifer Mattson, review of *Koyal Dark, Mango Sweet*, p. 37; March 1, 2007, Gillian Engberg, review of *My Dadima Wears a Sari*, p. 90l October 15, 2007, Gillian Engberg, review of *Keeping Corner*, p. 46.

Bulletin of the Center for Children's Books, July-August, 2004, Hope Morrison, review of *Blue Jasmine*, p. 483.

Cooperative Children's Book Center, August, 2004, Kathleen Horning, review of *Blue Jasmine*.

Kirkus Reviews, May 15, 2004, review of *Blue Jasmine*, p. 497; October 1, 2007, review of *Keeping Corner*.

Publishers Weekly, August 23, 2004, review of *Blue Jasmine*, p. 55; May 1, 2006, review of *Koyal Dark, Mango Sweet*, p. 65; November 5, 2007, review of *Keeping Corner*, p. 65.

School Library Journal, August, 2004, Lee Bock, review of *Blue Jasmine*, p. 128; April, 2006, Kathleen Isaacs, review of *Koyal Dark, Mango Sweet*, p. 148; June, 2007, Alexa Sandmann, review of *My Dadima Wears a Sari*, p. 124.

Voice of Youth Advocates, August, 2004, review of *Blue Jasmine*, p. 225.

ONLINE

Debbie Michiko Florence Web site, http://www. debbimichikoflorence.com/ (February 1, 2008), Debbie Michiko Florence, interviews with Sheth.

Kashmira Sheth Web log, http://kashmirasheth.typepad. com (February 1, 2008).

Papertigers.org, http://www.papertigers.org/ (May 1, 2007), Kristen Daniel, review of *My Dadima Wears a Sari*; (July 1, 2007) Mary Beth Cecchini, review of *Koyal Dark, Mango Sweet*.*

*   *   *

SPINELLI, Eileen 1942-

Personal

Born August 16, 1942, in Philadelphia, PA; daughter of Joseph Patrick (an engineer) and Angela Marie Mesi; married Jerry Spinelli (a writer), May 21, 1977; children: six children. *Religion:* Christian. *Hobbies and other interests:* Travel, herb gardening, old movies, anything to do with tea: tea parties, afternoon tea, collecting teapots.

Addresses

Home—PA. *E-mail*—eileen@eileenspinelli.com.

Career

Writer, 1960—. Creative writing teacher. Formerly worked as a secretary, a waitress, and as a telephone receptionist.

Member

Authors Guild, Authors League, Society of Children's Book Writers and Illustrators.

Awards, Honors

Christopher Award, 1990, for *Somebody Loves You, Mr. Hatch*; Oppenheim Toy Portfolio Platinum Award, 1999, for *When Mama Comes Home Tonight*; North Carolina Children's Book Award nomination, 2001, for *Lizzie Logan, Second Banana*; Bank Street College of Education Best Children's Books of the Year award, 2001, for *In My New Yellow Shirt*, 2003, for *Here Comes the Year*; Storytelling World Award, *Horn Book*, 2002, for *Sophie's Masterpiece*; CCBC Choice designation, 2003, for *Wanda's Monster*; Carolyn Field Award, 2004, for *Do You Have a Hat?*

Writings

The Giggle and Cry Book, illustrated by Lisa Atherton, Stemmer House (Owings Mills, MD), 1981.

Thanksgiving at the Tappletons', illustrated by Maryann Cocca-Leffler, Addison-Wesley (Reading, MA), 1982, new edition illustrated by Megan Lloyd, HarperCollins (New York, NY), 2003.

Animals of the North, illustrated by Laura D'Argo, New Seasons, 1990.

Teddy Bear and His Friends, illustrated by Mike Muir, New Seasons, 1990.

Somebody Loves You, Mr. Hatch, illustrated by Paul Yalowitz, Bradbury Press (New York, NY), 1991, reprinted, 2006.

Boy, Can He Dance!, illustrated by Paul Yalowitz, Four Winds Press (New York, NY), 1993.

If You Want to Find Golden, illustrated by Stacey Schuett, Albert Whitman (Morton Grove, IL), 1993.

Lizzie Logan Wears Purple Sunglasses, illustrated by Melanie Hope Greenberg, Simon & Schuster (New York, NY), 1995.

Naptime, Laptime, illustrated by Melissa Sweet, Cartwheel Books (New York, NY), 1995.

Where Is the Night Train Going?: Bedtime Poems, Boyds Mills Press (Honesdale, PA), 1996.

Lizzie Logan Gets Married, Simon & Schuster (New York, NY), 1997.

Lizzie Logan, Second Banana, Simon & Schuster (New York, NY), 1998.

Sophie's Masterpiece: A Spider's Tale, illustrated by Jane Dyer, Simon & Schuster (New York, NY), 1998.

Sadie Plays House: A Really Messy Sticker Book!, illustrated by Margeaux Lucas, Little Simon (New York, NY), 1998.

When Mama Comes Home Tonight, illustrated by Jane Dyer, Simon & Schuster (New York, NY), 1998.

Coming through the Blizzard: A Christmas Story, Simon & Schuster (New York, NY), 1999.

Tea Party Today: Poems to Sip and Savor, illustrated by Karen Dugan, Boyds Mills Press (Honesdale, PA), 1999.

Night Shift Daddy, illustrated by Melissa Iwai, Hyperion Books for Children (New York, NY), 2000.

Song for the Whooping Crane, illustrated by Elsa Warnick, Eerdmans (Grand Rapids, MI), 2000.

Six Hogs on a Scooter, Orchard Books (New York, NY), 2000.

In My New Yellow Shirt, illustrated by Hideko Takahashi, Henry Holt (New York, NY), 2001.

A Safe Place Called Home, illustrated by Christy Hale, Marshall Cavendish (New York, NY), 2001.

Kittycat Lullaby, illustrated by Anne Mortimer, Hyperion Books for Children (New York, NY), 2001.

Summerbath, Winterbath, illustrated by Elsa Warnick, Eerdmans (Grand Rapids, MI), 2001.

Summerhouse Time, illustrated by Emily Lisker, Simon & Schuster (New York, NY), 2001, illustrated by Joanne Lew-Vriethoff, Knopf (New York, NY), 2007.

Here Comes the Year, illustrated by Keiko Narahashi, Henry Holt (New York, NY), 2002.

Inside Out Day, illustrated by Michael Chesworth, Orchard Books (New York, NY), 2002.

Rise the Moon, illustrated by Raúl Colón, Dial Books (New York, NY), 2002.

Wanda's Monster, illustrated by Nancy Hayashi, Albert Whitman (New York, NY), 2002.

Bath Time, illustrated by Janet Pederson, Cavendish Children's Books (New York, NY), 2003.

The Perfect Thanksgiving, illustrated by JoAnn Adinolfi, Henry Holt (New York, NY), 2003.

Moe McTooth: An Alley Cat's Tale, illustrated by Linda Bronson, Clarion Books (New York, NY), 2003.

What Do Angels Wear?, illustrated by Emily Arnold McCully, HarperCollins (New York, NY), 2003.

Three Pebbles and a Song, illustrated by S.D. Schindler, Dial Books (New York, NY), 2003.

City Angel, illustrated by Kyrsten Brooker, Dial Books (New York, NY), 2004.

Feathers: Poems about Birds, illustrated by Lisa McCue, Henry Holt (New York, NY), 2004.

I Know It's Autumn, illustrated by Nancy Hayashi, HarperCollins (New York, NY), 2004.

In Our Backyard Garden, illustrated by Marcy Ramsey, Simon & Schuster (New York, NY), 2004.

Something to Tell the Grandcows, illustrated by Bill Slavin, Eerdmans (Grand Rapids, MI), 2004.

While You Were Away, illustrated by Renée Graef, Hyperion Books for Children (New York, NY), 2004.

Do You Have a Hat?, illustrated by Geraldo Valério, Simon & Schuster Books for Young Readers (New York, NY), 2004.

Now It Is Winter, illustrated by Mary Newell DePalma, Eerdmans (Grand Rapids, MI), 2004.

The Best Time of the Day, illustrated by Bryan Langdo, Harcourt, Brace (Orlando, FL), 2005.

When You Are Happy, illustrated by Geraldo Valério, Simon & Schuster (New York, NY), 2006.

When Christmas Came, illustrated by Wayne Parmenter, Ideals Children's (Nashville, TN), 2006.

I Like Noisy, Mom Likes Quiet, illustrated by Lydia Halverson, Ideals Children's (Nashville, TN), 2006.

Hero Cat, illustrated by Jo Ellen McAllister Stammen, Marshall Cavendish (New York, NY), 2006.

Where I Live, illustrated by Matt Phelan, Dial Books (New York, NY), 2007.

Polar Bear, Arctic Hare: Poems of the Frozen North, illustrated by Eugenie Fernandez, Wordsong (Honesdale, PA), 2007.

Heat Wave, illustrated by Betsy Lewin, Harcourt (New York, NY), 2007.

Callie Cat, Ice Skater, Albert Whitman (Morton Grove, IL), 2007.

Baby Loves You So Much!, illustrated by David Wenzel, Ideals Children's (Nashville, TN), 2007.

Hug a Bug, illustrated by Dan Andreasen, HarperCollins (New York, NY), 2008.

The Best Story, illustrated by Anne Wilsdorf, Dial Books (New York, NY), 2008.

Poetry included in anthology *Animal Friends,* edited by Michael Hague, Holt (New York, NY), 2007. Contributor of hundreds of poems to periodicals.

Author's works have been translated into Spanish.

Sidelights

A poet and teacher of creative writing, Eileen Spinelli has produced numerous books for young children that combine the author's love of rhyme with her understanding of how young people view the world. The mother of six children and an experienced bedtime-story reader, Spinelli has a good sense of what works and what does not work in the arena of children's pic-

Via her jaunty verse, Eileen Spinelli takes readers on a tour of a busy farmyard in **The Best Time of Day,** *a book featuring Bryan Langdo's watercolor art.* (Voyager Books, 2005. Illustrations copyright © 2005 by Bryan Langdo. Reproduced by permission of Harcourt, Inc. This material may not be reproduced in any form or by any means without the prior written permission of the publisher.)

ture books. Among her own picture-book contributions are *Somebody Loves You, Mr. Hatch, The Perfect Thanksgiving, Boy, Can He Dance!*, and *Summerhouse Time*, as well as poetry collections such as *The Giggle and Cry Book, Where Is the Night Train Going?: Bedtime Poems, City Angel,* and *Polar Bear, Arctic Hare: Poems of the Frozen North*, the last a collection of two dozen verses that introduces children to the fragile ecosystem of the Arctic region. Described by *Booklist* contributor Jennifer Mattson as a "reassuring urban lullaby," *City Angel* was written in response to the September 11, 2001 tragedy and celebrates a human ecosystem: the many cultures and traditions that coexist within New York City. Brought to life in paintings by Kyrsten Brooker, Spinelli's text for *City Angel* personifies the compassion and caring of city residents in the form of a winged black woman clad in white who "offer[s] . . . quiet acts of kindness in the form of smiles, hugs or an unseen helping hand," as a *Publishers Weekly* observed.

Born in Philadelphia, Pennsylvania in 1942, Spinelli was raised in Secane, a nearby suburb. Always an enthusiastic reader, she counted among her favorite authors Marguerite de Angeli. Publishing her first work of poetry in 1950 when she was eighteen, Spinelli continued to write poetry for adults during her few free hours while raising her six children. "Teachers and our public

library played a big part in my growing interest in books and writing," Spinelli once told *SATA*.

Spinelli began writing for a younger audience in 1979, after her children had grown old enough to allow her some free time. Her first book, a rhyming list book titled *The Giggle and Cry Book,* was published two years later. *The Giggle and Cry Book* would be followed by two other books of poetry: *Naptime, Laptime* and *Where Is the Night Train Going?* In *Naptime, Laptime* Spinelli portrays a variety of animals indulging in a mid-day snooze, from field mice to Arctic seals to a young child's own stuffed animal. In *Booklist,* contributor Carolyn Phelan praised Spinelli's text for being "simple enough to suit a toddler's attention span" while also containing enough humor to keep older listeners interested. *School Library Journal* critic Rosanne Cerny dubbed the book a "poetic paean to the perfect spot" to take an afternoon nap. Sleep also serves as the focus of *Where Is the Night Train Going?,* in which Spinelli collects poems about dozing. Calling the author's verse "consistently sweet and gentle, rather than distinguished or splashy," Liza Bliss commented in her *School Library Journal* review of *Where Is the Night Train Going?* that the book's words and pictures are perfectly matched in their expression of "a mild sense of humor" and ability to recognize "young children's sensibilities."

Spinelli's first prose work for children, *Thanksgiving at the Tappletons',* reached bookstore shelves in 1982. In an offbeat portrayal of the uniquely American tradition, the Tappletons start the day hungry and watch as, one by one, each courses of their evening meal sidesteps the dining-room table. The salad has been fed to the school rabbits; the baker is out of pies by the time Mr. Tappleton has a chance to stop by, and the Thanksgiving turkey winds up floating in a pond in the backyard. "For a Thanksgiving book without pilgrims and Indians, this one just might 'talk turkey,'" quipped *School Library Journal* contributor Betty Craig Campbell of Spinelli's humorous story, while *Booklist* reviewer Ilene Cooper deemed it "appetizing fare." *Thanksgiving at the Tappletons'* was re-issued with new illustrations by Megan Lloyd that depict the Tappletons as a family of wolves, and Spinelli revisited the holiday in a second picture book, *The Perfect Thanksgiving,* in which two families share the perfect holiday feast in very different ways, one with a formal, well-mannered feast and another with a relaxing and casual dinner. "The jovial celebration of a national feast day" in *The Perfect Thanksgiving* "highlights the common thread of loving kinship" woven through Spinelli's story, according to a *Kirkus Reviews* writer.

Spinelli's output of picture books has been nothing less than prolific. Her books range widely in theme, from humorous stories such as *Something to Tell the Grandcows,* that are based on animal characters, to rhyming bedtime lullabies that are able to soothe the most fractious youngster. Featuring an all-critter cast, *Three Pebbles and a Song* re-tells the traditional "ant and grasshopper" fable but finds mice in the title roles. Although he is encouraged to help his family gather food and nesting materials for the coming winter, Moses the mouse decides to sing and dance instead. During the colder winter months that follow, Moses profits from his family's industry, and they, in turn, are entertained by his singing and dancing. A *Publishers Weekly* reviewer wrote that Spinelli's story celebrates "art's power to invigorate and to sustain."

Cats frequently appear as central characters in Spinelli's books. In *Moe McTooth: An Alley Cat's Tale,* for example, Moe enjoys prowling the city streets until the cold weather sends him in search of a warm home. Adopted by a friendly human, the cat enjoys a cozy home in an apartment during the winter, but when spring rolls around Moe must chose between returning to his street life or losing his new friend. Another wild cat is the focus of *Hero Cat,* in which a mother cat finds a safe, cozy spot in an abandoned building, and there gives birth to five kittens. When the building is devastated by fire, she manages to save her litter, helped by some caring firemen. *Callie Cat, Ice Skater* introduces a young kitten who pursues her passion although it is not shared by her two best friends, and In *Booklist* Kathleen Odean called *Moe McTooth* "a special treat

A sultry summer day comes to life when Spinelli teams up with illustrator Betsy Lewin for Heat Wave. *(Harcourt, 2007. Illustrations copyright © 2007 by Betsy Lewin. Reproduced by permission of Harcourt, Inc. This material my not be reproduced in any form or by any means without the prior written permission of the publisher.)*

for cat lovers," while Carolyn Phelan wrote in the same periodical that *Callie Cat, Ice Skater* is "a rewarding picture book" with a "gently delivered message." "Spinelli's simple, short sentences" bring to life the drama of *Hero Cat,* noted Gillian Engberg, the *Booklist* critic adding that younger children concerned over the tiny kittens "will be reassured by the story of a parent's fiercely protective unconditional love."

Some of Spinelli's books are designed for bedtime sharing. In *When Mama Comes Home Tonight* a toddler anticipates reunion with his or her working mom, and all the fun they will have in the hours they will spend between dinner and bedtime. Inevitably, of course, the rhyming book ends with lullabies. *Booklist* contributor Stephanie Zvirin called the title "tender" and "the perfect book for lap sharing." *Night Shift Daddy* puts a new spin on the bedtime story. The dad in this rhyming tale tucks his daughter in and then goes out the door to work. In the morning he returns and listens to *his* bedtime story before the girl leaves home for a day of activities. In *Rise the Moon,* poems celebrate people and creatures who welcome the soothing light of the moon as it rises and bathes the world in its own special glow. A *Publishers Weekly* critic praised the work as a "poetic tribute to the moon and the many magical and mysterious ways it influences and inspires." In her *Booklist* review of *Rise the Moon,* Engberg deemed Spinelli's story "a beautiful, reassuring celebration of night."

Other picture books by Spinelli include *Heat Wave,* which opens a nostalgic window on to how people survived the heat of summer in the days before air conditioning, as well as *Somebody Loves You, Mr. Hatch.* In *Somebody Loves You, Mr. Hatch* a retiring bachelor seems to lead a monotonous life until he receives a Valentine box filled with candy from a mysterious admirer. A contributor to *Kirkus Reviews* called the picture book "charming," adding that it contains "a real plot" and an "amiable tone" that should appeal to young listeners. In *If You Want to Find Golden* a young boy and his mother spend a day together in the city where they live and discover a rainbow of color mixed in with their everyday activities. "From the white sugar-frosted doughnut at the diner to plump purple grapes at the grocery store . . . young readers will enjoy this dawn to dusk catalogue of colors," claimed Lisa Dennis in a *School Library Journal* review.

In addition to her picture books for younger children, Spinelli has also authored a series of books for older readers that features a spunky young protagonist named Lizzie Logan. Lizzie is introduced to readers in the middle-grade novel *Lizzie Logan Wears Purple Sunglasses.* A ten year old with a formidable imagination, Lizzie proves to be a loyal friend to neighborhood newcomer Heather, despite the incredible lies she sometimes tells. While noting that Spinelli's chapter book is not a true-to-life portrait of young people, a *Kirkus Reviews* critic noted that the story "buoyantly addresses

One of Spinelli's popular young heroines stars in **Lizzie Logan Wears Purple Sunglasses,** *a book featuring illustrations by Melanie Hope Greenberg.* (Simon & Schuster Books for Young Readers, 1995. Illustrations © 1995 by Melanie Hope Greenberg. Reprinted with the permission of Simon & Schuster Books for Young Readers, an imprint of Simon & Schuster Children's Publishing Division.)

the 'problem' of a great imagination in someone who is sensitive." In her *Horn Book* review, Nancy Vasilakis predicted that the book will "provide newly fluent readers with plenty of chuckles and a few anxious moments." Spinelli continues Lizzie's imaginative adventures in two more books, *Lizzie Logan Gets Married* and *Lizzie Logan, Second Banana.*

Biographical and Critical Sources

PERIODICALS

Booklist, December 15, 1982, Ilene Cooper, review of *Thanksgiving at the Tappletons',* p. 569; December 1, 1995, Carolyn Phelan, review of *Naptime, Laptime,* p. 641; July, 1998, Stephanie Zvirin, review of *When Mama Comes Home Tonight,* p. 1879; January 1, 2003, Gillian Engberg, review of *Rise the Moon,* p. 88; April 15, 2003, Kathleen Odean, review of *Moe McTooth: An Alley Cat's Tale,* p. 1479; September 15,

2003, Kay Weisman, review of *Three Pebbles and a Song,* p. 249; November 1, 2003, Gillian Engberg, review of *What Do Angels Wear?,* p. 506; March 1, 2004, Gillian Engberg, review of *In Our Backyard Garden,* p. 1186; April 1, 2004, Terry Glover, review of *Something to Tell the Grandcows,* p. 1370; August, 2004, Carolyn Phelan, review of *I Know It's Autumn,* p. 1944; October 15, 2004, Julie Cummins, review of *Now It Is Winter,* p. 411; January 1, 2005, Jennifer Mattson, review of *City Angel,* p. 875; October 15, 2005, Shelle Rosenfeld, review of *The Best Time of Day,* p. 60; March 1, 2006, Julie Cummins, review of *When You Are Happy,* p. 101; March 1, 2006, Gillian Engberg, review of *Hero Cat,* p. 101; April 15, 2007, Hazel Rochman, review of *Polar Bear, Arctic Hare: Poems of the Frozen North,* p. 48; May 1, 2007, Ilene Cooper, review of *Heat Wave,* p. 101; October 15, 2007, Carolyn Phelan, review of *Callie Cat, Ice Skater,* p. 50.

Bulletin of the Center for Children's Books, June, 2003, review of *Moe McTooth,* p. 423; November, 2003, Karen Coats, review of *The Perfect Thanksgiving,* p. 125; March, 2004, Deborah Stevenson, review of *Something to Tell the Grandcows,* p. 296.

Horn Book, September-October, 1995, Nancy Vasilakis, review of *Lizzie Logan Wears Purple Sunglasses,* p. 605; November-December, 2007, Nell Beram, review of *Heat Wave,* p. 668.

Kirkus Reviews, December 15, 1991, review of *Somebody Loves You, Mr. Hatch,* p. 1985; June 1, 1995, review of *Lizzie Logan Wears Purple Sunglasses,* p. 787; August 15, 2003, review of *The Perfect Thanksgiving,* p. 1079; January 1, 2004, review of *Something to Tell the Grandcows,* p. 41; March 1, 2004, review of *While You Are Away,* p. 230; August 15, 2004, review of *Now It Is Winter,* p. 813; September 15, 2005, review of *The Best Time of Day,* p. 1034; March 15, 2006, review of *When You Are Happy,* p. 301; February 15, 2007, review of *Polar Bear, Arctic Hare;* May 1, 2007, review of *Summerhouse Time;* May 15, 2007, review of *Where I Live;* June 15, 2007, review of *Heat Wave;* September 15, 2007, review of *Callie Cat, Ice Skater.*

Publishers Weekly, May 8, 2000, review of *Night Shift Daddy,* p. 221; December 16, 2002, review of *Rise the Moon,* p. 66; August 23, 2003, review of *Three Pebbles and a Song,* p. 63; September 22, 2003, review of *The Perfect Thanksgiving,* p. 65; January 17, 2005, review of *City Angle,* p. 55; July 9, 2007, review of *Heat Wave,* p. 52.

School Library Journal, March, 1983, Betty Craig Campbell, review of *Thanksgiving at the Tappletons',* p. 167; January, 1994, Lisa Dennis, review of *If You Want to Find Golden,* pp. 99-100; February, 1996, Rosanne Cerny, review of *Naptime, Laptime,* p. 90; April, 1996, Liza Bliss, review of *Where Is the Night Train Going?,* pp. 130-131; April, 2003, Marge Loch-Wouters, review of *Moe McTooth,* p. 138; September, 2004, Kathleen Kelly MacMillan, review of *Now It Is Winter,* p. 181; February, 2005, Martha Topol, review of *City Angel,* p. 110; January, 2006, Lisa S. Schindler, review of *The Best Time of Day,* p. 114; April, 2006, Carol L. MacKay, review of *Hero Cat,* p. 118;

May, 2007, Teresa Pfeifer, review of *Polar Bear, Arctic Hare,* p. 125; Nancy Brown, review of *Summerhouse Time,* p. 144; June, 2007, Judy Chichinski, review of *Heat Wave,* p. 125; July, 2007, Marilyn Taniguchi, review of *Where I Live,* p. 85.

ONLINE

Eileen Spinelli Home Page, http://www.eileenspinelli.com (January 10, 2008).

V-Z

van OMMEN, Sylvia 1978-

Personal

Born December 16, 1978, in Baarn, Netherlands. *Education:* Attended Constantijn Huygens Art Academy.

Addresses

Home—Rijnsburg, Netherlands. *E-mail*—sylviavan ommen@gmail.com.

Career

Author, illustrator, and animator. Illustrator for magazines, newspapers, and educational publications; cocreator, with Maurice van der Bij, of animated television show *de Show van Niks* ("The Show about Nothing").

Writings

(Self-illustrated) *Drops,* Lemniscaat (Rotterdam, Netherlands), 2002, published as *Jellybeans,* Roaring Brook Press (Brookfield, CT), 2004, published as *Sweets,* Winged Chariot Press (Kent, England), 2005.

(Self-illustrated) *De verassing,* Lemniscaat (Rotterdam, Netherlands), 2002, published as *The Surprise,* Front Street Books (Asheville, NC), 2007.

Marleen Westera, *Schaap en Geit,* Lemniscaat (Rotterdam, Netherlands), 2004, translated by Nancy Forest-Flier as *Sheep and Goat,* Front Street Books (Asheville, NC), 2006.

Marleen Westera, *Verteten—per twaalf exemplaren,* Lemniscaat (Rotterdam, Netherlands), 2008.

Sidelights

Sylvia van Ommen is the author and illustrator of the well-received picture books *Jellybeans* and *The Surprise.* Born in Baarn, Netherlands, van Ommen studied at the Constantijn Huygens Art Academy in Kampen and later contributed illustrations to a variety of magazines, newspapers, and educational publications.

First published in the Netherlands, *Jellybeans* centers on the philosophical musings of two friends: Oscar the cat and George the rabbit. While snacking on jellybeans in the park, the duo ponder the existence of heaven and the meaning of friendship. "The book is very pure, very basic," observed Ilene Cooper in *Booklist,* and a *Kirkus Reviews* critic applauded the "feather light treatment of the weightiest subject . . . all of it made charmingly comprehensible" by the author/illustrator's work. According to a contributor in *Publishers Weekly,* van Ommen's "spare artwork is as streamlined, childlike and winsome as her narrative, which is likely to inspire dialogue . . . about what might lie ahead."

In *The Surprise,* a wordless picture book, a fluffy sheep primps before a mirror, then dashes off to purchase some bright red dye. After her fleece is colored, the protagonist shears it off and heads to a poodle's shop, where the wool is spun into yarn. Returning home, the sheep grabs her knitting needles and transforms the yarn into a wonderful garment for a friend. "Van Ommen's charming compositions in thickly applied gouache clearly chronicle the sequence of events," Jennifer Mattson remarked in *Booklist,* and a *Publishers Weekly* reviewer similarly noted that the book's "bright, spare paintings offer just enough detail and information to keep pages turning." A contributor in *Kirkus Reviews* described *The Surprise* as "a feel-good tale in any language, bright in both mood and color."

Van Ommen also provided the artwork for Marleen Westera's *Sheep and Goat,* a collection of short tales about an unlikely friendship. Though quiet, reflective Sheep and gregarious, curious Goat appear to be mismatched in every way, their concern for one another is evident. "Simple, evocative drawings perfectly complement the story's warmth and generous spirit," noted a *Kirkus Reviews* critic. According to Elizabeth Bird, writing in *School Library Journal,* van Ommen's "pen-and-ink drawings are pitch perfect and more than a little extraordinary."

Biographical and Critical Sources

PERIODICALS

Booklist, April 15, 2005, Ilene Cooper, review of *Jelly-beans,* p. 1462; May 15, 2007, Jennifer Mattson, review of *The Surprise,* p. 53.

Guardian (London, England), November 12, 2005, Julia Eccleshare, "Head and Heart," review of *Sweets.*

Kirkus Reviews, April 15, 2005, review of *Jellybeans,* p. 483; November 1, 2006, review of *Sheep and Goat,* p. 1125; March 1, 2007, review of *The Surprise,* p. 233.

Publishers Weekly, April 11, 2005, review of *Jellybeans,* p. 54; May 14, 2007, review of *The Surprise,* p. 52.

School Library Journal, June, 2005, Marianne Saccardi, review of *Jellybeans,* p. 130; November, 2006, Elizabeth Bird, review of *Sheep and Goat,* p. 116; May, 2007, Marianne Saccardi, review of *The Surprise,* p. 110.

A wooly sheep creates the perfect gift for a special friend in Sylvia van Ommen's fanciful self-illustrated **The Surprise.** (Lemniscaat, an imprint of Boyds Mills Press, Inc., 2007. Copyright © 2003 by Sylvia van Ommen. Reproduced by permission of Boyds Mills Press, Inc.)

ONLINE

Luster Productions Web site, http://www.illuster.nl/ (December 20, 2007), "Sylvia van Ommen."
Show about Nothing Web site, http://www.theshowabout nothing.eu/ (December 20, 2007), "Sylvia van Ommen."
Sylvia van Ommen Home Page, http://www.sylviavanom men.com (December 20, 2007).

* * *

WAHL, Mats 1945-

Personal
Born May 10, 1945, in Malmö, Sweden.

Addresses
Home—Sweden.

Career
Novelist.

Awards, Honors
Nils Holgersson Medal, 1989; Nordiske Börnebogspriset, 1990; Augustpriset, 1993, for *Vinterviken;* ABF literaturpris, 1994; Janusz Korczak prize, 1994; Deutscher Jugendliteraturpreis, 1996; Kulturpriset Till Adam Brombergs minne, 2002.

Writings

NOVELS

Honungsdrömmen, Liberförlag (Stockholm, Sweden), 1980.
Hallonörnen, 1980.
Vinterfå gel, 1981.
Förstå else och handling, 1982.
Guntzborg Jöntzon, 1982.
Norrpada, 1982.
Döläge, 1983.
Ungdomspedagogik, 1984.
Halva sanningen, Raben & Sjögren (Stockholm, Sweden), 1984.
Havsörnsvalsen, 1985.
Hat, 1985.
Jiggen, 1985.
Husbonden (also see below), 1985.
Utbildning och klass, 1986.
Mannen som älskade kvinnor, 1986.
Den lackerade apan, 1986.
Anna—Carolinas krig, Bonniers (Stockholm, Sweden), 1986.
Skrinet, Carlsson (Stockholm, Sweden), 1986.

Jac Uppmuntraren, 1987.
Play It Again, 1987.
Sjöbo, 1988.
Maj Darlin, 1988.
Fanfars lajka, illustrated by Tord Nygren, translated as *Grandfather's Laika,* Lerner (Minneapolis, MN), 1990.
Kärlek i September, 1990.
Sagan om den lilla krå kodillen, 1990.
Därvarns resa, 1991.
Nå ra riktigt fina dar, 1992.
Vinterviken (title means "Winter Bay"; also see below), 1993.
Vildmarksfiskaren, 1994.
I ballong över Stilla havet, 1994.
Lilla Marie, 1995.
Nu seglar Vasa, 1995.
Emma och Daniel—Mötet (title means "Emma and Daniel: The Meeting"; also see below), 1996.
De övergivna, 1997.
3 Pjäser, 1998.
(With Sven Nordqvist) *Den långa resan,* 1998.
Emma och Daniel: Kärleken, 1998.
Emma och Daniel: Resan, 1998.
John-John, 1999.
Folket i Birka på vikingarnas tid, 1999.
Den osynlige, 2000, translated by Katerina E. Tucker as *The Invisible,* Farrar, Straus & Giroux (New York, NY), 2007.
Halva sanningen, 2001.
Så pa, 2001.
Tjafs, 2002.
Kill, 2003.
Svenska för idioter, 2003.
Å terkomst, 2005.
Den vilda drömmen, 2006.

OTHER

På spaning efter växandets punkt (reader), Liberförlag (Stockholm, Sweden), 1978.
Konsten att undervisa (reader), Liberförlag (Stockholm, Sweden), 1979.
(Adaptor with Kjell Sundvall) *Husbonden* (television film; based on his novel), Tiger Film/SVT Drama, 1989.
(Adaptor with Sara Heldt) *Vinterviken* (screenplay; based on his novel), FilmTeknik/Svenska Fiminstitutet, 1996.
(Adaptor with Ingela Magner) *Emma och Daniel—Mötet* (screenplay; based on his novel), Sone Film/ Omega Film, 2003.

Writer for television, including for *Sexton* (miniseries, 1996.

Adaptations
Halva sanningen was adapted for film, 2001; *Den osynlige* was adapted as a film by Mick Davis, directed by Joel Bergvall, and produced by Nordisk Film Production, 2002; it was also adapted by Davis and Christne Roum as *The Invisible,* directed by David S. Goyer, 2007.

Sidelights

Well known as a writer for young people in his native Sweden, Mats Wahl published his first book in 1978 and his first novel, *Honungsdrömmen,* two years later. A prolific author, Wahl has continued to produce fiction at a steady rate, averaging a book per year since 1980. Several of his novels have been adapted for film by the author; in addition his 2000 novel *Den osynlige* was adapted for film twice, in versions for both Swedish and English-language audiences.

Den Osynlige—translated into English as *The Invisible*—is the story of Hilmer Eriksson, a fifteen-year-old high schooler living in rural Sweden. Although Hilmer is living what most readers would describe as a perfect life—a good student, he has a nice girlfriend and excels at several hobbies—things are not going as smoothly as some would think. A particular problem is caused by an angry classmate named Annie. One morning things go from annoying to strange, when Hilmer realizes that he has suddenly become invisible. Recognizing that this condition began during a bike ride to a neighboring town, Hilmer determines to make sense of the mystery, doing so by "haunting" Detective Harald Fors, the policeman who has been assigned to investigate the teen's disappearance. "The intriguing premise of this suspenseful novel will pull readers right into contemporary Sweden," wrote a *Publishers Weekly* contributor, the critic also praising Wahl's use of a succinct text with shifting narratives to increase the plot's suspense. In what *Booklist* contributor Kathleen Odeon described as "skillful, understated prose," *The Invisible* reveals "the dark side of modern society" in a story Odeon characterized as "less a mystery than a human tragedy."

Wahl's award-winning 1993 novel *Vinterviken* focuses on John-John, a black boy who lives with his mother and stepfather in a Stockholm suburb. When the boy and friends rescue ten-year-old Patricia from a public pool, the girl's father rewards them by inviting them to his home in an affluent neighborhood. Here John-John meets Patricia's older sister, Elisabeth, and falls in love. The teen romance is constantly thwarted by Elizabeth's father, as well as by the many cultural differences in the worlds that the two teens inhabit. Part of a series of novels featuring two preteens, *Emma och Daniel—Mötet* introduces twelve-year old Emma, who lives in Lapland with her fisherman father Anders. In her home in northern Sweden, fishing occupies much of the girl's life and there is no electricity. When the widowed and lonely Anders invites Sara, a woman from Stockholm with whom he has been corresponding, to visit the family, Emma is upset. Even more upsetting is the fact that Sara is bringing her son Daniel, a boy Emma's age. Daniel is equally unenthusiastic about the visit: he misses his computer. When the two children join an elderly fisherman on a three-day fishing trip into the forest wilderness, tragedy follows, and they must join

together in order to find their way back to civilization. Emma and Daniel's adventures continue in *Emma och Daniel: Kärleken* and *Emma och Daniel: Resan;* in addition, the first book in the popular trilogy was adapted for film by Wahl in 2003.

Biographical and Critical Sources

PERIODICALS

Booklist, March 15, 2007, Kathleen Odean, review of *The Invisible,* p. 45.
Publishers Weekly, February 5, 2007, review of *The Invisible,* p. 61.
School Library Journal, April, 2007, Shannon Seglin, review of *The Invisible,* p. 150.
Voice of Youth Advocates, April, 2007, Heather Pittman, review of *The Invisible,* p. 58.

*   *   *

WALLACE, Nancy Elizabeth 1948-

Personal

Born May 16, 1948, in New York, NY; daughter of John and Alexine Wallace; married Peter E. Banks (a high school teacher). *Education:* University of Connecticut, B.A., M.A. (child development). *Hobbies and other interests:* Sailing, hiking, camping, theater, museums, gardening, bike riding.

Addresses

Home—Branford, CT. *Agent*—Sterling Lord Literistic, 65 Bleecker St., New York, NY 10012.

Career

Author. Yale-New Haven Hospital, New Haven, CT, director of Volunteer Services, coordinator of Child Life Program; preschool teacher, day-care teacher, and consultant, 1972-92. A Better Chance and Read to Grow (ABC; Connecticut literacy program), volunteer.

Member

Society of Children's Book Writers and Illustrators.

Awards, Honors

Honors award, National Parenting Publications honors award, 1995, for *Snow;* Gold award, Oppenheim Toy Portfolio, 2000, both for *Rabbit's Bedtime;* Best Book of the Year citation, Bank Street College of Education, 2000, for *Apples, Apples, Apples,* 2001, for *Count down to Clean Up!,* 2002, for *Pumpkin Day!,* 2003, for

Leaves! Leaves! Leaves!; ForeWord award, 2001 for *A Taste of Honey;* Best Books recommendation, Association of Booksellers, and International Honor Book designation, Society of School Librarians, both 2003, both for *Leaves! Leaves! Leaves!;* International Honor Book designation, Society of School Librarians, and Children's Book Council Showcase Nonfiction Picture Book designation, both 2004, both for *Seeds! Seeds! Seeds!;* Best Children's Books for Family Literacy award, 2005, and Connecticut Book Award for Best Illustrator, and Best Books for Babies honor, Beginning with Books, both 2006, all for *Alphabet House;* National Parenting Publications Honors Award, 2007, for *Shells! Shells!*

Shells!; Mockingbird Award, and Kids' Wings Award, both 2008, both for *Look! Look! Look!*

Writings

SELF-ILLUSTRATED PICTURE BOOKS

Snow, Golden Books (New York, NY), 1995.
Rabbit's Bedtime, Houghton Mifflin (Boston, MA), 1999, bilingual edition, with Spanish translation by Annie Garcia Kaplan, published as *Hora de dormir del conejo/Rabbit's Bedtime,* 2000.

Readers meet a group of silly but loving rabbit friends in Nancy Elizabeth Wallace's self-illustrated picture book **Tell-a-Bunny.** (Marshall Cavendish, 2000.

Tell-a-Bunny, Winslow Press (Delray Beach, FL), 2000.

Apples, Apples, Apples, Winslow Press (Delray Beach, FL), 2000.

Paperwhite, Houghton Mifflin (Boston, MA), 2000.

A Taste of Honey, Winslow Press (Delray Beach, FL), 2001.

Count down to Clean Up!, Houghton Mifflin (Boston, MA), 2001.

Pumpkin Day!, Marshall Cavendish (Tarrytown, NY), 2002.

Recycle Every Day!, Marshall Cavendish (Tarrytown, NY), 2003.

Baby Day!, Houghton Mifflin (Boston, MA), 2003.

The Sun, the Moon, and the Stars, Houghton Mifflin (Boston, MA), 2003.

Leaves! Leaves! Leaves!, Marshall Cavendish (Tarrytown, NY), 2003.

The Valentine Express, Marshall Cavendish (New York, NY), 2004.

Alphabet House, Marshall Cavendish (New York, NY), 2005.

The Kindness Quilt, Marshall Cavendish (New York, NY), 2006.

(With Linda K. Friedlaender) *Look! Look! Look!,* Marshall Cavendish (New York, NY), 2006.

Shells! Shells! Shells!, Marshall Cavendish (New York, NY), 2007.

Fly, Monarch! Fly!, Marshall Cavendish (New York, NY), 2008.

Author's original art and writings are archived at the Northeast Children's Literature Collection, Dodd Center, University of Connecticut.

Sidelights

Nancy Elizabeth Wallace is an author and illustrator noted for her colorful cut-paper collage art. Her first picture book, *Snow,* was warmly received by critics who praised both the nostalgic, fun-loving story and Wallace's illustrations. In this story, a grandfather rabbit recalls the fun he and his brother had long ago, when the first snow of the winter finally arrived. Wallace was praised for her ability to "capture . . . the quiet magic and cozy charm of a cold, snowy day with loved ones," by Roni Schotter in the *New York Times Book Review.* Likewise, Patricia Pearl Dole, writing in *School Library Journal,* noted that Wallace's illustrations, characterized by bright colors, spare shapes, and an auspicious use of white space, "gives a feeling of primitive exuberance to the pictures."

In *Rabbit's Bedtime* Wallace tells the story of a young rabbit preparing for bed and recalling the day's events in a simple rhyme. The action "is impressively captured in Wallace's distinct cut-paper artwork," remarked a contributor to *Kirkus Reviews.* Although *School Library Journal* critic Sue Sherif described the overall effect of the book almost too sweet, "the clean design and the book's small, square format make it a likely success," she added. Another rabbit is cast in *Tell-a-Bunny,* in

which Sunny the bunny asks her friends to spread the word about a surprise party she is planning for friend Earl. With each phone call, the facts about the party get more and more mixed up, and on the day of the party Sunny's guests arrive at her house at six in the morning rather than at six at night. "Whether or not kids are familiar with 'telephone,' they'll recognize the humorous confusion that miscommunication can bring," observed Steven Engelfried in a review of *Tell-a-Bunny* for *School Library Journal.*

In *Apples, Apples, Apples* Wallace adds a recipe for applesauce, instructions for making prints from apples, famous apple sayings, and an apple song to a story about a bunny family that goes to an apple orchard. Additional information about growing apples and the history of the fruit are planted within the book's illustrations, engaging the interest of older readers as well. "Bold shapes and monochromatic backgrounds keep the pictures clean and uncluttered," remarked Joy Fleishhacker in *School Library Journal,* and *Booklist* contributor Ilene Cooper praised Wallace's "wonderful paper-cut artwork."

Wallace's artwork and the innate attractions of the natural world work their magic in *Paperwhite,* as a young friend and an old friend plant a narcissus bulb in the dead of winter. Awaiting the arrival of the flower's bloom in spring, they make cookies and knit scarves, string beads, and play the piano. As in her other stories, Wallace's illustrations add further dimensions to her text; here they show the passing days through subtle changes in the light as little Lucy Rabbit arrives each day at 4:30. Praised by *School Library Journal* contributor Wendy Lukehart as "a lovely paean to the simple acts shared by friends," *Paperwhite* celebrates "both the wonders of nature and the pleasures of a loving intergenerational friendship," according to a *Publishers Weekly* contributor.

Like *Apples, Apples, Apples* and *Paperwhite, A Taste of Honey* instructs preschoolers while also entertaining them. In this story, young Lily Bear asks question after question of Poppy Bear. Along with Wallace's readers, Lily learns where honey comes from, starting with the jar on the shelf and leading inevitably back to bees. Sidebars allow the author to include additional information, but the main text and the colorful cut-paper illustrations are designed with preschoolers in mind. The result is "a picture book well designed to explain and entertain," according to Carolyn Phelan in *Booklist.*

In *Shells! Shells! Shells!* Buddy Bear and his mother visit the seashore, where Buddy learns what sort of creatures once occupied the many different shells deposited by the tide. Buddy returns in *Leaves! Leaves! Leaves!,* as a walk during a fall day generates a wealth of information about the colorful leaves that float from the sky. *Seeds! Seeds! Seeds!* finds the young cub the recipient of a special gift from his plant-loving grandfather: five craft projects that involve seeds of all sorts.

Cover of Wallace's self-illustrated ecology-minded picture book Recycle Every Day! (Marshall Cavendish, 2003. Copyright © 2003 by Nancy Elizabeth Wallace. Reproduced by permission.)

Praising *Seeds! Seeds! Seeds!* as "clearly written and brightly illustrated," Carolyn Phelan wrote in *Booklist* that Wallace's activity-filled picture books "will be an appealing addition to classroom units on seeds and germination." "Wallace successfully blends fiction and nonfiction, art and informational text" in *Leaves! Leaves! Leaves!,* according to *School Library Journal* contributor Rachel G. Payne, the critic adding that Buddy's "lively curiosity" will inspire young children to ask their own questions.

Alexander, Kiki, and Kat, three spunky mouse characters, star in another book by Wallace that has an echo-

ing title. In *Look! Look! Look!* the tiny rodents give a mini-lesson in art appreciation as they isolate and explore the different elements in a classic painting. In *Kirkus Reviews*, a reviewer called *Look! Look! Look!* "an accessible book, packed with learning opportunities," while *School Library Journal* contributor Andrea Tarr predicted that Wallace's entertaining volume "encourages originality while inspiring creativity."

Wallace introduces young children to civic-mindedness in the picture books *Count down to Clean Up!* and *Recycle Every Day!,* both of which feature her characteristic bunny characters. In the first book, ten bunnies, each with a unique color and sporting a clue as to its special interest, travel down the street. Although each bunny disappears into a shop along the way, all ten convene at a nearby park armed with the supplies they have acquired to help them perform their unique role in a group fix-up project. "Children will delight in figuring out who went where and who got what," predicted GraceAnne A. DeCandido in her *Booklist* review of *Count down to Clean Up!* Noting that Wallace makes use of found paper in her illustrations, Roxanne Burg concluded in *School Library Journal* that the author/illustrator "has cleverly combined the medium with a message of caring for the local community and its resources."

In *Recycle Every Day!* readers meet a young bunny named Minna. Because Minna hopes to win a poster contest about recycling, she talks with her parents to find out what sorts of things go into the activity. From composting to reusing and repairing to donating used clothing, the girl finds a wealth of subjects to include in her artwork. Noting that Wallace's "story is a vehicle for the Be Green message," a *Kirkus Reviews* writer predicted that "young readers won't mind," due to the games and recycling facts and challenges the author includes in the book. The *Kirkus Reviews* writer concluded that *Recycle Every Day!* provides readers with an "excellent introduction to this increasingly important subject," while in *Booklist,* Julie Cummins predicted that the book, with its simple story and cut-paper art, "will encourage children to make the world a cleaner, greener place." Minna returns in several other titles by Wallace, among them *The Kindness Quilt,* which inspires young readers with its focus on the little gestures that make "a better world," according to Cooper.

The seasonal picture book *Pumpkin Day!* celebrates a favorite autumn activity through the eyes of a loving rabbit family. During a day spent in a pumpkin field, the flop-eared family members learn about the different kinds of pumpkins and how they are grown. Soon pumpkins are carved into jack-o-lanterns, the seeds baked, and pumpkin muffins consumed. Wallace's illustrations include pumpkin facts on signposts and she includes a recipe so that readers can bake up pumpkin muffins at their own home. "The origami-and-paper collages placed against pure backgrounds are the best Wallace has done to date," concluded Cooper in her *Booklist* review of *Pumpkin Day!* In *Kirkus Reviews* a critic noted that, with "a bit of science" and "a dab of folklore," the author-illustrator crafts an "inviting" fall storytime offering. Another seasonal picture book, *The Valentine Express,* introduces the history and traditions surrounding the late-winter holiday, combining a simple story featuring Minna the rabbit with project ideas that will have "crafty youngsters . . . run[ning] for the scissors, glue and construction paper," according to a *Publishers Weekly* critic.

Wallace once told *SATA:* "I keep a quote by Joseph Campbell on my desk: 'If you follow your bliss, you put yourself on a kind of track that has been there the whole while, waiting for you, and the life that you ought to be living is the one you are living.'

"I had worked for years at Yale-New Haven Hospital (YNHH) on Pediatrics as a child-life specialist (therapeutic play) and coordinator of the program. We used play, art, music, creative writing, medical play, and puppetry to help infants, toddlers, preschool and school age children, and adolescents to cope with the stress of being in the hospital. These experiences gave children an important sense of normalcy, choice, and control, and the opportunity to express their thoughts, fears, fantasies, and misconceptions. In this acute-care setting, we worked with pediatric patients with burns, cardiac problems, spinal column injuries, cancer, and cystic fibrosis. I prepared children for surgery, medical tests, even to have limbs amputated; and provided play for children up to within hours of their death. I burned out.

"Next came Volunteer Services, administering the YNHH program with over one thousand volunteers, many in highly sophisticated patient support and educator roles. While I was director, we initiated a creative arts program; it won an American Hospital Association Award. Musicians visited patients' bedsides in the intensive-care units, art docents brought prints to patients and gave mini lectures, and comedians brought laughter to the AIDS floor. The power of the arts was clear to me. But it was one of those eighty-hour-a-week positions with no boundaries; there was always more, more, more that could be done. There was little time or energy for my family and friends. I needed to find better life balance.

"So, I registered for two adult education courses; a three-session Scherenschnitte class (a traditional form of paper cutting) and for what I thought was a ten-session children's-book-writing course. The emphasis would be on illustration; the other students were all artists! I thought, 'Okay, well, I'll try cutting paper for my illustrations.' After submitting an assignment, the instructor told me, 'You've found your medium.'

"I sent my work out and received rejections. Then one project was picked out of the 'slush pile' and at the first meeting with the editor, *Snow* was accepted on the spot. Because I was now a published author I was hired by LEARN to be an author-in-residence to work with inner-city and suburban school children, helping them to write and illustrate their own books.

"Because I was a children's book author and had worked at Yale-New Haven Hospital, when a committee with a vision of creating a Books for Babies literacy program formed in 1998, I was invited to join them and to write 'the book'! *Rabbit's Bedtime,* illustrated with cut paper, is about balance and taking time to do the important little BIG things in life. *Rabbit's Bedtime*—or the bilingual version, *Hora de dormir del conejo/*

***Wallace's popular cut-paper rabbit characters again take center stage in* The Kindness Quilt.** (Marshall Cavendish, 2006. Text and illustrations copyright © 2006 by Nancy Elizabeth Wallace. Reproduced by permission.)

Rabbit's Bedtime—is given to every newborn at three Connecticut hospitals; and Read to Grow keeps growing!"

Biographical and Critical Sources

PERIODICALS

Booklist, November 15, 1995, Susan Dove Lempke, review of *Snow,* p. 565; May 15, 2000, Helen Rosenberg, review of *Tell-a-Bunny,* p. 1750; October 15, 2000, Ilene Cooper, review of *Apples, Apples, Apples,* p. 448; November 15, 2000, Shelley Townsend-Hudson, review of *Paperwhite,* p. 651; January 1, 2001, Isabel Schon, review of *Hora de dormir del conejo/Rabbit's Bedtime,* p. 973; February 15, 2001,

Carolyn Phelan, review of *A Taste of Honey,* p. 1142; September 15, 2001, GraceAnne A. DeCandido, review of *Count down to Clean Up!,* p. 233; August, 2002, Ilene Cooper, review of *Pumpkin Day!,* p. 1963; February 15, 2003, Ilene Cooper, review of *Baby Day!,* p. 1078; April 1, 2003, Julie Cummins, review of *Recycle Every Day!,* p. 1404; November 1, 2003, Karin Snelson, review of *Leaves! Leaves! Leaves!,* p. 507; January 1, 2004, Carolyn Phelan, review of *The Sun, the Moon, and the Stars,* p. 870; April 15, 2004, Carolyn Phelan, review of *Seeds! Seeds! Seeds!,* p. 1449; November 15, 2004, Ilene Cooper, review of *The Valentine Express,* p. 594; November 1, 2005, Karen Hutt, review of *Alphabet House,* p. 54; *Look! Look! Look!,* p. 94; October 1, 2006, Ilene Cooper, review of *The Kindness Quilt,* p. 61; May 15, 2007, Carolyn Phelan, review of *Shells! Shells! Shells!,* p. 53.

Bulletin of the Center for Children's Books, November, 2000, review of *Paperwhite,* p. 124; October, 2002, review of *Pumpkin Day!,* p. 84; April, 2006, Deborah Stevenson, review of *Look! Look! Look!,* p. 376.

Kirkus Reviews, September 15, 1995, review of *Snow,* p. 1360; September 1, 1999, review of *Rabbit's Bedtime,* p. 1423; August 1, 2001, review of *Count down to Clean Up!,* p. 1134; August 1, 2002, review of *Pumpkin Day!,* p. 1146; February 1, 2003, review of *Baby Day!,* p. 242; March 1, 2003, review of *Recycle Every Day!,* p. 401; August 15, 2005, review of *Alphabet House,* p. 924; March 1, 2006, review of *Look! Look! Look!,* p. 242; August 1, 2006, review of *The Kindness Quilt,* p. 797; February 15, 2007, review of *Shells! Shells! Shells!*

New York Times Book Review, November 12, 1995, Roni Schotter, review of *Snow,* p. 42.

Publishers Weekly, November 6, 1995, review of *Snow,* p. 93; June 26, 2000, review of *Apples, Apples, Apples,* p. 74; September 4, 2000, review of *Paperwhite,* p. 107; March 19, 2001, review of *A Taste of Honey,* p. 99; December 6, 2004, review of *The Valentine Express,* p. 59.

School Library Journal, December, 1995, Patricia Pearl Dole, review of *Snow,* p. 93; November, 1999, Sue Sherif, review of *Rabbit's Bedtime,* p. 132; May, 2000, Steven Engelfried, review of *Tell-a-Bunny,* p. 156; September, 2000, Joy Fleishhacker, review of *Apples, Apples, Apples,* p. 211; October, 2000, Wendy Lukehart, review of *Paperwhite,* p. 141; June, 2001, Janet M. Bair, review of *A Taste of Honey,* p. 141; October, 2001, Roxanne Burg, review of *Count down to Clean Up!,* p. 133; November, 2002, Melinda Piehler, review of *Pumpkin Day!,* p. 140.

Teaching Children Mathematics, January, 2002, David Whitin, review of *Paperwhite,* p. 299; November, 2002, Melinda Piehler, review of *Pumpkin Day!,* p. 140; March, 2003, Gay Lunn Van Vleck, review of *Baby Day!,* p. 210; April, 2003, Carolyn Janssen, review of *Recycle Every Day!,* p. 142; September, 2003, Rachel G. Payne, review of *Leaves! Leaves! Leaves!,* p. 193; December, 2003, Deborah Rothaug, review of *The Sun, the Moon, and the Stars,* p. 140; June, 2004, Sandra Welzenbach, review of *Seeds! Seeds! Seeds!,* p. 121; December, 2004, review of *The Valentine Express,* p. 123; October, 2005, Susan E. Murray, review of *Alphabet House,* p. 131; March, 2006, Andrea Tarr, review of *Look! Look! Look!,* p. 204; November, 2006, Maren Ostergard, review of *The Kindness Quilt,* p. 115; May, 2007, Lynn K. Vanca, review of *Shells! Shells! Shells!,* p. 111.

ONLINE

Balkin Buddies Web site, http://www.balkinbuddies.com/ (January 15, 2008), "Nancy Elizabeth Wallace."

Winslow Press Web site, http://www.winslowpress.com/ (January 10, 2008), "Nancy Elizabeth Wallace."*

*   *   *

WEINHEIMER, Beckie 1958-

Personal

Born 1958, in Murray, UT; married; children: two daughters. *Education:* Brigham Young University, B.S.;

Beckie Weinheimer (Photo by Alan Kearl. Courtesy of Beckie Weinheimer.)

Attended University of California, Los Angeles; Vermont College, M.F.A. (writing). *Hobbies and other interests:* Traveling, watching movies, walking in the park, cleaning while listening to books.

Addresses

Home and office—Queens, NY. *E-mail*—beckie weinheimer58@yahoo.com.

Career

Author.

Awards, Honors

Best Books nomination, American Library Association, 2007, for *Converting Kate.*

Writings

Converting Kate, Viking Children's Books (New York, NY), 2007.

Sidelights

Beckie Weinheimer fell in love with writing as a high-school student, although she did not consider it as a profession until the death of her first daughter. Realizing that writing gave her a sense of identity at a difficult time in her life, she took writing courses at the University of California, Los Angeles, then enrolled in

Vermont College's M.F.A program. In an online interview for *Authors Den*, Weinheimer commented that her goal as an author is "to connect with those people who are looking for someone to understand them." Recalling the feeling of being "understood by an author I never met" as a reader, she explained that "want[ing] people to feel less alone. . . . is my goal."

In her debut novel *Converting Kate*, Weinheimer relates a coming-of-age tale that explores the issues of religion and identity. Sixteen-year-old Kate Anderson has just lost her father and moved with her fanatically religious mother to a small town in Maine where they help Kate's aunt manage a bed and breakfast. The death of Kate's father, as well as her mother's reprohibition of a traditional burial because of her extreme religious beliefs, causes the teen to question the faith she was raised with. *Converting Kate* follows Kate's journey as she breaks with the Holy Divine Church and discovers a new identity as she learns to think for herself. Calling Weinheimer's protagonist a "strong, self-reliant young woman, a *Publishers Weekly* contributor added that Kate's situation "will likely strike a chord with any teen who has struggled with a belief system that has been handed to them." A contributor to *Internet Bookwatch* deemed Weinheimer's first novel "deftly written, inherently fascinating, consistently entertaining, thoughtful and thought-provoking reading." In *Kliatt* Claire Rosser concluded that the novelist writes with "compassion and intelligence," while a *Children's Bookwatch* online reviewer described *Converting Kate* as a "skillfully written novel that underscores the evolution of a compliant young girl into a self-reliant young woman."

In her *Authors Den* online interview, Weinheimer advised would-be writers: "Read. Write. Follow your passions. Follow that voice in your head no matter how strange and different it is, because that is your voice and that is what sells books!"

Biographical and Critical Sources

PERIODICALS

Booklist, March 1, 2007, Ilene Cooper, review of *Converting Kate,* p. 80.
Bulletin of the Center for Children's Books, March, 2007, Deborah Stevenson, review of *Converting Kate,* p. 311.
Kirkus Reviews, February 1, 2007, review of *Converting Kate,* p. 130.
Kliatt, March, 2007, Claire Rosser, review of *Converting Kate,* p. 19.
Publishers Weekly, March 26, 2007, review of *Converting Kate,* p. 95.
School Library Journal, April, 2007, Joel Shoemaker, review of *Converting Kate,* p. 151.
Voice of Youth Advocates, February, 2007, Caitlin Augusta, review of *Converting Kate,* p. 535.

Cover of Weinheimer's young-adult novel Converting Kate. (Viking, 2007. Photograph of girl © 2007 by John Halpern, 2007. Photograph of stained-glass window courtesy of Getty Images. Reproduced by permission of Viking.)

ONLINE

Authors Den Web site, http://www.authorsden.com/ (December 15, 2007), "Beckie Weinheimer."
Beckie Weinheimer Home Page, http://www.beckiewein heimer.org (December 15, 2007).
Children's Bookwatch Web site, http://www.midwestbook review.com/ (November 1, 2007), review of *Converting Kate.*
Good Reads Web site, http://www.goodreads.com/ (December 15, 2007), "Beckie Weinheimer."
Internet Bookwatch Web site, http://www.midwestbook review.com/ (October 1, 2007), review of *Converting Kate.*

*   *   *

WHITE, Ruth C. 1942-
(Ruth White Miller)

Personal

Born March 15, 1942, in Whitewood, VA; daughter of John Edward (a coal miner) and Olive (a hospital food server) White; married (divorced); children: Dee Olivia.

Ruth C. White (Photo courtesy of Ruth White.)

Education: Montreat-Anderson College, A.A., 1962; Pfeiffer College, A.B., 1966; Queens College (Charlotte, NC), library media specialist certification, 1976. *Politics:* "Independent." *Hobbies and other interests:* Yoga, exercising, walking with her golden retriever.

Addresses

Home—Hummelstown, PA.

Career

Mt. Pleasant Middle School, Mt. Pleasant, NC, English teacher, 1966-76; Boys Town, Pineville, NC, house mother, 1976-77; Harleyville-Ridgeville High School, Dorchester, SC, librarian, 1977-81; Dougherty Junior High School, Albany, GA, librarian, 1981-85; Association for Research and Enlightenment Foundation, Virginia Beach, VA, librarian, 1986-97.

Awards, Honors

Best Children's Book by a North Carolinian designation, North Carolina chapter of the American Association of University Women, 1977, and Georgia Children's Book Award nomination, both for *The City Rose;* Newbery Honor Book designation, 1997, for *Belle Prater's Boy;* Notable Book designation, American Library Association (ALA), for *Sweet Creek Holler;* ALA Best Book for Young Adults designation, New York Public Library 100 Titles for Reading and Sharing selection, both for *Weeping Willow;* ALA Best Book for Young Adults, 2000, for *Memories of Summer.*

Writings

FOR CHILDREN AND YOUNG ADULTS

(Under name Ruth White Miller) *The City Rose,* McGraw (New York, NY), 1977.
Sweet Creek Holler, Farrar, Straus (New York, NY), 1988.
Weeping Willow, Farrar, Straus (New York, NY), 1992.
Belle Prater's Boy, Farrar, Straus (New York, NY), 1996.
Memories of Summer, Farrar, Straus (New York, NY), 2000.
Tadpole, Farrar, Straus (New York, NY), 2003.
Buttermilk Hill, Farrar, Straus (New York, NY), 2004.
The Search for Belle Prater, Farrar, Straus (New York, NY), 2005.
Way Down Deep, Farrar, Straus (New York, NY), 2007.
Little Audrey, Farrar, Straus (New York, NY), 2008.

Contributor to *Venture Inward.*

White's works have been translated into German, Dutch, Chinese, Indonesian, French, Polish, Afrikaans, and Japanese.

Adaptations

Many of White's books have been adapted as audiobooks.

Sidelights

Ruth C. White is the author of several award-winning novels for middle-grade and young-adult readers, and her works include *Sweet Creek Holler, Weeping Willow, Little Audrey,* and *Belle Prater's Boy* and its sequel, *The Search for Belle Prater.* White's stories are set in the South, in particular in the coal-mining region of western Virginia where the author grew up. Commentators have praised White for her characterizations, depiction of locale, and sensitive treatment of such difficult experiences as the death of a parent, divorce, abandonment, and rape. In 1997 White's much-acclaimed novel *Belle Prater's Boy* was named a Newbery honor book.

In her works, White focuses primarily on teenage girls, and the action in many of her novels takes place in the 1950s, when she herself was young. "I work with and write for adolescent girls because that was the time in my life when I was most confused and unhappy," she once explained. "I can relate to these girls now because I remember the pain of trying to grow up, trying to find my identity, and trying to be an individual in a conformist's world. Adolescents today have basically the same problems, only more of them."

Growing up in a poor western Virginian family during the 1950s provided White with both incentive and fodder for her later writing career. "Born in the poverty-stricken coal mining region of Virginia, I was the fourth daughter of a coal miner who died when I was six," she once commented. Although her family had no television, it was probably for the best: they read aloud and performed music together. In this setting, White developed her imagination and "managed to get the most out of the public school system and go on to a better life," building a career as a school teacher and librarian, and also gaining respect as a writer.

Although White published her first novel, *The City Rose,* in 1977, it was over a decade before her second book appeared. In *Sweet Creek Holler* six-year-old Ginny and older sister June must deal with the rumors that swirl around them when they move to a new town. The girls are actually the object of these rumors because their father was shot to death, leaving them and their beautiful mother to fend for themselves. During the six years they live in the small mining town of Sweet Creek Holler, the sisters witness the tragic effect gossip can have on sensitive souls. *Voice of Youth Advocates* reviewer Joanne Johnson praised White's "carefully drawn characters" and "well-thought out and presented" relationship between Ginny and a young friend. In *Horn Book,* critic Nancy Vasilakis judged the novel to be "stronger in its delineation of character and in its evocation of time and place than in its narrative development," yet she praised White's obvious "affection for the indigent folk of its Appalachian locale."

In *Weeping Willow,* set in 1956, White tells the story of fourteen-year-old Tiny, who is the eldest child in her family. As she grows into adulthood, Tiny must deal with her stepfather's unwanted sexual advances, as well as with the typical challenges of high-school life. Writing in the *Voice of Youth Advocates,* Myrna Feldman praised the novel's characters, setting, and details, deeming *Weeping Willow* an "exceptionally fine book" that is "honestly written and difficult to put down." "While the sweep of the novel is admirable," wrote *New York Times Book Review* critic Linda Lee, questionable is the novel's message that "incest is a bad thing, but it can be lived with." Praising the story's detailed setting and "strong" voice, Alice Casey Smith contended in a *School Library Journal* review that *Weeping Willow* "has too, too many threads that don't weave together." Betsy Hearne viewed the novel more favorably, however, writing in the *Bulletin of the Center for Children's Books* that *Weeping Willow* contains "vividly rendered" characters and a "plot following variably but believably from their [the characters'] patterns of action."

Belle Prater's Boy takes place in the fall of 1953, and here White explores the nature of friendship, loss, and love. Despite its title, the novel revolves around twelve-year-old Gypsy, who is known in Coal Station, Virginia, for her beautiful long hair and for having a father who died tragically seven years earlier. When her cousin Woodrow Prater moves in next door following the mysterious disappearance of his mother, Belle, he and Gypsy develop a close friendship that, according to a

Publishers Weekly reviewer, allows both preteens to "face tragedy and transcend it—and . . . pass along that gift to the reader."

Reviewers praised *Belle Prater's Boy* highly. Writing in *Kliatt,* Jana Whitesel deemed White's novel a "rare" book that "transcends age with its timeless story." In the *New York Times Book Review,* Meg Wolitzer declared that "it takes a writer of real lyricism and energy to tell a good young-adult story, and Ruth White is one." Several critics cited the author for her well-drawn characterizations and vivid depiction of locale, Wolitzer remarking that White's "vivid and accurate eye has helped her fashion an ideal backdrop for the story and its element of suspense." "White's characters are strong . . . and her storytelling is rich in detail and emotion," asserted Maeve Visser Knoth in a *Horn Book* review, while *Booklist* reviewer Stephanie Zvirin praised the book's "humor and insight," "solid picture of small-town life," "unpretentious, moving story," and "strongly depicted characters." *Belle Prater's Boy* "balances disturbing emotional issues with the writer's light touch," summed up a critic in the *Voice of Youth Advocates.*

The curiosity of many readers was sparked by the central mystery of *Belle Prater's Boy:* namely, what happened to Woodrow's Prater's mother? White provides the answer in *The Search for Belle Prater,* which was published more than nine years after the first book. In what a *Kirkus Reviews* contributor praised as an "elegantly conceived sequel" containing "tiny glints of magic," thirteen-year-old Gypsy narrates the adventures of the two seventh graders who—joined by friend Cassie Daulborne (who claims to have second sight) as well as by a teen runaway named Joseph—attempt to track down the missing woman. After receiving a mysterious phone call on the exact hour of his birth, Woodrow decides that his mother wishes to reestablish contact. Traveling to West Virginia, the group encounters racial prejudice, reunites Joseph with his family, and ultimately brings an answer to the question posed by the novel's title.

Calling *The Search for Belle Prater* a "worthy sequel" to the award-winning *Belle Prater's Boy,* Marie Orlando added in *School Library Journal* that the novel shares "the warmth, love, and humor" of the first book. Noting the deepening friendship between Woodrow and Gypsy, *Horn Book* contributor Cindy Dobrez added: "Characterization, dialogue, and setting are among White's many literary strengths, and she doesn't disappoint here."

Other novels by White have continued to focus on young characters coming to terms with their personal reality during the 1950s. In *Memories of Summer* thirteen-year-old Lyric witnesses her older sister, Summer, gradually decline mentally, becoming a stranger with schizophrenia; meanwhile, the young teen must also deal with a new culture as the family moves north to Flint, Michigan, where her widowed father finds work in an automobile plant. Praising White's novel as "affecting," *Kliatt* contributor Paula Rohrlick noted that *Memories of Summer* is based on White's experiences with her own sister, and added that the author includes "gentle humor . . . as well as pathos, and the tale is simply but movingly told."

In 1955, thirteen-year-old music-loving Tadpole shows up at the Kentucky home of ten-year-old cousin Carolina Collins, guitar in hand and fleeing from an abusive uncle. Carolina's mother, Serilda, is usually docile, but she fights to protect the troubled young boy in White's novel *Tadpole,* which a *Publishers Weekly* reviewer praised for its "homespun language" and "evocation of ordinary people as they stumble into enduring truths about human strength and vulnerability." Another ten-year-old is the focus of *Buttermilk Hill,* which finds wise and self-reliant Piper Berry weathering her parents' divorce by focusing on her own dreams and gaining insights and strength from both her friends and her poetry. Praising White's "down-home, approachable style," *Horn Book* contributor Christine M. Heppermann noted that *Tadpole* is full of "appealing characters" and "eloquently crafted images of . . . life in the Kentucky hills." A *Kirkus Reviews* critic also had praise for *Buttermilk Hill,* dubbing it a "poignant, compassionate exploration of the hopes and dreams that burn in the hearts of a small-town community in 1970s America," while in *Booklist,* Ilene Cooper praised White for maintaining "a good balance of happiness and hard knocks."

Way Down Deep introduces a unique cast of characters living in a small rural town in 1950s West Virginia. Three-year-old Ruby is found on the steps of the town's courthouse and is instantly accepted by all, Ms. Arbus in particular. A decade later, a man is caught trying to rob the town bank and he and his family are also accepted by local townspeople. As secrets are revealed, it is this family that ultimately sheds light on the secrets in Ruby's past. Cooper, writing in *Booklist,* noted that "at the heart of the story are profound questions that readers will enjoy puzzling out," while *Horn Book* contributor Betty Carter remarked that *Way Down Deep* contains "an undeniable charm." In a *School Library Journal* review, D. Maria LaRocco called the novel "captivating and thoughtful on many levels." As LaRocco added, *Way Down Deep* "offers humor, mystery, and a feel-good ending that a multitude of readers will find satisfying."

Biographical and Critical Sources

PERIODICALS

Booklist, September 15, 1977, review of *The City Rose,* p. 197; October 1, 1988, review of *Sweet Creek Holler,* p. 329; June 15, 1992, Stephanie Zvirin, review of *Weeping Willow,* p. 1827; April 15, 1996, Stephanie Zvirin, review of *Belle Prater's Boy,* p. 1434; September 1, 2000, Debbie Carton, review of *Memories of Summer,* p. 109; May 1, 2003, Gillian Engberg, review of *Tadpole,* p. 1598; August, 2004, Ilene Cooper, review of *Buttermilk Hill,* p. 1937; February 15, 2005, Cindy Dobrez, review of *The Search for Belle Prater,* p. 1079; March 1, 2007, Ilene Cooper, review of *Way Down Deep,* p. 85.

Bulletin of the Center for Children's Books, June, 1992, Betsy Hearne, review of *Weeping Willow,* p. 284; April, 2003, review of *Tadpole,* p. 336.

Christian Science Monitor, July 10, 2001, review of *Memories of Summer,* p. 20; April 17, 2003, review of *Tadpole,* p. 21.

English Journal, November, 1993, Margaret B. Shelley, review of *Weeping Willow,* p. 79.

Five Owls, January, 2001, review of *Memories of Summer,* p. 68.

Horn Book, November-December, 1988, Nancy Vasilakis, review of *Sweet Creek Holler,* p. 785; September-October, 1992, Nancy Vasilakis, review of *Weeping Willow,* p. 589; September-October, 1996, Maeve Visser Knoth, review of *Belle Prater's Boy,* p. 601; May, 2001, Kristi Beavin, review of *Memories of Summer,* p. 362; May-June, 2003, Christine M. Heppermann, review of *Tadpole,* p. 358; September-October, 2004, Betty Carter, review of *Buttermilk Hill,* p. 600; May-June, 2005, Betty Carter, review of *The Search for Belle Prater,* p. 334; May-June, 2007, Betty Carter, review of *Way Down Deep,* p. 293.

Journal of Adolescent & Adult Literacy, March, 2001, review of *Memories of Summer,* p. 581.

Kirkus Reviews, June 1, 1977, review of *The City Rose,* p. 581; September 1, 1988, review of *Sweet Creek Holler,* p. 1330; June 1, 1992, review of *Weeping Willow,* p. 725; July 15, 2000, review of *Memories of Summer,* p. 1048; August 1, 2004, review of *Buttermilk Hill,* p. 750; April 1, 2005, review of *The Search for Belle Prater,* p. 428; March 1, 2007, review of *Way Down Deep,* p. 10.

Kliatt, January, 1993, review of *Weeping Willow,* p. 13; May, 1998, Jana Whitesel, review of *Belle Prater's Boy,* p. 42; July, 2002, Paula Rohrlick, review of *Memories of Summer,* p. 25; March, 2005, Janis Flint-Ferguson, review of *The Search for Belle Prater,* p. 16; March, 2007, Janis Flint-Ferguson, review of *Way Down Deep,* p. 20.

New York Times Book Review, November 13, 1988, Beverly Lowry, review of *Sweet Creek Holler,* p. 20; August 23, 1992, Linda Lee, review of *Weeping Willow,* p. 26; October 27, 1996, Meg Wolitzer, review of *Belle Prater's Boy,* p. 44; February 11, 2001, review of *Memories of Summer,* p. 26.

New Yorker, November 18, 1996, review of *Belle Prater's Boy,* p. 102.

Publishers Weekly, August 12, 1988, review of *Sweet Creek Holler,* p. 460; May 18, 1992, review of *Weeping Willow,* p. 71; March 11, 1996, review of *Bell Prater's Boy,* pp. 65-66; July 31, 2000, review of *Memories of Summer,* p. 96; December 23, 2002, review of *Tadpole,* p. 71; November 8, 2004, review of *Buttermilk Hill,* p. 56; February 19, 2007, review of *Way Down Deep,* p. 169.

Riverbank Review, fall, 2000, review of *Memories of Summer,* p. 35; spring, 2003, review of *Tadpole,* p. 44.

School Library Journal, September, 1977, review of *The City Rose,* p. 132; October 1988, Katharine Bruner, review of *Sweet Creek Holler,* p. 165; July, 1992, Alice Casey Smith, review of *Weeping Willow,* p. 91; April, 1996, Cindy Darling Codell, review of *Bell Prater's Boy,* p. 158; August, 2000, Cindy Darling Codell, review of *Memories of Summer,* p. 192; March, 2003, Connie Tyrrell Burns, review of *Tadpole,* p. 242; September, 2004, Miriam Lang Budin, review of *Buttermilk Hill,* p. 219; April, 2005, Marie Orlando, review of *The Search for Belle Prater,* p. 143; April 1, 2007, D. Maria LaRocco, review of *Way Down Deep,* p. 152.

Tribune Books (Chicago, IL), July 27, 2003, review of *Tadpole,* p. 5; April 22, 2007, Mary Harris Russell, review of *Way Down Deep,* p. 9.

Voice of Youth Advocates, December, 1988, Joanne Johnson, review of *Sweet Creek Holler,* p. 244; October, 1992, Myrna Feldman, review of *Weeping Willow,* p. 234; June, 1997, review of *Belle Prater's Boy,* p. 87; December, 2000, review of *Memories of Summer,* p. 356; December, 2004, review of *Buttermilk Hill,* p. 397; April, 2005, Lucy Schall, review of *The Search for Belle Prater,* p. 52.

ONLINE

BookPage, http://www.bookpage.com/ (August 5, 2007), Dean Schneider, review of *Tadpole.*

Ruth C. White Home Page, http://www.ruthwhite.net (August 5, 2007).

TeenReads.com, http://www.teenreads.com/ (August 7, 2007), Donna Volkenannt, review of *Way Down Deep.*

Looking Glass Review Online, http://www.lookingglass review.com/ (August 7, 2007), review of *Way Down Deep.*

Ruth C. White

Ruth C. White contributed the following autobiographical essay to *SATA* in 2007:

Introduction

At some point in the nineteenth century, the English Comptons helped to settle the rugged hills of Southwest Virginia. Olive Compton, born in 1916, was one of their direct descendants. She grew up on the very top of Compton Mountain in Buchanan County. It was the most isolated place in Virginia at that time, and Olive lived there from her birth to her marriage having very little communication with the outside world. She didn't even have a radio or a telephone.

Growing up with twelve sisters and brothers, Olive worked in the gardens, helped tend the livestock, and assisted with housework and the younger children. Each day she and her other school-age siblings walked about two miles down the mountain to a small country school at Whitewood in the valley. Olive's favorite subjects were reading and geography.

Hannibal Compton, Olive's uncle, was an educated man, a schoolteacher and an early historian of the region, and he had a whole library of excellent quality right up there on the top of Compton Mountain. So, as a young girl, Olive would spend hours reading his books, and she found that reading could take her away to a more desirable place and time, and to more interesting people and events than she had ever known. By the time she had reached eighth grade, Olive was fairly self-educated through her reading, which was probably a good thing, because eighth grade was as far as one could go at the Whitewood school, and her parents did not have the money to send any of their children away to a county high school.

In the 1920s and 1930s, coal mining became the chief industry in Buchanan County, and Whitewood grew into a booming coal town. At the age of seventeen, while attending church in the valley, Olive met a young miner who loved to read as much as she did. His name was John Edward White, known affectionately by one and all as John Ed.

John Ed and Olive married and quickly became the parents of five daughters. Audrey Virginia came first in 1936; Yvonne Marie in 1939; Eleanor June in 1940; Ruth Carol in 1942 and Elizabeth Gail in 1944. True to

Southern tradition, Ruth Carol, like John Ed, was called by both names, and so was the baby, Elizabeth, a.k.a. Betty Gail. Unfortunately, Betty Gail died at the age of seven months, which brought me, Ruth Carol, to the rank of baby of the family.

My sisters and I had more entertainment and more contact with the outside world than our mother had as a girl, but we still became avid readers mostly through her influence. She read aloud to us even after we were old enough to read for ourselves.

Since reading was such a big deal in my family, and I loved a good story above all else, I knew that I would be a writer someday, even before I started school, and I never wavered from that goal. What I did not know was that I would be writing about those days in which I was living. I had visions of stories involving princesses and swashbuckling heroes, lovesick cowgirls and faraway places with strange-sounding names. It was only after I grew up and away from the Appalachian region that I

Olive White, age twenty-eight, holding Betty Gail and Audrey beside her, age eight. Front left to right: Eleanor, Ruth Carol, and Yvonne (Photo courtesy of Ruth White.)

realized what a wealth of unique story material I had stored up in my memories during those early years. Therein lay my greatest asset as a writer.

Today, upon reaching a certain age, I find that I cannot remember what happened last week, but I remember well those childhood years in the Appalachian Mountains as if they never ended, and that is where I actually began writing these novels, which only today are finished and published.

Some of my most pleasant memories of childhood involve crawling into one bed with all of my family on cold winter evenings while Mom read to us from *Little Women, Heidi, Lassie Come Home,* or some other such wonderful treasure. But it was Laura Ingalls Wilder, a Midwesterner, who was the first, and probably the most important influence on my own writing. My sisters and I felt that we were growing up with the Ingalls girls.

Although all of my published books are definitely fiction, just as Mrs. Wilder's were, there is an element of truth, or many elements of truth, in each of them. In most of my books I have used the Appalachian setting, interwoven the culture and dialect of that region, and used characters that I knew there. I have also used the names common to the Appalachian region, both people and places, and repeated jokes, stories, and songs that I remember from childhood.

In addition to telling the stories of the mountains, five of my books, *Sweet Creek Holler, Weeping Willow, Memories of Summer, Tadpole,* and *Little Audrey,* tell some part of my own life as a child. In short, I have taken my reality and turned it into fiction.

My Childhood as Recalled in My Books

My earliest memories (1945–48) are of living not far from Whitewood and Compton Mountain in a place called Jewell Valley Coal Camp. A coal camp was a place where the coal miners lived with their families. In our camp all the houses were exactly alike—brown square wooden boxes with two families living in each one. A partition ran down the center to divide the living quarters. We had no running water inside the house, meaning no indoor toilets, and not much else in the way of modern convenience.

The miners were paid with scripts instead of money, which could be spent only at the company store. We lived in the coal camp from the time I was three until just after I turned six. My sisters attended school at Jewell Valley, but we were gone before I made it to first grade, and kindergarten did not exist in that time and place. *Little Audrey* covers those years of living in the coal camp with my father, mother and three sisters. As I was beginning the story, I decided to write it as close to the truth as possible. First of all, I would use the real names of places and people, including my family. I

would include real events as they happened, to the best of my recollection, or if I couldn't remember something, I would ask one of my sisters to help me out.

At the time the story takes place, my sister Audrey was the only one of us old enough to tell a tale. So I have her as the narrator of *Little Audrey.* When I was ready to start the first page, I closed my eyes, took myself into Audrey's head, and used her senses. I saw myself on the dirt road running through Jewell Valley. I saw the hills and the camp. I saw and smelled a beautiful spring day. I heard a voice beside me. It was an old friend, Virgil. Because I felt so completely in the moment, I began writing in the present tense: "It is a golden day in May, 1948. The air fairly sparkles with sunshine." And the story began to flow. I did not have to struggle at all with the plot, the characters, the setting. Everything was there already, waiting for me to place it upon the page, and the present tense felt so natural that I decided to stay with it.

As the story opens Audrey has been very ill, first with scarlet fever, and then with a botched tonsillectomy, which nearly killed her. At this point she has been back in school for a month, and is struggling to regain her health. While relating information about her school life and the everyday problems of bullies and best friends, she casually brings up the subject of sisters, referring to Yvonne, Eleanor, and me as the "three little pigs," and further labels me the "runt piglet."

Audrey recognizes and laments the fact that her parents chose to have more children than they could properly care for. Then, without much fanfare or self-pity, she reveals the most painful burden her family must carry, namely that her father, John Ed, has become a serious alcoholic who neglects his wife and kids. In her own words, or as close as I could come to Audrey's words at that time, she describes the hardships of living in poverty, along with the hopes and dreams of a little girl inspired by a very special teacher, a good friend, and a strong mother who holds the family together.

At the end of the book, John Ed is killed, and I wanted the reader to be left with the impression that his death, though very sad, was not the worst tragedy that could have happened, but in truth was the best thing for the rest of the family. Though the mother and children mourn for the person John Ed once was, they have not actually seen that person in a long time. Without him they find a way to leave the hills and make a better life for themselves.

In reality, my father had become an alcoholic by the time we moved to Jewell Valley. He spent every weekend away from his family, drinking with others like him, and he actually was killed one night while he was drunk. As in the story, I was six years old, and my sisters were seven, eight, and eleven. Mom was forced to take us out of the coal camp and find another way to live. She was only thirty years old at that time and she didn't have any prospects of securing employment because jobs for women simply did not exist.

With a small amount of insurance money from the mining company and some help from John Ed's father, Mom bought a little brown house for us in a narrow hollow tucked away among the hills near Grundy, Virginia. The place was called Little Prater. There we survived on a monthly check from Social Security. Of course we were very poor, but I think we were actually somewhat happy, at least content, living a quiet simple life there from 1948 to 1954.

When I am visiting schools, I often tell young people that my childhood was both traumatic and wonderful. It was traumatic in that my father was killed suddenly and violently when I was very young. My mother, sisters, and I were forced to live in poverty, and every day was a struggle to survive. But it was also wonderful in that we had a loving mother and relatives, and we had each other. We didn't have to worry about being kidnapped, molested, or murdered. Those thoughts never entered our heads. We were, in fact, as carefree as the little wild animals that scampered up and down the hillsides.

In fact we did a lot of scampering up and down the hillsides ourselves. On pretty days we sometimes left our house after breakfast and played in the hills all day. We came home only long enough to eat our "beans and 'taters." In summer we had fresh vegetables and fruits, and we were healthy most of the time.

My sisters and I were not only avid readers but also great mimics. We had no television, but there were movie theaters in nearby Grundy, and we were lucky to see the latest movies from Hollywood, which we would later act out. We would write down all the dialogue we could remember from a good movie and learn it for our own entertainment. Being the aspiring writer, I also wrote original plays for my classmates, and they would help me act them out.

We attended a little four-room country schoolhouse that was perched up on a hillside there in Little Prater. You might think such a backwoods school would not be very successful in educating its poor student body, but in this case you would be wrong. Our teachers were excellent, and in spite of everything, my sisters and I were blessed to receive a sound basic education.

Somehow or other we managed to have a radio all those years, and we picked up every song that came along, thus developing a remarkable repertoire of folk, country, bluegrass, spiritual, and popular music. To this day we know the words to scores of forgotten songs. We are a wealth of music trivia. I often use the lyrics of some these songs in my books.

Sweet Creek Holler is the fictional account of an Appalachian girl whose coal-miner father has been killed. In this book I took the four girls in my family and combined them into the two main characters—Ginny and June Marie Shortt. Ginny is the narrator, and the story covers her life from ages six to twelve, living with her sister and widowed mother in a shack up a "holler." Ginny and Junie go through many of the normal girl things in growing up, but they also experience some interesting mystical events.

I have always enjoyed reading stories involving mysterious and supernatural happenings, and I find that most young people feel the same. In my own books, I don't want to over-do that angle, but I do like to include a touch of mysticism, just enough to tweak the imagination. In *Sweet Creek Holler* I manage this with two ghost girls who happen to be about the same size as Ginny and June Marie.

During those years of living in Little Prater, my paternal grandfather and grandmother, whom we called Poppy and Granny, lived in Feds Creek, Kentucky, just over the state line not far from us. Poppy worked in a mine there. I often visited them, and I have happy memories of those visits. In fact, Kentucky was so special to me I decided to set a novel in that time and place. It turned out to be *Tadpole*.

Even though *Tadpole* is set in Kentucky, and we actually still lived in Virginia at that time, the story is based on our real lives. I tried to portray all four of the girls in my family as we were. The oldest and most sociable one, Kentucky, is Audrey, who, as a child, had more friends than all the rest of us combined. The next oldest, Virginia, is Yvonne, who was more concerned about her looks than the rest of us, and she was as pretty as a flower. Georgia is Eleanor, the brainy sister, who studied all the time and made straight A's, but she was also quite lovely. And then of course there was Carolina who thought she was nobody, based on myself.

The character of Tadpole is based on my favorite cousin who was an orphan. In the book, he acquired his nickname by swallowing a live tadpole on a dare. An hour later he chucked it up again, and it was still alive, so he threw it back into the creek where it swam away. He tells Carolina that the tadpole is probably a big bullfrog by now, and all the other frogs call him Jonah.

In reality, my cousin's nickname was Toad, and when I last saw him in 2004, he told me he didn't remember where his nickname came from. What he did remember about his childhood was being passed around from one relative to another, just like Tadpole in the book.

When kinfolk visited in those days, it was a special time, almost like a holiday, but I, being the youngest, was sometimes ignored by older cousins. Writing fiction, however, allows you to re-write the past, and give yourself happy endings. So in this book, Tadpole, who picks the guitar and sings, appreciates little Carolina as nobody has done before, and helps her in finding some self-esteem as the talented one.

The Inseparables, at Grundy High School graduation, 1960. Left to right: Gipsy, Roberta, Ruth Carol, and Garnette (Photo courtesy of Ruth White.)

Here again, I couldn't resist a few mystical events. One of these, by Tadpole's account, is the death of his melancholy cousin, Eugene. Tadpole is distraught over this loss until he notices that in a certain painting, which has always been Eugene's favorite, a new figure has emerged, and it happens to be Eugene himself, as happy as a pup!

In a similar vein, Tadpole sometimes hears a voice that guides him, and which he reveals to Carolina as the adult Tadpole, come back through the years to assist him in growing up, because he had no parents. Then there's the mystical window at his uncle's house through which Tadpole can see the past. There he watches his mother and Carolina's mother as little girls playing in the yard.

Of course I had to give Tadpole a happy ending in letting him go to Nashville to become a singing star. In reality I'm afraid he did not have such good fortune. He ran away from his relatives and joined the army as soon as he was old enough. He later settled down in Rising Sun, Maryland, married, and became the father of twin boys.

In my own real life, as my sisters and I began to grow up, our requirements grew as well, and my mother struggled desperately to fulfill our needs. Eventually,

she did manage to find a job working in the kitchen of Grundy Hospital where she worked long, hard hours for little pay.

In 1955 there was much talk about the booming auto industry in Michigan. It was rumored that they were hiring a great number of men and women and paying good wages. So my mother made the decision to take my sisters and me to Flint, Michigan, in search of a better life. I can only imagine how much courage it must have taken for this quiet, shy person from Compton Mountain to leave the hills and all her relatives, to say goodbye to the only home she had ever known, and move to a large industrial city up North. On top of that to be responsible for four teenage girls must have been almost overwhelming for her.

On a bus we left Grundy mid-morning one September day and continued riding through the night, carrying all of our possessions in suitcases and a few boxes. In Ohio we saw flat land for the first time in our lives. I think in that moment we all felt the enormity of this great life change, and steeled ourselves for the unknown. It was indeed a very difficult move for all of us, but particularly so for Audrey, the oldest. Shortly after our move to Flint, she began to show signs of a mental breakdown, but she managed to hang on bravely for a few more years. In the end it was a crushing disappointment in love that overwhelmed her, and schizophrenia swallowed up the sister we once knew. This memory was almost too painful for me to dwell on, but it was an important part of my life. So here again my reality turned to fiction.

Memories of Summer tells the story of sixteen-year-old Summer Compton as she is descending into madness. It is told through the eyes of her sister, Lyric, who is thirteen. In this story I wanted to emphasize not only the suffering of the schizophrenic, but also the effects of mental illness on the entire family. In several of my other books, I have a widowed mother taking care of her family alone, because that had been the case with my family. But one day my sister Eleanor said to me, "Have you ever thought what our lives would have been like if Mom had been the one to die, and Dad had lived?"

Actually, I had never thought of that, but I did at that moment. Believe me, I am very glad that I had a wonderful mother who raised me and my sisters in a way that nobody else in the world could have done, but for the sake of variety in my storytelling, I decided that in my next book I would have the father be the survivor who took care of the kids, and that's the case in *Memories of Summer.*

In this book, as Claude Compton and his two daughters arrive in Michigan, the city of Flint is commemorating its centennial year with elaborate celebrations. Coming from Glory Bottom, Virginia, the girls find everything exciting and fascinating. For the first week they wander

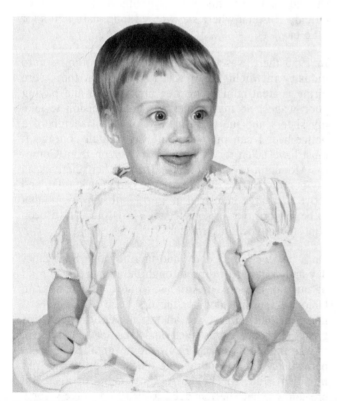

Dee Olivia Fisher born October 2, 1963 (Photo courtesy of Ruth White.)

around the city alone, laughing and singing, enjoying all the sights and sounds, and having glorious adventures. Then comes Monday morning and school. Lyric manages to re-enter the real world, and adapt to this new life, but Summer cannot. It is the beginning of her breakdown.

Several months of anguish follow, not only for Summer, but also for Lyric and their father. Summer is tormented by voices and people who exist only in her mind. She has always had an unreasonable fear of dogs, which she refers to as wolves, and now she begins having nightmares about them. The sisters have always been extremely close; then strangely enough, one night Lyric finds herself in one of Summer's nightmares. In this way, she gets into Summer's mind, and experiences the horror her sister is going through. Summer is diagnosed with schizophrenia, and at the end of the book, is committed to Pontiac State Hospital, while Lyric and her father settle into a new life in Michigan, and find some degree of happiness.

The true events of my sister's descent into darkness were too painful to write about. Furthermore, it is not a story for young people. By the time Audrey was committed to Pontiac State hospital at the age of twenty-three, she had given birth to two beautiful sons. She was confined and treated for years, but, like Summer, she never regained her sanity. My mother raised her children, Johnny and Mike.

As it turned out, Mom was not able to work for the auto industry as she had so counted on. It seems men were hired at any age, but women over thirty-five could not find employment at the factories, and she was thirty-nine. That's how things were in those days. So again Mom worked in the food-service department of a hospital in Flint. The pay and working conditions, however, were better than she had been used to in Virginia.

My sister, Yvonne, stayed in Michigan, eventually married a General Motors man, and became a wonderful mother to four fine boys. Eleanor also stayed, eventually married a factory man, and became mother to two very fine children—a girl and a boy.

And I? Well, in reality, at the tender age of thirteen, I found Flint to be a harsh environment compared to the home we had left behind, and I was acutely homesick for the mountains. In those days, with the extended family in Southern culture, it was common to live for a period of time with a relative, for different reasons. If Junior didn't behave, for example, he might be sent to live with Uncle Jim for a time, or if you needed to be closer to the high school, you might stay with Grandma nine months out of the year, etc.

So, it was decided that I could go live for a while with an aunt and uncle back in Virginia, until I thought I could manage Michigan again. I went home to the hills

Ruth at home in Virgina Beach, 1986 (Photo courtesy of Ruth White.)

on a Greyhound bus, believing, along with my mother, that I would return to her in Michigan in a matter of weeks or a few months at the most. As it turned out, I spent the next four years with my aunt and uncle in Virginia, attended Grundy High School there, and graduated in 1960. That was reality.

Weeping Willow is the fictional account of those four years. In this book I came so close to that fine line between fiction and reality, that even I hardly knew where one ended and the other began. So it is not surprising that this is my favorite of all my books. This is the story of Tiny Lambert, who is more like me than any other character I have created. Though I did not suffer the abuse that Tiny suffered, the rest of the book is to me like a photograph of a particular time and place. Yet, with the issues in this story, it could take place in the twenty-first century. The themes are as old as the hills themselves.

The mysticism in *Weeping Willow* comes in the form of Willa, a little girl only Tiny can see. She has curly red hair and shows up to comfort Tiny in difficult times. It appears that Willa is simply an imaginary friend, until she returns suddenly at the worst moment of all for Tiny. Now Tiny is a teenager, and so is Willa. Later, Tiny learns that her missing father had curly red hair. It was my intention to leave the reader with the impres-

sion that in times of need, Tiny's father has come to her in a form she can relate to. In the end Tiny feels a hole in her heart, which Willa once occupied, and she knows that Willa will never come again, because Tiny has grown up.

I had some wonderful English teachers at Grundy High School who helped me and encouraged me to write. Two of them were Miss Hart and Mrs. McElroy. My grades were never something to brag about, but I managed to be an average student without working too hard.

It was at Grundy High School that I met Roberta Smith, the best friend of my life. She supported me in my writing by reading every word I wrote. She, in turn, loved to create poetry, and I encouraged her in that. I still have some of her poems.

Besides Roberta and me, there were three others in our close circle of friends. They were Garnette, Gipsy, and Vicki. We called ourselves the "Inseparables," not only because we were all in the high school band, but we also did everything else together. In *Weeping Willow* the characters of Rosemary and Bobby Lynn are composites of these four girls. That's why the book is dedicated to them, along with the Grundy High School Class of 1960. Many of the characters in my books love music and are talented in that area. This is the case in

Weeping Willow, because high school and junior college were the years when my own musical interests peaked. I played clarinet and also sang.

In fact, like Tiny Lambert, I won the local talent contest the year I was a senior. Two weeks later I won another one in a nearby town. In my mind, those two wins, even today, stand alongside my Newbery honor (to be discussed), as an equal source of pride. As the years went by, I belonged to different singing groups and studied piano, but without much success. Other priorities took over my life, and my involvement with music fell by the wayside, though my love for it remains to this day.

In reality, upon graduation from high school I had a rare opportunity to go to college. At this point nobody in my family had ever even thought of such a thing, but it was almost as if some good spiritual entity gently took control of my life and manipulated me into a good education. With the help of the Buchanan First Presbyterian Church and the Junior Woman's Club, both in Grundy, I found myself partially funded for college. Of course I would also have to work, which I was willing to do.

There is a picturesque little college down in North Carolina called Montreat, which I still dream about and think of sometimes with a feeling much like homesickness. Going there was the first major turning point in my life, for it lifted me out of the backwoods and introduced me to a wider world.

At Montreat I met young people like me from all over the world. At that time the school was similar to Berea in Kentucky, in that it offered a liberal arts education to anybody who was willing to work, and work I did. I served in the cafeteria three meals every day, and also helped in the dean's office.

Somehow I managed to continue with my writing, and was encouraged by my teachers. I wrote for the school newspaper, which was called *The Dialette,* and I continued privately to write stories, which I dreamed would one day grow into novels.

It is my intention to do a sequel to *Weeping Willow,* which will focus on Tiny's years at Mountain Retreat College, and also on her relationship with Cecil, who is the boy next door. This will be a crossover book, connecting *Weeping Willow* and *Buttermilk Hill,* which is discussed further on.

My First Publication, The City Rose

It was at Montreat that I met my husband, Larry Fisher. After two years of college, I moved with him to his hometown, Mt. Pleasant, North Carolina, near Charlotte. Then came the most important role of my life, as I gave birth to a beautiful baby girl, whom we named Dee Olivia. When she was two years old, I went back to finish my degree at nearby Pfeiffer College, and became a teacher.

I began teaching language arts at Mt. Pleasant Junior High. It was there that I discovered both my favorite age group, and the very best in young-adult literature, which made me nostalgic for my childhood. I realized that, of all the reading I had done during my sixteen years of education, I had come full circle back to the literature I loved most—specifically the young-adult novel.

I started teaching in 1966, and the schools in North Carolina had been only recently integrated. In one of my classrooms I had two African-American students, both girls and both good readers. Once a week I would take my classes to the library to select their own books. It was my favorite day of the week. I noticed that my two African-American girls searched and searched the stacks for reading material, but they were not very excited with what they came up with. In trying to help them find the best books, I finally managed to get it out of them that they wanted to see books with African-American girls on the covers, and there were very few such publications at that time.

Then I would write one, I told myself. Yes, I had always wanted to be a writer, and here was a hole in children's literature that I would try to fill. I set about writing a book with an African-American girl as the main character, but of course the first novel is not so simple. I found myself working on it for years.

In 1969 my marriage ended, and I became a single mother. Dee and I lived in a trailer while I continued to teach and she attended the same school where I worked. In 1973 I met and married a man by the name of Joe Miller who lived in a neighboring town.

By this time I had come to the realization that I would be happier as a school librarian so that I could help young people with their reading. I could also indulge my love for children's literature. So I attended classes at nearby Queens College in Charlotte and earned certification in library science. Though I had done only average academic work in high school and at Montreat, and had barely squeaked through Pfeiffer, I found it was easy to make good grades at Queens, as I loved my subject so much.

In my spare time, what little there was of it, I continued to work on my book. I had definitely underestimated how long it would take to finish such a project, and get it published. Today many people ask me how I managed to find a publisher for that first book, and I always reply that I was simply lucky. I had a copy of *Writer's Digest,* which included a list of publishers looking for new authors and willing to read unsolicited manuscripts. Being a student for so many years, the name McGraw-Hill had become familiar to me from seeing it on textbooks. So I decided I would send my manuscript there first, where it fell into the hands of a young editor by the name of Eleanor Nichols. She worked with me on revisions for about a year before she accepted the book for publication.

Ten years had gone by since I had started my novel, and the girls I wanted to write it for were long gone from school. But no matter, I thought, I had finally managed to publish my first book, and other young girls and boys would read it.

The City Rose, published under my married name of Ruth White Miller, came out in 1977, when books with African-American children as the main characters were no longer rare, but the demand was growing. It is about a young girl who moves to North Carolina to live with an aunt after a fire destroys her family in Detroit. It was fairly well received for a first novel, and soon became an Avon paperback. Today it is out of print, but used copies can be found on the Internet.

Dee and Buttermilk Hill

As the Beatles put it so aptly, while I was busy with other things, life was happening. My little girl, Dee, was growing up. She had her own life and many friends and relatives in Mt. Pleasant. They were fairly nice years for her. In *Buttermilk Hill,* which is based on Dee's childhood, I have used my own memories, as well as Dee's, to paint this picture of small-town life in the 1970s. Piper Berry is the main character, and she lives with her divorced hippie mother and a golden retriever in a trailer. Piper also happens to be the daughter

of Tiny Lambert from *Weeping Willow.* So this book shows you not only what happens to Tiny when she grows up, but also what happens to her daughter.

Dee was never a poet as Piper Berry is in *Buttermilk Hill,* but she was very much like Piper in other ways. She loved animals, for one thing, and she loved her relatives, especially her grandmother Fisher. I decided to make Piper a poet when I read some poems written by two good friends of mine, Virginia Grant and Nora Baskin. I asked them if they would write some poems for the main character in my new book, and both graciously agreed.

During the time I spent in North Carolina I saw little of my mom and sisters in Michigan. Mom was busy with Audrey's boys and trying to work. Yvonne and Eleanor were also busy raising their own children. Eleanor did manage to continue her education. She eventually earned a master's degree from Oakland University in Michigan. She graduated with honors and became a reading specialist.

A Few Unsettling Years

In 1977 my husband and I took on a job as house parents at Boys' Town, a home for troubled boys in Pinev-

Eleanor and Ruth in Nashville, 1989 (Photo courtesy of Ruth White.)

Family reunion at Breaks Park, 1996. Front left to right: Mom, Ruth, and Yvonne. Eleanor is behind Yvonne—Toad (or Tadpole) is behind Ruth (Photo courtesy of Ruth White.)

ille, North Carolina, near Charlotte. Dee, of course, moved there with us, and was not very happy about it. Looking back, I can hardly blame her.

I will never forget the experience of working there with adolescent boys. It was fulfilling, but at the same time heart-wrenching to see so many young boys struggling to find their place in life. I admired the other house parents there who had been at it so competently for several years, and I had to conclude that I did not have what it takes to be a successful houseparent. Not everybody is cut out for such a demanding job. We left after only a year.

At this point, Joe, Dee, and I moved to Summerville, South Carolina, near Charleston because we had always loved the area. There I began my career as a school librarian at Harleyville-Ridgeville High School in nearby Dorchester. This school was in a very poor district, and many of my students were troubled with family and money problems, racial tensions, drug and alcohol abuse, giving birth out of wedlock, poor academic achievement, etc. It was a challenge for me, and I did not have the time or energy to think of my writing for the years I was there.

In the meantime, Dee was happy and attending one of the best public schools in the South—Summerville High

School, a very large facility near Charleston. She made friends easily and graduated from there in 1981. She chose to go to college at my old alma mater, Montreat, back in the mountains of North Carolina. I was delighted with her choice.

That same year my marriage ended and I left my job in South Carolina to move to Albany, Georgia, and live with my sister, Eleanor. General Motors had transferred her husband to a new plant in Albany, and Eleanor found a position teaching at Deerfield, a private school.

Yvonne remained busy with raising children in Michigan, while Audrey was in and out of hospitals and half-way houses. On several occasions Mom tried to care for Audrey at home, but it simply didn't work out. She was too ill for home care.

In Albany, I found employment as a school librarian at Dougherty Junior High School. There followed some very troubling years for both Eleanor and me. We were almost forty years old, which certainly seems young to me now, but together we went through a bout of depression and soul searching. We talked a lot about metaphysics and our recent fascination with noted psychic Edgar Cayce. We talked about visiting the Association for Research and Enlightenment in Virginia Beach, (the

ARE) which was built around the psychic readings of Cayce. But we never quite made it.

We also recalled our youth in the mountains and how it had shaped us. I wanted to write about those years, and my second book began to form in my mind. When I finally started the actual writing of *Sweet Creek Holler,* a floodgate of old memories, old sorrows and grief, and, yes, nostalgia, opened up. It was my first experience with writing as catharsis. It was better than psychotherapy.

After five years in Albany my book was no closer to completion, my job was growing stale, and I felt I needed a dramatic change to re-awaken my passion for life. That's when I made the impulsive decision to move to Virginia Beach and try to get a job at the ARE Library. As soon as that decision was made, I felt excitement stirring in my bones, and my life took on new meaning. In July of 1986, I made that move, and it was the second important turning point in my life (the first being Montreat). I found a small three-bedroom house to rent, then invited my mother, who was almost seventy by then, and Dee, who was between jobs, to join me there. They both accepted, and we three settled into a period of togetherness and happiness.

Mom was delighted to stay at home at last and not have to work. She took care of the house. Dee, having the right personality for dealing with people, was quick to find a job in selling. At first I did some substitute teaching in the public schools, but within a matter of months I was hired as a librarian at the ARE's metaphysical library, one of the most fascinating libraries in the world. And right outside my office door I could see all of the more than fourteen thousand psychic readings done by Edgar Cayce, bound in brown leather and perused each day by scholars, holistic healers, and spiritual teachers from all over the world. I felt that I was home.

At the ARE I learned more than I can even describe. The people I met there ranged from some real kooks to the highly intelligent and enlightened. I felt that I was in an intense classroom, and I liked to imagine this place was a spiritual junction for old souls. I devoured hundreds of metaphysical books. I attended conferences, lectures, church and social events with like-minded people. It was as if I were hungry for the contacts, the stories, the information, the mystery and mysticism.

Publishing My Second Book, Sweet Creek Holler

In no time at all I was finished with *Sweet Creek Holler.* Since McGraw-Hill had gone out of the children's book business, I had to find a new publisher. This time I wrote a query letter with the intention of sending it to children's book editors. In this letter I first mentioned

Ruth and Dee at the Newberry Banquet, 1997 (Photo courtesy of Ruth White.)

The City Rose, then described my new book, and asked the editor to contact me if interested in seeing *Sweet Creek Holler.* Then I made copies of the letter and sent it to thirty different publishers. In no time at all I had nineteen positive replies. I numbered the replies as they came in and set about sending my manuscript to each publisher sequentially.

Of course computers were rare in those days, so my books were typewritten, and electronic book submissions were unheard of, so hard copies had to be laboriously put through a copy machine and sent to each publisher one at a time. Three publishers rejected *Sweet Creek Holler* before a reader at Farrar, Straus & Giroux of New York read it, liked it and gave me a phone call. It was October of 1986, and it was the most welcome phone call of my life.

Margaret Ferguson was a young editor at FSG that autumn and she was assigned to my book. We worked very well together, and have done the same on all my books since. *Sweet Creek Holler* was well received in 1988, earning very good reviews, including one in the *New York Times Book Review,* which was quite thrilling. It was also named to ALA's Notable Books list.

Several changes took place within my family in the late eighties. First of all, Eleanor went to work in management for General Motors, and was first assigned to the new Saturn plant in Spring Hill, Tennessee. Her family moved with her.

Second, Dee took a job in Myrtle Beach, South Carolina, where she stayed with an old friend from her Mt. Pleasant days. It was her intention to earn enough money to go back to college, and eventually she did manage to earn her degree in business.

And third, Audrey's two sons, John and Mike, now with families of their own, came to Virginia Beach to start a business together, and Mom moved in with Mike and his family.

So I was on my own, but not lonely. I found that I actually enjoyed the solitude. I also had more time for my writing and my growing spirituality. I became active in the Unity Church, and attended ARE events and conferences. I began writing book reviews and short articles for *Venture Inward,* which is the magazine of the ARE And I met some truly interesting people from all over the world. It was a time of great personal growth, in which I found emotional and mental health.

Reunion and Loss

It was either Janis Ian or Janis Joplin who said, "You never get over high school," and this was the case with me. Memories of those high school years still haunted me. In 1990, I traveled back to Grundy for my thirty-year high school reunion. Of course it was not my first

visit back to my roots, but it was the most significant, because four of the Inseparables, who, after high school, had been separated to four different states, would be together again. Roberta, a teacher in Bristol, Tennessee, was married with three sons; Garnette, a nurse in Roanoke, Virginia, was married with a son and a daughter; and Gipsy was an unmarried music teacher in nearby Elk Horn City, Kentucky. Vicki was married with two daughters and one son in Pembroke Pines, Florida. She had been two years behind us in high school, and was not present for the reunion.

Roberta, Garnette, and I stayed at Gipsy's house the first night. It was wonderful and bittersweet. Of course the magic of the teenage years had long left us, but we still had enough in common to renew the close ties we had shared those thirty years previous. Now at forty-eight, we simply picked up our conversation as if it had been interrupted only yesterday. The next night we met with our other classmates for the official reunion. It was unforgettable.

I had already started writing *Weeping Willow* before the reunion, but when I returned home, the book bloomed with new life. I finished quickly and it was published in 1992, dedicated to my good friends and our most special class of 1960.

The year after that, in July, 1993, I lost my sister, Audrey, to lung cancer. After all the years of anguish, her suffering was finally ended. Then sadly, in October of the same year, my dear friend, Roberta, died during an asthma attack.

Ruth at ALA, 1998 (Photo courtesy of Ruth White.)

Writing Belle Prater's Boy

In both *Sweet Creek Holler* and *Weeping Willow,* the main characters are children living in poverty in Southwest Virginia in the 1950s. Of course I was writing from experience. So when I was searching around for a new story idea, I had to realize that being poor is only one of the problems young people face in all generations. Children who do not have to worry about money still have difficulties in their lives. The loss of a parent is a good example, through death, divorce, desertion, etc.

With this in mind, I decided to set my next story—still in my beloved Virginia mountains in the 1950s—but in brighter, more comfortable surroundings. As for characters, I knew only that Gypsy and Woodrow would be the city mouse and the country mouse, but there would be no animosity between them. They would have much to learn from each other.

But I had no idea where the story was going from there. So I placed Gypsy and Woodrow in this small, middle-class, close-knit community and in my mind I said to them, "Now, tell me your story."

I didn't realize then that Woodrow's mother, Belle Prater, would turn out to be the pivotal focus of the book. But right from the start she intrigued me, and I guess that's how she managed somehow to take over the story. Though we never meet her, she haunts every page, from first to last.

In this story I deliberately inserted the theme of appearances versus reality on several levels. There's the contrast between the two sisters—Love, who is a beauty, and her plain sister, Belle; Gypsy, the town's little golden girl, and Woodrow, the cross-eyed kid from the sticks; the obvious creature comforts and loveliness of Residence Street as opposed to the shack up on Crooked Ridge; and the social world where Love Ball Dotson reigns supreme versus the dark world of Blind Benny, who wanders out only at night.

Besides the publication of *Belle Prater's Boy,* another very important event for me occurred in 1996. The descendants of John Ed and Olive Compton White met at the Breaks Interstate Park on the Virginia/Kentucky state line near Grundy for a family reunion. Mom, now almost eighty years old, reigned over the festivities with a wonderful smile on her face the whole time.

All of Mom and Dad's surviving children and grandchildren, along with spouses, came from a half dozen states to be there. We rented cabins tucked away in the Appalachian woods, and for three days reminisced together. There was good food, and much singing and laughter, and yes, a few tears as well.

The Newbery Honor

On the January morning of the Newbery announcements in 1997, I headed out to work at the ARE Li-

Yvonne and Ruth on Mackinac Island, 2004 (Photo courtesy of Ruth White.)

brary as usual, not realizing that my life was about to change. My editor, Margaret Ferguson, called me at work around 9:30 and gave me the news that *Belle Prater's Boy* had won a Newbery honor. It was one of the most amazing moments of my life. I was thrilled, to say the least.

When I returned home that evening I found the Newbery Committee had left a message on my answering machine, also giving me the news and congratulating me. That day and the next I think I received flowers from about a dozen different sources.

In June of that year I was invited to the ALA convention in San Francisco, where Dee and I attended the Newbery banquet and met all of the other ALA winners. *A View from Saturday,* by E.L. Konigsburg took the medal that year, and there were three other honor books.

Belle Prater's Boy was the breakthrough book that made me feel like a real writer. After its success I was able to quit my nine-to-five job at the ARE Library and become a full-time writer. I started accepting invitations to visit schools and book events all across the country. Dee usually travels with me to the most interesting places. We have met many fascinating people and experienced some wonderful adventures together. To date, I have traveled to eighteen states discussing my books with young people and their parents, teachers, and librarians. What a great job!

Still, I stayed in Virginia Beach to study metaphysics and haunt the ARE for two more years. Finally I was able to verbalize my new-found belief system in this way: *Spirituality is a reverence for life; care and compassion for the poor, the sick, the elderly, children and animals; living in harmony with the earth; valuing people over things; and respecting yourself.*

I try to use these tenets in living my life day by day.

The Millennium and Beyond

I have always had a knack for knowing when it is time to go, and this insight came to me in 1999. I felt that I had learned all I needed to learn at this particular crossroads, and now I wanted to spend more time with Dee. In Pennsylvania she had become quite successful, owning her own business and a home near Hershey, where you can smell the chocolate when the wind is right.

Two weeks before the millennium I moved away from the South for the second time in my life, to live with Dee. Together we bought a beautiful golden retriever, Dory, who added much to our lives. We had always been close, but that winter, as we played in the snow with our dog and spent many wonderful days and nights together, we grew even closer.

My own mom spent some of those carefree days with us. She had begun dividing her time among her children and grandchildren. She spent a few months with Dee and me, a few with Yvonne, and a few with Eleanor, but she always returned to live with Mike, whom she had raised. I think she felt more at home with him.

Dee, Ruth, and Mom on Mom's last birthday, Pennsylvania, 2000 (Photo courtesy of Ruth White.)

In 2000, I published *Memories of Summer,* a book about a schizophrenic girl, similar to Audrey's story. It was designated as a best book for young adults by the ALA. Mom was the first to read it, and I am afraid it brought back too many sad memories for her. She cried.

In May of 2001, while at Mike's house, Mom lay down on the couch to watch her favorite television program and never got up again. At the age of eighty-four, this gentle, soft-spoken lady from Compton Mountain, who had always loved her family above all else, died. I wonder if, at that moment, she saw herself as a girl sprawled under a tree on that isolated mountain top in the hills of Virginia, reading a good book. And I know I must write Olive's story before I die.

A Period of Productivity

Tadpole and *Buttermilk Hill* were followed by *The Search for Belle Prater.* This book begins a few months after *Belle Prater's Boy* ended. On New Year's Eve the Ball household receives a mysterious phonecall from Bluefield, West Virginia. Woodrow is quite sure it is his mother, Belle Prater, calling. After that, he and Gypsy will not be satisfied until they go by themselves on the bus to Bluefield to search for Belle. The book describes how they search for Belle and what they find in the end.

Way Down Deep has little to do with my own life, except for the Appalachian setting. The idea came from a newspaper article I read years ago about a little girl abandoned in a field near a town in the Midwest. Nobody ever learned her identity, or how she came to be there. This story haunted me for years, and finally I decided to build a story around such an incident. Unfortunately, in real life the child died, but the town, not willing to have the unknown girl forgotten, erected a monument for her.

As I began my version of the story I had no idea how I would solve the mystery of Ruby's sudden appearance in the little town of Way Down Deep, but I knew that the ending would come to me. I also knew I would not let her die. That was too sad for a children's story. As I wrote, and the characters took shape in my mind, the mystery did solve itself naturally. I felt that it ended the only way it could have done—in a burst of mysticism!

These Happy Golden Years

For many years my sister, Yvonne, and I, had not seen much of each other because we lived so far apart. I did not know her four boys and their families well, and they did not know Dee and me. But all of that began to change after the 1996 reunion at the Breaks. Yvonne and her husband, Bob, loved the state park in Virginia as much as I did, and we began meeting there for a week each summer whenever possible.

Proud "Gammy" Ruth with Pate in May, 2007 (Photo courtesy of Ruth White.)

In the meantime, Yvonne and Bob were building a wonderful log cabin in Millington, Michigan, near Flint. They sent me pictures, and finally I had to go see it for myself. It is a grandparent's dream to have such a place. In a park setting with a stream running through it, it has an elaborate tree house for the grandchildren, and seven meticulously tended wooded acres. Dee and I began to spend a few days each year with Yvonne and Bob at their "estate," and Yvonne and I have caught up with the years and reminisced about our childhood days in Virginia. We also see Eleanor and her family occasionally in Tennessee where she has a beautiful home on the top of a hill, also with about seven acres surrounding her house. One of her children lives on the same land within sight. It is gratifying today to see how well my sisters have turned out with their beautiful families and homes. In spite of the hard times, the lean years, we finally all made it to a safe and happy place.

In 2006, Dee married William Anderson, and once again I knew it was time to go. So I left her house, but didn't go far. I moved into a condo of my own only about a block from Dee and William.

On May 27, 2007, Dee gave birth to a fine baby boy, William Paisley Anderson, IV, called Pate for short. As my first grandchild, he is, of course, the most magnificent child in the world! I can see myself now surviving to a ripe old age, living here near Dee, William, Pate, and maybe more little ones, sharing their lives and writing more books.

Today my life is very full. I spend my days walking in the park with my golden retriever, Dory—yes, she's eight years old now—helping care for Pate and writing whenever I can find the time. But there's always time to do what you love to do.

A Note to My Readers

To those young people who have a sincere desire to write, my advice to you is do it! READ, READ, READ! Then WRITE, WRITE, WRITE! Your background doesn't have to hold you back. Start where you are now. And nobody can stop you.

WYNNE-JONES, Tim 1948-
(Timothy Wynne-Jones)

Personal

Born August 12, 1948, in Bromborough, Cheshire, England; immigrated to Canada, 1952; son of Sydney Thomas (an engineer and lieutenant colonel in the British Army) and Sheila Beryl (a homemaker) Wynne-Jones; married Amanda West Lewis (a writer, calligrapher, director, and teacher), September 12, 1980; children: Alexander, Magdalene, Lewis. *Education:* University of Waterloo, B.F.A., 1974; York University, M.F.A. (visual arts), 1979. *Hobbies and other interests:* Cooking, crosswords, cross-country skiing.

Addresses

Home and office—Perth, Ontario, Canada. *Agent*—Leona Trainer, Transatlantic Literary Agency, 72 Glengowan Rd., Toronto, Ontario M4N 1G4, Canada. *E-mail*—twj@ perth.igs.net.

Career

Writer. PMA Books, Toronto, Ontario, Canada, designer, 1974-76; University of Waterloo, Waterloo, Ontario, instructor in visual arts, 1976-78; Solomon & Wynne-Jones, Toronto, graphic designer, 1976-79; York University, Downsview, Ontario, instructor in visual arts, 1978-80; Vermont College, currently instructor in MFA in Writing for Children and Young Adults program. Red Deer College Press, children's book editor, 1990-96. University of New Brunswick, instructor in maritime workshop; Children's Literature New England, lecturer in summer institute; writing instructor at Banff School of Fine Arts, Red Deer College, St. Lawrence College, Algonquin College, and University of Ottawa. Writer-in-residence, Perth and District Public Library, Perth, Ontario, 1988, and Nepean Public Library, Nepean, Ontario, 1993.

Member

International PEN, Writers Union of Canada, Association of Canadian Television and Radio Artists, Society of Composers, Authors, and Music Publishers of Canada, Canadian Society of Children's Authors, Illustrators, and Performers.

Awards, Honors

Seal First Novel Award, Bantam/Seal Books, 1980, for *Odd's End;* I.O.D.E. Award, 1983, and Ruth Schwartz Children's Award, 1984, both for *Zoom at Sea;* ACTRA Award for best radio drama, 1987, for *St. Anthony's Man;* Governor General's Award for Children's Literature, 1993, Canadian Library Association (CLA) Children's Book of the Year award, 1993, and *Boston Globe/ Horn Book* Award for Fiction, 1995, all for *Some of the Kinder Planets;* Notable Books for Children citation, American Library Association, and Mister Christie

Award shortlist, 1994, both for *The Book of Changes;* Governor General's Award for Children's Literature, 1995, and Young-Adult Book of the Year designation, CLA, Mister Christie Award shortlist, and Books for the Teen Age citation, New York Public Library, all 1997, all for *The Maestro;* Vicky Metcalf Award, Canadian Authors Association, 1997, for body of work; Children's Book of the Year designation, CLA, 1998, for *Stephen Fair;* Books for the Teen Age citation, New York Public Library, 1999, for *Lord of the Fries;* Arthur Ellis Award, Crime Writers of Canada, and Edgar Allen Poe Award shortlist, 2001, and Ruth Schwartz Award shortlist, Ontario Arts Council, Red Maple Award shortlist, Ontario Library Association and London *Guardian* Children's Fiction Prize shortlist, all for *The Boy in the Burning House;* Rocky Mountain Book Award, 2005, for *Ned Mouse Breaks Away;* Boston Globe/Horn Book Honor Book designation, 2007, for *Rex Zero and the End of the World.*

Writings

FOR CHILDREN

Madeline and Ermadello, illustrated by Lindsey Hallam, Before We Are Six (Hawkesville, Ontario, Canada), 1977.

Zoom at Sea, illustrated by Ken Nutt, Douglas & McIntyre (Toronto, Ontario, Canada), 1983, illustrated by Eric Beddows, HarperCollins (New York, NY), 1993.

Zoom Away, illustrated by Ken Nutt, Douglas & McIntyre (Toronto, Ontario, Canada), 1985, illustrated by Eric Beddows, HarperCollins (New York, NY), 1993.

I'll Make You Small, illustrated by Maryann Kovalski, Douglas & McIntyre (Toronto, Ontario, Canada), 1986.

Mischief City (verse), illustrated by Victor Gad, Groundwood (Toronto, Ontario, Canada), 1986.

Architect of the Moon, illustrated by Ian Wallace, Groundwood (Toronto, Ontario, Canada), 1988, published as *Builder of the Moon,* Margaret K. McElderry Books (New York, NY), 1988.

The Hour of the Frog, illustrated by Catharine O'Neill, Little, Brown (Boston, MA), 1989.

Zoom Upstream, illustrated by Eric Beddows, Groundwood Books (Toronto, Ontario, Canada), 1992, HarperCollins (New York, NY), 1994.

Mouse in the Manger, illustrated by Elaine Blier, Viking (New York, NY), 1993.

The Last Piece of Sky, illustrated by Marie-Louise Gay, Groundwood Books (Toronto, Ontario, Canada), 1993.

Some of the Kinder Planets (short stories), Groundwood Books (Toronto, Ontario, Canada), 1993, Orchard (New York, NY), 1995.

(With Amanda Lewis) *Rosie Backstage,* illustrated by Bill Slavin, Kids Can Press (Toronto, Ontario, Canada), 1994.

The Book of Changes (short stories), Groundwood Books (Toronto, Ontario, Canada), 1994, Orchard (New York, NY), 1995.

The Maestro, Groundwood Books (Toronto, Ontario, Canada), 1995, Orchard (New York, NY), 1996, published as *The Survival Game,* Usborne (London, England), 2006.

(Reteller) *The Hunchback of Notre Dame,* illustrated by Bill Slavin, Key Porter Books (Toronto, Ontario, Canada), 1996, Orchard (New York, NY), 1997.

(Reteller) Bram Stoker, *Dracula,* illustrated by Laszlo Gal, Key Porter Books (Toronto, Ontario, Canada), 1997.

Stephen Fair, DK Ink (New York, NY), 1998.

On Tumbledown Hill, Red Deer College Press (Alberta, Ontario, Canada), 1998.

Lord of the Fries, and Other Stories, DK Ink (New York, NY), 1999.

The Boy in the Burning House, Douglas & McIntyre (Toronto, Ontario, Canada), 2000, Farrar, Straus & Giroux (New York, NY), 2001.

(Editor) *Boy's Own: An Anthology of Canadian Fiction for Young Readers,* Penguin (New York, NY), 2001.

Ned Mouse Breaks Away, illustrated by Dusân Petrîĉiĉ, Groundwood Books (Toronto, Ontario, Canada), 2003, Farrar, Straus & Giroux (New York, NY), 2005.

A Thief in the House of Memory, Groundwood Books (Toronto, Ontario, Canada), 2004.

The Boat in the Tree, illustrated by John Shelley, Front Street (Asheville, NC), 2007.

Rex Zero and the End of the World, Farrar, Straus & Giroux (New York, NY), 2007.

Rex Zero, the King of Nothing, Farrar, Straus & Giroux (New York, NY), 2008.

On Tumbledown Hill, illustrated by Dusân Petrîĉiĉ, Red Deer Press (Calgary, Alberta, Canada), 2008.

Short fiction included in anthologies such as *My Dad's a Punk: Twelve Stories about Boys and Their Fathers,* edited by Tony Bradman, Kingfisher (Boston, MA), 2006; *All Sleek and Skimming,* edited by Lisa Heggum, Orca, 2006, *First Times,* edited by Marthe Jocelyn, Tundra Books, 2007; and *Click* (serial novel), Scholastic, 2007. Author of libretto for children's opera *A Midwinter Night's Dream* and a musical version of *Mischief City.* Contributor of book reviews to Toronto *Globe and Mail,* 1985-88, and to periodicals including *Chickadee, Quill & Quire,* and *Horn Book.*

Author's work has been translated into several languages, including French and German.

NOVELS; FOR ADULTS

Odd's End, Little, Brown (Boston, MA), 1980.

The Knot, McClelland & Stewart (Toronto, Ontario, Canada), 1982.

Fastyngange, Lester & Orpen Dennys (Toronto, Ontario, Canada), 1988, published as *Voices,* Hodder & Stoughton (London, England), 1990.

RADIO PLAYS

The Thinking Room, produced by Canadian Broadcasting Corporation, 1981.

The Road Ends at the Sea, produced by Canadian Broadcasting Corporation, 1982.

The Strange Odyssey of Lennis Freed, produced by Canadian Broadcasting Corporation, 1983.

The Testing of Stanley Teagarden, produced by Canadian Broadcasting Corporation, 1985.

The Enormous Radio (from the story by John Cheever), produced by Canadian Broadcasting Corporation, 1986.

St. Anthony's Man (from his own story), produced by Canadian Broadcasting Corporation, 1987.

Mr. Gendelman Crashes a Party, produced by Canadian Broadcasting Corporation, 1987.

Dust Is the Only Secret, produced by Canadian Broadcasting Corporation, 1988.

We Now Return You to Your Regularly Scheduled Universe, produced by Canadian Broadcasting Corporation, 1992.

Sidelights

A British-born Canadian, Tim Wynne-Jones has proven himself a versatile and perceptive writer on many levels. Whether writing children's picture books, young-adult titles, or adult fiction and plays, his message of the power of fantasy and fiction comes through loud and clear. As he once commented, "I like to tell stories—to entertain and instruct—about ordinary people in extraordinary circumstances or extraordinary people in very ordinary circumstances." Considered one of Canada's most popular authors among preschoolers and primary graders, Wynne-Jones captures the mystery, fantasy, and wonder of childhood in his books while also addressing such realistic concerns as the conquering of personal fears and the relationship between children and their parents. He is known and appreciated for his rich language, zany plots, and a sophistication of theme that does not proclaim itself didactically, but that "reverberates beneath the simple surface of image and dialogue," as Gwyneth Evans noted in *Twentieth-Century Children's Writers.*

The son of an engineer, Wynne-Jones was born in Cheshire, England, in 1948, but grew up in Ottawa, Ontario, Canada. His introduction to children's literature came during his involvement in a research project at the University of Waterloo. A group of sociology students was studying racism and sexism in books for young readers, and Wynne-Jones, studying visual arts at the time, was included as someone on the creative side of things. In an interview with Dave Jenkinson in *Emergency Librarian,* Wynne-Jones explained that having examined a plethora of children's books and finding fault with many of them, "the group decided that, because they knew what was wrong with children's books, they could then write good ones. It was a great lesson in how you do *not* write a children's book."

Although the publishing venture created by the student grant project was short lived, it did produce Wynne-Jones's first creative effort, *Madeline and Ermadello,* a "quietly charming story about a young girl's fantasies," according to *In Review* contributor Linda Smith. Ermadello is Madeline's friend, the third in a trio that includes her carpenter father, Ernie, and her next door neighbor, Barnell. Ermadello is special: because he is imaginary, Madeline can make him be anything she wants him to be. The quiet climax to this picture book comes when Madeline introduces Ermadello to her real-life friends at a tea party. A *Children's Book News* reviewer concluded that *Madeline and Ermadello* "is a charming story of friendship that younger readers are certain to enjoy."

Wynne-Jones's first book highlights the elements of fantasy and wonder that have become common to his work for children. It was several years, however, before Wynne-Jones published a second picture book. During this time he worked as a designer at a publishing company, as a visual arts instructor at both Waterloo University and York University, and as a graphic designer in his own company. He also earned an M.F.A. in visual arts and was married. Then he wrote and published his first adult novel, a psychological thriller titled *Odd's End,* which won him Canada's prestigious Seal First Novel Award and a cash prize of 50,000 dollars. Understandably, Wynne-Jones stuck with adult fiction for his next title, *The Knot,* but he returned to children's books in 1983.

"I didn't start writing children's books because I had children," Wynne-Jones told Jenkinson in his *Emergency Librarian* interview. "I'd always had ideas for children's stories." Although a visual artist himself, Wynne-Jones does not illustrate his own books. Rather, he visualizes stories with the illustrations of other artists he respects. One such artist is Ken Nutt (Eric Beddows), an acquaintance whose artwork Wynne-Jones wanted to see in book form, and the direct inspiration this collaboration was the family cat, Montezuma—or Zuma for short. Writing early one morning, Wynne-Jones observed the cat sitting on the kitchen counter batting at water from a dripping faucet. The idea for an adventure-loving and water-loving cat came to the author quickly. "The story, *Zoom at Sea,* was written in 20 minutes," Wynne-Jones later told Jenkinson. Brought to life in Nutt's art, Zoom the cat goes to the home of the mysterious Maria, who helps him realize a lifelong dream of going to sea. Linda Granfield, writing in *Quill & Quire,* noted that *Zoom at Sea* features a "perfect balance of text and illustration" that combine to inspire children and adults alike to "live our dreams."

Wynne-Jones initially had no intention of creating a sequel to *Zoom at Sea,* but after his mother-in-law suggested further possibilities for Maria's magical powers, *Zoom Away* was launched. In this story, a trip upstairs to Maria's attic becomes the magical metaphor for a trip to the North Pole. Zoom goes in search of the nautical tomcat, Uncle Roy, who set sail for the North Pole and has not been heard from since. Again, Nutt's simple black-and-white illustrations "complement . . . per-

fectly" Wynne-Jones's text, according to Bernie Goedhart in *Quill & Quire.* Goedhart concluded that the two "seem destined to carve themselves a permanent niche in the world of Canadian picture-books." Although reviewers such as Jon C. Stott in *Canadian Literature* contended that Wynne-Jones's simple text lacks "depth," others disagreed. Sarah Ellis, writing in *Horn Book,* commented that "*Zoom Away* is one of those rare picture books that combines absolute simplicity with mythic resonance. . . . The story is bigger that its plot." Drawing comparisons to such elemental Canadian myths as the search for the Northwest Passage and the romance involved in such adventure, Ellis concluded that the "satisfaction we feel at the book's safe ending goes beyond the satisfaction of putting a tired child to bed." Reviewing both "Zoom" titles for *Canadian Children's Literature,* Ulrike Walker placed the books in the context of mythic test or quest tales. According to the critic, the "Zoom" stories are "remarkable works" that "bear eloquent witness to the complex levels of realization which all of us must undergo before we reach that stage we label 'adult.'"

If Zoom travels to the Arctic via Maria's attic, the next obvious question—and one posed to Wynne-Jones by a student: What would a trip to the basement hold in store for Zoom? The answer comes in the third "Zoom" book, *Zoom Upstream.* Set in ancient, cat-revering Egypt, *Zoom Upstream* has Zoom following a mysterious trail through a bookshelf to Ancient Egypt, where he joins Maria in a further search for Uncle Roy. When Maria shows Zoom five silver buttons from a sailor's coat, the clues ultimately lead the two to Uncle Roy and safety. The book's ending was described by Janet McNaughton in *Quill & Quire* as "more like a beginning," with the trio sailing away in search of the source of the Nile. *Zoom Upstream* is "a very special book," concluded McNaughton.

With *I'll Make You Small,* Wynne-Jones moves away from the voyaging world of cats to the more prosaic but no-less-dangerous world of the suburban neighborhood. Young Roland's next-door neighbor, crotchety old Mr. Swanskin, threatens to make Roland shrink in size if he catches the boy trespassing on his property. When Swanskin is not seen for several days, Roland is sent by his mother to investigate, only to find the eccentric old man repairing toys he broke during his own childhood. The gift of a pie saves Roland from Swanskin's threats, and he learns the man's secret: that he was made to feel small as a child. "A child who likes scary stories, but is too young for [Edgar Allen] Poe or [Alfred] Hitchcock, should enjoy this book," commented Bernie Goedhart in *Quill & Quire.*

Another popular picture book from Wynne-Jones, and one that *Five Owls* contributor Anne Lundin compared to Maurice Sendak's popular *Where the Wild Things Are, Architect of the Moon* was published in the United States as *Builder of the Moon.* In this story, young David Finebloom receives an urgent message one night

Through a shared challenge, two stepbrothers become friends in **The Boat in the Tree,** *Tim Wynne-Jones's story featuring art by John Shelley.* (Front Street, an imprint of Boyds Mills Press, Inc., 2007. Illustrations copyright © 2007 by John Shelley. Reproduced by permission.)

via a moonbeam and flies away, building blocks in hand, to repair the moon. Lundin noted in her review that "Wynne-Jones's text is spare, simple, poetic," while Walker wrote in *Canadian Children's Literature* that the author's "subtle work" "does not enclose but encourages the child to take a decisive step toward change." Also writing in *Canadian Children's Literature,* Michael Steig noted that *Architect of the Moon* features a "visual text" in which pictures and text "achieve . . . a highly gratifying level of literary and artistic complexity and interest."

Other books by Wynne-Jones that have found fans among many young readers include *The Hour of the Frog, The Last Piece of Sky, The Boat in the Tree,* and *Ned Mouse Breaks Away,* all of them well received by critics. Illustrated by John Shelley, *The Boat in the Tree* captures the world of an imaginative child who uses his love of boats to build a relationship with a newly adopted older brother. Geared for early elementary-grade readers, *Ned Mouse Breaks Away* tells what *School Library Journal* contributor Eva Mitnick deemed a "sur-

real story [that] is both quirky and matter-of-fact": it describes a bewhiskered political prisoner who decides to gradually escape from prison by mailing bits of himself to a close friend. As more and more of Ned is boxed up and mailed out to his friend's seaside home, the once-jailed rodent is gradually reassembled there to enjoy the sunshine. Meanwhile, his still-imprisoned parts are gradually changed out for tin replacements that fool Ned's guards, whittling the real Ned down to only one bit: the hand he uses to address each of his packages. Noting the book's "goofy" cartoon art by Dusân Petriĉiĉ, Mitnick dubbed *Ned Mouse Breaks Away* "funny, light, and deliciously different," and a *Publishers Weekly* critic wrote that Wynne-Jones's "breezy novel brims with chuckles."

Turning to short fiction, Wynne-Jones has produced several collections that have a special appeal for young readers. His award-winning *Some of the Kinder Planets* contains nine stories in which children make encounters with other worlds, both metaphorically and realistically. Reviewing the work, Deborah Stevenson commented in

Cover of Wynne-Jones's teen short-story collection Some of the Kinder Planets, *featuring art by Christian Potter Drury.* (Puffin Books, 1996. Text copyright © 1994 by Tim Wynne-Jones. Cover copyright © 1994 by Christian Potter Drury. Used by permission of Puffin Books, an imprint of Penguin Putnam Books for Young Readers, a division of Penguin Putnam Inc. All rights reserved.)

the *Bulletin of the Center for Children's Books* that the writing "is thoughtful, inventive, and often humorous," while a *Publishers Weekly* reviewer noted that "ordinary moments take on a fresh veneer in this finely tuned short-story collection."

More short stories are offered up in *The Book of Changes,* descrobed as a "fine collection" by a *Kirkus Reviews* critic and "a delight" by *Quill & Quire* contributor Annette Goldsmith. Told from the point of view of male narrators, the seven stories in the collection "hold wonder and fascination for inquisitive readers," according to *School Library Journal* reviewer John Sigwald. "Wynne-Jones deals in moments, and these are carefully chosen and freshly realized," Sarah Ellis remarked in *Horn Book.* In "The Clark Beans Man," for instance, a boy uses a Donald Duck impersonation to fend off a schoolyard bully; in "Dawn," a teenager on a bus trip develops a brief friendship with a tough-looking older girl. Nancy Vasilakis, also writing in *Horn Book,* concluded that in *The Book of Changes* "Wynne-Jones tells his readers . . . that we all have the power to create the music of our own lives." Noting that the author

attempts to "conjure up a sense of wonder" in *The Book of Changes,* Goldsmith wrote that the "wonderful moments in this book . . . will stay with readers." In *Horn Book,* Vasilakis concluded: "Wynne-Jones tells his readers in these perceptive short stories that we all have the power to create the music of our own lives."

Other story collections by Wynne-Jones include *Lord of the Fries, and Other Stories* and the edited collection *Boy's Own: An Anthology of Canadian Fiction for Young Readers.* A reviewer in the *Bulletin of the Center for Children's Books* observed of *Lord of the Fries, and Other Stories* that the author's "creative plotting and faith in the power of imagination . . . keeps events sparking along in absorbing and unpredictable ways."

With the young-adult novel *The Maestro,* Wynne-Jones again broke new ground for himself. The story focuses on fourteen-year-old Burl and his struggle for survival after he flees his brutal father and seeks shelter in a remote cabin by a Canadian lake. The cabin is inhabited by Nathaniel Gow, a musical genius who is himself in flight from the mechanized world. Gow—patterned after real-life Canadian musician Glen Gould—allows Burl to stay at his cabin while he travels home to Toronto. When Burl learns of Gow's subsequent death, he tries to claim the cabin for himself, then goes on a mission to save Gow's final musical composition, confronting his abusive father along the way. Roderick McGillis, writing in *Canadian Children's Literature,* noted that while *The Maestro* is "redolently Canadian," it also offers much more. "Its prose is dense and its themes move into challenging areas for young readers," McGillis remarked. Stevenson concluded in a *Bulletin of the Center for Children's Books* review that "Wynne-Jones has displayed a knack for the unusual made credible in his short story collections" and that it is "nice to see that skill expanded into a well-crafted and accessible novel." Writing in *Quill & Quire,* Maureen Garvie commented that *The Maestro* is "tightly and dramatically scripted" and that Wynne-Jones's first young-adult novel is a "peach."

The author turns to psychological suspense in *Stephen Fair,* about a fifteen year old who is plagued by nightmares. With the support of his friend Virginia, Stephen begins to question his troubled family life, including his mother's erratic behavior and the disappearances of his father and older brother. "Wynne-Jones is an impressive stylist," remarked a critic in reviewing *Stephen Fair* for the *Bulletin of the Center for Children's Books,* "and his depiction of Stephen's family, friends, and thoughts are unforcedly deft." A *Kirkus Reviews* writer noted that the author reveals his characters' feelings "through quick, telling details and comments, or heavily symbolic background events," and a *Publishers Weekly* reviewer declared that Wynne-Jones "maintains the suspense while Stephen slowly unveils family secrets."

Taking place in rural Ontario, *The Boy in the Burning House* focuses on Jim Hawkins, a teen who lives with his mother. Maintaining a living on the family farm has been difficult since the disappearance of Jim's father, and Jim is quick to anger when neighboring teen Ruth Rose starts rumors about the death of Jim's dad and the complicity of her upstanding minister stepfather in the man's disappearance. Although most people ignore the troubled young woman's stories, Jim takes portions to heart, beginning an investigation that uncovers arson and murder and resolves a story that "spins out taut as a bow string," according to *Booklist* critic GraceAnne A. DeCandido. In *Publishers Weekly* a contributor dubbed *The Boy in the Burning House* "an action-packed thriller" in which Wynne-Jones's "swift-moving plot will keep the pages turning," and *Horn Book* reviewer Lauren Adams wrote that the book's "gripping, fast-moving" storyline "offers the pure adrenaline rush of a thriller." Noting that the author has gained many fans on the strength of his ability to create "quirky, offbeat characters," Adams concluded that *The Boy in the Burning House* "does not disappoint."

Described by a *Publishers Weekly* contributor as a reading experience akin to "entering a dream," *A Thief in the House of Memory* introduces readers to sixteen-year-old Declan Steeple, a boy who is, like Jim in *The Boy in the Burning House,* also dealing with parental abandonment. Since his mother's departure six years before, Declan has lived with his father and little sister Sunny, and more recently with his father's girlfriend, Birdie. As questions about his mother's disappearance draw him into the past, the teen is compelled to return to the family's large estate, Steeple Hall, which now stands empty atop a hill overlooking his new home. On one visit to the mansion, Declan and Sunny discover the body of a housebreaker. When the dead man turns out to be someone who once knew his mother, his appearance generates revelations that ultimately hold the answers to Declan's own past. Wynne-Jones's novel serves as "part mystery and part psychological study of how the past affects the present," according to the *Publishers Weekly* contributor, while in *Horn Book* Vicky Smith called *A Thief in the House of Memory* "equal parts tricky and haunting," and "unambiguously memorable." In *Booklist,* Carolyn Phelan praised the middle-grade coming-of-age novel as "original" and "vividly written," adding that the author's "narrative conveys a strong sense of Declan's uneasiness, as past and present overlap in an unsettling way." A "rich and rewarding novel," *A Thief in the House of Memory* "will appeal most to thoughtful readers who appreciate a sad and bittersweet read," concluded *School Library Journal* contributor Karyn N. Silverman.

Based on Wynne-Jones's childhood and geared for pre-teen readers, the "Rex Zero" stories include *Rex Zero and the End of the World* and *Rex Zero, the King of Nothing.* Set in 1962, *Rex Zero and the End of the World* introduces readers to Rex Harrison as the eleven year old and his family adjust to life in their new home in Ottawa. As Canadians grow concerned over the possibility of a nuclear Armageddon sparked by cold-war tensions between the United States and the USSR, Rex finds those fears filtering down into his own world. When he discovers a strange creature, his first thought is that it has been mutated by exposure to radiation.

However, when it turns out to be a panther named Tronido that has escaped from the local zoo, efforts to capture the creature help the boy make new friends and adjust to a new way of life. In his humorous and lighthearted present-tense narrative, Rex "paints a universe both hopeful and realistic, one that readers may well want to visit," concluded a *Publishers Weekly* contributor, while in *Horn Book* Julie Roach wrote of *Rex Zero, the King of Nothing* that Wynne-Jones's "timely piece of historical fiction also casts a haunting light on kids growing up in a world filled with fear." Praising the novel as "delightfully nerve-wracking, eccentric and optimistic," a *Kirkus Reviews* writer took special delight in the many details of mid-twentieth-century popular culture that salt Wynne-Jones's story. "Any distance created" by the nostalgic setting of *Rex Zero and the End of the World* "is more than made up for by the intricately flavored details of Rex's life," the reviewer concluded.

Noting that he never composes plot outlines before beginning to write a novel, Wynne-Jones once explained: "I write the same way I read (though not as fast, unfortunately). I never quite know what's going to happen on the next page. I want to surprise myself and by

Cover of Wynne-Jones's short-story collection **Lord of the Fries,** *featuring artwork by Kyrsten Brooker.* (DK Ink Books, 1999. Jacket art copyright © 1999 by Kyrsten Brooker. Reproduced by permission of DK Publishing, Inc.)

so doing, hopefully, surprise my reader. Sooner or later, I get an idea where the story is going. That's what happens when I read, too. But even when I know where I want to take a story, I keep my options open. You never know when one of your characters will come up with a better idea than you!"

Biographical and Critical Sources

BOOKS

Children's Literature Review, Volume 21, Gale (Detroit, MI), 1990, pp. 226-231.

Twentieth-Century Children's Writers, 4th edition, St. James Press (Detroit, MI), 1995, pp. 1049-1051.

PERIODICALS

Booklist, September 1, 2001, GraceAnne A. DeCandido, review of *The Boy in the Burning House,* p. 97; March 1, 2005, Carolyn Phelan, review of *A Thief in the House of Memory,* p. 1186; March 1, 2007, Hazel Rochman, review of *Rex Zero and the End of the World,* p. 86, and Gillian Engberg, review of *The Boat in the Tree,* p. 90.

Bulletin of the Center for Children's Books, May, 1995, Deborah Stevenson, review of *One of the Kinder Planets,* p. 328; October, 1996, Deborah Stevenson, review of *The Maestro,* p. 81; March, 1999, review of *Lord of the Fries, and Other Stories,* p. 260; May, 2005, review of *A Thief in the House of Memory,* p. 412; April, 2007, Elizabeth Bush, review of *Rex Zero and the End of the World,* p. 349.

Canadian Children's Literature, number 60, 1990, Ulrike Walker, "A Matter of Thresholds," pp. 108-116; number 70, 1993, Michael Steig, "The Importance of the Visual Text in *Architect of the Moon:* Mothers, Teapots, et al.," pp. 22-33; number 81, 1996, Roderick McGillis, review of *The Maestro,* pp. 58-59.

Canadian Literature, spring, 1987, Jon C. Stott, review of *Zoom Away,* p. 160.

Canadian Review of Materials, January-February, 1994, Joyce MacPhee, "Profile: Tim Wynne-Jones," p. 4.

Children's Book News, June, 1979, review of *Madeline and Ermadello,* p. 2.

Emergency Librarian, January-February, 1988, Dave Jenkinson, "Tim Wynne-Jones," pp. 56-62.

Five Owls, May-June, 1989, Anne Lundin, review of *Builder of the Moon.*

Horn Book, May-June, 1987, Sarah Ellis, review of *Zoom Away,* pp. 378-381; January-February, 1995, Sarah Ellis, reviews of *Some of the Kinder Planets* and *The Book of Changes;* February, 1996, Nancy Vasilakis, review of *The Book of Changes,* pp. 76-77; November-December, 2001, Lauren Adams, review of *The Boy in the Burning House,* p. 759; May-June, 2005, Vicky Smith, review of *A Thief in the House of Memory,* p. 334; March-April, 2007, Vicky Smith, review of *Rex Zero and the End of the World,* p. 207; January-February, 2008, Julie Roach, review of *Rex Zero and the End of the World,* p. 26.

In Review, winter, 1978, Linda Smith, review of *Madeline and Ermadello,* p. 70.

Kirkus Reviews, July 15, 1995, review of *The Book of Changes,* p. 1032; April 1, 1998, review of *Stephen Fair,* pp. 503-504; April 1, 2005, review of *A Thief in the House of Memory,* p. 429; February 1, 2007, review of *Rex Zero and the End of the World,* p. 131; February 15, 2007, review of *The Boat in the Tree.*

Kliatt, September, 2001, Paula Rohrlick, review of *The Boy in the Burning House;* May, 2005, Michele Winship, review of *A Thief in the House of Memory,* p. 19.

Publishers Weekly, May 1, 1995, review of *One of the Kinder Planets,* p. 59; March 16, 1998, review of *Stephen Fair,* p. 65; September 24, 2001, review of *The Boy in the Burning House,* p. 94; February 3, 2003, review of *Ned Mouse Breaks Away,* p. 76; May 9, 2005, review of *A Thief in the House of Memory,* p. 71; February 5, 2007, review of *Rex Zero and the End of the World,* p. 60.

Quill & Quire, August, 1985, Bernie Goedhart, review of *Zoom Away,* p. 38; October, 1986, Bernie Goedhart, review of *I'll Make You Small,* p. 16; December, 1986, Joan McGrath, "Poems for Kids Conjure up a Cockeyed World," p. 15; November, 1992, Janet McNaughton, review of *Zoom Upstream,* p. 33; October, 1994, Annette Goldsmith, review of *The Book of Changes,* p. 38; December, 1995, Maureen Garvie, review of *The Maestro,* pp. 36-37.

School Library Journal, March, 1984, Linda Granfield, review of *Zoom at Sea,* p. 72; October, 1995, John Sigwald, review of *The Book of Changes,* pp. 141-142; October, 2001, Alison Follos, review of *The Boy in the Burning House,* p. 176; April, 2003, Eva Mitnick, review of *Ned Mouse Breaks Away,* p. 144; April, 2005, Karyn N. Silverman, review of *A Thief in the House of Memory,* p. 144; May, 2007, Caitlin Augusta, review of *Rex Zero and the End of the World,* p. 146; June, 2007, Ieva Bates, review of *The Boat in the Tree,* p. 127.

Voice of Youth Advocates, February, 2007, Alison Follos, review of *The Boy in the Burning House,* p. 503; April, 2007, Angela Semifero, review of *Rex Zero and the End of the World,* p. 59.

ONLINE

Tim Wynne-Jones Home Page, http://www.timwynne-jones.com (February 1, 2008).*

*   *   *

WYNNE-JONES, Timothy
See WYNNE-JONES, Tim

*   *   *

ZOLOTOW, Ellen
See DRAGONWAGON, Crescent